★ BUZAN'S ★
BOOK OF
GENIUS

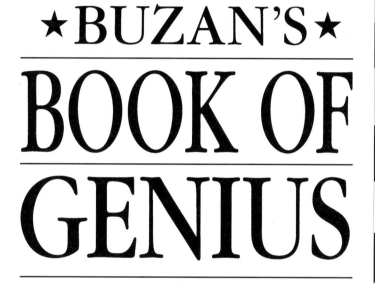

★ BUZAN'S ★
BOOK OF
GENIUS

and how to
UNLEASH YOUR OWN

★ ★ ★ ★ ★ ★ ★ ★ ★ ★ ★ ★

TONY BUZAN AND
RAYMOND KEENE

STANLEY PAUL

LONDON

We dedicate this book to the new Medici, Their Serene Highnesses Reigning Prince Hans-Adam II, Prince Philipp and Princess Isabelle von und zu Liechtenstein.

First published in 1994

1 3 5 7 9 10 8 6 4 2

Copyright © 1994 Tony Buzan and Raymond Keene

First published in the United Kingdom in 1994 by
Stanley Paul and Company Limited,
an imprint of Random House,
20 Vauxhall Bridge Road, London SW1V 2SA.

Random House Australia (Pty) Limited,
20 Alfred Street, Milsons Point, Sydney,
New South Wales 2061, Australia.

Random House New Zealand Limited,
18 Poland Road, Glenfield,
Auckland 10, New Zealand.

Random House South Africa (Pty) Limited
PO Box 337, Bergvlei, South Africa.

Random House UK Limited Reg. No. 954009

ISBN 0 09 178551 0

Managing editor: Nicky Thompson
Designer: Nigel Partridge
Picture researcher: Nadine Bazar
Production controller: Susan Denton
Diagrams and maps: Anthony Duke
Index: Hilary Bird

Typeset by SX Composing Limited, Rayleigh, Essex
Colour origination by Dot Gradations Limited
Printed and bound in Great Britain by
B.P.C. Paulton Books Limited, Bristol.

CONTENTS

ACKNOWLEDGEMENTS   6

INTRODUCTION   7

PART ONE

DEVELOPING YOUR MENTAL SKILLS   11

PART TWO

THE HALL OF FAME   63

PART THREE

MENTAL WORLD RECORDS   239

AN INVITATION TO READERS   248

BIBLIOGRAPHY   248

FURTHER INFORMATION   249

INDEX   251

ANSWERS   255

PICTURE ACKNOWLEDGEMENTS   256

ACKNOWLEDGEMENTS

The authors and editor would like to express their profound thanks to the following, all of them experts in their field, who in various ways made enormous contributions to this book.

Very special thanks are due to Paul Collins, ultra marathon record holder, concert violinist and Alexander teacher; Vivian Davies, Keeper of Egyptian Antiquities, The British Museum, London; Dr Jacqueline Eales, Lecturer in History, the University of Kent, Canterbury; Annette Goodman, Associate, Imperial Society of Teachers of Dance; Ted Hughes, the Poet Laureate; Patricia Utermohlen, Lecturer in the History of Art (ICA).

We would also like to acknowledge the help of Sean Adam, Les Blackstock, Philip Bond, Brian Clivaz and the staff at Simpson's-in-the Strand, John Graham, Bob Heller, Dr Frank James, Con McCarrick, Vanda North, Dominic O'Brien, David Spanier, Brian Timmins, Dr Marion Tinsley, Sir Brian and Lady Mary Tovey, Joseph Petrus Wergin, David Woo and Benjamin Zander.

Not forgetting Michael Attenborough, Lesley Bias, Jan Bowmer, Anabel Briggs, Clare Clements, Carol Coaker, Professor Michael Crawford, Natacia Diot, Professor Nathan Divinsky, James Farnsworth Young, Michael J Gelb, Lorraine Gill, Nicky Goudge, Garry Kasparov, Sandy Long, Jeff Malyon, Barry Martin, Marion Paull, Professor Jonathan Schaeffer, Jean Sewell, Julian Shuckburgh, Julian Simpole, Dr Andrew Strigner, Sheikh Talib, Amelia Thorpe, Veron and Mike Thompson, Trevor Turner and Phyllida Wilson.

INTRODUCTION

$$e + M = C^{\infty}$$

The book you hold in your hands is an adventure into the worlds of genius – your own and that of some of the greatest minds in history – and it has a number of main purposes.

A MANIFESTO FOR THE MIND

It is a natural function of the human brain to learn, and especially to explore and expand its own mental powers – to unlock and unleash larger and larger portions of the vast, substantially dormant potential of the super bio-computer that everyone carries around. This book provides you with a manifesto for the mind and will assist you in achieving that goal. We hope that you will find it informative, educational, exciting, stimulating, easy-to-understand and relevant to your personal needs.

We have redefined genius, based on our examination of the nature of intelligence and its growth, as well as on our survey of the Great Minds who rose to the top in their disciplines. In this book we have broken many misconceptions and false beliefs about the qualities of genius, thus leading to a new understanding of its nature and a new ability to nurture it.

CONTRIBUTING TO A NEW RENAISSANCE

One of our hopes for this book is that it will raise the general global awarenes of intelligence, Mental Literacy (explained on pages 32-33) and genius. It will contribute to the new Renaissance of the Mind that has already begun and which will flower in the 21st century. During our research we have discovered that, without doubt, nurture (proper education and environment) is more important than nature (genetic make-up) in determining genius. And we have provided you with principles and formulae that will make the accessing of genius easier and more enjoyable.

HOW THE BOOK IS ORGANIZED

To accomplish all the goals above, and to allow you to unleash your true potential in the most effective way, we have written the book in a manner that is in itself a formula for the realization of genius. This formula is revolutionary, yet staggeringly simple.

First, we outline a programme that will allow you, the reader, to check to what extent and in which areas your mental skills compare with the positive characteristics of the Great Minds in the Hall of Fame. Then we demonstrate how the principles derived and the lessons learned from those Great Minds can, in fact, be easily assimilated and adopted by everyone.

Having established these new parameters for the mind, in the Hall of Fame we describe the lives and achievements of 100 Great Minds of the past (including a few of the present). We analyse the achievements of this mega-grouping of history's greatest intellects, and isolate the key qualities which have propelled them towards their brilliant sucesses. Inevitably, many common and replicable factors have emerged from this investigation into genius-in-action.

Once your own mental levels have been established and the characteristics of genius identified, the way for you to achieve and maintain your own peak of mental fitness will become clear. This book reveals what incredible heights of mental performance are achievable, have been achieved in the past and are, in fact, open for everyone to attain.

PART ONE: DEVELOPING YOUR MENTAL SKILLS

In this section of the book, we introduce you to a total Genius Quotient (GQ) self-check. First you go on a grand tour of the 20 Characteristics of Genius and grade yourself accordingly (and honestly!). Following this, we guide you through information and exercises on standard IQ, including your verbal, numerical/logical, and engineering/spatial intelligences. This part of the book also contains explanations of and investigations into your six other significant intelligences.

For each area of intelligence, we give you scores, gradings and advice on improvement and development. All your intelligences combine to give you an overall Multiple Intelligence.

After the Characteristics of Genius and the various intelligence tests, we describe the importance of understanding how the brain functions and how to achieve a healthy mind in a healthy body – both of which are essential if you want to make the most of yourself. Part One concludes with sections on the Brain Principles: Formulae for Genius; Memory; Creativity; Speed Reading, Mind Mapping and Mind Sports. A modern genius needs to be in command of all these areas.

A HEALTHY MIND IN A HEALTHY BODY

The ancient Greeks and the Italians, who nurtured two of the greatest Renaissances and flowerings of genius in the history of mankind, believed in the principle of *mens sana in corpore sano* (a healthy mind in a healthy body). In this section of the book, we introduce you to facts about your body that are as amazing as those about your brain. We explore the inter-relation between the brain and the body, and give you action steps for developing, simultaneously, your mental and physical genius. As well as general fitness, we show how diet, drugs, sleep and rest, sex and mental attitude affect your performance.

THE BRAIN PRINCIPLES: FORMULAE FOR GENIUS

In this section, we introduce you to six new Brain Principles that lead to accelerated learning and the rapid development of overall intelligence. Once you have read about these, you will learn why James Joyce, in his book *Ulysses*, made the statement, *'A man of genius makes no mistakes. His errors are volitional and are the portals of discovery.'*

MEMORY

Geniuses are renowned for displaying a great memory, an ability to learn how to improve it, and tremendous concentration. And in surveys around the world, memory and concentration are most regularly cited as the main problems people experience with using their brains. In this section of the book, we explain the underlying principles of memory, and outline methods that will help you to improve your powers of recall.

CREATIVITY

This is the quality most commonly connected with genius. It is similarly the most commonly misunderstood and ill defined. Here we suggest a new definition of creativity and offer new insights into it. Einstein's $E = mc^2$ revealed the explosive and infinite nature of the relationships between energy, matter and the speed of light in the physical universe. Similarly, our new formula reveals the even more explosive nature of the relationships between energy, memory and creativity. A multiplicity of infinities are available to the internal universes of the human mind.

$$e \twoheadrightarrow M = C^\infty$$

The formula above, and at the beginning of this introduction, shows that *Energy plus Memory produces Infinite Creativity.* As you read through this part of the book, especially the sections on Creativity, Memory and Mind Mapping, the meaning and power of this equation will become increasingly clear. In essence, the equation proves that the ability of the human brain to solve problems and to create is limitless, so long as the equation is correctly applied. The great geniuses of history used it to supreme effect, as you will discover in Part Two.

SPEED READING

As you are reading at the moment, although you may think that you are reading with your eyes, you are in fact reading with your brain! In this section, we explore this essential approach to reading in depth. Your ability to assimilate and to learn new information after applying the principles which we have outlined will increase substantially and dramatically.

MIND MAPPING

Here we introduce you to Radiant Thinking, and its natural extension, the Mind Map. This revolutionary new form of remembering, creating, analysing, organizing, solving problems and communicating is a natural expression of our equation linking Energy, Memory and Creativity. Mind Mapping will help you to unleash your multiple intelligences in a way that you would not have thought possible.

MIND SPORTS

The benefits of physical exercise have long been recognized. Every school includes sports, athletics and games in its curriculum, and physical and aerobic fitness have become a great growth industry in the last couple of decades. However, what has not been universally understood, until now, is that what physical sports can do for the body, Mind Sports can do for the brain. Playing games of strategy like chess and draughts, card games like bridge and poker, the oriental giants like go and shogi or simply doing a crossword provides you, in essence, with a portable gymnasium for the mind. What is more, it has been discovered that exercising your brain in this way, and listening to classical music, can in fact increase your IQ!

PART TWO: THE HALL OF FAME

In this major section of the book, we identify our choice of the towering geniuses of the past five millennia. Many of these 'Great Minds inspired each other and they will act as superlative collective role models for you. Among our earliest geniuses are the Builders of the Great Pyramid at Giza, a massively enduring structure that would not be obliterated even if it sustained a direct hit by a modern thermo-nuclear weapon. We then proceed via Aristotle, Alexander the Great, Leonardo da Vinci, Columbus, Shakespeare, Newton, Goethe and Einstein to Professor Stephen Hawking, whose vision of the universe leads the way for modern cosmology.

The profiles of these Great Minds all probe specifically for the particular qualities which foster genius and allow it to be unleashed, to flourish and ultimately to triumph. It is in these pages that you will find the destruction of so many of the popular and, dare we say, ridiculous misconceptions about genius.

COMMON MISCONCEPTIONS

The super-intelligent child or prodigy is often assumed to be a thin, pale, hunched, thick-bespectacled, anti-social and non-physical nerd! Similarly, the great creative genius is frequently portrayed as disorganized, unkempt, dishevelled, dirty, forgetful and probably insane. Geniuses are also reputed to peak early, losing their abilities in mathematics, physics and lyric poetry in their early twenties, and losing their abilities for science, music, art and novel writing in their early thirties. The catalogue of misconceptions grows with the assumptions that most geniuses were sickly as children, celibate, orphaned and destitute.

It has also been constantly stated that the genius was a 'one-in-a-million' exception who had been given some special divine spark of genius not available to the average run-of-the-mill human being. This argument assumes that the basic nature of a genius is inborn and is not a product of education, care, love or nurture.

On the opposite sides of these misconceptual coins is the 'thick Jock' hypothesis – the assumption that anyone involved in high physical activity will necessarily be of a lower mental capability.

FACTS ABOUT GENIUSES

In this book we reveal an amazing discovery – the brain is actually connected to the body! We say this humorously and also in deadly earnest. As you will see from the above misconceptions about genius and intelligence, for the last few centuries the human race has, if you like, decapitated itself, disconnecting conceptually the mind from the body. Our study of the geniuses in the Hall of Fame proves that *all* our societal prejudices are exactly the *opposite* of the truth.

Great intelligence is characterized by robust health, greater physical size, advanced social skills and, importantly, a sense of humour. The creative genius has all these skills and is, in contradiction to the stereotype, meticulously organized, scrupulously clean and possessed of an exceptionally powerful memory. Recent studies also, not surprisingly, show that those who engage in physical activity are, across the board, superior in their multiple intelligences.

In addition to debunking the misconceived myths, our survey of geniuses also concludes that their intelligence, creativity, productivity and work rate tended to accelerate with age, many of their greatest triumphs being at the end of a long life. To our delight, longevity is another characteristic of genius.

Another point is that geniuses very rarely spent their time 'isolated in attics'. They were more often to be found exhibiting their lust for life in the midst of celebrations, parties and social events – excellent role models for us all!

NATURE VERSUS NURTURE

We also directly disagree with the 'spark of genius' school of thought. The basic nature of genius is in all human beings; it is nurture of that nature which is all important. This view has been held by many of the great geniuses themselves, including Maria Montessori, Morihei Ueshiba and F.M. Alexander. This approach to genius is supported by the Japanese musician, inventor, author and teacher Shinichi Suzuki, who founded his world-famous Suzuki Music Schools based on nurture helping nature. Suzuki's understanding is best described in his own words.

ALL JAPANESE CHILDREN SPEAK JAPANESE

'This thought struck me like a flash of light in the dark. Since they all speak Japanese so easily and fluently, there must be a secret; and this must be training. Indeed, all children everywhere in the world are brought up by a perfect educational method: their mother tongue. Why not apply this method to other faculties? I felt I had made a tremendous discovery. It was just taken for granted; people in general think that the ability children display is inborn . . .

'If a child cannot do his arithmetic, it is said that his intelligence is below average. Yet he can speak the difficult Japanese language – or his own native language – very well. Isn't this something to ponder and think about? In my opinion, the child who cannot do arithmetic is not below average intelligence; it is the educational system that is wrong. His ability or talent simply has not been developed properly. It is astonishing that no one has discovered this before, although the situation clearly has existed throughout human history.'

Two of Suzuki's conclusions were:

1 We must study how to develop talent through education.

2 We must realize that talent, not only in music but in other fields as well, is not inherited.

THE MAGNET OF GENIUS

We totally agree with Suzuki. Our investigations also reveal, time and again, that *genius attracts while absolute genius attracts absolutely.* It is no accident, for example, that the incandescent intellectual environment in the city state of Athens during the fifth and fourth centuries BC populated by Phidias, Aeschylus, Sophocles, Euripides, Socrates, Plato and Aristotle should have been so irresistible to High Renaissance minds. Those fascinated by the Athenian Golden Age include Michelangelo, Leonardo, Machiavelli and Raphael, all contemporaries from the Italian city states some 2000 years later.

SEEING THE HEEL – BUT MISSING ACHILLES

From our study of the geniuses it has emerged that their focus was on the positive rather than the negative. One of the fundamental principles on which this book is based is therefore that any individual society or civilization which wholeheartedly accepts and applauds greatness and genius in others is far more likely to achieve greatness or genius itself. The cynical debunking of heroes of the past has, unfortunately, become a farcical contemporary industry that produces little of value.

We entirely agree that uncritical idolization of all aspects of the public and private life of any 'hero' is naive and counter-productive. Great men and women will often exhibit weaknesses, sometimes associated with their enormous energy and lust for life. This must obviously be recognized. However, constant dredging for such peccadillos and the consequent defamation of their character and entire work serves little useful purpose.

Nelson, Einstein, Jung, Goethe, Hawking... the list of those who have come into the firing line of late is endless. What concerns us more importantly in this book are the thoughts, the plans and the realizations of the visions which the Great Minds chose as their own.

We encourage you to select those qualities in the lives of the great geniuses that most ideally reflect your own personal goals and aspirations, and to combine these with the exercises and examples in Part One. Together they will contribute to your own personal Genius Development Programme.

PART THREE: MENTAL WORLD RECORDS

We are delighted that in this book we have brought together for the first time the most impressive mental world records and achievements particularly in the field of memorization. Our purpose is to show the quantifiable peaks to which every individual can aspire. We are confident that you will find these 'Everests of the Mind' awe-inspiring. We include them as a challenge and an enticement! Remember that your brain improves its capacity whenever you learn new things and conquer new mental terrain.

Finally, as you progress through this book, we wish you the greatest of enjoyment and the greatest of success. You are entering a community that is the natural right of everyone, and which was most beautifully expressed by Herman Melville, the American novelist and poet, when he said, *'Genius, all over the world, stands hand in hand, and one shock of recognition runs the whole circle round'.*

We hope that *Buzan's Book of Genius* will be that one shock of recognition.

TONY BUZAN AND RAYMOND KEENE
AUGUST 1994

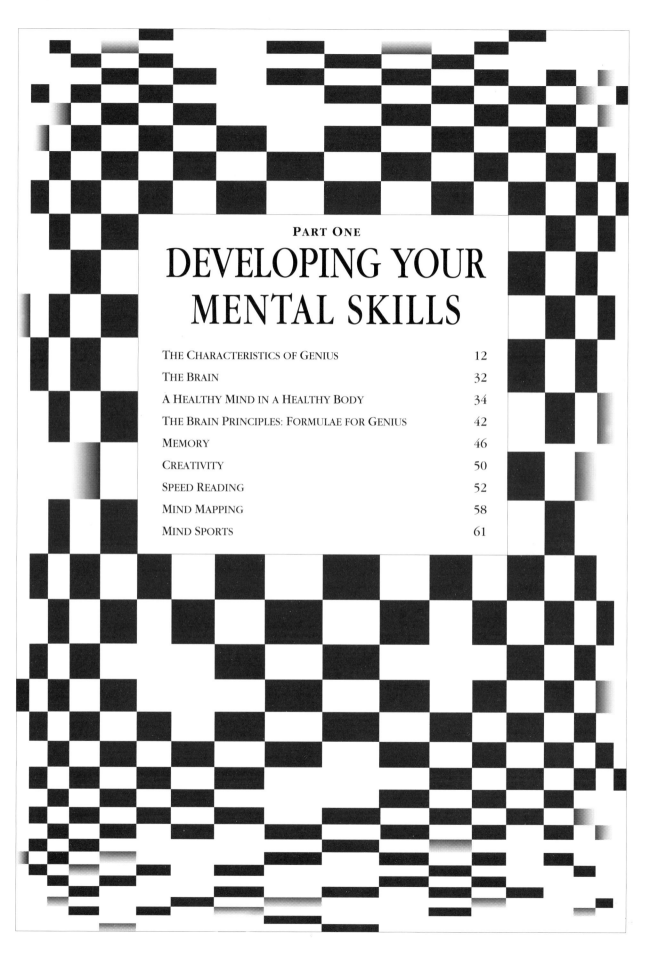

PART ONE

DEVELOPING YOUR MENTAL SKILLS

THE CHARACTERISTICS OF GENIUS   12

THE BRAIN   32

A HEALTHY MIND IN A HEALTHY BODY   34

THE BRAIN PRINCIPLES: FORMULAE FOR GENIUS   42

MEMORY   46

CREATIVITY   50

SPEED READING   52

MIND MAPPING   58

MIND SPORTS   61

THE CHARACTERISTICS OF GENIUS

'PLANET EARTH PROVIDES THE ULTIMATE INTELLIGENCE TEST. IT IS THE INDIVIDUAL'S ABILITY TO DEAL WITH THE INTRICATE MULTIPLICITY OF CHALLENGES, WHICH THE ENVIRONMENT PROVIDES ON A SECOND-BY-SECOND BASIS, THAT ULTIMATELY DETERMINES THE LEVEL OF OUR INTELLIGENCE AND OUR CONSEQUENT CHANCES OF SURVIVAL.'

TONY BUZAN

While we researched the 100 geniuses introduced in our Hall of Fame, as well as many others who did not make our list, 20 essential characteristics of genius emerged. These recur constantly in all successful geniuses, whether they come from the world of the arts, science, religion, business, politics, sports, theatre, or the professions. These 20 qualities (listed opposite) constitute the championship and leadership characteristics of genius.

In this romanticized rendering by William Blake (1757-1827), Isaac Newton is holding dividers, 'measuring the universe'.

THE 20 QUALITIES OF GENIUS

1 Vision
2 Desire
3 Faith
4 Commitment
5 Planning
6 Persistence
7 Learning from mistakes

8 Subject knowledge
9 Mental literacy
10 Imagination
11 Positive attitude
12 Auto-suggestion
13 Intuition
14 Mastermind group (real)

15 Mastermind group (internal)
16 Truth/honesty
17 Facing fears/courage
18 Creativity/flexibility
19 Love of the task
20 Energy
　　(physical/sensual/sexual)

MULTIPLE INTELLIGENCE TEST 1
YOUR GENIUS QUOTIENT

To find out your Genius Quotient (GQ), you need to rank yourself honestly in the above genius characteristics. It is essential in this test and in all the others in this book that you are as truthful with yourself as you possibly can be, for only by knowing where you are *truly* ranked can you establish your benchmarks and thus start a programme of properly unleashing the genius within you. (As you will discover, honesty is one of the overriding qualities of the great geniuses, so make an effort to be truthful.)

In order to compare yourself with the great geniuses, give yourself marks in relation to each characteristic on a scale of 0-100 (0 = non-existent; 100 = perfect or absolute). For example, for the first characteristic, Vision, if you feel that you have *no* life vision whatsoever, and are completely goal-less, give yourself a 0. On the other hand, if you feel that your vision is completely clear, and the total focal point of your life, give yourself 100.

As you read through the following definitions of the 20 traits of genius, think about how the specific qualities apply to yourself. Later, you may find it intriguing to 'give the test' to each of the 100 geniuses in this book, thus devising a personal rating system of them for yourself, and comparing it with our 'official' ranking list. For your own assessment, make sure that you consider each quality very carefully, and rate yourself accurately not in comparison to your daydreams or wishes, but in comparison to the great geniuses and your own current *real* level. Read the definition for each trait, and then enter your personal mark in the table on page 18 before moving on to the next trait. Continue by giving yourself marks for each genius quality.

1 VISION

The degree to which the goal of succeeding in your life's ambition is absolute, imaginatively seen, precisely formulated, clearly stated, and comprehensively understood. It is the 'guiding light' of the individual (or team). One of the 'greatest of all time' in this department was he who is famous for that very quote – the boxing champion Muhammad Ali. His visions of victory were so complete that he would describe in detail the round-by-round progress of many of his fights, culminating in the round and type of victory, as long as eight months before the fight. Not only were his predictions eerily accurate, they were so strong and so perfectly described that they were etched into the minds of his opponents, who subsequently usually shared his vision for the fight and co-operated in it completely – in contributing towards their own downfall.

2 DESIRE

The degree of the passion or wish to accomplish your visions, goals and mission. The great geniuses often described their own desire as 'burning' or like an overriding hunger. Faraday's desire to explore the world of electricity, even though he was a humble bookbinder, was so strong that he willingly took the job of washing test tubes in the laboratories of the masters so that he could glean their knowledge and learn his trade. Similarly Michelangelo's desire to complete certain master works from appropriate pieces of marble was so overriding that he used to manage the engineering projects necessary to extract the stone, and, in many cases, wait years for the correct and precious blocks he desired.

3 FAITH

All the geniuses we have studied had a belief in themselves and their Mastermind Groups; they had the mental, and therefore the physical, power to accomplish their vision. Faith has to be particularly strong because it is often, in the case of the genius, attacked by those who don't yet understand the vision. As Jonathan Swift (1667-1745), the Anglo-Irish poet and satirist, stated in *Thoughts on Various Subjects* (1711):

'When a true genius appears in the world, you may know him by this sign: that the dunces are all in confederacy against him.'

4 COMMITMENT

This combines the previously mentioned desire to win, and the faith in oneself that the goal can be attained. Commitment is specific in that it is an agreement to act on the vision, desire and faith. Most geniuses and world champions usually state their commitment publicly, write it down as a personal incentive, gather a small or large band of people under the same 'commitment banner' or do all three.

The great World Chess Champion and genius, Garry Kasparov, is often cited as one of the individuals most committed to becoming World Champion ever known. After having fought the gigantic Soviet chess machine which wanted his main rival, Anatoly Karpov, to remain champion, Kasparov not only was illegally denied the title, but fought back in a second match to gain it. Subsequently he had to battle against the International Chess Federation (FIDE) which also tried to deny him the World Championship. Such was Kasparov's commitment that he took on both FIDE and his opponent, while at the same time setting up a new international chess organization – The Professional Chess Association. Due to his commitment he won all battles, and remains the greatest chess player ever.

5 PLANNING

Planning involves the clarity of definition, focus and precision of the short-, medium- and long-term plans for accomplishing the overall vision (incorporating the communication of such plans to appropriate individuals and groups).

The quintessential example of planning is Ch'in Shi Huangdi, the first Ch'in Emperor.

Not only did he plan in detail and general concept the reorganization of China – the greatest and oldest civilization – he also completed the Great Wall of China, a masterpiece of macro- and

ADVICE FROM A GENIUS

One of the most insightful quotes on commitment comes from Johann Wolfgang von Goethe, the holder of the mental world record in Used Human Vocabulary (50,000 words), pictured skating here, with his mother and fiancée in the background.

'Until one is committed, there is hesitancy, the chance to draw back, always ineffectiveness. Concerning all acts of initiative (and creation), there is one elementary truth the ignorance of which kills countless ideas and splendid plans: that the moment one definitely commits oneself, then Providence moves too. All sorts of things occur to help one that would never otherwise have occurred . . . Whatever you can do or dream you can . . . Begin it now.'

micro-cosmic detail. Ch'in even carried his planning into his life after death, creating in extraordinary detail and scope a second realm with a replica 6000-strong army to protect him. Each individual member of the terracotta force was given the face of one of Ch'in's soldiers.

6 PERSISTENCE

Most great geniuses and champions are capable of continuing the pursuit of their goals in the face of adversity and when others would give up. Persistence was admirably demonstrated by the great American Draughts/Checkers World Champion (a 50-year reign), the exceptionally physically fit 65-year-old, Dr Marion Tinsley. He played for eight hours a day, five days a week, for two weeks, against the implacable Chinook computer (the world's official number two player with a database of 27 *billion* positions) and crushed it in the final game, leaping up and proclaiming 'A victory for human beings!'

Perhaps the most famous story of persistence concerns Thomas Edison. After he had tried over 5000 ways to get electricity to produce light, and was accused of being insane for not giving up, he replied that since he was the only person who knew of so many ways his experiments did not work, he must therefore be the one who was nearest to the truth.

7 LEARNING FROM MISTAKES

Great geniuses have an uncanny ability to consider each and every 'mistake' no matter how unpleasant, as an experience that could be a useful stepping stone towards the next success. As James Joyce (1882-1941), the Irish novelist, wrote in *Ulysses* (1922), '*A man of genius makes no mistakes. His "errors" are volitional and are the portals of discovery.*'

Alberti, da Vinci, Michelangelo, Titian, Rembrandt, Cézanne, Picasso and Dali all built their successes from a series of minor failures. And where would we be now if Orville and Wilbur Wright had not learned from their own!

8 SUBJECT KNOWLEDGE

Geniuses, Olympians and champions are renowned for their voracious thirst for and comprehensive grasp of knowledge of their particular subject (and often that of many others!). A simple glance at such names as Aristotle, Aquinas, da Vinci, Copernicus, Shakespeare, Newton, Goethe, Darwin and Einstein confirms that to aspire to genius one has to acquire a vast and fundamental knowledge-base in the field you wish to pursue, and from which great new thoughts can spring.

9 MENTAL LITERACY

Standard literacy is an understanding of the knowledge of the alphabet and how to expand it into words and eventually sentences, paragraphs and books. Numeracy (numerical literacy) is the understanding of the alphabet of numbers and the ability to combine and interlink them in increasingly sophisticated ways.

Mental literacy is the king of literacies. First, it is the knowledge of the alphabet of the physical structure and nature of the brain, including its major and minor parts such as the cerebral cortex and the brain cell. Second, it is an understanding of the alphabet of the brain's behavioural skills, especially memory, creativity, learning, and general thinking skills.

Even though mental literacy is a relatively new concept resulting from the sudden explosion of knowledge concerning the physical functioning of the brain, the great geniuses of the past latched on to the fact that whichever organ enabled them to think was the prime organ and should be encouraged. This is why so many of the geniuses became great teachers, and why most of them were renowned for having developed extraordinary memories, especially Homer, Alexander the Great, da Vinci, Pitt the Elder, Thomas Jefferson, Mozart, Napoleon, Stravinsky, and Gates.

Indeed, Dominic O'Brien, the 1993 World Memory Champion and 1994 Brain Trust Brain of the Year, practises a full range of mental (and physical) skills for at least four hours a day, taking himself for walks and runs in the morning on which he applies every facet of his mind to the perception, imaging and remembering of multiple *loci*, pathways and maps in his mind.

10 IMAGINATION

The ability to create internal images, to 'see thought' and to visualize the outcome of plans and goals. All the great visionaries in this book used their imaginations to create such a powerful internal vision that their entire life was spent, much like Michelangelo's, removing that which was not of the vision itself until only the vision remained – in reality. Imagination made real.

11 POSITIVE ATTITUDE

A realistic, positive attitude is enthusiastic, optimistic, up-beat, 'can-do' and open to every opportunity for getting the best out of any situation. It is, rather than starry-eyed wishful thinking, an accurate assessment of events with a focus on maximizing opportunities. A positive attitude permeates the great minds of history, and is especially identifiable in those who have been involved in combat, such as Alexander the Great, Suleyman the Magnificent, the Duke of Wellington, Mahatma Gandhi and Muhammad Ali. Other examples abound from the recent world of sports, including World Champions such as Chionofuji (sumo), Daley Thompson (decathlon), Steve Ovett and Sally Gunnell (athletics), Mark Spitz (swimming) and Mary Lou Retton (Olympic gymnastics).

Greg Norman's performance against Nick Faldo in the final round of the 1993 British Open, described as one of the greatest final rounds in golf history, is a useful example. *The Sunday Times* reported: 'Norman, however, turned every negative into a positive, as though crushing defeats were essential pieces in the jig-saw of great golf. *"The whole crux is that you believe in yourself. I can bounce back from whatever they throw at me,"* said Norman.'

12 AUTO-SUGGESTION

The degree of active, positive 'self-talk' directed towards the accomplishment of goals. We all 'self-talk' and psychological researches have shown that as much as 90% of it tends to be negative – for instance, 'I'm too tired', 'I'd never be able to do that', 'I'm stupid'. Our geniuses have a ratio that was at least 90% positive! Indeed they even 'auto-suggested to themselves' out loud. Dickens used to talk to his characters, and Einstein used to pace up and down his studio roaring with laughter at his conversations with his formulae and the universe. Watch great athletes and you can actually *see* them expressing their positive attitude, vision and commitment through active instructions to themselves – they become their own best coaches.

13 INTUITION

The ability to 'sense' or 'feel' accurately the possibilities and probabilities for accomplishing a goal in all situations. Intuition may be described as a Super Logic in which the human brain compares its historical matrix of multiple quadrillions of bits of data with a new matrix of experience. It is what causes that sudden flash of insight (Archimedes and his 'Eureka!'), that sudden stroke of military genius (Nelson), that sudden deep realization that something will succeed (Walt Disney and *Fantasia*). The feeling we experience in such situations is the body's reaction to the brain's calculations. In most cases the intuition is correct, and is a skill that can be learned and developed. The great geniuses

trusted theirs to a far greater extent than their contemporaries trusted their own.

14 MASTERMIND GROUP (REAL)

The Mastermind Group refers to those individuals who make up the immediate personal and professional 'circle of advisers and influences' who assist the individual (genius) in the achievement of the vision and goals. The grading should be based on the excellence of the quality of the group. Geniuses are conspicuously *not* isolated individuals, but are surrounded, from an early age on and throughout their lives, by the best minds of the time. Lao-Tzu had Confucius and Buddha; Confucius – Buddha and Lao-Tzu; Plato had Socrates; Alexander the Great had Aristotle; and so the catalogue progresses to more recent times where Crick had Watson and Watson had Crick; and Bill Gates was not only surrounded by but subsequently hired the best minds on the planet

Lao-Tzu and Confucius, both 6th-century Chinese philosophers, formed part of each other's Mastermind Group.

as his advisers. In estimating your score for this characteristic, consider your 10 closest 'Mastermind' advisers (they are likely to include friends and colleagues and may include your family).

15 MASTERMIND GROUP (INTERNAL)

In our studies we have found no exception to the rule that great geniuses have internal role models or heroes – either from history, from those in the present but who are not personally known, or from myth. It is remarkable how many of the geniuses in this book had each other as role models and heroes and, indeed, some of them may already be, or may become, part of your own personal internal Mastermind Group.

When you rate yourself for this category, your rating should reflect not only the strengths of your group, but also the clarity with which you see the individuals, the depth of the knowledge you have about them, and the frequency with which you 'consult' them.

16 TRUTH/HONESTY

Great geniuses tend to be true to themselves, true to their friends, and true to the concept of truth. To them truth is both a beacon and a balm, and their works frequently refer to it. From Milton we have: *'Beholding the bright countenance of truth in the quiet and still air of delightful studies.'* And from Shakespeare: *'Time's glory is to calm contending Kings, To unmask falsehood, and bring truth to light.'* When you are rating yourself for this genius characteristic, remember to be honest!

17 FACING FEARS/COURAGE

It is often assumed that 'great minds' have less fear than those around them. The opposite appears to be true. The vision of past geniuses was so great, and their commitment to it so absolute, that their fear of losing it or becoming involved in circumstances that lessened their chances of gaining it, was proportionally gigantic in comparison to those who had little 'reason for living'. The strength of the geniuses was that they were capable of facing those fears, admitting them, and then using them appropriately to face the fears and adversity with courage. The appropriate attitude to the enormous danger of fear, and 'overcoming' it, was succinctly expressed and summarized in the 'obliteration of obliteration' mantra by psychologist Frank Herbert in *Dune*, his novel concerning the development of the ultimate genius:

'Fear is the little death that brings total obliteration. I will face my fear. I will permit it to pass over me and through me. And when it is gone past I will turn the inner eye to see its path. Where the fear has gone there will be nothing. Only I will remain.'

18 CREATIVITY/FLEXIBILITY

This quality of genius refers to your personal degree of ability to generate new ideas, see things from different perspectives, to solve problems in original ways, to think with your multiple cortical skills in a synaesthetic way (linking the senses), and to maintain an open, quick, curious and exploring mind. As you read about the great geniuses in this book, you will find that most great military victories were won not by the strengths or size of the military force, but by the creativity and flexibility of the thinkers within those martial groups. Similarly, all great scientific and artistic ideas came from this same skill.

19 LOVE OF THE TASK

This is expressed as an all-consuming passion and enthusiasm for not only the particular vision in mind, but also for the wider implications and applications of the field. Our research has shown that the enthusiasms of the great minds of history consistently led them to polymathy (a great and varied knowledge), and more often than not was such an irrepressible fountain of inspiration that it poured out from them in their willing role as great teachers. Socrates, Euclid, Suleyman the Magnificent, Bach, Faraday, Maria Montessori, and Martha Graham, to name just a few, all dramatically emphasize the point that those who *really* can do, *do teach*! When rating yourself in this section, include your willingness to pass on your special knowledge to others, regardless of the obstacles.

20 ENERGY (PHYSICAL/SENSUAL/SEXUAL)

Without exception, the great geniuses were and are known to exude physical, sensual and sexual energy to an unusual degree. It is our contention that these expressions are natural and to be expected when a mind has a vision to which all the other 19 attributes of genius are attached. The story of Ivan Pavlov's sheer energy transforming the life of the great English psychologist, Dr Robert Thouless, is a marvellous case in point. And no one should be surprised about Einstein's enthusiasm for the opposite sex!

CALCULATING YOUR GENIUS QUOTIENT (GQ)

Fill this chart with the marks you award your-self for each of the 20 qualities of genius. Rate yourself again after a couple of months, or after you have made a concerted effort to improve in specific areas, and use the chart as a record of your progress. Try to be as honest as possible when rating yourself; if you find this difficult, it may be helpful to ask someone who knows you well for his or her opinion. When you have added up your score for all the genius qualities, check your GQ in the analysis on the opposite page.

		Your score. Note: 0 = non-existent 100 = perfect									
	Date										
	GQ check	1st	2nd	3rd	4th	5th	6th	7th	8th	9th	10th
1	VISION										
2	DESIRE										
3	FAITH										
4	COMMITMENT										
5	PLANNING										
6	PERSISTENCE										
7	LEARNING FROM MISTAKES										
8	SUBJECT KNOWLEDGE										
9	MENTAL LITERACY										
10	IMAGINATION										
11	POSITIVE ATTITUDE										
12	AUTO-SUGGESTION										
13	INTUITION										
14	MASTERMIND GROUP (REAL)										
15	MASTERMIND GROUP (INTERNAL)										
16	TRUTH/HONESTY										
17	FACING FEARS/COURAGE										
18	CREATIVITY/FLEXIBILITY										
19	LOVE OF THE TASK										
20	ENERGY (PHYSICAL/SENSUAL/SEXUAL)										
	TOTAL SCORE										

SCORING AND ANALYSIS

While studying the geniuses and compiling the characteristics, we have observed three intriguing facts.

The first is that the characteristics seem to be more than just individual qualities. They are almost like a chemical, mathematical or physics formula which requires all its elements for it to be properly balanced. Second, this balance is of an extraordinarily delicate nature. The concept of genius characteristics can be thought of as a ventipede (an imaginary 20-legged creature akin to the centipede). In a centipede, the loss of one of its 100 legs would be relatively unimportant, and easily managed. In the ventipede, however, the loss of even one of its legs (characteristics) has the same devastating effect on the whole body and its effective function and locomotion as does the loss of a single leg to a biped. The point is that when developing your own genius characteristics it is essential to make sure that you nurture them *all* on an on-going basis.

Third, the 20 terms used to describe the characteristics have been considered very carefully, and are, in a sense, the supreme distillation of the concepts they express. Many other words and expressions exist that describe qualities of excellence in human beings, and you will find that these will be either synonyms for the 20 characteristics or will be subsumed under them. For example, words such as 'innovative' and 'proliferate' will be subsumed under the characteristics of 'creativity/flexibility' and 'energy'. In your future reading try to clarify the characteristics in your own mind.

The scoring and analysis which follows will help you to establish personal goals and will give you guidelines for the continuing development of your own genius, and your championship and leadership qualities.

SCORING AND ANALYSIS

2000 – 1900 (100 – 95%)

A score in this percentile places you in the genius bracket in the individual GQ test and possibly in all the following Olympian tests. You will be a natural leader in whatever you wish to accomplish.

1900 – 1800 (95 – 90%)

This score indicates that you are on the verge of overall genius. With a little extra effort and training in the area, or areas, of relative weakness you will rapidly reach genius level.

1800 – 1600 (90 – 80%)

An exceptionally good score. With such high marks you will generally be near the top, and occasionally at the top, of your chosen endeavour. Look at where your weaknesses are, and immediately embark on a programme of continuing self-development.

1600 – 1400 (80 – 70%)

Above average. Have a good look at your test results, and examine in depth your strengths and weaknesses, using the former to help you to develop skills in the latter.

1400 – 1000 (70 – 50%)

You are in the average range. This simply means that your personal characteristics of genius have been partly developed and still have a long way to go. You need to do some brain training – perhaps read more than usual, learn a language or take up a new sport.

Below 1000 (below 50%)

Assuming you have not underestimated yourself, your score shows that you are idling on by far less than 1% of your brain's conscious capacity. Get your brain in gear without any delay! Think about your attitude to life and what you want to achieve. Then go for it.

YOUR MULTIPLE INTELLIGENCE QUOTIENT (MIQ)

The history of the development of our knowledge about intelligence is fascinating. Often the quest for knowledge resulted in dead ends; nevertheless the efforts of researchers increasingly led to more profound and useful insights.

Experiments in intelligence testing by 'scientific' means started at the beginning of the 20th century. Philosophers had always been interested in the cognitive powers of the brain, especially the intellectual pursuits of thinking and the perception of the universe. They now raced against the earliest psychologists who were initially searching for physiological bases for intelligence. These included the possibility that the relative speed of impulses throughout the nervous system might reflect fundamental differences in intelligence.

Early experiments included measuring the 'knee-jerk response', with the result that no correlation between the speed of response and intelligence was found. The next and most obvious route was to measure the size of the brains of exceptionally bright and exceptionally dull people. Some very minor differences were found, but these were so slight as to be statistically insignificant.

The birth of intelligence (IQ) tests followed. They were invented by Alfred Binet (1857-1911), a Frenchman who abandoned a successful law career in his early 20s because he had become so fascinated by the new discoveries in physiology, psychology, mesmerism and hypnosis. It is often assumed that intelligence tests were designed to control, suppress and manipulate the masses, and to retain power for the ruling classes. As is so often the case with the history of the development of great ideas, exactly the opposite in fact turns out to be true.

Binet had been particularly influenced by the views of John Stuart Mill who, at the time, was proposing a psychological theory suggesting that our more complex mental acts develop from the association of simpler acts with one another. Binet was also intrigued by the study of mental abilities and disabilities, and was concerned by his observation that all students in higher education and universities at the turn of the century came exclusively from the upper and ruling classes. He therefore set out to devise tests that were based on a child's intellectual aptitude alone, especially the abilities of judgement, comprehension and reasoning. He produced a series of questions which he constructed so that they could be understood and solved regardless of class, creed, or any previous special school learning. He asked thousands of children hundreds of questions, and noted which questions, when answered correctly, would predict success in school, and which questions, when failed, would predict difficulty in school. Binet then calculated what the average four, five, and six-year-old test scores would be, and gave them a value of 100 IQ points – a normal IQ. Any child who

had a test score below average would have an IQ below 100, and any child who had a test score above average would have an IQ score of more than 100. The score any child actually achieved was described as his or her mental age. Thus, for example, if a six-year-old child scored what an average eight-year-old child would score, the six-year-old was given a *mental age* of eight. An IQ was calculated by the ratio of mental age over chronological age – in this example: $\%$ = 1.33. Binet then multiplied the score by 100 to give, again in this example, an IQ of 133.

How often is an IQ above the norm, and how often below? The distribution of intelligences cover a fairly smooth 'bell' curve. 50% of the population fall into the average range, 30% into the low and high ranges, 14% into the very low and very high ranges, and 3% into the exceptionally low and 'genius' ranges.

Although these tests were originally supposed to give absolute scores that did not change throughout life, a number of questions began to be raised about the IQ test as a comprehensive test of human intelligence. First it was discovered that mental abilities of nearly all kinds were positively linked – when people were good at one thing they were likely to be good at others. Thus if a person has a good vocabulary there is a very high probability that the same person will also be good at mathematics and have a better than average memory. Similarly, if a person has a good memory, they will more than likely have a large vocabulary and be good at mathematics. This suggested that training in one area could affect performance in other areas, and therefore change the 'absolute' IQ.

It was also noticed that certain children tended to increase their IQs dramatically as they grew

This diagram shows the normal distribution of IQ scores. Half of people tested fall into the average range, while only 3% have a 'genius' level IQ.

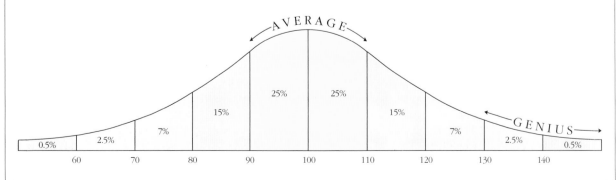

older, while others tended to remain fairly constant. No explanation was found other than that some form of training had been taking place that was having a major effect on the development of the child's intelligence. A third and more disturbing observation was that many people with 'genius' IQs were often singular failures in their personal, academic and professional lives, indicating some form of imbalance.

This gave rise in the 1970s to a revolution in ideas about what intelligence really is and means – a revolution headed by Professor Howard Gardner, Tony Buzan, and Professor Robert Ornstein. Professor Gardner summed it up when he stated that there are a number of different kinds of intelligence, that intelligence is never completely in the head, and that a true intelligence involves an interaction between whatever is in your head and the opportunities that are around you in the environment.

The more these multiple intelligences have been investigated, the more different intelligences have arisen! In this book we identify 10 major intelligences, which include the verbal and numerical intelligences which form the base of traditional IQ testing. The 10 multiple intelligences are:

1 Genius Quotient
2 Verbal Intelligence
3 Numerical/Logical Intelligence
4 Engineering/Spatial Intelligence
5 Sensual Intelligence
6 Body/Kinaesthetic Intelligence
7 Creative Intelligence
8 Intra-personal Intelligence
9 Inter-personal Intelligence
10 Spiritual Intelligence

The pages which follow explain each of your multiple intelligences, and provide self-check tests. Each test consists of 10 questions, the answers to which will enable you to check the current levels of both your particular intelligences and your combined multiple-intelligence quotient (MIQ). The first test you have already taken to establish your GQ. The next two tests measure your traditional IQ, and the remaining seven your other multiple intelligences. Analyses of the scores are included for each test, and for your overall multiple intelligence quotient.

Most questions require you to rate yourself. As mentioned before, make sure that you answer the questions as honestly as you can. You need to know where you are *truly* ranked to establish your starting levels. Then you can begin a programme of intelligence development that will give you real feedback on your improvement. *All* intelligences can, like any natural organism, be nurtured and grown, and your brain's capacity increases when you learn new things. In other words, even though you may have been led to believe otherwise in the past, the more you learn, and the more you expand your knowledge, the more you will be capable of learning and will feel inspired to learn.

YOUR TRADITIONAL IQ

Traditional IQ, as mentioned above, covers a specific range of verbal and numerical or mathematical skills which are normally combined into a single number designating your 'official IQ'. In tests 2 and 3, the two areas of skill have been separated, so that you may differentiate between your verbal and numerical IQ.

Complete both of the following tests in the time and manner indicated.

MULTIPLE INTELLIGENCE TEST 2
VERBAL INTELLIGENCE

Verbal or linguistic intelligence is one of the major factors in traditional IQ testing. Vocabulary (knowing the meanings and definitions of words), and a concomitant knowledge of the multiple interrelationships between words, has been found to be the single intelligence most highly correlated with success in academia and the professions.

Give yourself 15 minutes maximum to complete the 10 questions of your Verbal Intelligence Test. Feel free to go back over any questions within your time limit. If you are finished before the 15 minutes are up, you are advised to look at your answers again. When the allotted time has expired, check your answers (see page 255), fill in the score chart on page 22, add up your total points and then read through the scoring and analysis (also on page 22).

1 QUAD is to OCT
as TRI is to . . . .

2 Which is the odd one out?

Sempre	Allegro
Forte	Spumante
Vivace	Mosso
Molto	

3 Rearrange the following
letters to make four words:
a) RETOCX . . . .
b) RABIN . . . .
c) HINTK . . . .
d) ERATCEIV . . . .

4 Fill in the missing word:
INFANT is to INFANCY
as ADULT is to . . . .

5 Which is the odd word out?
a) NOLI . . . .
b) TERIG . . . .
c) GROMNLE . . . .
d) NELFEI . . . .
e) ACT . . . .

6 Insert the missing letter:

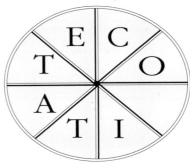

7 Fourteen : One
as Stone : . . . .

8 Guitar : Cello
as Segovia : . . . .

9 Land : Sea
as . . . . : Strait

10 Insert a word that means
the same as the two words
outside the brackets:
STICK (. . . . .) WAGER

SCORE CHART									
1	2	3	4	5	6	7	8	9	10
TOTAL									

SCORING AND ANALYSIS

1000 – 850

You obviously have a high verbal IQ, and could consider joining MENSA, the High IQ Society.

850 – 750

You are in the generally high IQ bracket and probably find yourself skilled in all verbal areas. Push yourself into the genius range.

750 – 650

High average. Consider training in vocabulary and linguistic skills, and improve the volume, comprehension and speed of your reading.

650 – 500

Average but do not be discouraged by this. Follow the advice given for the above score.

500 – 0

The fact that you have been able to read this questionnaire and a summary proves that your brain is capable of getting a far higher score. Train yourself! For instance, try to read more and look up any words that you don't know.

MULTIPLE INTELLIGENCE TEST 3
NUMERICAL/LOGICAL INTELLIGENCE

This intelligence, the second major factor in standard IQ tests, refers to the ability to manipulate and play with the 'numerical alphabet'.
Give yourself 15 minutes maximum to complete the 10 questions of your Numerical/Logical Intelligence Test. Feel free to go back over any questions within your time limit. If you are finished before the 15 minutes are up, you are advised to look at your answers again. When the allotted time has expired, check your answers (see page 255), write your score on the opposite page, add up your total points and then read through the scoring and analysis for this particular test.

1 Insert the missing number:
14, 17, 20, ...

2 Insert the missing number:
93, 85, 77, ...

3 Fill in the missing number:

1	12	12
3	4	12
10	20	

4 What is the missing number?

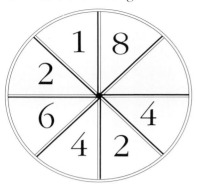

5 Fill in the missing number:
I N T 5 L L I – 5 N T
6 Fill in the next number:
1, 4, 9, 61, 52, 63, 94 . . . . . .

7 Insert the missing number:

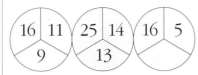

8 Insert the missing number:

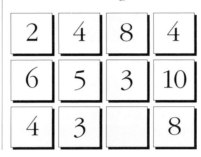

9 Find the missing number:

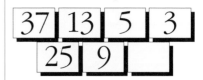

10 What is the next number in this series?
9, 11, 21, 23, 33, 35, ...

SCORE CHART									
1	2	3	4	5	6	7	8	9	10
TOTAL									

SCORING AND ANALYSIS

1000 – 850

A mathematically genius-high IQ. (If you questioned why 850 to 1000 instead of 950 to 1000, demote yourself to the next bracket!)

850 – 750

You are in the superior IQ bracket for numerical logical intelligence. Embark on a self-improvement programme to push yourself into the genius range.

750 – 650

High normal numerical IQ, indicating that you probably have done well in mathematics at school, and love certain mathematical games. Play more in this field, and improve.

650 – 500

Normal. Your formal training has not emphasized this aspect of your intelligence, but you can easily learn the necessary mental skills.

500 – 0

If you have had no trouble calculating the scores, move yourself up a bracket! This score indicates that your mathematical training is incomplete, and needs to be given a fresh start.

MULTIPLE INTELLIGENCE TEST 4
ENGINEERING/SPATIAL INTELLIGENCE

This intelligence enables us to think about the intricate inter-relationships in the world of three dimensions. This intelligence can involve wide spaces, such as those required of the astronomer, the sailor or the airline pilot, or the more local spaces of the painter, the architect, the sculptor, the mechanical engineer or the surgeon. Incidentally, chess, although often considered a mathematical/logical game, is primarily one that requires spacial intelligence.
In scoring this test, give yourself 0 if the statement is absolutely untrue, and 100 if it is explosively true; or as directed. Again, compare yourself with others to make your scoring more accurate. The answers for questions 1 and 2 are on page 255.

1 Someone has bought the abstract painting shown below, but cannot remember which way up it is supposed to be. Can you identify whether it corresponds to picture number 1, 2, 3 or 4 and also say whether side a, b, c or d should be at the top? Maximum time 5 minutes.

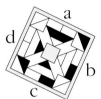

2 How many triangles are there in this structure? . . . . Maximum time 3 minutes.

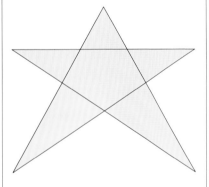

3 I enjoy games such as draughts, chess and go.
SCORE . . . .

4 I am one of the best people I know at giving, receiving and understanding directions.
SCORE . . . .

5 I love maps and map reading, and can always translate them accurately into the real world.
SCORE . . . .

6 When I make notes, I always use shapes, colours and diagrams to help me understand better.
SCORE . . . .

7 I am the person to whom others come when mechanical objects and other forms of machinery need fixing.
SCORE . . . .

8 I loved and regularly received top marks in geometry.
SCORE . . . .

9 I am fascinated by astronomy, including the relative distance and position of objects in the universe, and

their shapes and structures.
SCORE . . . .

10 I am, or would have loved to have been, an engineer, an architect, a sculptor, or similar.
SCORE . . . .

SCORE CHART									
1	2	3	4	5	6	7	8	9	10
TOTAL									

SCORING AND ANALYSIS

1000 – 950

A genius score. You would have had much in common with Leonardo da Vinci!

950 – 900

You have an extraordinary spatial intelligence, and are probably one of the leading thinkers in this area in your field. Keep increasing this intelligence – it will continue to expand the dimensions of your internal universe.

900 – 800

An exceptionally good score of which you can be proud. With a little more training you will be able to achieve even greater spatial awareness.

800 – 700

Above average. Check your scores and take steps (in three dimensions!) to improve.

700 – 500

Average. This score indicates that you probably did not have the best teachers in mathematics or the sciences. Give this area another try.

500 – 0

If you have walked across at least one street with traffic on it during this week – and avoided being knocked down – then your engineering and spatial intelligence is far better than you are giving yourself credit for. Re-evaluate.

MULTIPLE INTELLIGENCE TEST 5 SENSUAL INTELLIGENCE

We have discovered that most of the great creators and mnemonists (memorizers) have highly developed senses. In addition to this they also tended to blend and link all

their senses. When you give yourself scores for this test, choose a score of 0 if the statement is absolutely and incontrovertibly untrue, and 100 if it is explosively true.

1 I enjoy, with a passion, dancing.
SCORE . . . .

2 I would describe myself as 'sartorially intelligent' – a genius at clothes design. My clothes are colour coordinated, tactile, and regularly receive positive comments from those around me.
SCORE . . . .

3 I am able to recall visual information with immediacy and stunning clarity.
SCORE . . . .

4 I am especially sensitive to smells, and the olfactory sense plays a large role in my life's major memories.
SCORE . . . .

5 I would be placed in the top percentile of those who live to eat; the bottom percentile of those who eat only to live.
SCORE . . . .

6 I consider myself a particularly sensual person.
SCORE . . . .

7 I love playing with children.
SCORE . . . .

8 I love all aspects of nature and am regularly in contact with the land, rivers, lakes, and the oceans. I also like all forms of weather.
SCORE . . . .

9 I regularly describe experiences in one sense with the language of the others.
SCORE . . . .

10 I consider sex to be a multi-faceted multi-sensual activity, and regularly engage all my senses in the experience.
SCORE . . . .

SCORE CHART									
1	2	3	4	5	6	7	8	9	10
TOTAL									

SCORING AND ANALYSIS

1000 – 950

You have reached the peak of sensual intelligence and obviously use your senses to the full. Continue to enjoy!

950 – 900

You are almost at genius level. Think about which senses you appreciate or use the least, and then push yourself into the higher bracket – having as much fun as you can while you do so!

900 – 800

You are using the massive range of your sensory intelligences well. For even more pleasure, pursue even more pleasure!

800 – 700

Above average. You are already well on the way to experiencing a far more enjoyable and 'in contact with the world' life. Continue the pursuit.

700 – 500

Average. This suggests that there is a lot to be desired and you should be desiring it. Think about what is missing in your life, then rectify the situation.

500 – 0

You are depriving yourself, others, and the world the benefit of an intelligence that is obviously being concealed. Start to release it.

MULTIPLE INTELLIGENCE TEST 6
BODY/KINAESTHETIC INTELLIGENCE

Athletes solve problems or 'make things' with their whole bodies or parts of their bodies. Dancers, actors, surgeons, and indeed everyone who uses his or her body to solve a problem or make something, share this intelligence.

Give yourself a score from 0 – 100; 0 would mean that you are the least fit person you know, and 100 would mean that you are the most fit.

1 I exercise aerobically (cardiovascularly) at least four times a week for 30 minutes or more, at an extremely hard and fast pace. (If you don't know the meanings of aerobic or cardiovascular, you will probably score 0!)
SCORE . . . .

2 I am physically coordinated, balanced and poised.
SCORE . . . .

3 I am exceptionally strong at lifting, pulling and pushing with every one of my major bodily muscle groups.
SCORE . . . .

4 I am unusually flexible in all directions with all joints.
SCORE . . . .

5 My ongoing resistance to major and minor illnesses means that I am consistently in 'rude' health, and rarely miss a day of work.
SCORE . . . .

6 My stamina is extraordinary. I can go on and on in physical, mental, sexual, social and professional situations.
SCORE . . . .

7 My diet is particularly healthy, and would be the envy of an Olympic athlete. It incorporates fresh food, little sugar and salt, few refined foods, and balanced and varied items.
SCORE . . . .

8 I manage my activity/rest time intelligently, incorporating regular and good sleep, at least three good breaks during a working day, and at least six weeks a year in which I am completely away from my main profession or pastime.
SCORE . . . .

9 I relish all thoughts of physical activity and consider the expression of myself in physical/sporting terms to be a major theme of my life.
SCORE . . . .

10 The same for sex!
SCORE . . . .

SCORE CHART									
1	2	3	4	5	6	7	8	9	10
TOTAL									

SCORING AND ANALYSIS

1000 – 950

A physical genius! You are probably a major athlete, dancer or other form of physical star. Keep it up throughout your life!

950 – 900

You are or can be a national level performer. Get some advice from Olympians, and join them.

900 – 800

A very encouraging score. You are near the top of your field, and with a little more effort could reach national or international prominence. Learn from the greats, and keep trying.

800 – 700

Above average. You are probably in good shape and are one who generally enjoys the physical aspects of life. Review your score, and see if there are areas in which you wish to improve.

700 – 500

Average. This could be dangerous! Your brain needs a good body to support it. The majority of the geniuses in this book were physically as well as mentally fit. Follow their example! Try to take more exercise.

500 – 0

At least you found the energy to turn the pages and complete the test! For your own survival's sake, give your physical life a complete check-up, and embark on the exploration and improvement of your physical being. You owe it to your body and your brain.

MULTIPLE INTELLIGENCE TEST 7
CREATIVE INTELLIGENCE

Whereas the verbal and numerical intelligences tend to focus on a more analytical, logical thought process, creative intelligence refers to the more radiant, explosive thought process which leads one into new realms of thinking and expression. In scoring this test, give yourself 0 if the statement is absolutely and incontrovertibly untrue, and 100 if it is explosively true. Compare yourself with a group of 100 others – either known to you or the geniuses in this book – to make your scoring more accurate.

For one of the questions, you will need a pen or pencil and paper, plus a watch or clock with a second-hand so that you can time yourself. Get these ready before you start the test.

1 I could easily attain and would enjoy getting a Degree in art.
SCORE . . . .

2 I could easily attain and would enjoy getting a Degree in music.

SCORE . . . .

3 I could easily attain and would enjoy getting a Degree in creative writing.

SCORE . . . .

4 I could easily attain and would enjoy getting a Degree in theatre and acting.

SCORE . . . .

5 I regularly make people roar with laughter.

SCORE . . . .

6 People often say I am crazy,

mad, unpredictable, a 'one off', etc.

SCORE . . . .

7 I regularly attend the theatre, art exhibitions, concerts and other cultural events.

SCORE . . . .

8 I enjoy all forms of musical expression.

SCORE . . . .

9 I consider myself an exceptionally creative and productive individual.

SCORE . . . .

10 This is the test for which you need pen, paper and watch. If may help if you ask someone else to time you. When you are prepared, write down in 60 seconds all the uses you can possibly think of for a paperclip.

SCORE . . . .

SCORE CHART									
1	2	3	4	5	6	7	8	9	10
TOTAL									

SCORING AND ANALYSIS

SCORING (QUESTION 10)
In this creativity test, based on work on creative thinking by American psychologist E. Paul Torrance, coming up with three to four possible uses of a paperclip is average; eight is excellent, 12 is very unusual and 16 is exceptional. Score 10 points for each use, with 100 points maximum.

1000 – 950

We expect to see you on the international stage, at the opening of your major art exhibition, at the launch of your next international bestseller, or receiving the Nobel Prize! Realize that this intelligence *improves* with age, and keep it up!

950 – 900

A national level creative master, you are on the verge of international fame.

900 – 800

An exceptionally good creativity score. As this intelligence is one of the most susceptible to improvement, give it a nudge, and get into the genius category.

800 – 700

Well done! This is an above average score. Check into your attitudes and knowledge of creativity, improve them, and boost your score and your basic intelligence norm.

700 – 500

Average. In this test, especially, average means that your training in creativity has either been small, weak, or misdirected. Learn such skills as lateral and radiant thinking, and, if possible, take courses on the nature of your brain, memory and creative thinking.

500 – 0

This score should really be impossible! Have you been honest with yourself? Your brain is better than you think so encourage it by taking courses on the subjects mentioned above or at least start by reading relevant books. Use your imagination to the full.

MULTIPLE INTELLIGENCE TEST 8
INTRA-PERSONAL INTELLIGENCE

This form of intelligence concerns self-knowledge and self-fulfilment, and is fundamentally about understanding yourself. It is

about having a good mental model or map of yourself, and being able to operate with an accelerating learning curve on the basis of that knowledge.

In scoring this test, give yourself 0 if the statement is absolutely and incontrovertibly untrue, and 100 if it is explosively true.

1 I am truly self-confident.
SCORE . . . .

2 I am able to cry in appropriate emotional situations.
SCORE . . . .

3 My attitude to life is fundamentally and overridingly positive.
SCORE . . . .

4 People generally consider me a happy, enthusiastic and energetic person.
SCORE . . . .

5 I am the main controller of my own life.
SCORE . . . .

6 I relish others displaying affection towards me.
SCORE . . . .

7 I regularly and consistently tell those close to me that I love them.
SCORE . . . .

8 I am mentally literate, understanding the physical and behavioural alphabets of my brain.
SCORE . . . .

9 I am physically literate, understanding comprehensively the forms and methods of attaining physical fitness, the nature of an

appropriate diet, and the required rhythms of rest and sleep on a short- and long-term basis.
SCORE . . . .

10 In communication, my body language is always congruent with my message, and I regularly use varied and open-armed gestures.
SCORE . . . .

SCORE CHART									
1	2	3	4	5	6	7	8	9	10
TOTAL									

SCORING AND ANALYSIS

1000 – 950

A genius score. You are the perfect friend.

950 – 900

You are the kind of person everybody loves to know. With such a high score, and with such obvious energy and enthusiasm, it will be easy for you to enter the genius range.

900 – 800

A good high score. As

intelligence in this area is a prime factor in your success and life, consider improving even further.

800 – 700

Above average. You are generally mature, and will benefit from further work in this area.

700 – 500

Average. You undervalue yourself – wrongly. Re-evaluate! Think about how you

relate to others and whether you are currently suppressing your emotions and feelings.

500 – 0

This score indicates that although you have 'told the truth' in your scoring, the truth you believe in is not true! Study and take courses in communication, physical exercise and health, and radiant thinking. Make an effort to adopt a positive attitude and take control of your life.

MULTIPLE INTELLIGENCE TEST 9
INTER-PERSONAL INTELLIGENCE

This intelligence refers to the understanding of others – what motivates them, their various personalities, how they function, what their perceived needs are and, in short, 'what makes them tick'.

The superb playwright is an

example of a person with a developed inter-personal intelligence, for to write (or to act) in a play or even to understand a play fully, you need a high degree of inter-personal intelligence. This is why Shakespeare is considered

to be England's genius of geniuses.

To score yourself from 0 – 100, 0 would mean that you were the least skilled in this category, and 100 would mean that you are the most skilled. Be as honest as you can.

1 I listen with understanding and compassion, and am well known for doing so.
SCORE . . . .

2 Whenever I am involved in negotiation, the result is always a win/win – in other words both sides are satisfied and think they have gained.
SCORE . . . .

3 I am able, and love to, lead teams of different and differing people to achieve given goals.
SCORE . . . .

4 I delight in the multiplicity of human characters, and am sensitive to all different personality types.
SCORE . . . .

5 People regularly come to me to help them gain insight. I *do* help them to gain it.
SCORE . . . .

6 I am known for my personal warmth, compassion and capacity for affection.
SCORE . . . .

7 In social gatherings I am often the leader in helping others to relax and laugh.
SCORE . . . .

8 In conversation or in public speaking I maintain meaningful eye contact.
SCORE . . . .

9 I am able to communicate my own point of view successfully without antagonizing others.
SCORE . . . .

10 I receive consistently good service in restaurants and hotels.
SCORE . . . .

SCORE CHART									
1	2	3	4	5	6	7	8	9	10
TOTAL									

SCORING AND ANALYSIS

1000 – 950

You are probably already a leader, an international business personality, or a major coach of some sort. If you are not, consider becoming one!

950 – 900

A top level communicator and leader on a national scale. You could easily make the international level if you wish.

900 – 800

You are near the top of the field in inter-personal intelligence, and are probably an especially popular person with colleagues and friends. As this is one of the most important intelligences, consider honing your skills even further.

800 – 700

Above average. Continue to enjoy yourself with others, focus on those areas where you gave yourself a lower score, and consider improving.

700 – 500

Average. Inter-personal intelligence is a skill which should be encouraged. Reflect on your relationships with others. Are you *really* listening to what they say. Try to think more about what they mean and feel.

500 – 0

Give yourself and others a break! Realize that both they and you are far more fascinating and intriguing than you may currently believe. Open up a bit more.

MULTIPLE INTELLIGENCE TEST 10
SPIRITUAL INTELLIGENCE

Spiritual intelligence is the comprehensive intelligence described by the American psychologist A.A. Maslow (1908-70) as the ultimate human goal in the hierarchy of needs. It usually manifests itself when all other intelligences are simultaneously operating at an especially high level.

Score yourself from 0 – 100, where 0 would mean that you were the least able in this category, and 100 would mean that you are the most able. (In this test, saints would score hundreds, and devils would only achieve zeros!)

1 My life has a sense of complete and positive purpose to it.
SCORE . . . .

2 I feel a great connnection to, and often 'feel at one' with, the universe.
SCORE . . . .

3 People feel that I am 'congruent' in that I understand and have a deep knowledge of myself. I do what I say.
SCORE . . . .

4 I am known for my playful, irrepressible and bubbling sense of humour.
SCORE . . . .

5 I am at peace with myself.
SCORE . . . .

6 Other life forms generate in me a sense of awe, wonder, love and respect.
SCORE . . . .

7 Others consider me far more mature and wise than average.
SCORE . . . .

8 I am able to combine successfully humility with self-confidence. (I am not arrogant but know what I can achieve).
SCORE . . . .

9 I am able to express myself fully on all levels and in all ways.
SCORE . . . .

10 I am amazed at my capacity for wonder!
SCORE . . . .

SCORE CHART									
1	2	3	4	5	6	7	8	9	10
TOTAL									

SCORING AND ANALYSIS

1000 – 950

A genius score – approaching sainthood!

950 – 900

An extremely superior score. You need no advice!

900 – 800

You are comparatively wise, and are obviously living a very fulfilled life. Continue on the path.

800 – 700

Above average. With the spiritual strengths you obviously already possess, strengthen those areas where you are currently weaker.

700 – 500

Average. As this intelligence incorporates peace of mind, laughter and fulfilment, it is *very* well worth while developing it further as soon as you possibly can.

500 – 0

Such a score will probably indicate that you are not happy with yourself or your lot. But remember that you have the power to change your current circumstances. You need to make your life more meaningful both to yourself and to others, so think about how you can improve things. Try to consider your life objectively or talk about it with someone whose opinion you trust and value.

OVERALL SCORING AND ANALYSIS OF YOUR MULTIPLE-INTELLIGENCE QUOTIENT AND TRADITIONAL IQ

Your total Mental Intelligence Quotient is taken by combining the scores from your Genius Quotient, your Multiple Intelligence Quotient and your traditional IQ scores. To find your total score, divide your GQ by two, leaving all the other scores in your Multiple Intelligence Test and your standard IQ tests as they are. Add these together to give you a possible total of 10,000. Fill in this chart to establish your combined score, and then compare your results with the scoring and analysis opposite.

TEST	SCORE
TEST 1 GENIUS QUOTIENT	
TEST 2 VERBAL INTELLIGENCE	
TEST 3 NUMERICAL/LOGICAL INTELLIGENCE	
TEST 4 ENGINEERING/SPATIAL INTELLIGENCE	
TEST 5 SENSUAL INTELLIGENCE	
TEST 6 BODY/KINAESTHETIC INTELLIGENCE	
TEST 7 CREATIVE INTELLIGENCE	
TEST 8 INTRA-PERSONAL INTELLIGENCE	
TEST 9 INTER-PERSONAL INTELLIGENCE	
TEST 10 SPIRITUAL INTELLIGENCE	
TOTAL	

OVERALL SCORING AND ANALYSIS

10,000 – 9500

A score in this percentile places you in the multiple genius bracket. You are up there with Leonardo da Vinci and Shakespeare! With such a vast and comprehensive range of brain and body skills you could be a world leader in virtually any field you choose. If you are not already, you should be getting close!

9500 – 9000

This score indicates that you are probably in the genius range in many of your separate intelligences, and are pushing the genius level in the remainder. It is very unlikely that you are weak in *any* intellectual arena. With the range of talents already available to you, why not use them to strengthen any weaknesses? Aim higher!

9000 – 8000

An exceptionally good score. With such high marks you will generally be near the top, and occasionally at the top, of your chosen field of endeavour. But even with such a score you may have one or two areas of specific weakness. Identify what these are and then strengthen these weak links in your intellectual chain.

8000 – 7000

Above average, and still excellent. With such a score, you should thoroughly review the tests and your results, examining in depth your strengths and weaknesses. Your weaknesses are sufficient to place unnecessary obstacles in your pathway, so use your identified strengths to develop your weaker areas. Adopt a positive attitude in everything that you do.

7000 – 5000

You are in the average range. This simply means that your multiple intelligences have been only partly developed and have a long way to go before they reach their full potential. Do some brain training – read books, take up mental challenges, stimulate your mind in whatever way you can and you will soon reap the benefits.

below 5000

You are using less than 1% of your brain's conscious capacity so there is plenty of scope for improvement! Your life will be more positive and satisfying if you work on increasing all your intelligence levels. It is never too late to begin but you must want to help yourself on the road to success. Look back at your tests and results – and start using your brain now!

THE BRAIN TRUST/USE YOUR HEAD CLUB

If you really want to improve yourself, why not join The Brain Trust/Use Your Head Club? This international organization (charity number 1001012 and previously known as The Brain Club) was established to help people to increase their mental, physical and spiritual awareness. The club is a forum for expanding on many of the issues raised in this book and will encourage you to wake up your brain!

You can either choose to study in your own home and/or to meet others who also wish to expand their vast range of mental skills. By attending your own 'mental gymnasium', you can improve on the following:

1 Memory.
2 Mind Mapping®.
3 Learning and study.
4 Mathematics.
5 Physical performance.
6 Communication.
7 Game skills.
8 Range/speed reading.
9 Creative thinking.
10 Your IQ.
11 The Arts.
12 Vocabulary building and language learning.
13 Personality development.
14 Special skills.

The Use Your Head Club grades levels of achievement for the different areas within the club and awards certificates as you reach advancing levels of competence. For details on how to join, contact:

The Use Your Head Club, P O Box 1821, Marlow, Buckinghamshire, SL7 2YW. Telephone (01628) 477004.

THE BRAIN

'SURROUNDED BY A FOREST OF ENEMY SPEARS –
ENTER DEEPLY AND LEARN TO USE YOUR MIND AS A SHIELD.'
MORIHEI UESHIBA (1883-1969)

The more that you know about the brain, the more you will recognize that there are vast areas which you are not using to the full. Similarly, once you have understood your brain's true potential and capacity, you will find it easier to unleash your own genius.

Amazingly, the fact that the brain is located in the head was only generally accepted 500 years ago – even the great Aristotle thought that many of the mental functions were centred on the heart. Despite the fact that we know more about the nature and function of the brain than many past geniuses, many misconceptions about the brain are still commonly held.

For instance, it is a myth that after the age of 21 the average human loses between 1000 and 10,000 brain cells a day. When the human brain is fed, exercised and nurtured by learning, rather than lose cells, it actually grows more sophisticated inter-connections. Similarly, it is widely believed that the brain's general mental abilities decline with age at an accelerating rate. It is true that the majority of people find that their mental abilities *do* decline with age, but this is not a natural phenomenon. This decline takes place because people use synergistically incorrect formulas to train themselves to become worse as they grow older. If you follow all the advice in this book, you will be able to encourage your brain to do what it is naturally designed to do – improve with age.

Another popular misconception is that certain mental habits can never be changed. This is far from the truth. So long as you provide your brain with an appropriate vision, commit yourself to that vision and then apply the characteristics of genius to accomplish your particular goal, then you should be able to achieve it easily.

MENTAL LITERACY

If you have read about the characteristics of genius (see page 12), you will have already dis-

---

FACTS ABOUT THE BRAIN – THE HUMAN COMPUTER

The brain is about the size of two clenched fists and, on average, weighs an incredibly light 3 lb (1.4 kg).

∘ ∘ ∘

Within your brain there is enough atomic energy to build any of the world's cities many times.

∘ ∘ ∘

The number of neurons or nerve cells in your brain is approximately 12 trillion (more than two and a half times the number of people currently living on the planet).

∘ ∘ ∘

Your brain cells contain 1000 trillion trillion protein molecules. Each brain cell has the physical possibility of connecting with 100,000 adjoining brain cells.

∘ ∘ ∘

Your body provides your brain with information through a network of 500,000 touch detectors; 200,000 temperature detectors; and four million pain sensitive structures.

∘ ∘ ∘

Your brain listens with your ears. These both contain 24,000 fibres that are able to detect enormous ranges and subtle distinctions in the air's molecular vibrations.

∘ ∘ ∘

Through your olfactory system (your nose!), your brain is able to detect one molecule of 'smell' in one part per trillion of air.

∘ ∘ ∘

The function between brain cells where communication crosses is called the synapse. In the synapse, an electrical impulse shunts chemical messengers between two brain cells, transmitting thought. No one knows how this is done.

THE LEFT AND RIGHT SIDES OF THE BRAIN

RIGHT SIDE		LEFT SIDE
RHYTHM		WORDS
SPATIAL AWARENESS		LOGIC
GESTALT (WHOLE PICTURE)		NUMBERS
IMAGINATION		SEQUENCE
DAYDREAMING		LINEARITY
COLOUR		ANALYSIS
DIMENSION		LISTS

Nobel Prizewinner Professor Roger Sperry of California spent many years researching into the cerebral cortex (the layer which covers the brain). Among his discoveries, which have subsequently been confirmed and expanded upon, he found that the two sides of the brain (which are often referred to as the left and right hemispheres) split the major intellectual functions between them. He assigned these different functions as illustrated above.

Since Sperry's research, it has been found that the mental skills he correctly identified are in fact distributed *throughout* the cerebral cortex. It is therefore misleading and extremely unhelpful to describe people as having a dominant left or right side of the brain. Everyone has the potential to develop *all* his or her mental skills. If you currently misbelieve that you have a more dominant right side of the brain, for instance, then it simply means that you have not yet fully developed the skills originally attributed to the left hemisphere of the cerebral cortex.

covered that mental literacy is one of the prime factors contributing to genius. It is quite astounding that, although billions of dollars are spent worldwide on research into traditional verbal literacy and numeracy, the most important 'alphabet' of all – that of the human brain – has to date been largely ignored. Once you have mastered this fundamental literacy, you will be able to acquire all the other types of literacy much more easily.

In fact, to be mentally literate is to understand two 'alphabets' about your brain. The first is the 'alphabet' of the brain's biology. This includes acquiring information about the cerebral cortex and its functions, the nature of brain cells and their potential, the nature of the brain's biological extensions (the senses) and the general functions of the different areas of the brain.

The second 'alphabet' relates to your brain's behaviour, including general learning, memory, creativity, your different areas of intelligence and your whole range of mental skills (there are more than you might think). This book is devoted to raising your levels in all these areas.

THE BRAIN'S POTENTIAL
Have you ever considered how many internal 'maps of thought' it is possible for your brain to create? Think about this now and then jot down your answer on a piece of paper or make a mental note of it before reading any further. The great Russian neuro-psychologist, Professor Petr Anokhin, spent the final years of his distinguished career investigating the answer to this question with the aid of the most advanced electron-microscopes, brain scanners and supercomputers. His conclusion was: 'We can show that each of the 10 billion neurons in the human brain has a possibility of connections of one with 28 noughts after it! If a single neuron has this quality of potential, we can hardly imagine what the whole brain can do. What it means is that the total number of possible combinations/permutations in the brain, if written out, would be 1 followed by 10.5 million kilometres of noughts!'

'No human yet exists who can use all the potential of his brain. This is why we don't accept any pessimistic estimates of the limits of the human brain. It is unlimited!'

A Healthy Mind in a Healthy Body

'WORLD CHAMPION GARRY KASPAROV LAYS IMMENSE EMPHASIS ON PHYSICAL FITNESS AND MAKES NO SECRET OF HIS ENORMOUS PHYSICAL PREPARATION. HE SEES CHESS AS A BATTLE OF THE MIND AND RECOGNIZES THAT WITHOUT A SUPREMELY FIT BODY TO BACK IT UP THE MIND CANNOT FUNCTION.'

RAYMOND KEENE

The image of the genius as a frail, pallid, sickly and half-blind individual is exactly the *opposite* of what our researches have found to be true. In nearly every instance, geniuses are robust, energetic, vibrant, and maintain exceptional physical wellbeing. Wittingly or unwittingly, they subscribe to and practise the Classical ideals of a healthy mind in a healthy body (*mens sana in corpore sano*). Alberti could jump, feet together, over the heads of his fellow athletes; Leonardo da Vinci was known as the strongest man in Florence; and today Kasparov weight-trains, runs and boxes in preparation for mental combat over the chess board.

Modern research is consistently confirming that the Greeks and Romans were correct. The more the remarkable human body is nourished, cared for and trained, the more the brain that resides in it and depends upon it for nutrition, oxygen, sensing and locomotion, will itself flourish. So if you want to improve your mind, you should start by improving your physical fitness.

In this chapter we consider the main elements of physical health that lead to mental health and the raising of the general intelligences, and give specific action steps for developing your own healthy mind and healthy body.

The main elements in developing complete physical health are:

1 General Physical Fitness
2 Diet
3 Drugs
4 Sleep and Rest
5 Sex
6 Mental Attitude

1 GENERAL PHYSICAL FITNESS

AEROBIC TRAINING

Aerobic training refers to any training that is literally 'with oxygen'. In more practical terms it refers to training that builds up your stamina and endurance by providing a greater supply of oxygen throughout your body and brain.

Forms of exercise that specifically encourage aerobic fitness include running, swimming, long-distance skiing, fast and long-distance walking, rowing, physical lovemaking, and using the growing range of aerobic training machines. To enable you to perform these activities and to empower body movement, locomotion, and environmental sensitivity, your body has 200 bones, 500 totally co-ordinated muscle systems, and over seven miles (11 km) of nerve fibres!

THE AEROBIC FORMULA

The aerobic formula is exceptionally simple, and has profound effects. To become and stay aero-bically fit ('oxygen fit') you need to exercise only three times a week, starting with a five-minute warm-up and exercising aerobically for 20 minutes. During this time your heart should maintain a beat of between 120-180 beats per minute (depending upon your age and current condition). Follow this exercise with a five-minute warm-down period. The exercises should be done ideally on alternate days, and can be combined with strength, flexibility and poise training. The effects of even this modest amount of exercise on the body and brain are astonishing.

THE EFFECTS OF AEROBIC TRAINING ON THE BRAIN AND BODY

Human lungs are composed of many millions of tiny grape-like globes called alveoli. These are spaces which are surrounded with a network of fine blood vessels called capillaries. Air, containing oxygen, is drawn into these spaces when we breathe in and the oxygen diffuses into our red blood cells through the thin capillary walls. When we breathe out, the remaining air plus waste products from the blood, such as carbon dioxide, are eliminated from the lungs.

Oxygen is carried around your body by the haemoglobin in your red blood cells. The ability of your lungs to function is entirely dependent upon the 'breathing fitness' of the muscles of your rib-cage and diaphragm, and these 'breathing muscles' can get fit only by aerobic training.

An aerobically fit person can process *twice as much* oxygen in any given time period as an unfit person. In addition the lungs of a healthy person will also expel wastes and poisons from the body with a far greater efficiency. It is obvious from this that aerobic training has significant effects on the blood.

Blood, Energy and Health

Aerobic training sends a constant message to the brain that more oxygen is required than is currently available. As a result the body produces more blood, and within that blood more oxygen-carrying haemoglobin, more red blood cells to carry the haemoglobin, and more blood plasma to the red blood cells. The total supply of blood in the body and brain is thus increased considerably. Studies by Dr Kenneth Cooper and others have shown that an average-sized man may increase his blood volume by nearly a quart in response to aerobic conditioning. Equally important, the number of red blood cells per unit volume also increases, meaning that the density of oxygen in the blood is greater.

The increased volume of haemoglobin thus allows more oxygen to be delivered to all parts of the body, and more waste to be carried away. In addition to an increased volume of blood, aerobic exercise increases the blood supply to the muscles. This increases the flexibility of all the blood vessels, decreases the resistance to blood flow, and creates masses of extra capillaries to take blood to the further extremes of the body.

Quite simply, aerobic training increases your supply of energy, decreases the probability of various diseases, allows the body, its brain and senses to function more naturally, and increases the probability of a long life. All these qualities characterize genius.

The Effect of Aerobics on the Heart

Aerobic training, as well as increasing the vital capacity of the lungs, the volume of blood and the flexibility of the cardiovascular system, increases the size and strength of the body's most important muscle – the heart. An athlete's heart is a larger, stronger and more healthy muscle than average, is highly efficient, and pumps more blood with each beat and with less effort. An unexercised heart is smaller, weak – like any unexercised muscle – and possesses smaller chambers into which the blood flows and from which it is pumped out. In a happy design of nature, the heart also feeds itself. The coronary arteries which feed the heart muscle its own supply of blood and oxygen are correspondingly stronger in a healthier, strong heart.

The more fit the heart, the slower its beat and the greater volume of oxygen it pumps out with every beat. A healthy (genius level) heart beats 60 times a minute or less, whereas an unfit heart beats at a rate of 80 beats a minute. Therefore it is obvious that an unhealthy heart, weaker and pumping less effective blood, has to do far more work than the healthy heart. Paradoxically, the more you 'work your heart' through a healthy aerobic training programme, the less work your heart has to do. It is really like the ultimate athlete, who works more effortlessly, gracefully and efficiently in periods of relaxation, times of normal activity, and in moments of extreme demand and exertion. Like the superior athlete, a healthy heart has exceptional stamina and endurance.

The Effect of Aerobics on the Brain

The brain is the prime beneficiary of aerobic fitness. Each brain cell is a tiny and incredibly sophisticated processing plant, with its own incoming and outgoing transport systems, its storage facilities (memory) and its nuclear power plant for creating energy, heat, new thought, and new protoplasm – the material of which it itself is made. Every second that your heart pumps blood into your brain (40% of the blood supply goes directly to its awaiting cells) it is feeding the brain the ultimate energy source for thinking – oxygen. It is essential that your brain gets the 'highest octane'.

To put in perspective the importance that evolution has placed on the brain, it weighs only two to three per cent of your total body weight, and yet will take as much as 40-50% of all the oxygen you inhale. The other systems receive, in their combined total, half of the remaining resources and include the skeletal system, the heart itself, the lungs, the muscle systems, and the general nervous system. Evolution considers your brain to be by far the most important part of you. You should too.

AEROBICS AND THE MUSCULAR SYSTEM

Because the whole body is usually exercised in an aerobic exercise programme, the muscles benefit as well. Obvious benefits such as muscle speed and endurance are supplemented by muscle tone. Aerobically fit muscles tend to be leaner, finer and longer than untrained muscles. This is because more of the entire area of the muscles is close to the nerve and blood supply routes. The muscles in turn, when they are in use, act as 'mini hearts' pumping more fresh oxygen around the system and to the brain.

THE DIGESTIVE SYSTEM

In an aerobically fit body, the entire digestive system will be fed more regularly and cleansed more effectively. Conditions such as hyper-acidity will tend to decline, hormonal levels will balance, and the regular healthy expansive breathing and strong and steady beating of the heart will massage the entire system, keeping it and the overall body more relaxed and at ease. In such a condition, all nutrition that is ingested will be more effectively processed.

SLEEP

Aerobic exercise increases the quality of sleep and will often lessen the amount required.

In another seminal study, Dr Kenneth Cooper had two groups stay in bed, flat on their backs, for three full weeks. The first group exercised three times daily on bicycle ergometers strapped to their beds, while the other group was allowed no exercise. The exercise group had normal sleep patterns throughout, sleeping for seven to eight hours a night. The group which was not allowed to exercise slept erratically or developed a chronic insomnia. They also tended to want to sleep for longer, and when they were awake they were comparatively listless. Aerobic fitness gives your brain a deeper rest and integrating period for one quarter to one third of every day.

THE PSYCHOLOGICAL EFFECTS

Because of the intimate connection between the brain and body, physical fitness can now be seen to be in many ways equivalent to mental fitness. As Cooper says, '*A definite relationship has been found between physical fitness and mental alertness and emotional stability. In the first place, improved endurance performance makes the body less susceptible to fatigue, and consequently less likely to commit errors, mental or physical. Your performance can be sustained longer without the necessity for frequent breaks.*' This relates directly to the qualities of energy, stamina, persistence, and focus of the great geniuses.

Further evidence of the validity of the *mens sana in corpore sano* principle comes from a study by Dr Appleton and Dr Kobes at the United States Military Academy at West Point. They made a study that directly compared the physical aptitude and health of their cadets and their success at the academy. Over four years, the cadets who were fit had an attrition rate half that of their unfit class-mates. The drop-out rate was also especially high among non-athletes, who found themselves incapable of absorbing the academic curricula simply because they did not have the alertness and stamina to maintain the necessary mental effort.

Similar tests have shown highly positive correlations between performances in physical tests and exercises, and academic and leadership qualities. They have also revealed a positive correlation between physical health and mental outlook. Those in good aerobic condition tend to be more self-confident, more optimistic, more determined and generally have a greater love of their jobs and professions, a generally higher energy level, and a greater lust for life.

STRENGTH

Muscular strength is an important part of overall health, and refers to the ability of all your muscles and muscle systems to lift, pull and rotate.

THE MUSCLE STRENGTH FORMULA

As with aerobics the formula for gaining muscle power is simple. Once again, the exercise needs to be repeated three times weekly, and can take between 20-60 minutes depending on the number of muscles and muscle groups being strengthened.

Within the three times weekly formula, another simple formula resides – three times five (3×5) – which should be applied to whatever exercise you are doing.

As an example, suppose that you are doing a simple lift (or 'curl') for your biceps – the large muscles in your arm that enable you to lift things. You need a weight that you can only *just* lift five times before becoming fatigued. Lift the weight five times, and then take a one-minute rest. During this rest the blood will flow to your muscles (aerobic fitness will help you here!) and the muscles will be 'pumped up' ready for the second set of five lifts. These will probably be slightly easier than the first five, because you are now fully pumped up. Rest for another minute, and then complete the third five repetitions. These will be the most difficult, because your muscles will now be tired and stretched from the previous reptitions, and you should be able only just to make the final lift of these last five.

This formula (3 × 5) should be applied to every muscle and muscle group you are training. After the third repetition of five, the body realizes that in order to cope with this new demand, it will be necessary to increase the volume and strength of the muscle, and will add more muscle tissue during your days of rest, thus building up bulk, size and strength of your muscular system. The low repetitions will produce the more bulky muscle. When the weight becomes easier, which it will, simply add more, keeping to the 3 × 5 formula.

Higher repetitions, anywhere from 6-20, will progressively increase the aerobic fitness of the muscle, making it leaner and longer rather than bulky, and providing slightly less immediate 'power strength' and more 'stamina strength'.

The advantages of maintaining muscular strength include general physical safety, greater functional ability, considerably greater self-confidence, and respect from others. Both chess champions Bobby Fischer and Garry Kasparov have publicly stated that one of the main reasons for becoming physically strong was because it made them feel stronger *in all senses* during mental competition.

FLEXIBILITY

Flexibility fitness refers to the ability of your body's joints to move freely in all the directions for which they were designed. When the body is flexible the muscles are able to extend to their full length and thus avoid the danger of damage. The nervous system is also able to send its messages in a smooth flow to any part of the body without being blocked by areas of muscular rigidity and tension. Similarly, oxygen can flow more freely through blood vessels and capillaries in a body free of restrictions and blockages.

The deep-rooted need for flexibility can be seen regularly in the desire of ourselves and animals to stretch (one of the best instructors in this area of physical fitness is the cat!). Stretching is one of the best 'flexibility exercises' and can be naturally performed on a daily basis. It should also be combined with aerobic and muscular training, where it can form a major part of the warm-up and warm-down.

Exercises that are specifically designed to increase flexibility include dance, yoga, gymnastics, aikido and aerobic 'stretchercises'.

POISE

It is possible to be aerobically, muscularly and flexibly fit, and yet still to be 'off balance'. Perfect poise is the perfect balance of the body when all aspects of the muscular and skeletal systems – especially the positioning of the head, spine and joints – are properly aligned. It is interesting that Leonardo da Vinci, arguably the most cortically balanced individual of all time, was also renowned for his exceptional poise and the extraordinary grace and balance of his movements.

Proper poise allows fluidity of movement, and a natural flow of all energies throughout the system. It is often described as a 'balanced resting state' in which the body, no matter what its position, is fundamentally alert and ready to spring effectively into action. Excellent disciplines for the attainment of poise include certain forms of dance and yoga, aikido, and the Alexander Technique, the scientific and practical technique for aligning the body as it was designed to be aligned which was developed by F.M. Alexander, a genius also mentioned on page 56.

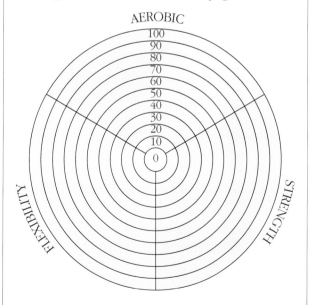

Use this chart to help you to maintain a balance between your aerobic training, flexibility and strength. Give yourself from 1 – 100 for each.

SUMMARY OF GENERAL PHYSICAL FITNESS

To be comprehensively fit, you should not neglect any of the four areas described above – aerobics, strength, flexibility, and poise. The first three require specific exercises and routines, and are best worked into an overall exercise programme. Sports which combine all three to a good degree, and which are therefore most effective for someone wishing to conserve time while becoming fit, include rowing, swimming, running, the martial arts (especially aikido), gymnastics and long-distance skiing.

It is useful to keep records. On the previous page you will find a general physical fitness chart on which you can graph your relative levels of fitness giving yourself both a current picture of your 'fitness balance' as well as goals.

2 DIET

Does the quality of the food you eat make a difference to your physical health and, most importantly, your brain-power? The answer is a resounding 'yes', with increasing evidence supporting the case. A diet that will keep your mind and body healthy needs to consist of foods that have specific value for the heart and cardiovascular system, the digestive system, the brain and the nervous system. Through the centuries, certain dietary principles have been discovered that are constant and common to all healthy eating and physical disciplines.

GENERAL PRINCIPLES

1 Eat fresh food wherever possible. Fresh food has the advantage of being 'complete' and containing more vitamins, minerals and nutrients than food which has been frozen or tinned.

2 Eat a diet rich in variety. A varied diet allows the body to select from a wider range of possibilities those things it particularly needs at any moment in time. Eating the same foods regularly, or the same foods on certain given days, gives rise to the probability of a clogging of the system, or a depletion of some necessary element.

3 Look at yourself. On a regular basis stand, both front on and side on, naked in front of a mirror. Look at yourself as you would a wild animal and decide whether you look as healthy and fit as you should. If not, take appropriate dietary and other action and, if you are satisfied with your appearance, continue the good practice.

4 'Listen' to yourself. Much of our eating behaviour is simply habit. We often say 'yes' to every proffered snack or tit-bit, 'yes' to every possible cup of tea or coffee, and 'yes' to ourselves when looking at an item on the menu that we 'know we like'. When selecting food, especially in company, imagine that you are on your own, and go for food and drink which you would *actually* choose if you had the widest choice available and were eating what you really *felt* like. When two-year-old children were placed in a large castle-type building with every possible food available, the experimenters became most concerned on the first day when one little boy stuffed himself with chocolates, and another chose to eat over 10 bananas. By the end of two weeks, however, every child had selected for itself a totally balanced diet. Let your body use its natural intelligence to select what it needs.

A GOOD BASIC DIET

Each individual requires a diet specifically tailored to his or her individual body's chemistry, general activity and specific physical activities. There are, however, certain food groups that can make up a good basic diet from which individual variations can then be created.

VEGETABLES AND FRUIT

Vegetables should form the base of any healthy diet. They are rich in nutrients, and contain ample fibre for cleansing the digestive tract and keeping it muscularly fit and flexible. They are quickly and easily digested, and can, if eaten with appropriate knowledge, form a complete diet in themselves. Similarly, fruit should be included in a balanced diet.

NUTS, SEEDS AND WHOLE GRAINS

These are all highly concentrated sources of 'brain food'. Incidentally, since they contain all the genetic information necessary for plant life, they may in a sense be considered to be the brains of plants.

FISH

Fish has traditionally been considered *the* 'brain food' and research by Professor Michael Crawford, Director of the Institute for Brain Chemistry and Human Nutrition, has confirmed this assumption. 60% of the brain is built from a specialized fat or liquid, most of which we cannot manufacture in our own systems but have to take in from the food chain. The primary source of these essential fats is fish. Crawford goes so far as to posit the theory that the development of human intelligence and genius is largely due to the development of societies around lakes, river-basins and coastlines where the supply of this essential brain food is abundant.

MEAT

Meat can be highly nutritious, and should be eaten by those who desire it two or three times a week maximum. The danger with many meats is that they can be suffused with synthetic chemicals. It is therefore best to eat wild meat and game where possible.

BRAIN FOODS

Most of the foods mentioned in the basic healthy diet contain various items that are good for the brain (and what is good for the brain is good for the body!). Specifically, the brain and its nervous system are nourished by certain amino acids (the constituents of protein; the B complex of vitamins; the essential fats found abundantly in fish; and the minerals potassium, magnesium, iron and zinc). Any healthy diet should include food that contains these essential nutrients.

The more aerobically fit the body is, the more the digestive system is able to ingest its food, and the more efficiently and effectively the blood can deliver the nutrients to the entire brain and body.

THE INTELLIGENT DIET

The intelligent diet will naturally contain appropriate sugars and salts. It is therefore unnecessary and in many cases harmful to add additional salts and sugars to food. Similarly, any refined or processed food will tend to be more difficult to ingest, and may contain elements that are damaging to general health.

The adage 'you are what you eat' we now know to be true. Eat with intelligence and become more intelligent.

3 DRUGS

The word 'drugs' conjures up a host of fears and evils, and it is true that the addictive drugs heroin, cocaine, crack, ecstasy, and marijuana, generally have majorly negative effects on the human nervous system. Their possible side-effects include memory loss, paranoia, neurological damage, social maladaptability, depression and death. Occasionally they can be prescribed under expert supervision. The two drugs named as the most dangerous by the United Nations are nicotine and alcohol, and both have an effect on the brain and the body.

NICOTINE

Every time nicotine is inhaled, a yellowish-brown coating of oil smothers the 600,000,000 alvioli of the lungs, making it far more difficult for oxygen to pass through into the blood-stream, and therefore depriving the brain of some of its needed supply of energy. It is much like an oil slick covering the ocean, preventing the oxygen-breathing animals and organisms below it from surviving. As a result of this assault on the system, general functioning and life-expectancy are affected in the following ways:

1 – 20 cigarettes per day
A general increase in upper respiratory and cardio-vascular ailments, with life expectancy reduced by two years.

20 – 40 cigarettes per day
A two- to three-fold increase in the probability of most major ailments, especially cancer, and a life expectancy reduced by five to 10 years.

40 cigarettes plus per day
A five to 10 times greater probability of most major ailments, and a life expectancy reduced by 12 to 15 years.

ALCOHOL

A useful way to look at this drug is to take the perspective of a Martian, examining the effects of varying amounts of this particular liquid on the brain, nervous system and muscular system of the inhabitants of Earth. Prolonged use causes massive memory loss, disintegration of vital organs, vocabulary and language impairment, disintegration of the muscular system, eventual loss of brain cells, loss of balance and coordination, and a reduced life expectancy.

On the up-side for those readers who enjoy drinking, studies have shown that moderate drinking, especially when the drink is taken with food, combined with good exercise, can relax the mind and body, and may even in some instances be helpful to the cardiovascular system. Some studies show that those who drink in moderation have an additional two years' life expectancy. As with the advice on diet, it is essential to 'listen' to your body's *real* needs.

4 SLEEP AND REST

In which of the following situations do you suddenly come up with bursts of creative ideas, floods of memory, or the solutions to problems on which you have been working?

	Yes	No
In the bath		
Taking a shower		
While shaving		
While putting on make-up		
In the toilet		
In bed		
During sleeping/dreaming		
Walking in nature		
While driving		
When jogging/swimming		
While doodling		
While listening to music		

Most people check at least one of the above, and the majority of people check most of them. This is because rest is a necessary part of mental as well as bodily function. It is much like a mental inhalation and exhalation, where inhalation is equivalent to active learning and the assimilation of data, and exhalation is equivalent to sorting, integration and rest.

The qualities common to the situations in which people are most creative and most capable of reviewing memories are rest, relaxation and solitude. It is at these times that we can daydream about apples and gravity, bodies and water, sunbeams and the structure of the universe, and whatever great idea *you* next allow yourself to have.

In other words, to function most effectively, your brain needs regular breaks as well as regular periods of activity. If you do not take them, your brain will make you do so anyway. You will call it a loss of concentration, nervous tension, or in more extreme cases a nervous breakdown – all instances of your brain *insisting* that you take a break and balance yourself.

Sleep, one of the deepest forms of rest, is a period where the brain integrates the day's and life's experiences, shifting, sorting and filing, as well as solving problems. Dreams are a natural part of this process, and are one of the creative genius's greatest sources of inspiration.

In a study done at the University of British Columbia in the early 1960s, students were able to register for a psychology course on dreams. At the beginning of the year they took a large number of personality and aptitude tests, and then began their studies. To their bemusement, all the professor asked them to do was to say whether or not they had had any dreams since their last class and, if they had, to describe them in detail, and then engage the class in conversation about the dreams.

As the year progressed, the students were given psychometric tests regularly, and the class procedure remained the same. By the end of the year the number of students reporting dreams had risen from a very few to the entire class. In the psychometric tests, self-images had increased, creativity scores had risen, academic performance had been reported as generally improved, and expressions of self and creative pursuits had increased dramatically. The students had also taken up many new hobbies.

The conclusion of the study was that a focused attention on dreaming would greatly enhance general wellbeing and creative output. This is confirmed in the lives of those with great minds, where dreaming and fantasy are often the wellsprings for great new ideas and paradigm shifts.

In a well-exercised and well-fed body, sleep will be deep and curative, and will often provide, from an infinite source of creativity, major insights and revelations.

5 SEX

The largest sex organ in the body is not between the legs – but between the ears! As a general fitness activity, physical sex can provide one of the most complete work-outs, involving extreme levels of aerobic, strength and flexibility fitness.

Sex also stimulates the intellectual skills, and the same principles apply to it as apply to most other things in terms of learning, memory, creativity and pleasure. The more cortical skills and the more senses that there are involved, then the more complete, stimulating and literally 'orgasmic' the experience is.

It is easy to see, from the brain's point of view, why romance is so intellectually stimulating, motivating, memorable, remarkable and wonderful, as well as being something that we all wish to enjoy – because all the cortical skills are used and all senses are totally involved. Intense conversations, flowers, planning, foods, wines, poetry, beautiful locations, nature, aromas and touch are all the pleasurable ingredients of romance. It is this combination of sexuality, love and total focus that has inspired many of the world's great geniuses to their greatest works of art, poetry, literature, music and conquest. The works of Beethoven, Picasso and Dali were often claimed by their creators to be inspired solely by this triumvirate.

The multiple intelligences and sexuality are all part of the same finely woven fabric. This explains why most of the world's great geniuses, no matter what their field, were known for their prodigious sexual appetites, which were once thought to be an aberration rather than a signature of genius. Intelligence, in its widest interpretation *is* sexy!

6 MENTAL ATTITUDE

Mental attitude has a direct correlation with both physical health and mental fitness. An attitude of fear, indecision, indifference, inflexibility, and negativism produces stress, ill-health and a generally deteriorating set of mental skills. Studies by the British Medical Association and the American Medical Association have shown that as much as 80% of disease (dis-ease) is caused by these mental attitudes.

An open-minded, committed, flexible, courageous, curious and optimistic mental attitude will produce a body that is physically more healthy and freed from stress, and a mind which is more alert and capable of dealing with the constant 'intelligence tests' that day to day living requires.

Initial results in this area show that the more genius-compatible of these two attitudes may actually encourage the growth of more sophisticated and intricate 'wiring' between brain cells. Such a general mental attitude has also been found to be identical to that which characterizes older people who may be described as successful. A positive mental attitude will greatly contribute to a longer and healthier life.

YOUR NEXT STEP FORWARD

In order to develop the healthiest mind in the healthiest body, the following action steps, based on the material in this chapter, are highly recommended.
1 Do basic training, especially aerobics, for at least 20 minutes at least three times a week.
2 Strengthen your muscular system.
3 Try to become and remain even more flexible.
4 Develop and improve your poise.
5 Create a Mastermind Group of health advisers. They might include specialist doctors, coaches, instructors and an Alexander teacher (see page 56).
6 Find time to play – one of the best forms of all-round exercise, especially when you can play with children.
7 Know yourself better. Measure your weight and strength and consider your state of health on a regular basis.
8 Incorporate regular rest periods in your life.
9 Establish and monitor a basic healthy diet.
10 Mind Map (see page 58) your current levels and future goals (put the latter into practice).

THE BRAIN PRINCIPLES: FORMULAE FOR GENIUS

'SCIENCE SEEKS KNOWLEDGE. LET THE KNOWLEDGE LEAD US TO WHERE IT WILL, WE STILL MUST SEEK IT. TO KNOW ONCE FOR ALL WHAT WE ARE, WHY WE ARE, WHERE WE ARE, IS THAT NOT IN ITSELF THE GREATEST OF ALL HUMAN ASPIRATIONS?'
SIR ARTHUR CONAN DOYLE (1859-1930)

As we discover more about the brain, funda-mental principles on which its operation is based are revealed. In this chapter, six of these principles, all essential for the realization of genius, are introduced.

THE SYNERGISTIC PRINCIPLE

Earlier models and concepts of the human brain often assumed that its capabilities were bounded, and the mathematics on which it was based were somewhat limited. Recent research has shown that the brain is a synergistically mathematical organ. In a synergistic system 1 plus 1 equals more than 2. This 'more than 2' can stretch literally to infinity. Thus we can confi-dently say that the capability of the brain is lim-itless, an idea echoed by Petr Anokhin in his physiological investigation of the capacity of the individual brain cell and its interconnections.

A simple proof of the fact that the brain does have this extraordinary potential lies in the everyday and universal habit of daydreaming. In a daydreaming situation you can take yourself (*one* person) plus *one* other person and can cre-ate in your mind romantic novels, murder mys-teries and horror stories that would rival today's blockbuster films.

The synergistic principle means that each one of us is self-creating in two major spheres: the mental and the physical. Once the synergistic principle is combined with Radiant Thinking and Mind Mapping, your brain can go on associating, without hesitation, for ever. Thus everyone's ability for divergent thinking, the opposite of the convergent thinking tested in IQ tests, is not only limitless, but is capable of creating its own inter-nal universes of knowledge, networks of thought, memory banks and uniquely innovative and inspirational ideas.

Further research into the brain's function while it is thinking provides strong evidence for the fact that if the brain is thinking and learning vigorously, each brain cell will actually produce more 'connection points' with which to commu-nicate with other brain cells, thus creating a more sophisticated, intricate, and complex bio-com-puter. What we think, the way we think, and the way we think about thinking, literally changes the biological structures of our brains. All this is particularly good news, and means that the human race's attitude and approach to brain-storming can alter dramatically and for the better.

Before becoming too 'heady' over this idea, it is important to consider the computer acronym GIGO, standing for 'Garbage In, Garbage Out'. It was thought for some time that this principle applied to the brain in the same way as it does to computers. This is a false assumption, how-ever. For the brain, the appropriate acronym is GIGG – standing for 'Garbage In, Garbage GROWS'! Because the brain operates synergisti-cally, the rubbish we put into it finds a wonder-ful nesting place and *multiplies*. This means that as well as being self-creating, the brain can sim-ilarly be self-destructive. And not only self-destructive, but synergistically self-destructive, meaning that it has an almost limitless power to be so. A simple check of your own life, or cur-rent affairs, and of the history of your own community, nation and world will confirm phe-nomenal examples of both exquisite self-gener-ating creativity – as in the great Greek and Italian Renaissances – and horrific examples of individ-ual and mass destruction.

There is good news within this bad news. The brain is fortunately not *designed* to self-destruct. It will do so in only one situation – and this situ-ation has three elements. The human brain will only self-destruct when

1 It has the wrong formula.
2 It believes the formula to be true.
3 It acts upon it or practises it.

The irony of this is that the more loving, intel-ligent, creative, and powerful an individual or group is, the more rapidly it will self-destruct when it has the wrong formula, believes it to be true and practises it. A good example of this is that of a particularly strong, flexible and aerobically fit individual who becomes stuck in a swamp or quicksand. If that individual believes that the correct formula for escaping from the situation is to thrash about with full physical vigour, then all that supreme power will be directed, unwittingly, to an almost instantaneous disappearance below the surface.

It is essential therefore that we find the correct formula. *Buzan's Book of Genius* is a massive exploration of all those formulae which are positively synergistic, and which create the natural state for the human brain – the natural and ongoing Renaissance of genius. The brain principles outlined in this chapter are further examples.

THE SUCCESS PRINCIPLE

For much of this century it was assumed that the human brain is a trial and error mechanism. This formula was nearly correct, but unfortunately placed the emphasis incorrectly. For if the brain were a trial and *error* mechanism, we would have been born, and tried error, error, error and died. In fact, we were born, and tried success, success, success; then error, check, adjust, success, success and so on. In other words, the brain is a trial and *success* mechanism.

The instant we recognize this, our whole attitude about ourselves changes, and instead of considering ourselves 'only human', we realize the positive aspects of being human, with a massive range of talents, abilities and potentials.

THE PYGMALION EFFECT

Considering ourselves in a more positive light produces a self-induced Pygmalion Effect. The Pygmalion Effect describes the reaction that occurs when children are considered by their parents, friends and teachers to be bright, intelligent and successful. If this happens, the children automatically become more of each of these qualities. When children are considered to be dull, bad, and failures, they will similarly manifest those qualities and have less chance of being successful. To consider ourselves the product of trial and error produces a negative Pygmalion Effect. To consider ourselves as we are, based on trial and *success*, creates greater opportunities for the positive synergistic spiral to lock in, and changes the internal bio-chemistry and structure of our brains to our benefit.

THE RED RUM BRAIN PRINCIPLE

The story of the racehorse Red Rum typifies one of the most important of the brain principles for success – persistence.

Red Rum was a little horse of undistinguished career, when he was entered in the English Grand National – the most challenging and dangerous of all steeplechase races, requiring the field of often as many as 40 starting horses to run for four and a half miles over 30 high and dangerous fences. In many of the Nationals, as few as seven horses actually completed the course, the others either falling, refusing, and in some more horribly extreme cases, dying.

In his first Grand National, Red Rum, smaller than most of the other horses, was initially in the rear of the field but gradually fought his way up among the leaders. To everyone's surprise, and the bookmakers' dismay, the little outsider eventually won handsomely.

Winners of the Grand National very rarely repeat their victory, partly because they are handicapped with extra weight the following year. Also, the odds against any horse successfully completing the course twice are extremely high. Red Rum, however, was an exceptional horse who made the National his own. He went on to win two out of the four Nationals he subsequently raced, coming second in the other two, despite his age and handicapping. Rummy's determination to succeed has not been equalled by any other horse and he became a national hero. On his retirement, he remained a popular crowd-puller, attending events and raising money for charity.

What Red Rum accomplished was the touching of an inner core of awareness. The awareness that one of the brain's great attributes, and indeed one of the greatest attributes of genius, is the ability to persist, to continue to try for success, no matter what the odds, no matter how many the setbacks, and no matter how long the journey. This quality of intelligence is often misnamed 'stubbornness, pig-headedness, bullheadedness, and thick-headedness'. These terms reflect only on the negative, and ignore the real essence of persistence, and how it is essential for the flowering of our intellects.

Thomas Edison, one of the most creative and flexible minds ever, and one who 'helped us see the light' in many ways, summed it up succinctly when he commented '*Genius is one per cent inspiration, 99 per cent perspiration*'. He certainly persisted with experiments to find solutions.

*Genius composer Wolfgang Amadeus Mozart, shown here aged
30, adopted such a positive attitude towards life that we have
named the Amadeity Principle of genius after him.*

THE GOETHENDIPITY PRINCIPLE

On a trip to Africa, co-author Tony Buzan was invited to speak on the Development of Genius on a radio show. He was warned that the interviewer, once a national British sporting hero, was renowned for his abrasive, attacking and aggressive style of interviewing. To Tony's delight, the interview turned out to be one of the most positively provocative, wide-ranging and mutually enthusiastic he had ever experienced. What was planned as a half-hour show turned into a two-hour marathon that simply flashed by.

The experience had been so stimulating for both the disc jockey and for Tony that after the show they chatted about what had made it so extraordinary. They discovered that their careers had been remarkably similar, both having been interested in sports, both having studied a wide range of subjects at university, both having become fascinated by learning and the development of the brain's potential, and both having specifically worked on their intellectual and communication skills in order to be able to express their points of view more clearly.

Shortly afterwards, a friend of Tony's commented on the excitement generated by the programme: 'How lucky it was that you two met – a real serendipity'. But was this really the case? Surely if two intelligences had devoted so much of their lives to almost identical forms of pursuit, and were following a similar vision, their meeting was not 'luck' or serendipitous? Surely it was something more meaningful and more in tune with the way all living organisms of a similar 'form' have innumerable ways of 'sensing' each other's presence?

Searching for the right word to express his thoughts, Tony remembered Goethe's comment on vision, commitment and genius (see page 164) and, coining a word to describe his meeting with the disc jockey, decided that it wasn't serendipity, but *Goethen*dipity which had brought them together. Goethendipity is the concept that the people you meet, and the circumstances in which you find yourself, will relate incredibly closely to the power of your personal vision, the commitment you have to it, the persistence with which you pursue it, your appropriate practice of the brain principles, and the degree of your development of the other characteristics of genius.

THE AMADEITY PRINCIPLE

In the early 1990s, psychologists studying Mozart's letters revealed a finding that they considered most odd: they had 'discovered' that Mozart was, to use their jargon, 'psychotically positive'. They mis-named him this because they had found a letter in which he had written to his wife that a new opening performance of one of his operas had gone exceptionally well. Mozart had happily described all the positive aspects of the performance, mentioning only at the end that it had not met with critical acclaim, and that the audience had numbered only 10 people!

Mozart, like most other leading geniuses, intuitively realized that it was far more productive for his creative processes and musical composition to focus on excellence rather than to dwell on the negative. He was, contrary to the psychologists' assumptions, *appropriately* positive.

This brain principle and quality of genius, in his especial honour, we have named Amadeity.

THE VIE BRAIN PRINCIPLE

The VIE principle is an acronym standing for Veneration, Inspiration and Emulation. It refers to the consistently observed fact that all great geniuses had role models, 'heroes', and Mastermind Groups of real and imaginary advisers from whom they drew their inspiration, and whom they used as role models in order, through emulation, to achieve personal goals.

In the pursuit of your own genius, it is essential to provide yourself with such role models. One of the main functions of *Buzan's Book of Genius* is to provide, in the portraits of the 100 great geniuses, a vast range of many of the greatest minds in history from which you can select your own particular role models and real and/or internal Mastermind Groups.

THE BRAIN PRINCIPLES – ACTION STEPS

1 Constantly search out and check for the synergistically correct formulae.
2 When you are in a negative synergistic spiral, remember that you can always get out of this 'black hole' by focusing on your positive vision.
3 Whenever you feel like quitting, remember Red Rum, and keep going.
4 Encourage Goethendipity.
5 Practise Amadeity.
6 Develop your own personal Pygmalion Effect on yourself. Check your comments to others and your own self-talk, scanning it for negatives and positives. Accentuate the positive!
7 Select the 10 main Mastermind members of your internal and real Mastermind Groups. Start on-going 'meetings' with them.

MEMORY

*'MEMORY CONFERS BOTH THE FREEDOM TO BREAK FROM ACCEPTED
WISDOM AND THE POWER TO CREATE THE NEW.'*
RAYMOND KEENE

In surveys Tony Buzan and his colleagues have conducted around the world, memory is consistently named as the major problem facing individuals. The reason why it is such a problem is not to do with the 'natural state' of the memory; it is more due to the fact that the way we have trained it is synergistically designed to disintegrate those very skills we are trying to use to help us to recall. What are the *real* limits of the potential of our memories?

Professor Luria, Russia's most eminent psychologist during the latter half of this century, and the best student and protégé of Petr Anokhin, tells a remarkable story about a man named Shereshevsky. Luria explains: 'The actual beginning dates back to the 1920s, when I had only recently begun to do work in psychology. It was then that a man came to my laboratory and asked me to test his memory.

'At the time the man, Shereshevsky, was a newspaper reporter and he had come to my laboratory at the suggestion of the paper's editor. Each morning the editor would meet with his staff and hand out assignments for the day – lists of places he wanted covered, information to be obtained in each and so on. The list of addresses and instructions was usually fairly long, and the editor noted with some surprise that S (Shereshevsky) never took any notes. He was about to reproach the reporter for being inattentive when, at his urging, S repeated the entire assignment *word-for-word*. Curious to learn more about how the man operated, the editor began questioning S about his memory. But S merely countered with amazement: Was there really anything unusual about his remembering everything he had been told? Wasn't that the way other people operated? The idea that he possessed certain particular qualities of memory which distinguished him from others struck him as incomprehensible . . .

'When I began my study of S it was with much the same degree of curiosity psychologists gen-

erally have at the outset of research, hardly with the hope that the experiments would offer anything of particular note. However, the results of the first test were enough to change my attitude and to leave me, the experimenter, rather than my subject, both embarrassed and perplexed.

'. . . as the experimenter, I soon found myself in a state verging on utter confusion. An increase in the length of a series of numbers or words to be memorized led to no noticeable increase in difficulty for S, and I simply had to admit that the capacity of his memory *had no distinct limits* . . . Experiments indicated that he had no difficulty reproducing any lengthy series of words whatever, even though these had originally been presented to him a week, a month, a year or even many years earlier. In fact, some of these experiments designed to test his retention were performed (without his being given any warning) 15 or 16 years after the session in which he had originally recalled the words.'

Luria concluded that to all intents and purposes, Shereshevsky's memory was not only phenomenal, it was *perfect*.

Such a story might seem impossible, were it not for the mounting evidence about the physical and behavioural aspects of the brain which seem to indicate that, in a natural state, memories can indeed approach the levels attained by Shereshevsky and Magliabechi (see page 52).

The evidence for the brain's capacity and memory is further supported by the record-smashing accomplishments of Dominic O'Brien, the first World Memory Champion and Brain of the Year in 1994. As he has explained, he was a poor student in school, with a relatively weak memory. It was only by becoming mentally literate, physically fit, and by training his memory appropriately that he is now able to accomplish feats that are astounding psychologists, trailblazing the way for fellow mnemonists and mental athletes and matching the accomplishments of Shereshevsky.

To demonstrate for yourself the extraordinary power of your own memory, two simple exercises will prove to you that yours is unbelievably efficient and competent, and in all probability limitless in its capacity.

First, think about how many bits of data (words, numbers, visions, sense impressions and memories) you already have stored in your memory. It is obviously multiple-multiple quadrillions. Think next about how you hold an animated conversation with a friend. While you are listening attentively, and understanding everything your friend says, what you are in fact doing is instantaneously accessing, from your staggeringly gigantic database, *without any pre-warning*, randomly spoken sounds which would not be *exactly* the same as any sounds you have ever heard before. Your brain has therefore to compare and contrast and select information instantaneously on an on-going basis so rapidly that it is, like Red Rum's victories, mathematically impossible. And yet you do it in a smooth and flowing way that is so natural that *you don't even notice* that what you are performing when you chat away, is something that no known computer can come *even close* to duplicating, and which, if you could explain it, would make you one of the greatest scientists in history.

The second exercise is an exercise in Radiant Thinking and pre-Mind Mapping. Draw a circle to represent the sun in the centre of a page. With radiating branches emanating from the circle, quickly write down all the associations you have with the word 'sun'. You will probably end up with between 10 and 40. Next consider whether you can write down words associated to the words that you have connected to 'sun'. Of course you can and of course in each instance it will be more than one. Do this. Consider next whether you can continue this process. Once again of course you can. What you are doing when you are finding associations is simply accessing more of the elements of your database. How long will it be possible for you to continue this process? Obviously forever! With this simple demonstration you have just proved that, theoretically, and even actually at this moment, you have already acquired an infinite database and have the capability of adding infinities to it.

THE SECRETS OF MEMORY

What, then, are the secrets that enable those such as Shereshevsky and all those listed in the Mental World Records Memory section to achieve such astonishing results? Fortunately the answer is simple. Your memory operates on these three basic principles:

1 Association.
2 Imagination.
3 Order and structure.

In memory and learning for the last few centuries we have tended to focus on the left-dominant skills, discouraging or diminishing in importance activities such as daydreaming, wild imaginings, general fantasizing, music and art. In this way we have taken away almost totally one of the tripods of memory, causing the entire structure to crash.

To revivify our memories we need to make active use of all our cortical skills, to consider the thoughts of Leonardo da Vinci, and to apply the specific memory techniques developed by the ancient Greeks called *mnemonics* (after the Greek goddess of memory, Mnemosyne). In addition we should develop our Radiant Thinking and Mind Mapping skills.

Leonardo da Vinci, who, as well as being one of the greatest all-round geniuses ever, was one of the great memorizers, said that the average human 'looks without seeing, listens without hearing, touches without feeling, eats without tasting, moves without physical awareness, inhales without awareness of odour or fragrance, and talks without thinking'. In this 'sensory blindness' the memory is literally disassociated from the universe around it, and as association is one of the pillars of memory, the universe, or all our experience, tends to be forgotten.

Da Vinci's rule for memorization is identical to his own life's vision which was to develop the senses, in his case all of them and especially vision. To follow his advice, and inevitably to improve your powers of memory, learn to look as a child or artist looks; to listen like a musician; to talk like a poet; to move like an animal or dancer; to detect odours like a deer; and to eat and drink as if you were a master chef.

There is a simple system, developed by Buzan and Vanda North, world rated mnemonist, which allows you to use your cortical skills, apply your senses, and guarantee that you are using association, imagination and order in your memory tasks. All you have to do is to remember the phrase 'smashin' scope', and you will have, in a simple acronym that refers to the 'smashing scope' of your memory, all the major elements of the mnemonic technique.

A POETRY CHALLENGE

At the 1993 World Memory Championships, one of the competitions required the contestants to memorize as much of a poem as they could within an allotted time span of 15 minutes. Then they had to write down as many lines as possible, with correct punctuation and spelling. To ensure that there was no chance of anyone knowing the poem in advance, the Poet Laureate Ted Hughes (born 1930) wrote a 54-line poem especially for the occasion. He titled it *Anamnemonicker* because his chosen words and style make the poem deliberately difficult to remember. For instance, the tenses change from present to past and back to present within the first four lines. In addition, he used words (such as 'armour', 'star', 'rapier', 'shining' and 'steel' in the first few lines) which conjure up similar mental images. Associating words with pictures in the mind usually helps people to remember but where words lead to similar visual impressions this can be misleading for the memorist. Poems which have a rhyme scheme, rhythm, patterns, repeated words and are written in short verses are obviously much easier to memorize than poetry which does not. Think about how little time it takes children to memorize nursery rhymes (which contain all these elements) and which poems and verses you yourself can recite from memory. Test your powers of recall by trying to memorize as much of *Anamnemonicker* as you can within 30 minutes and then writing it down. Also, Hughes applied his genius to write the poem as a conundrum. Can you solve it? The answer is on page 255 (and the poem is much easier to understand when you know what it is about!).

ANAMNEMONICKER

A Knight in armour falls pushed off his star
By the crow of a cock. A wedding ring
Bounced off a coffin but a finger caught it.
A rapier dances away shining. A black
Cloak is flung aside while the owner
Flogs himself with nettles in a garden.
An *ignis fatui* face, pale, gray bearded,
Ponders a tuft of primroses. Too late
For the hoop of steel. Too late for the nightbird
Hurrying into the snare. A corpse in steel
Toppled by drunkards, calls from the foot of a cliff.
A sulphur coffin, the crypt's candelabra,
Warms the worm which serves as daily bread
For the mole. A different worm is dinner
To the carp which serves as brighter shadow
To the half-dressed and half-witted. A pair
Of Siamese Twins hunt with a pedigree Dachshund.
What was a passport is a twist of paper
Hiding a fiery poem and the egg of a blowfly.
Prison bars bend under a trumpet blast
Blown by the mask of a black knight who butchers
The ring-finger with a hammer of nettles.
A pigeon vomits a lily and a virgin
Hides her face in a bible of lies. A dagger
Slashes the air around its resting place.
Suddenly carves a nun out of nothing.
A rose devours itself and drops fragments.
A dark horse broods crow's eggs in a mare's nest.

It all comes out in a mirror. Even the dog
Dashes from its kennel, sniffs at a king
Sleeping on flowers bewailed by a laughing
   woman.
A mouse chokes on its fable. A royal stag
Stumbles under its arrow. The watchful flute
Refuses to make music for dancing weasels.
A cup of blood quenches heaven. Shackles
Are shaken at fear. Burbling, the new baby
Is invulnerable but the rat must perish.
A crown in a back pocket hurts as bad
As a boil that must be lanced. Maybe the ship
Will take it all away. A dripping sponge
Mops at the blood. But an angel adjusts
Its binoculars and all is recorded.
The army marches after a mad owl.
A sword burst into wild flowers, then flames,
Then melts, pouring into a mould. A letter
Dipped in ocean opens the two-faced door
To the serpent's fang that sleeps hidden
In a vial of tears wept by weeds.
A skull referees for two madmen
Fighting over a phantom . . . two idiots
Going off their heads in the front row.
A water skeeter becalms the storm brewing
Its pearl in the dregs of a teacup. A secretary
Reads out the minutes to a row of tombs.

TED HUGHES, POET LAUREATE

S *Synaesthesia and sensuality.* Whenever you are trying to remember something, attach, as da Vinci recommends, as many of your senses as possible to what it is you are trying to retain and recall.

M *Movement.* This increases the number of 'pictures' your brain is registering, and therefore increases the probability that you will remember something if you 'make it move'.

A *Association.* Your brain remembers by linking and joining things together. Think of *anything*, and you will find that your brain immediately adds other associations to it, much as you did with the exercise on the word 'sun'. Memory techniques work especially well if you link any item you want to remember with something you already know, producing a new 'smashin' scope' image that is so memorable you actually *do* remember it.

S *Sexuality.* Everyone has a superb memory in this arena. Activate it when you are endeavouring to remember!

H *Humour.* Make things you want to remember witty. Humour provides image and movement, thus increasing the possibility that you *will* remember it.

I *Imagination.* This is one of the cornerstones of memory, and the more it is used, the better the memory performance will be. Indeed, as Einstein said, 'Imagination is more important than knowledge. For knowledge is limited, whereas imagination embraces the entire world, stimulates progress, giving birth to evolution.' It also gives birth to a greater memory.

N *Number.* This provides order and structure, and allows you to 'place' things in your infinite memory filing system that are easily accessible and therefore recallable.

S *Symbolism.* Using especially provocative, imagistic and colourful symbols for things you wish to recall will enhance your power to do so.

C *Colour.* Colourful notes are more memorable than monotone dull notes. A colourful life is more memorable than a dull life. Using colour will enhance your memory.

O *Order/sequence.* Various forms of ordering, in conjunction with the use of number, increase the sophistication of your brain's filing system, and make it more like an automated, streamlined library, rather than like a rubbish dump.

P *Positivity.* When you are in a positive frame of mind, your brain and senses are literally more open to the world and universe around them. In this more open state they will function far more effectively, and in functioning far more effectively will allow you to register sensory impressions more clearly and immediately. This is the biological equivalent of expanded memory capacity.

E *Exaggeration.* When you are trying to remember something that seems to be difficult to remember, make it gigantic, colour it lavishly, increase its dimensions, and accelerate or enormously slow down its motion. In this way you will be making a 'bigger' impression on your brain, which will consequently be more memorable.

The 'smashin' scope' system is the approach to memory that Shereshevsky developed naturally, and which Dominic O'Brien trains himself with every day in his rigorous mental workouts. It is also the same system, used and adapted to each individual's needs and preferences, that has enabled all of the world record holders in the Mental World Records section to accomplish their amazing yet nevertheless relatively easily attainable memory feats.

When you develop your memory in these ways, which are the ways in which it was designed to be used, you will simultaneously be developing all aspects of your potential genius, and will therefore be improving at the same time your intelligence, your reading speed, your note-taking capability, your general thinking skills, your creative and innovative thinking, your ability to envision your goals, your humour, your general communication skills and your overall potential. Remember to develop your memory!

MEMORY – ACTION STEPS

1 Start a personal memory development programme.
2 Make a daily habit of developing your senses.
3 Use and develop your imagination.
4 Encourage your own sense of humour and fun.
5 Use the principles of 'smashin' scope' whenever you wish to remember anything.
6 Study the habits of the great memorizers.
7 Develop your Radiant Thinking and Mind Mapping skills (see page 58). Use Mind Maps to help you to remember the important things in your life.
8 Go for Mental World Records.
9 Develop your powers of association – play the game of linking anything with something else in an imaginative and witty way. This is more fun if you play it with a group of friends.
10 Remember to remember!

CREATIVITY

*'CREATIVE THINKING MAY MEAN SIMPLY THE REALIZATION THAT THERE
IS NO PARTICULAR VIRTUE IN DOING THINGS THEY WAY THEY HAVE
ALWAYS BEEN DONE.'*
RUDOLPH FLESCH, PHILOSOPHER

Creativity is as essential to your survival as breathing. It allows you to be flexible and inventive in your approach to all kinds of problems; gives you humour, spontaneity and release from stress; and is the inexhaustible well from which all great geniuses drink. Creativity is usually thought of as a rare god-given gift that is available only to those one-in-a-hundred-million blessed or lucky artists, writers and musicians. Nothing could be further from the truth. It is in fact a skill natural to each human brain, and like other skills it can be developed through training and the application of the correct principles.

WHAT IS CREATIVITY?

In their hunt for the Holy Grail of creativity, thinkers and writers have come up with relatively vague descriptions of the personality of creative geniuses, suggesting that they tend to be iconoclastic, interested in unrelated fields (how can *any* field be unrelated to any other?) and that they seem to have a strange tolerance for ambiguity. The creative individual is often thought of as messy, possessing a poor memory, disorganized, relatively unkempt and unclean, and 'way out'.

There are essences of truth in these vague personality descriptions, and there are reasons for the comprehensibly inaccurate assumptions about what a creative genius 'looks like'. This will become clear when you complete the following self-check.

CREATIVITY SELF-CHECK

Rate yourself on a scale of 0 – 100, giving yourself 0 if the statement describes you not at all and 100 if it describes you perfectly and you are highly skilled in the area.

1 I am instantaneously and spontaneously able to associate new and unique ideas with pre-existing ones.

2 I use many different colours in most aspects of my creative thinking.

3 I use different conceptual shapes and structures in my creative thinking processes.

4 I am easily able to combine unusual elements.

5 In my mind's eye I am capable of magnifying or diminishing any object or structure.

6 I am instantaneously capable of changing and adjusting my conceptual positions.

7 I regularly and with enjoyment rearrange and link pre-existing concepts.

8 Similarly, I regularly reverse pre-existing concepts.

9 It is natural for me to respond aesthetically to any appealing object.

10 It is natural to me to respond to any emotionally appealing object and also to express emotion.

11 I am capable of responding equally well to an object which appeals to either my sense of sight, touch, hearing, smell, taste or kinaesthetic awareness.

12 I find it easy and enjoyable to use interchangeable shapes and codes.

Each of the above statements encapsulates one of the 12 major mental skills necessary for the development of full creativity. As you can see, each one of these is readily trainable.

It is equally easy to see how these characteristics identify the behaviour of the major geniuses in this book. As an exercise, pick any one of the 100, and match the grid of his or her life's expression against the grid of the questions you have just answered. You will find, virtually without exception, that each genius behaved, to an exceptional degree, exactly as the 12 characteristics of creativity would suggest they should have.

In this light it is also easy to see why, with only a shallow investigation of the nature of genius, and with the false assumption that it is an untrainable attribute, those who have not developed their own creativity would describe those who have as iconoclastic, strange, and deviant. Because deviant, in the best sense of what the word means, is what the creative genius is: a deviator from the norm, who can see things from far greater ranges and from far more original perspectives than average thinkers.

The consistent cries of 'Eureka!' that echo down through the history of genius, echo in themselves the consistent verbal expression of those who have gone beyond the norm, and in so doing have made the great realizations that have allowed the progress of the development of intelligence.

Psychologist Dean Keith Simonton of the University of California in Davis calls the ability of the creative genius the ability to permutate 'mental elements' – images, phrases, flashes of memory, sounds, rhymes, abstract concepts and the senses. The more open-minded the individual, the more the natural intelligence is able to fill the brain with more of these elements (memory once again aiding creativity). Simonton uses the image of a child with buckets of Lego as being a highly creative person. He or she has a greater chance of forming novel combinations of ideas, images or symbols that constitute a masterpiece than does someone who possesses only a few Lego bricks, because they have chosen not to develop their natural thinking skills.

In addition, the creative genius will tend to blend the senses, readily transferring one sense to another. It is no coincidence that all great mnemonists do exactly the same thing. Picasso was so developed in all his sensory modes that he saw numbers as patterns, not symbols of quantities: the number two became a folded pigeon wing and the number zero an eye. Alexander Fleming, the discoverer of Penicillin, painted with germs! He would culture a batch of micro-organisms, each a different hue, paint them on to a Petri dish and wait for them to grow into pictures. Another example is the French composer Olivier Messiaen who reported that he could see the 'colour' of a musical tone.

THE DANCE OF CREATIVITY AND MEMORY

In exactly the same way as you matched the 12 characteristics of the brain's creative behaviour with the life of the geniuses, match them with the principles of memory, including the development of the senses, and smashin' scope. You will find that they are virtually identical. This indicates, contrary to much modern theory, that memory and creativity are part of the same Möbius strip. The main difference is simply that the brain uses all these techniques to aid its memory by literally recreating the past in the present. For the purpose of creative thinking the brain uses exactly the same elements for casting a 'memory of the present' into the future, making it an eventual reality.

The process of creative thinking is also identical to that of proper memory and mnemonic techniques in that it combines element (a) with element (b) to produce a memorable and creative image (c). Newton combined an apple (a) with a head (b) to produce gravity (c). Archimedes combined water rising (a) with the mass of his body (b) to produce a new theory of the measurement of volume (c).

USING MIND MAPS

A note-taking, note-making and thinking tool that combines all the elements of memory and creativity is the Mind Map (see page 58). To develop your own creativity you are strongly encouraged to learn this Radiant Thinking skill.

SUMMARY

The world's creative geniuses were those who 'locked in' to the fact that they could *unlock* the limitless creative energies of their minds by using their full range of cortical skills. They used and developed their senses, and extended their knowledge, mental literacy and creativity by applying the 12 creative thinking principles. You can unleash your own genius by following their example.

CREATIVITY – ACTION STEPS

1 Start your own creativity development programme.
2 Create for yourself a *Creative Thinking Zone*.
3 Practise breaking your own moulds in clothes, personality and habits.
4 Make time to play with children – and with the child in yourself.
5 Develop your Radiant Thinking skills.
6 Make a habit of using Mind Maps as an aid to memorization and creative and innovative thinking.
7 Choose role-model geniuses who you consider especially creative for your Mastermind Group.
8 Read more widely and become polymathic.
9 Make friends with people of all ages.
10 Meet new people; explore new cultures.
11 Work on solving massive problems.
12 Develop your sense of humour, which helps you to stretch your mind's ability to accept ambiguity and juxtapose opposites.
13 Start (or continue) to write poetry.
14 Develop your artistic skills.

SPEED READING

'READING IS TO THE MIND WHAT EXERCISE IS TO THE BODY.'
SIR RICHARD STEELE (1672-1729), ESSAYIST AND POLITICIAN

The remarkable visual instrument of your eyes and their super-bio-computer brain can together accomplish a vast range of reading speeds, comprehension and memory. We know that Thomas Jefferson, John Stuart Mill and John F. Kennedy were voracious readers who could apparently read at around 1000 words per minute. However, the most phenomenal example of what the eye/brain combination *can* accomplish makes even these speeds seem slow.

HOW MAGLIABECHI THE LIBRARIAN BECAME THE LIBRARY

Antonio di Marco Magliabechi was a contemporary of Spinoza, Sir Christopher Wren, Sir Isaac Newton and Leibniz. He was born on 29 October 1633 in Leonardo da Vinci's birthplace, Florence. His parents were so poor they were unable to provide him with any formal education, and at a young age he was apprenticed to a local fruit dealer. Magliabechi spent his spare time in the shop trying to decipher what was on the pamphlets and journals that were used to wrap the groceries.

One of the shop's regular customers was a local bookseller, who noted the young man's

attempt to read the strange hieroglyphics before him. The bookseller took him to his own shop and was amazed to find that Magliabechi could almost immediately recognize, remember and identify all the books after only a brief familiarization with them. With the bookseller's help, Magliabechi eventually learned to read properly and began to combine his new-found reading ability with phenomenal memorizing techniques which he developed and which enabled him to remember in its entirety (including punctuation) nearly everything that he read.

A sceptical author decided to put the lad's growing reputation for speed reading and memory to the test and gave Magliabechi a new manuscript that he could in no way have seen before, telling him to read it for pleasure. Magliabechi duly read the manuscript at a remarkable speed and returned it almost immediately, confirming that he had read it in its entirety. A little while after the event, the author pretended that he had lost his manuscript and asked Magliabechi if he could help him to remember some of it. To his astonishment the young man wrote out for him the entire book, transcribing perfectly every single word and every punctuation mark as if he had been copying from the original.

As time went on Magliabechi read at greater and greater speeds and memorized increasingly large numbers of books. He eventually became so famous for the speed at which he devoured and memorized knowledge that experts in all subjects came to him for instruction and source material in their own areas of interest. Whenever he was asked questions he provided answers by quoting verbatim from the books that he had read and automatically memorized.

As his reputation spread, so did his wealth, and he was eventually hired by the Grand Duke of Tuscany to act as his personal librarian. In order to be able to handle the volume of material in an entire library, Magliabechi decided to develop his speed reading abilities even further

FACTS ABOUT YOUR EYES

An eye contains 130 million light receptors. Each of these receptors can take in at least five photons (bundles of light energy) per second.

○　　○　　○

Your eyes can distinguish between over one million different colours.

○　　○　　○

The CERN Laboratory in Switzerland has estimated that to build a machine which could duplicate the incredible sophistication of our eyes would require equipment costing about £45 million ($68 million). This mechanical 'eye' would be the size of a small house!

and apparently did this to almost super-human dimensions. Contemporaries reported that he could simply 'dip' into a page, apparently absorbing the contents in their entirety with only one or two visual fixations, much to the amazement of those whom he allowed to watch him. He developed a reputation for having read and memorized the entire library!

Like most geniuses, Magliabechi continued to develop his abilities as he progressed with age. The more he speed read and memorized, the faster he was able to read and the more he was able to remember. The story goes that in his later years he would lie in bed surrounded by volumes each of which he would devour in less than half an hour, memorizing them in turn until he fell asleep. This he continued to do until his death in 1714 at the age of 81.

If Magliabechi's eye/brain system was capable of such incredible reading and memory accomplishments, why do the rest of us crawl along at speeds which make us functionally illiterate? The answer appears to lie not in the fact that we do not have the basic ability, but that we have actively and unwittingly trained ourselves to *become* slow. In other words, we have adopted belief systems, reading practices and habits that are synergistically self-destructive of our abilities to read at any speed and with any reasonable comprehension.

FALSE BELIEFS ABOUT READING

The following beliefs about reading are commonly held and taught in most schools around the world. Each one of them is demonstrably and dangerously wrong, as the remainder of this chapter will reveal. As you read the statements think about whether you were taught and/or believe that they relate to proper, 'correct' reading behaviour.

1 To read well you need to read 'slowly and carefully'.

2 You should always read word-for-word.

3 You should understand 100% of everything you read.

4 You should try to remember 100% of everything you read.

5 You should not subvocalize (sound the words to yourself) as you read.

6 The eye moves smoothly along the lines as it reads.

7 If you miss something while reading you should skip back to make sure you 'get it'.

8 Children should not read with their fingers on the page underneath the word, because it slows them down.

9 You should overcome any problems of comprehension and understanding before moving on to the following text.

10 You should read the book page by page, never reading the end 'until you get there'.

11 You should not skip words.

12 You should note important items when you get to them.

13 Variation in levels of motivation will not affect reading speed.

14 Your notes should be in sentence or list form and should always be 'neat'.

15 You should immediately look up the meaning of any words you do not understand.

16 As you read faster, your comprehension drops.

17 It is unnatural to read quickly.

18 You cannot appreciate the material if you read it quickly.

19 You can only read and understand what your eyes directly focus upon.

All the above statements are incorrect, so if you agreed with any of them, change your opinion immediately. True to the formula for synergistic self-destruction, they will only make you progressively *slower*, will increasingly *decrease* your ability to remember, and will on-goingly eat away at both your concentration and your confidence in a most unproductive way.

What actually happens when you read is a profoundly complex process that is simultaneously easy to understand and to put into practice. The remainder of this chapter is devoted to exploding the myths about reading, and explaining how your eye and brain *really* work and *can* work for you when you read.

THE BASIC MECHANICS OF READING

Your eye is the most sophisticated 'camera' on the planet. To see something clearly (to photograph it) it must 'hold the object still' for a fraction of a second, before it moves on to the next object. When translated into reading, this means that the eye must 'fix' on a few words, 'photograph' and register them, and then move to the next few words where the process is repeated. With this knowledge about the physical action of the eye, it is easy to distinguish between a slow and a faster or range reader (the term applied to someone who can read well over a wide *range* and variety of speeds).

Slow readers read one or two words at a time,

'fix' on these words for as much as one and a half seconds, regularly 'skip back' to check for accuracy and understanding, and regularly have their eyes wandering off the page, distracted by external events or internal images – daydreaming!

Speed or range readers take in three to six words per fixation, 'fix' on these words for as little as a half or even a quarter of a second, 'skip back' only very occasionally, and keep their eyes focused on the page and their brains focused on the content of that page.

To put all this in perspective, a slow reader will read roughly 100 words per minute, a normal reader will read about 200 words per minute, a traditional 'good reader' will read 400 words per minute and a range reader will read 1000 plus words per minute.

READING SPEEDS AND WORDS PER SECOND

Slow reader
100 words per minute = 1.6 words per second

Normal/average reader
200 words per minute = 3.3 words per second

Traditional 'good' reader
400 words per minutes = 6.6 words per second

Range reader
1000 words or more per minute = 16.6 words or more per second

---

YOUR FIELD OF VISION

Your eyes have two main types of vision – the sharp or central focus and the peripheral or wide vision. Your central focus can see clearly six words at a time horizontally *and vertically*. This means that a good range reader will be reading three things at the same time: the six horizontal words at the centre of the vision; the cluster of words above those six already read, constituting a *review*; and the cluster of words shortly to be read, constituting a *preview*. A range reader will take full advantage of this sharp focus.

VISUAL FIELD – PERIPHERAL/WIDE

Of the 260,000,000 light receivers working for you while you read, 220,000,000 are devoted to your peripheral vision. This is because it is from the world outside your central focus that food,

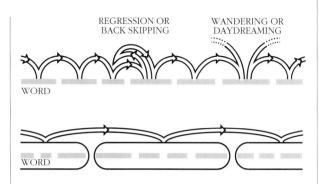

ABOVE A slow reader has a number of bad habits (shown in the top diagram). These include having only a small fixation span, backskipping and regression, and letting the brain wander. The eyes of a speed or range reader have a wider fixation span.

BELOW When a speed or range reader uses the eye/brain system properly, the field of vision encompasses a large circled area (top) on a page. Similarly, peripheral vision extends beyond the page (bottom).

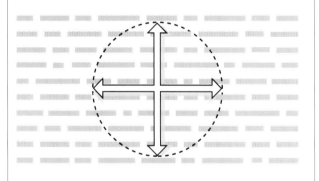

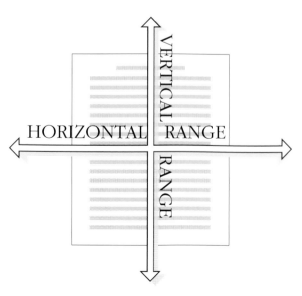

danger, possible mates and millions of other items of interest come. In other words, you need that massive percentage of your vision devoted to what goes on around you in order to ensure your survival.

This dominant part of your vision is also a lot clearer than has previously been believed. You can check the evidence of this from your own life. If you have ever bought a new or second-hand car, let's imagine a little red one, inevitably when you took it for your first drive you noticed similar little red cars everywhere – heading towards you, in side alleys, and even in the rear-view mirror! This is because your brain, behind the lens of your eyes, was scanning the environment for items of interest, and little red cars were of interest. The fact that you can pick them out *wherever they are* in your visual field, shows just how clear this wide vision is. To check this for yourself, place a pointer in the middle of a page, keep your eyes focused on it, and see how much you can actually see with your peripheral vision, especially things like diagrams, headings and page numbers. You will often find that you can also see much of the opposite page.

CYCLOPEAN PERCEPTION

If the eye is focused on the central circle of sharp-focus words, what then is it that is actually *seeing* everything around it? Paradigm-shifting work done by Bela Julesz at the Sensory and Perceptual Processes Department of Bell Telephone Laboratories has proven that every-one in fact has a 'central eye', and that this cen-tral eye is the brain.

Because of the way we have constructed our lives and environment, what our eyes centrally focus on is normally that to which the brain is paying attention. It is almost as if we have become glued to the smaller, more 'tunnel vision' part of our visual field. In its natural state the brain is far more alert, using its own massive internal eye to scan the entire range of informa-tion coming through the lenses, and at times focusing on everything at once. This is a visual skill actively developed by all great artists, par-ticularly in the visual and martial arts. It was probably this vast eye/brain potential that Magli-abechi developed to its full, enabling him to take in pages of books at a glance.

COMPREHENSION

The reason why some people are taught to read 'slowly and carefully' is because it used to be the opinion that slower equalled higher comprehen-sion, and faster equalled lower comprehension. All research shows this to be an especially invid-ious negative synergy. According to this wrong formula, the slower you go, the less you under-stand, which then means that you have to go even more slowly and will end up with even less comprehension. The fact is that the faster you read, the more your comprehension *increases*. A simple experiment will show you how this is true. Read the first of the following statements as it is laid out, taking it in slowly and each set of letters one at a time. Then read the second state-ment reading the words as they are grouped.

1 It is in teresting to find out a bout the act ivities of the human brain.

2 All studies of human genius have shown that they all pay special attention to developing their full range of mental intelligences.

Your brain works more naturally and more comfortably at speeds of 400 words per minute and up, where the clustering of words is mean-ingful. This increase in speed allows an auto-matic increase in the ability to understand, because the information is organized in chunks that make sense. This automatically spills over into memory, because when things are grouped and linked meaningfully, memory automatically improves.

In addition to improving your understanding and increasing your memory, a higher reading speed will in many instances raise your standard IQ. Most IQ tests are given in written form, and if your eye/brain system is absorbing the infor-mation at a higher rate and more efficiently, it will be able both to analyse the information more appropriately and rapidly, and you will therefore have more time to devote to the actual solving of each problem as opposed to reading about them as the seconds tick by.

TECHNIQUES FOR IMPROVING READING SPEED AND COMPREHENSION

Armed with this knowledge about the amazing power of your eye and brain, you can now approach reading in a more exciting and more rewarding way. Techniques and hints to help you improve rapidly, and to continue improving for the rest of your life, are as follows:

1 Take in more words per visual fixation.

2 Do not linger for too long on any group of words – your eye/brain system is *easily* capable of 'photographing' at very high speeds.

3 Keep your eyes moving progressively onward.

4 Stay focused on the page.

5 Use your Cyclopean Perception, constantly scanning for key words and ideas.

6 Use sub-vocalization. Because your senses intermingle naturally, you will automatically, at some deep level, sound the words as you read. Whenever you come to a particularly important key word or phrase, internally 'shout it out', thus emphasizing it and registering it more strongly for both understanding and recall.

7 Establish an interested and positive mental state – your brain and senses will become more 'open' thus taking in more and naturally accelerating your speeds.

8 Read with good poise and posture (see below).

THE BEST POSTURE FOR READING

Ideally both your feet should be flat on the floor. Your back should be upright and you should aim for gently lengthening your musculature. The various curves in your back give you essential support. If you try to sit up so that your back is 'too straight' or try to flatten these curves you will end up exhausted.

If you are sitting on a chair or stool and are reading rather than writing, you may find it more comfortable to hold the book in your hands. Alternatively, if you do prefer to lean a few degrees forward over a desk or table, try resting the book on something so that it is at a slight angle. Above all, make sure that you are sitting on a firm base. Anything soft or too comfortable, like a cushion which gives way, will ultimately send you to sleep!

Sitting in a correct position for reading accomplishes many things for you.

Circulation For your brain to operate at peak efficiency, it requires a maximum flow of both air and blood. When the upper spine and especially the neck are bent into a curve, both the windpipe and the main arteries and veins in the neck are constricted. When you sit up straight the flow opens.

Field of Vision A good position allows your eyes to make full use of both your central and peripheral vision. Your eyes need to be at least 20 in (50 cm) from the written material.

Energy Flow Electricity flowing up your spinal column is necessary to maximize the power of your brain. Adopting an upright stance while maintaining the slight, natural curves in the spine have been proved to give more power and springiness to the column. Lower back pain and shoulder aches are also minimized with upright posture.

Alertness When the body is erect the brain knows that something active and important is happening. When the body is bent or slumped it is telling the brain – through the inner ear and the

THE ALEXANDER TECHNIQUE AND ITS FOUNDER

Today, an increasing number of people are turning to the Alexander Technique for help with 'medical ailments' like back pain, breathing disorders and postural difficulties. This technique of psycho-physical reintegration for promoting poise, balance and presence is now taught at all the major conservatoires of music and drama and is practised by thousands of people.

The technique was developed by and named after Tasmanian-born F.M. Alexander (1869-1955). He was a Shakespearean actor, scholar, amateur violinist and adventurer, who specialized in one-man recitals and whose promising stage career was interrupted by a persistent tendency to lose his voice in mid-performance. Leading throat specialists and voice coaches failed to provide him with any lasting remedy, so Alexander determined to find a solution himself.

He embarked on a lifelong self-examination of the way in which his body and mind inter-

acted. When he initially studied himself with the aid of a mirror, he noticed that as he spoke he tended to shorten his neck muscles, thereby pulling his head down and back. Alexander reasoned that this habit was responsible for his vocal problems. Moreover, he discovered that his tendency to shorten his stature began to manifest itself as soon as he started to *think* about speaking.

To summarize, F.M. Alexander found that by changing our ways of *thinking* we can free ourselves from physical misuse. In his own words, *'we can throw away the habits of a lifetime if we use our brains'*.

The Alexander Technique should be learned from a trained teacher. A catalogue of such teachers can be obtained by writing to The Society of Teachers of the Alexander Technique, 20 London House, 266 Fulham Road, London, SW10 9EL.

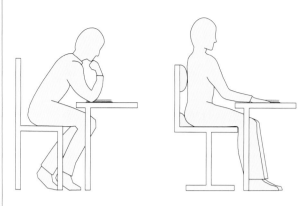

Try not to sit hunched over a table or desk while reading (left). It is much better for your brain if you sit in a more upright position (right).

balance mechanisms — that it is time for sleep, especially when the head is tilted too far from the vertical. When your body is alert your brain is alert.

The guide/pointer For millions of years the eye, the forefinger and the brain have been a team which has empowered the human brain to excel in observing; throwing; communicating; drawing; and in the last 5000 years in writing and reading.

We all naturally use our fingers to read in many situations anyway. Do *you* use a finger, a pointer, or a pen when you are adding up a column of numbers? Looking up a word in a dictionary? Searching for a name and number in a telephone directory? Reading instructions on a packet? The reason why we do this is because the guide helps the eyes to focus and concentrate. It is why all young children start to read by placing their hands underneath the words on the page and it is wrong to tell children to take away their hands or fingers. Using them as a guide may slow them down, though there is no harm in encouraging them to move the guide faster.

Ideally you should use a thin pointer such as a pencil when you are reading, and your eye will then automatically follow the guide. The guide will naturally concentrate your attention and will create a physical/mental memory pattern which will aid your recall. The ideal speed for maximizing comprehension when you start range reading is 600–700 words per minute. As most books and typed letters have 10 to 12 words per line, a reading speed of one line per second allows the eye to read at 600–700 words per minute. From this new base you can launch yourself towards a target of 1000 words per minute and then aim even higher.

To maximize your memory and recall, as well as to accelerate your speed, it is of prime importance that your reading is continuous. The guide is an extremely useful tool to help the speed and range reader achieve this because if you use it you reduce back-skipping and regression, increase the width of your fixation, establish a proper reading rhythm, improve concentration, increase understanding and memory, and accelerate speed.

Mark the book People and many animals have, from the very beginning, marked or branded things to 'claim their possession' – cave drawings, house names and numbers, cattle brands, corporate logos and personal signatures to name just a few. If you mark the important key words, concepts and images as you read, especially if you use colour which stimulates the visual cortex, your brain will 'own' that information. In other words you will both understand and remember it more completely.

Mark any problem areas as you read Do not stop to solve them. 80% of the time your brain will solve the problem as you read on. If you fail to solve the problem by doing this, it will still be easier to understand it in the context of what follows as well as what went before it.

Assess the book Before you read the main bulk of a book, there are a number of things you can do to help you to read it quickly and remember effectively.

1 Flip through the entire book, looking for charts, graphs, headings and major points of interest to get a feel for it.

2 Read the front and back covers and the fly leaves.

3 Read the table of contents.

4 Glance through the index, if there is one.

5 Check the bibliography, if there is one.

6 Scan the introduction and the beginning of the first chapter.

7 Read the last chapter, the summary and any conclusions.

8 If you are still interested, read the first and last page of the other chapters in the book.

9 Make a few notes about the book in Mind Map form (see page 58) on a single sheet of paper, and ask yourself if you really want to study the book in greater depth, or whether you now have enough information to satisfy your original goals. Usually only two or three out of any 10 books will really rate an in-depth read. For poetry, novels and other 'pleasure' reading most of the above does not apply, so you need to adjust your techniques appropriately.

MIND MAPPING

'THE MIND MAP IS THE ULTIMATE THINKING TOOL. IT WILL HELP YOU TO IMPROVE YOUR MEMORY AND POWERS OF CONCENTRATION, AS WELL AS TO CLARIFY AND STRUCTURE YOUR THOUGHTS.'

TONY BUZAN

If you have already read *The Mind Map Book*, written by Tony Buzan with his brother Barry (published by BBC Books), you will need no introduction to this exciting and innovative approach to taking and making notes. But for those who have yet to become Mind Mappers, what follows is a brief explanation of Mind Maps and some of their many applications. To find out more, in addition to referring to *The Mind Map Book*, you may find two other books particularly helpful. One is *Use Your Head* (also BBC Books), in which Tony Buzan first introduced Mind Maps. The second is *Get Ahead* (Buzan Centre Books) by Vanda North with Tony Buzan. This is a visual guide to Mind Mapping theory and practice by the world's leading trainer of trainers in Radiant Thinking and Mind Mapping techniques.

MIND MAPS VERSUS TRADITIONAL NOTES

Mind Mapping is as vital to our modern Information and Space Age as linear note-taking was to the Industrial Age and it will help you in many ways. Linear note-taking mainly relies on only a few of the brain's cortical skills, namely the use of words, lists, lines, and a certain amount of analysis. It also tends to be in only one colour (most frequently blue, black or grey). So this note-taking system – which is rapidly becoming outdated – has two enormous disadvantages: it employs only half of our intellectual capabilities and fails to use colour, which is one of the prime tools for learning, creativity and memory. Monochrome or single-colour notes are monotonous and boring, and when the brain is bored, it turns off and goes to sleep (which is why so many people actually drop off to sleep in lectures and libraries!).

Mind Maps incorporate colour, dimensions and visual images as well as words. Ideally they should be drawn using a pad of A3 white paper and a dozen or so brightly coloured felt-tip pens with good writing nibs, and a good selection of different coloured highlighters.

Mind Maps have numerous advantages over taking and making notes in the traditional, linear fashion. These include:

1 Saving you time – you note and read only relevant, key words and images.

2 Allowing you to concentrate on the real issues.

3 Stimulating your brain and your amazing powers of creativity.

4 Improving your powers of recall.

MIND MAPS AND RADIANT THINKING

Radiant Thinking is the natural way in which the brain functions. When you think of a word or idea, your brain immediately conjures up associated words or thoughts, which spring from this central concept. And of course, there are hundreds and thousands more associations which connect to these thoughts. The process goes on forever, radiating outwards from the initial idea.

The external expression of Radiant Thinking is the Mind Map. In the same way that in Radiant Thinking our thought processes are associative and proceed from or connect to a central point, a Mind Map always radiates from a central image. Remember that both your thoughts and your Mind Maps have an infinite number of possible associations.

HOW TO MIND MAP

To learn the true art of Mind Mapping, you need to consult *The Mind Map Book*, the bible on the subject. But as a starting point, here are some basic guidelines and principles which will help you to understand what is involved. Remember that whatever the subject, your Mind Map is personal to you and will be an aid to your thinking and memory. Mind Maps are not static or restrictive and can always be added to or revised at a later date. It is *most* important that you put aside any pre-conceived ideas before you Mind Map.

Mind Maps were used to make notes on all the geniuses in this book before the articles were written. If you look at Tony Buzan's Mind Map on Leonardo da Vinci (on the next page), you will see how the many aspects of this genius's life can be taken in at a glance. Linear notes on Leonardo would have taken up pages and pages and made the writing process much longer.

BASIC LAWS FOR MIND MAPPING

1 Start your Mind Map with a central image and try to use at least three colours for this. Do not worry about your artistic skills and if you think that you cannot draw, forget this immediately.

2 You can make visual aspects of your Mind Map as simple or as complicated as you like, though you will find that you will take more pride in your Mind Map (and remember it better) if you take time over it, and make it as beautiful as possible. Your images should be clear and should vary in size.

3 Order your thoughts radiating out from the central image in the sequence of their importance, emphasizing key words. For instance, there were many sides to Leonardo. He was not just a painter, but was also an inventor and scientist, with knowledge spanning many areas. Tony used images to remind him about what Leonardo had invented, and words for the different branches of science that his knowledge encompassed.

4 Print key words on lines (which form the skeleton of the Mind Map). Use only one word per line, making the length of the lines fit the words. Try to keep the radiating lines as horizontal as possible, so the words sitting on them are easier to read. Print the words in capital letters, varying their size according to their importance. Keep the letters upright, as the brain finds these easier to read (and so they will also be easier to remember). Among other things, you may find that it helps to use favourite colours to emphasize different key words.

5 Vary the thickness of the lines according to their importance, with thicker lines towards the centre of the Mind Map.

6 Use spacing as appropriate and in an organized fashion. If you reach a 'mental block' when you are Mind Mapping, add a line or two to this unfinished area and continue with another part of the Map. The blank lines will encourage your brain to complete the Mind Map at a later date.

7 Connect lines to each other – linking and associating ideas with loops, curves and arrows. Use symbols (like ticks, crosses, smiling and sad faces, to indicate likes and dislikes) and add your own codes whenever they are appropriate.

8 To help your memory, use images or words that relate to the senses wherever possible. As well as taste, touch, sight, hearing and smell, remember to include references to physical sensations (kinaesthesia).

TIPS WHEN MIND MAPPING

Before you start to Mind Map, you should prepare your state of mind and make sure that you are comfortable in your environment.

1 Be positive and do not worry if your first Mind Maps are not as good as you would like. You can always improve them in future.

2 Let your mind be free. If 'silly' thoughts come into your mind, commit them to paper in your Mind Map. They may be just what you need to change your point of view or to come up with a totally original concept. Encourage your creativity and free-flowing thoughts.

3 Train your brain by copying other Mind Maps and images around you.

4 When you are about to embark on a Mind Map, make sure that your environment is as welcoming and pleasing to you as possible. Surround yourself with your favourite things.

5 It is better to draw on a pad which is flat rather than tilted at an angle. Apart from this, if you prefer to work with music in the background, then do so but make sure that it is not going to be distracting. Work in natural light if you can. Also, make sure that your chair and table or desk will allow you to sit in an upright, relaxed position.

6 Check that the room temperature is not too warm and if possible work near a window so that your brain is receiving fresh air.

USING YOUR MIND MAPS

You may be surprised at the number of ways in which Mind Maps can help you. In addition to being the perfect tool for taking and making notes, the Mind Map is ideal for problem solving, planning and paradigm shifting. (A paradigm shift is a change in thinking about an established assumption. For instance, Einstein's theory of relativity involved a paradigm shift, as did the first suggestion that the earth is not flat.) Mind Maps can and have been used with excellent results for planning and making speeches, communicating, teaching and managing.

Students can use Mind Maps to learn subjects and prepare for exams. If this applies to you, you should review your Mind Map after various intervals. Spend about one hour studying and learn-

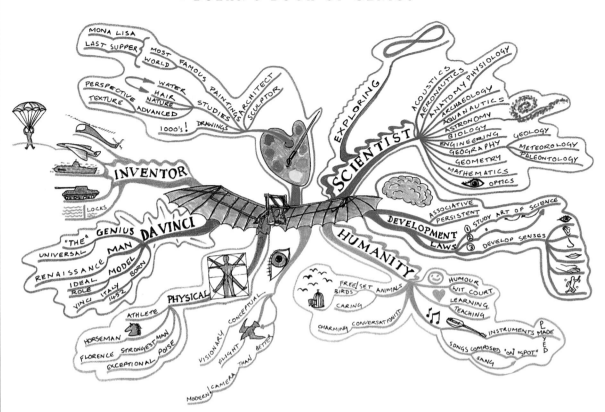

ing your Map and then review it after anything between 10 and 30 minutes. Then review it after a day, a month, and at three-monthly intervals thereafter. Drawing your Mind Map at speed from memory will also help. This will enable you to check any mistakes and identify any weak areas. If you find any areas on your master Mind Map difficult to recall, draw a mini Mind Map of the specific problem areas.

MIND MAP ACTION STEPS

To gain full value from this book, you are highly recommended to Mind Map your favourite geniuses, as well as the preceding sections in Part One. Doing this will increase *all* your mental abilities and will start you on a positive synergistic spiral towards the realization of your own genius. As you launch yourself into a Mind Mapping programme, you should be encouraged by the notebooks of the great minds of history. Many of the great geniuses – including Alberti, da Vinci, Galileo, Newton, Watt, Jefferson, Brunel, Darwin, Curie, Einstein and Picasso – understood that to express their genius fully they needed to make notes 'on the outside' that accurately reflected what was going on 'inside' their heads. Take the following steps to embark on unleashing your genius and making the most of Mind Mapping:

This Mind Map by Tony Buzan is a summary of the life of Leonardo da Vinci. The Mind Map has multiple purposes. It was used as the basis for writing the article about da Vinci in this book; it acts as a comprehensive summary of da Vinci's life; it gives a 'whole picture' of the genius; it can be used as an instantaneous review; and it can be referred to again in future. Note how the different elements in the Mind Map make full use of dimension, colour and image and how aspects of da Vinci's life are emphasized and associated.

1 Mind Map this book or the articles on geniuses in the Hall of Fame which particularly interest you.
2 Become a key-word detective when reading books, attending lectures and making notes.
3 Start to make Mind Map notes as part of your daily life.
4 Use colour and create a colour coding system for your notes.
5 Develop your artistic ability.
6 Experiment with three-dimensional symbols and using codes.
7 Mind Map yourself!
8 Make a group Mind Map with your family, friends or colleagues for the purposes of planning a holiday, studying or completing a project.

MIND SPORTS

*'PLAYING MIND SPORTS LIKE CHESS AND GO OR DOING A
CROSSWORD CAN SERVE AS A GYMNASIUM FOR THE MIND AND KEEP
YOU MENTALLY FIT.'*
RAYMOND KEENE

Playing mind sports is an excellent way of exercising the brain and is just as important as maintaining physical fitness is essential for a healthy body. There are hundreds of games which you can choose to play to keep your brain active while enjoying leisure time. Depending on your enthusiasm and skill, you may wish to play your chosen game at competition level, or simply to increase your knowledge and expertise by playing with friends and fellow enthusiasts. You will also find that reading books and magazines on mind sports is a useful way to increase your knowledge.

GAMES OF STRATEGY

The games which are perhaps most testing for the brain and which are played by more people across the world than any other are those which involve strategy. Many of the world's most popular board games have produced a superior class of world champion – great minds who are not only skilled at the game but are polymaths who are mentally and physically fit (as we have shown, the two are inextricably linked).

CHESS

Chess, with go, can rightly be regarded as the king of board games. Millions of people either play chess, are fascinated by it, or follow the exploits of its leading practitioners – and the World Chess Federation is the largest mind sports organization in the world.

Chess is one of many board games where two players essentially battle against each other with their minds and by physically moving pieces on the board in turn. The object of the game, played on a battlefield of 64 squares between White and Black armies, is to capture (or checkmate) the opponent's king. There are hundreds of books which explain the game's strategy and tactics. In addition, a network of clubs and societies exist to promote the playing of chess and to encourage the creation of chess tournaments.

PAST CHESS CHAMPIONS

The World Chess Championship was inaugurated in 1886, 35 years after the first chess tournament was held in London, and won by Wilhelm Steinitz (born 1836) of Austria. The three great players who followed him were Emanuel Lasker of Germany, who reigned as world champion from 1894 to 1921; Jose Capablanca of Cuba (champion from 1921 to 1927), and Alexander Alekhine of Russia and France (champion from 1927 to 1935 and 1937 to 1946).

After the Second World War, chess was dominated by the USSR, where it became established as the national game. The overwhelming figure in the USSR chess movement was Mikhail Botvinik, world champion on and off from 1948 to 1963. In 1972 the American Bobby Fischer briefly smashed the Russian hegemony, but after his withdrawal from the title, the world championship again reverted to the Russians. Garry Kasparov has held the title since 1985.

SUPER MENTATHLETE

Kasparov is the supreme example among mind sports practitioners of the motto 'a healthy mind in a healthy body'. Before he plays chess, he trains physically by running, playing tennis and swimming. He is also a polymath and Shakespearean scholar who can quote Shakespeare at length in both Russian and English. Since he became champion, Kasparov has contested a marathon series of battles against Anatoly Karpov for the world championship. These chess-board clashes require immense physical and psychological resilience as well as intellectual fitness.

DRAUGHTS

An early form of draughts (or checkers as it is known in the United States) may have been played in Egypt as far back as 1600 BC. But the modern game can be said to originate from Spain in the 16th century and France in the 17th, when manuals of the game were published.

In the UK and the US, the game is played on the dark squares only of an 8 × 8 board which is chequered light and dark (technically black and white) like a chess board. Each of the two players has 12 draughtsmen which they move in turn up the board, trying to capture their opponent's pieces by making a short diagonal leap as they do so. Pieces may be promoted to kings when they reach the other end of the board.

THE CHAMPION PLAYER

In the world of draughts, Dr Marion Tinsley is the greatest player the world has ever seen and when he loses a game it causes a sensation. Born in Irontown, Ohio, in 1927, Tinsley was introduced to the game by chance when he was fascinated by two books on draughts that he came across in his local library. His phenomenal memory and analytical skills enabled him to make great strides, and at an early age he won almost every tournament he entered.

Tinsley's success continued over the years and in 1954 he was recognized as world champion. In recognition of his decisive domination and contribution to the game, in 1992 he was awarded the title of World Champion Emeritus. In the same year, in the first ever championship between man and machine, Tinsley took on the Canadian computer program Chinook in an epic contest. Tinsley emerged triumphant after the 39 games, with four won, two lost and 33 games drawn. As we went to press in the summer of 1994, Tinsley was again battling against Chinook. Whatever the result, he remains the dominant human draughts champion, with a record that will be hard for anyone ever to equal.

Dr Marion Tinsley was the first to play a computer in a draughts championship.

GO

This ancient board game is about 4000 years old and is thought to have originated in China, where it is called *wei ch'i* (the surrounding game). However, it reached Europe in the 19th century via Japan (where there are over 10 million players).

Go is an extremely subtle game played between two people, though recently pair go for four players has been introduced. The aim in chess – to take enemy pieces and checkmate the king while protecting one's own pieces – remains constant throughout the game. In go, however, taking prisoners, the acquisition of territory, the invasion of enemy territory and the establishment of influence that counteracts an opponent's ability to form territory all fluctuate in relative value during the course of the game. Moreover, while chess is a single battle, the go board is spacious enough for several independednt conflicts which may only be related in the closing stages of the war.

THE GAME THAT SEEMS EASY

The standard go board is a 19 × 19 grid, though beginners may use boards that are as small as 9 × 9. 'Stones' are placed on the intersections of the lines on the grid. Half are white and half are black, and they do not move. This probably sounds simple – and it is – especially as there are only a few easy rules. However, whereas most games become less complex as pieces are removed, the go board starts empty and increases in complexity as more pieces are added. Unfortunately, many commercial versions of the game offer no enlightenment about strategy. If you have such a set, it is a good idea to read a book on the game, as the rules will not be any help in your choice of even where to place the first stone. One warning: you will need to play at least half a dozen times before you begin to feel that you know what you are aiming at, and at least another six or so times before you can hope to form any overall plans!

OTHER BRAIN-TESTING GAMES

In addition to the above, there are many card, word and board games which will exercise your brain, while providing you with hours of enjoyment. These include scrabble, poker, bridge, cribbage, backgammon, shogi and Chinese chess. Think about what type of mental exercise most appeals to you – then have fun playing the game of your choice!

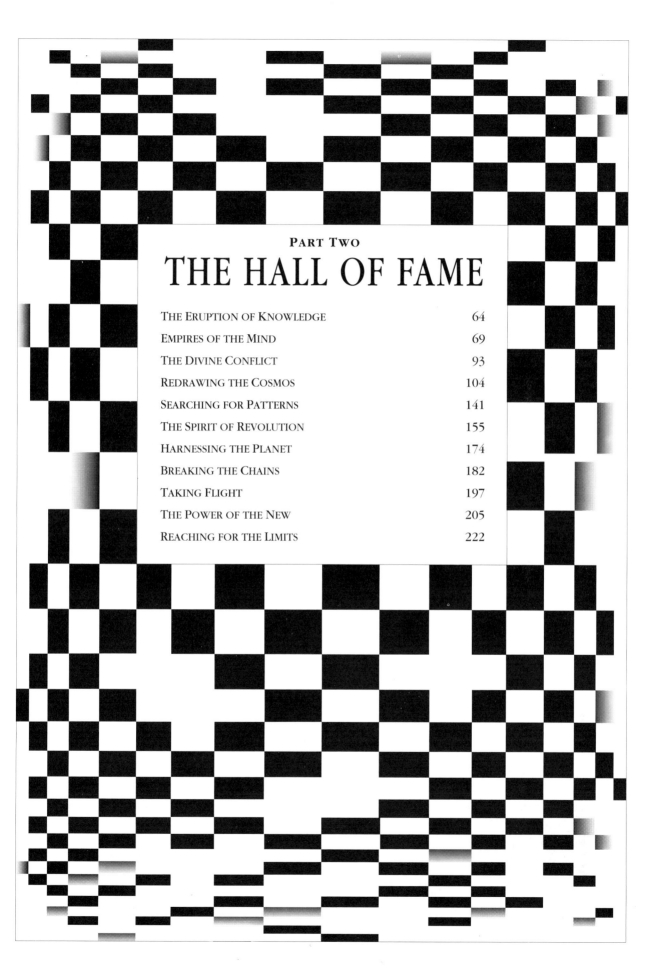

PART TWO
THE HALL OF FAME

THE ERUPTION OF KNOWLEDGE   64

EMPIRES OF THE MIND   69

THE DIVINE CONFLICT   93

REDRAWING THE COSMOS   104

SEARCHING FOR PATTERNS   141

THE SPIRIT OF REVOLUTION   155

HARNESSING THE PLANET   174

BREAKING THE CHAINS   182

TAKING FLIGHT   197

THE POWER OF THE NEW   205

REACHING FOR THE LIMITS   222

THE ERUPTION OF KNOWLEDGE

*'THINK OF IT, SOLDIERS; FROM THE SUMMIT OF THESE PYRAMIDS, FORTY
CENTURIES LOOK DOWN UPON YOU.'*

NAPOLEON BONAPARTE, 21 JULY 1798

VYASA *c.*500 BC

ENERGY

The Mahabharata, written in Sanskrit, is India's
greatest epic poem. It was first written down by
Vyasa *c.*500 BC, over 2000 years after it was created. The poem consists of 100,000 stanzas, is 15
times longer than the Bible (indeed, it is the
longest poem ever composed) and includes both
a shortened version of the other great Sanskrit
epic, the *Ramayana*, as well as the *Bhagavad
Gita*. The latter is an explanation of the working
of the universe, recounted by the demi-god
Krishna to the hero Arjuna, to justify the latter's
resolve to combat evil on earth.

EPIC WORK

The Mahabharata, or the 'Poetical History of
Human Kind', is the Sanskrit or Hindu equivalent
of *The Iliad* and *The Odyssey*. As with the Greek
epics, *The Mahabharata* is based on ancient
stories and legends. Similarly, nothing certain is
known of the life of the author or narrator, apart
from the existence of the poem itself, and that his
name was Vyasa. *The Mahabharata* is so deeply
embedded in Indian consciousness that it is at
the origin of thousands of myths, beliefs,
thoughts, legends and teachings which are still
very much part of Indian life.

TRUTH

The full story concerns an internecine struggle
between rival cousins, the five Pandava brothers
and the 100 Kauravas. This conflict, over who
will rule, has seismic consequences – culminating in an immense battle, which leaves millions
dead, and where the fate of the world is at stake.

As with the siege of Troy in *The Iliad*, *The
Mahabharata* is said to be based on actual historical events – in this case, a battle fought at
Kurukshetra in 3200 BC, which evidently had
enormous reverberations. Unlike *The Iliad*,
though, where both sides exhibit heroic and barbaric qualities, in *The Mahabharata*, the Pandava

are essentially a representation of Good, while
the Kauravas embody Evil.

The themes of the poem include religious
teaching, self-discovery, journey, exile and loss,
resurrection, predestination, chance, immortality,
games, war, political and social ambition, the
end of the world and Paradise. And finally, the
law, both cosmic and private, on which the fate
of the world rests.

EVERYTHING CONNECTS

An Indian saying has it that 'Everything in *The
Mahabharata* is elsewhere. What is not there is
nowhere.' Despite the difficulty of the hieratic,
highly stylized nature of the poem to a Western
audience, and the problems connected with stag-
ing it, *The Mahabharata* has, arguably, become
the most widely watched television drama ever
made. Indian film producers have ambitiously
turned the epic into a series of 90 45-minute
episodes, which has been shown around the
world. Meanwhile, English director Peter Brook
has directed a 9-hour-long stage version which,
in spite of its length, has captivated capacity
audiences throughout Europe, the Far East and
America.

THE BUILDERS OF THE GREAT PYRAMID *c.*2550 BC

WONDER OF THE WORLD AND LADDER TO HEAVEN

The oldest (and sole surviving member) of the
Seven Wonders of the Ancient World is the Great
Pyramid, situated on the plateau of Giza, a few
kilometres south-west of modern Cairo. It was
built as a tomb for Khufu (or Cheops), second
king of the Fourth Dynasty, who reigned for 23
years. It served not only as a repository for the
king's body, but also as a vehicle for his resurrection. The Egyptians considered the pyramid to
be a solid representation of the sun's rays, forming a ramp on which the dead king could ascend
to heaven. Those responsible for the pyramid's

design and construction are nowhere identified, though the *vizier Hemiunu*, who included among his many titles 'king's overseer of works', would have been involved in a supervisory role.

BEAUTY AND MAGNITUDE

For thousands of years the Great Pyramid has inspired wonder and admiration, not only for its size, but also for the skill of its execution. By any standards it is an impressive monument. Rising originally to a height of 482 ft (147 m) – the top 30 ft (9.5 m) are now missing, it was – until the last century – the tallest structure built by man. Its four sides are each about 738 ft (230 m) long, and its base covers about 13 acres (54,000 m²),

Robert Louis Stevenson (1850-94) wrote
'Along the sounding coast its pyramids
And tall memorials catch the dying sun'.

an area which could accommodate Westminster Abbey, St Paul's Cathedral and the cathedrals of Florence, Milan and St Peter's at Rome, all at the same time. It is orientated to the cardinal points of the compass with quite remarkable accuracy, the maximum error being a little over a twelfth of a degree. Its core masonry consists of over 2,300,000 separate blocks of limestone, each weighing about 2½ tonnes, while the casing blocks, made from fine white limestone and fitted together with great precision, weighed up to

THE INTERNAL DESIGN OF THE GREAT PYRAMID

*There appear to have been two major changes of plan in the pyramid's internal design. The main features are shown in the diagram below. **1** is the original entrance and descending passage, situated in the pyramid's north face and orientated towards the circumpolar stars – the 'imperishables', as the Egyptians called them. **2** is the original, subterranean burial chamber, which was abandoned before completion. **3**, a passage ascending through the masonry of the pyramid, marks the first change of plan. **4**, traditionally but wrongly referred to as the 'Queen's Chamber', was probably a second attempt at a burial chamber for the king, though it may have been intended for some other ritual function; it too was left unfinished. **5** is the 'Grand Gallery', 154 ft (47 m) long by 28 ft (8.5 m) high and leading directly to the final burial chamber. **6** is a rough passage thought to have been an escape route for the workmen detailed to plug 3 from the inside. **7** is the king's final burial chamber, built of red granite. (His black granite sarcophagus is still in place, though long ago emptied of its contents.) The chamber has a quite remarkable ceiling, consisting of nine enormous slabs, each weighing about 50 tonnes; it is surmounted by a structure in the form of five cell-like compartments, the topmost having a pointed roof, which was probably designed to relieve the pressure on the ceiling below. **8** and **9** are narrow shafts running from the burial chamber to the outside of the pyramid. They may have served as ventilation-shafts for the workers inside the pyramid, but it is also possible that they had a religious function.*

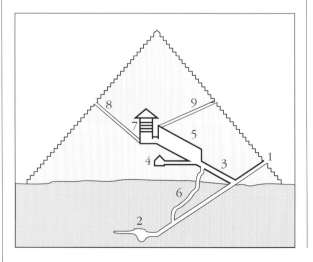

16 tonnes each. This limestone casing would originally have made the Great Pyramid gleam brightly in the Giza light.

SUPREMELY DEDICATED WORKFORCE

It has been suggested that a permanent force of no more than 4000 men was employed on the pyramid's construction, with additional labour levied during the season, when the River Nile overflowed its banks and agricultural work halted. It was not built by a vast slave army, as is often popularly imagined. The ancient Greek historian, Herodotus, claims that the Great Pyramid took only 20 years to build, and even this may be an over-estimation.

BELIEF

The Great Pyramid is one of the great works of man, an awesome testimony to the architectural, engineering, and organizational genius of the ancient Egyptians, as well as to their motivation and the strength of their religious beliefs.

HOMER – 8TH CENTURY BC
THE TRIUMPH OF MEMORY

Just as the ancient Egyptians achieved immortality through the Pyramids, so too did the Greeks through their myths and legends.

The most enduring recorder of those myths was Homer, the author of the most powerful legend of them all, the siege and fall of Troy. He created both *The Iliad*, which penetrates the everyday essence of the siege of Troy, and *The Odyssey*, the adventures of Odysseus (Ulysses), who travelled for 10 years to reach home after the siege had ended.

The imaginative pull of Homer's work has reverberated down the succeeding centuries and all over the world those who study Classics read his work in translation or in the original Greek. He is the man most frequently quoted by the great writers of the following generations. For instance, Shakespeare turned to Homer for inspiration, as did Chaucer, Milton, Goethe, Pope, Corneille, Racine and James Joyce, who even wrote his own *Ulysses*. More recently, the prizewinning West Indian contemporary poet, Derek Walcott, has written an epic poem, *Omeros*, which reaches back to the original creation of Homer.

Homer composed at a time when the written word was not necessarily the norm. His poems were 'epics', intended to be recited at public gatherings and at feasts allowing contemporary

This battle scene depicts the fall of Troy, which Homer immortalized in his epic The Iliad.

heroes to glory in their own achievements and those of their heroic ancestors. Powerful deeds of the past were recalled in declamatory style, in public, in order to inspire the present. Homer was aware of the power of the mind over the body and this is stressed in the poetry. The spoken meter was powerful, the beat was insistent with key phrases being repeated as an aid to memory. And it was only relatively late in their existence that the poems were written down.

INSPIRATION

Now, instead of having to memorize the two poems and declaim them, people can read them for themselves. They have been translated all over the world and serve as a constant reminder of ancient Greece, keeping the memory of that race alive, as Homer had intended. Alexander the Great even carried a copy of Homer's poems with him on campaign.

His work survives, but little is known of Homer's personal life – even the place of his birth is in doubt. Although Smyrna, Rhodes, Argos and Athens have all contended for the honour, he was probably born in a Greek colony on the coast of Asia Minor. Tradition has it that he was blind (there is a famous painting by Rembrandt, *The Blind Homer*, in the Mauritshuis Museum in The Hague) but even this singular detail of Homer's life has not been confirmed.

IDENTITY

Whenever hard facts about the life of a genius are hazy or lost in the mists of time, there is a tendency on the part of some critics to doubt the individuality, or even the existence, of such great men of the past (e.g. the arguments concerning the authorship of Shakespeare's plays). There are those who allege that Homer must have been a committee, that there was no one individual who could be identified as Homer. Surely this is nonsense. The homogeneity of the works themselves is counterproof to such an argument.

PRODUCTIVITY

As this book will demonstrate, immense productivity combined with sustained and superlative quality is well within the grasp, in any field, of one great mind. This is backed up by *The Great Books of the Western World*, compiled by the influential *Encyclopaedia Britannica*: 'In recent times, although both the inclusion of additional material and the probability of later interpolations are admitted, most scholars believe in one *Iliad*, one *Odyssey* and one Homer as author of them both.'

It has been established that the works of Homer (and of him alone) were recited at the Panathenaic festivals – the annual celebration of the goddess Athena's birthday – and that there was a fixed order for these recitations. The text of Homer which has come down to us today was compiled by Aristarchus, a librarian from Alexandria in Egypt, and his edition of 150 BC was, thereafter, regarded as authoritative. It is significant that the city of Alexandria was founded as a centre of Empire, commerce and learning, by Alexander the Great, who held Homer in such high esteem himself.

POSITIVE ATTITUDE

What do we learn from Homer? First, his was a colossal attempt at achieving perpetual memory.

He sought to make his civilization remembered, both by his followers in Greece and by the rest of the world, for all eternity – and he achieved it. We see also a magnificent celebration of life.

LAO-TZU 580-480 BC
THE OLD MASTER

Lao-Tzu, which means the Old Master, was the founder of Taoism, a set of precepts guiding personal and public life, which still competes for the allegiance of the Chinese people with both Confucianism and Buddhism, the other great Oriental philosophical and moral systems. He was a curator of the Royal Library at Loh in Honan province and his text, the *Tao Te Ching*, is the sole surviving record of his teaching of how things came into being and his belief that the phenomena of nature exist together quietly and without discord.

THE JOY OF LIFE

There is a classic Chinese painting called *The Vinegar Tasters*. In it Lao-Tzu's contemporaries, Confucius and Buddha, are both seen sampling vinegar from a vat and looking appropriately

Lao-Tzu believed in a simple way of life and that people should live in harmony with nature.

sour-faced. But Lao-Tzu, also tasting the vinegar, is smiling. What Lao-Tzu teaches is that the negative can be transmuted into the positive. From his point of view, bitterness comes from an inability to relish and appreciate life in all its facets. Life itself, once understood, is sweet. Lao-Tzu postulated a harmony which exists naturally between heaven and earth and which can be experienced by all people at all times. Earth, according to him, was in essence a reflection of the cosmos and run by the same laws. These laws not only affect the orbits of distant planets, but also the birds in the fields and the fish in the rivers and seas.

According to Lao-Tzu, the more men interfere with the natural balance governed by universal laws, the further harmony retreats into the distance. When arbitrary rules are imposed from the outside, discord becomes inevitable.

THE WAY

Lao-Tzu advocated wholehearted participation in one's personal life, rather than rejecting the world with its ups and downs. The principle he identified behind everything in heaven and earth he called Tao, 'the way'. According to the Tao, the key to good government in human affairs, is to leave mankind alone!

EVERYTHING CONNECTS

The lesson we can learn from Lao-Tzu and his 'Way' is that life is to be enjoyed – imposing rules for no good reason is bound to fail. Every negative situation conceals a positive. He rejoiced in all aspects of life. Like Da Vinci, Lao-Tzu ultimately taught that everything in the world and the universe is inextricably interconnected, everything relates to everything else.

The method by which Lao-Tzu reached his conclusions is unknown, but those conclusions have been echoed by great minds and have reverberated through the strands of subsequent secular and religious philosophies, moral codes and even scientific systems for centuries since.

'We read in the *Historical Record* of Ssu-ma Chi'en that Confucius went to consult the archivist or librarian Lao-Tzu, and after his visit said: "Birds fly, fish swim, animals run. The running animal can be caught in a trap, the swimmer in a net, and the flyer by an arrow. But there is the Dragon; I don't know how it rides on the wind or how it reached the heavens. Today I met Lao-Tzu and I can say that I have seen the Dragon!"' (Borges)

EMPIRES OF THE MIND

'WONDERS ARE MANY, AND NONE IS MORE WONDERFUL THAN MANKIND.'
SOPHOCLES (496-405 BC)

SAPPHO (BORN *c*.650 BC)

Throughout history women have been portrayed as the inspiring muses of male achievements. The nine daughters of Zeus and Mnemosyne were the original Muses of Greek mythology. This could be seen as a symbol for the union of supreme energy (Zeus) with perfect Memory (Mnemosyne) leading to infinite Creativity. They were the goddesses of literature and the arts and each was associated with a specific area of culture; thus Calliope was the muse of epic poetry, Clio of history, Erato of lyric poetry, Euterpe of the flute, Melpomene of tragedy, Polyhymnia of sacred song, Terpsichore of dance, Thalia of comedy and Urania of astronomy.

Sappho and Phaon *(with whom she was supposedly in love) by Jacques Louis David.*

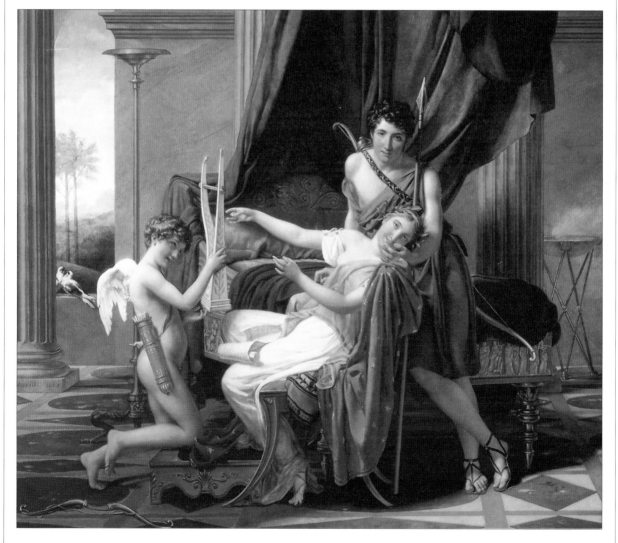

FEMALE INSPIRATION

Sappho, the greatest female poet of classical times, was not content simply to inspire the genius of others. She was herself inspired and her moving love poetry was widely praised by ancient writers, including Plato. She experimented with a variety of metres, including the sapphic, which was imitated by the Roman poet Horace (65-8 BC) and is evidently named after her. Only fragments of her lyric poetry survive, although she wrote nine books of odes, as well as elegies, hymns and epithalamia (songs celebrating marriage).

MARRIAGE AND PASSION

Sappho was born on the isle of Lesbos; later she moved to Sicily, married Cercylas and bore a daughter, Cleis. Female companionship was clearly important to Sappho – one of her poems expresses the poet's passion for a young woman – and she gathered a group of female acolytes, which gave rise to the word Lesbian. Sappho's passionate poetry is a lasting reminder of female inspiration in the ancient world.

CONFUCIUS (KUNG FU TSE) 551-479 BC

EDUCATION IS A POSSESSION THAT NONE CAN TAKE AWAY

'I once spent a whole day without food and a night without sleep, for the purposes of meditation, but found no consolation in it.'

Confucius was able to preach a firm moral code, albeit one without the benefit of divine revelation. He was also one of the earliest figures in the history of philosophy. He was born 551 years before the birth of Christ, 100 years before Aristotle, and was a virtual contemporary of Buddha, Lao-Tzu, Pythagoras and Socrates.

A CHINESE PHILOSOPHER BORN IN LU

Confucius did not bend his standards to the requirements of the world, but set a standard for the world to follow. He described the relation between rulers and governed as it should be, whereas Machiavelli, the political philosopher of the Renaissance, described that relationship as he thought it really was. Confucius was an idealist, hoping to improve the manners and morals of the people and their rulers.

STUDYING THE PAST TO UNDERSTAND THE PRESENT

There are numerous intriguing parallels between the two men. Both, for example, held high polit-

'Study the past, if you would divine the future' is just one of many pieces of advice from Confucius.

ical honours. In the year 501 BC, Confucius was appointed Governor of the town of Chungtu. The next year he was Minister of Works and the year after that he became Minister of Justice. Also, as was the case with Machiavelli, Confucius was dismissed by his political masters. In 497 BC he left Lu and did not return until 485 or 484 BC. On his readmission to Lu, he was well received but did not re-enter political life. In his final years, he put the finishing touches to his labours on the writings of the ancients. Like Machiavelli, Confucius drew his conclusions about the present from his study of the past.

THE GOLDEN RULE

Confucianism is a moral system without any religious base. Confucius was emphatically a moral and secular teacher and his greatest single pronouncement was his formation of the golden rule which is common to all religions: *'What you do not wish done to yourself, do not do to others. Only this law is necessary. It is a foundation and principle of all the rest.'* What we do not find in Confucius are expressions of fervent piety, and his model or ideal man does not commune with God or crave forgiveness from any deity. The only classical work assigned to Confucius is the *Chun Chiu*, which embraces events in the history of Lu from 722 to 481 BC. Compiled soon after his death, however, were the Confucian analects, or memorabilia, which gave abundant information on the Master's sayings and doings. They were first published in English as *The Morals of Confucius* in 1691.

LITERATURE – HISTORY – MUSIC
Literature and history formed the core of his education, but he also mastered the art of music, intended to inculcate in the pupil a sense of rhythm and proportion. The enlightenment that earned Confucius the title of Master did not come with a blinding flash; he moved towards it slowly and deliberately. *'At 15 I set my heart on learning; at 30 I took my stand; at 40, I came to be free of doubts.'*

BANNED BY MAO
Confucius's doctrines belong to common human wisdom; they are not specifically 'Chinese' in character. Fundamental to the political thought of Confucius is reciprocity: the subject owes absolute loyalty to the Prince, while the Prince or ruler owes absolute care to the subject. It is interesting to note that Chairman Mao actually banned the works of Confucius, whose moderation is in stark contrast to his totalitarianism.

THE THREE ENEMIES OF VIRTUE
Here is Confucius's simple, practical advice to young and old: *'He that applies himself to virtue has three enemies which he must subdue – incontinence, when he is yet in the vigour of his age, when the blood boils in his veins; contests and disputes when he has arrived at a mature age; and covetousness when he is old.'*

LOVE THY NEIGHBOUR
Confucius believed in harmony, hierarchy, social order and patriotism and laid particular emphasis on ritual. Though non-religious, there is also a curious Christian ring to his writings: *'Acknowledge thy benefits by the return of other benefits, but never revenge injuries.'* Five hundred years before Christ, he taught *'Love your neighbour as yourself'*.

THE ATTRACTION OF EXCELLENCE
Confucius urged that the Ruler or 'Prince' (cf: Machiavelli) should set an example of virtue which his subjects would then follow. This was his interpretation of the history of the Chinese rulers and he regarded history as essential to the study of virtue in human society. Confucius maintained that if those in government were virtuous, the wicked would, in theory, conform their lives to their example. *'When distant subjects are unsubmissive, one cultivates one's moral quality in order to attract them.'*

THE IDEAL STATE
Confucius developed an idealistic theory of reciprocal political duties, but governments were not always sufficiently enlightened to operate it. The best summary of Confucius's might be 'Imagining the ideal state'. He envisioned the most perfect empire of human affairs and that vision has endured for almost three millennia.

PHIDIAS 500-432 BC
'Ancient writers held that he added something to human understanding of the Gods.'

The Artist, as hero, originally makes his entry into the annals of genius in the 5th century BC, the Golden Age of Athens. Phidias, the contemporary and artistic counterpart of Plato and Sophocles, was considered the greatest sculptor of Greece, but he was more than that. He was a multi-dimensional talent who was also a painter, architect, designer, organizer, administrator, mathematician and scientist.

THE SCIENCE OF ART AND THE ART OF SCIENCE
The interest in mathematics and science in Athens helped to stimulate a profound reciprocal relationship with all forms of artistic endeavour, in a way that was not to be emulated until Brunelleschi, Donatello, Leonardo da Vinci and Michelangelo, the artists of Florence and Rome almost two millennia later. Greek statues were designed with regard to a network of mathematical proportions. Natural forms were seen and expressed in geometric terms, while geometric forms, such as Phidias's columns for the Parthenon, were treated as live and growing organisms. It is said that, on entering a temple designed by Phidias, the outwardly strict and severe marble columns dissolve into the sensation of a sacred grove of tall, swaying trees.

HONOURING WISDOM – THE PARTHENON
Certainly, the supreme work, which ensures Phidias's enduring memory and fame, is the

Parthenon in Athens. In the 5th century BC the city was overflowing with wealth, after the influx of tribute derived from its victories in the Persian war. At that time, Phidias received from Pericles, the Athenian statesman and general, the magnificent commission to extend the chief works of public art with which the city was to be adorned. These included the Temple of the Parthenon, which celebrated Athens' role at the head of the coalition of Greece which defeated the Persian invasions, as well as honouring Athene, the patron goddess of wisdom and Athens itself. (It is fascinating to observe that, around 1000 years later, when Constantinople, a Greek-speaking city, became capital of the Roman Empire, the chief religious edifice, created by the Emperor Justinian, was the Church of Santa Sophia, also a monument to wisdom!)

ENGINEERING INTELLIGENCE

Phidias was created Superintendent of all public works in Athens and had a team of architects, sculptors and stonecutters at his disposal. However, it was Phidias personally who, during the years 447–438 BC, designed and directed the work on the Parthenon. He was also individually responsible for carving the epicentre of the entire divine complex – the great cult statue, almost 40 ft (12 m) high, of the goddess of the Parthenon herself, Athene Chryselephantine – a long name which simply means Athene, encrusted with gold and ivory.

QUALITIES OF GENIUS

The qualities which characterized Phidias's sculpture were vitality of expression, the anatomical reality and celebration of the nude human body, the drama and grandeur of his divine figures, and the strength and living elegance of his marble columns. He also made detailed observations of animals, notably horses and bulls.

WONDER OF THE WORLD

Phidias left Athens, for Olympia, the most sacred spot in Greece, where he worked on his final masterpiece, the statue of Olympian Zeus, King of the Gods. Phidias's Zeus, constructed like his Athene in gold and ivory, was a triumph, recognized as one of the Seven Wonders of the Ancient World. The statue was 42 ft (13 m) high, while the height of the temple ceiling itself was 45½ ft (14 m). The pedestal was 3 ft 4 in (1 m) high, 21 ft (6.5 m) wide and 32 ft (9.75 m) long.

DIVINE PROBLEMS

When the statue was finished and ready to be moved from the workshop to the temple, Phidias faced two problems. The first was lack of light. The temple had only a single doorway and no windows, and so only a small amount of sunlight could penetrate to the back of the sanctuary where the statue was to stand. The second problem was the dry Greek climate. Phidias needed to ensure that the elephant ivory panels would not crack and break as they slowly dehydrated.

OLYMPIAN INTELLIGENCE – OLYMPIAN SOLUTIONS

The sculptor solved both problems with a remarkable degree of intelligence. Set into the floor around the base of the statue, a rim of white marble surrounded a rectangular paving of blue/black limestone, forming a shallow basin about 5 in (13 cm) deep. Into this olive oil was poured, to create a gigantic mirror. This reflected the light coming through the doorway on to the statue behind, enhancing the splendour and richness of the gold-and-ivory surface of the statue. The oil also acted as a humidifier, keeping the air in the temple slightly damp, and so preventing the statue from splitting and cracking.

DIVINE REMAINS

At Olympia, extensive remains still survive of the sacred precinct and the stadium where games were held in front of 40,000 spectators. As far as the statue of the Olympian Zeus is concerned, only the platform and the column of bases of the temple remain. For more than 800 years it dominated the temple, exciting the admiration of all who saw it. Then, in AD 391, the Christian emperor Theodosius I of Constantinople banned the Olympic Games, closed the temple of Zeus and ordered Phidias's workshop to be converted to a Christian church. In AD 426, Theodosius II shipped the statue to his palace in Constantinople but it was destroyed in a fire in AD 475.

ENDURING FAME

It was the highest possible honour to be invited to work at Olympia, for its symbolic significance to the Greeks was incalculable. During the celebration of the four-yearly Olympic Games, wars between Greek states were suspended, while the victors in the various disciplines, which included poetry and memory as well as physical sports, achieved instant heroic status, as well as fame, both immortal and universal. Meanwhile, those who cheated in the Games, however small the infraction, brought not just disgrace on themselves, but also heaped years of contumely on their native cities.

OLYMPIAN INSPIRATION

In all respects, the ancient games at Olympia were an inspiration for the future, in terms of their code of fair play, their striving for maximum achievement and their aspiration towards non-violent resolutions. They were the forerunners of the modern Olympic Games, revived by Baron Pierre de Coubertin at Athens in 1896, and of the more recent Olympics for mental sports, such as mathematics, computers, bridge and chess. Incidentally, the head of a horse from Phidias's frieze on the Parthenon was used as a model for the knight in the Staunton chess set, which is used in major competitions today.

CRAFTSMEN AND ANONYMOUS MASTERS

Until the 1400s, the concept of the artist as hero or genius simply did not exist. Whether sculptor,

According to legend, Aeschylus died when an eagle dropped a tortoise on his head.

layer of mosaics, painter or architect, the personality of a particular artist has been irretrievably lost. At other times, as with the construction of the Pyramids, or throughout the Christian Byzantine or Medieval periods, the artist himself was seen as a simple craftsman, and not even his name was recorded. Rather than being revered as a superhuman intelligence, the artist's personal identity was submerged in his service for the state or religion.

THE ANONYMOUS MASTERS

As a result, works of art are often attributed to quasi-anonymous 'Masters', whether it be the Master of Mérode, the Master of Wittingau, or numerous others of similar appellation. Even where the name of an artist *is* known, as with Giotto in the 13th century, the issue is clouded by disputes over attribution. We have to wait for 2000 years, from Phidias to Donatello and Brunelleschi, before this situation is corrected and the artist assumes, once again, a position in the Pantheon of genius.

AESCHYLUS 525-456 BC

CONTESTS OF THE MIND

The Greeks treated drama and poetry very much as fiercely competitive sporting events. It is important to bear this in mind when studying the three great Greek dramatists, Aeschylus, Sophocles and Euripides, who were contemporaries in 5th-century BC classical Athens – the so-called 'Golden Age' of the Athenian empire.

FATHER OF TRAGEDY

Aeschylus was known as the 'father of Greek tragedy'. He was born near Athens at Eleusis, the town of the Mysteries. Apart from his dramatic talents, Aeschylus's life was amazingly active and physical. He fought for Athens in the wars against Persia, being wounded at Marathon in 490 BC (a land battle) and at Salamis in 480 BC (a naval engagement). These were the victories which propelled Athens on the path to empire. In fact, Aeschylus's play, *The Persians*, is a celebratory eyewitness account of the Athenian destruction of the Persian fleet at Salamis.

PRODUCTIVITY

Aeschylus wrote over 60 plays (like Shakespeare, he is reported to have acted in his own works) and seven of these have come down to us, including his masterpieces – *Prometheus Bound, The Seven Against Thebes* and the *Oresteia*

Trilogy; this includes *Agamemnon* – perhaps the greatest Greek play to have survived from the classical period – *The Choephori* and *The Eumenides*, otherwise known as *The Furies*.

SETTING A RECORD

In 485 BC, Aeschylus achieved his first victory as a poet in the Athenian drama competitions. He subsequently took 13 prizes in the tragic poetry contests, his last victory coming in 458 BC when he was 67 years old. The winning entry was his great *Oresteia Trilogy*.

INNOVATION – LAW REPLACES VENGEANCE

Aeschylus's plays centre on the struggle between violence and reason. There is an immense grandeur to his theories of theology, providence,

inherited sin, personal vengeance and reconciliation. What we see in the early plays of Aeschylus is a first stage of the working out of a family curse. In *The Seven Against Thebes*, for instance, the curse ends in the total annihilation of the family concerned. In his more mature work, he addresses the conflict between opposing concepts of right, leading through successive crises to resolution in a rational compromise. In his plays, revenge, justice, force and persuasion are ultimately reconciled.

HERALDING CHRIST'S TEACHINGS

Aeschylus was the first to show (in writing) the principles by which, in a society, the primitive blood lust of vengeance for a past crime cannot satisfactorily be assuaged by reciprocal vendetta. It must either be dealt with by the impartial process of law, or the cycle of revenge must be broken by forgiveness at some point.

SOPHOCLES 496 – 405 BC

COMPETING WITH AESCHYLUS

Born at Colonnus, near Athens, Sophocles was a multi-talented poet, athlete, soldier and statesman. One of the great figures of Greek drama and a contemporary of both Aeschylus and Euripides, Sophocles had to give up his ambitions to appear on stage personally, as was customary with poets in the classical Greek age, because of a weak voice. This made him all the more determined to succeed as a writer. His triumph eventually came when he defeated Aeschylus at the dramatic contest in 468 BC.

BREAKING THE RECORD

Sophocles went on to win first prize at the great Dionysian Festival no fewer than 18 times – thus smashing Aseschylus's record. Over 62 years, Sophocles wrote two plays a year and he was still writing successfully at the age of 87. He competed for the tragic prize 31 times, winning 18 victories and always coming second when he did not win. He wrote seven major plays, all of which survive, plus over 100 other works – most of which have not survived. His greatest masterpiece is *Oedipus Tyrannus* (Oedipus the King). Aristotle based his aesthetic theory of drama in his book *The Poetics* on this play and also evolved from it his theory of the Tragic Flaw.

Sophocles was an innovative tragedian, introducing a third actor and scene painting to his plays.

The best-preserved ancient Greek theatre is at Epidaurus, where plays are still performed.

As a schoolboy, Sophocles was noted for his physical beauty. He won prizes in literature and numerous trophies in athletics. He also studied music thoroughly under the tutorship of Lamprus. Sophocles' life paralleled the golden age of Athens – the great Athenian period of the city's rise from the battle of Marathon in 490 BC to its decline. Sophocles' death, appropriately enough, came on the eve of Athens' defeat in the Peloponnesian War against Sparta.

VERSATILITY

Sophocles' career was not confined to literature. In 443 BC he became President of the Athenian Treasury, and in 440 BC, as General of the Athenian army, he served with Pericles in the Samian War. Finally, to top his political career, he was elected one of the 10 elders in the Athenian government, running the state.

MEMORY AND VISION

When he was 87, Sophocles is said to have been accused by his own son of being unable to manage his property. However, Sophocles refuted this patricidal and impudent charge magnificently. He convinced his judges of his competence by reciting from memory a lengthy chorus from the new play he had just finished writing! After that there was no doubt. Sophocles was intent on raising the intellectual level of Athens. In honour of the Muses, he formed a 'company of the educated', a society of cultivated Athenians who met to discuss poetry and music. It is said that Sophocles never left Athens, except in the service of the city, and he died in the glorious metropolis where he had lived and worked for almost nine decades.

There has been much debate among scholars about whether Aeschylus, Sophocles or Euripides is the greatest Greek tragedian. However, in terms of genius, particularly taking into account his contribution to the city state, Sophocles undoubtedly towers above the other two.

EURIPIDES 484-406 BC
WISDOM AND CREATIVITY

It was at the festival of Dionysus, the Greek god of Wine and Creativity, that the laurels for drama were distributed in the 5th century BC. Euripides won five of these extraordinarily important prizes – the equivalent of Olympic gold medals of the mind! Euripides wrote his dramas late in the age of Pericles, a time when the traditional values and beliefs of the Greek world were being eroded. Euripides' works reflected this growing uncertainty. The Gods as reconcilers, as represented by Aeschylus, were losing their hold on the minds of the Greeks, and attention was turning towards purely human concerns, rife with doubt, questioning, and complexity. Sophocles, who admired Euripides' work, as did Socrates, said: 'I paint men as they ought to be. Euripides paints men as they are.'

DIONYSUS

Greek tragedies were presented as trilogies – three plays followed by satyr entertainments, which were wild fantastic pantomimes, honouring Dionysus. The festivals were held near the Acropolis in Athens in the theatre of Dionysus, a huge amphitheatre which seated 15,000. The actors wore masks, and were accompanied by a singing chorus, all the performances being augmented by music which has, sadly, been lost.

FRENZY

Euripides' most famous play is *The Bacchae*. This is an extraordinary and terrifying tale of the power of religious hysteria, mob rule, madness and irrationality destroying human life. The play represented a caustic commentary on the manifold evils of the Peloponnesian War, then raging between Athens and Sparta. As it approached the end of its golden age, Athens suffered terribly in the 30-year war against Sparta; plague hit the city, and faith was weakened in Athenian institutions. The fierce themes of this play represented the disillusionment that the inhabitants of democratic Athens experienced during the war.

FLEXIBILITY

Euripides earned the title 'Philosopher of the Stage'. He held a prominent position in Athens, acted politically as the consul for Magnesia and possessed an enormous library, a rare thing for a private Greek citizen. In his youth he trained as a professional athlete and then turned from boxing to painting as a career. Several paintings attributed to him were exhibited publicly in later times. Euripides was a friend of the philosophers. We know that Socrates relished his writing; it is said that Socrates never even deigned to visit the theatre unless the performance was by Euripides, whose total output was between 80 and 90 plays.

SAVED BY MEMORY

Such was the beauty of Euripides' verse that Athenian prisoners, held captive in Syracuse after the disastrous campaign by Athens against the city in 415 BC, escaped death and received their freedom if they could recite from memory passages from his works to their captors. Towards the end of his life, Euripides was invited to Macedonia by King Archelaus, and he spent his final years at the Macedonian court. So highly valued was he, that, at his death, the king cut off his own hair as an expression of his grief.

GROUP PSYCHOLOGY

The main themes of Euripides' plays, marking them out as relevant to the concerns of succeeding ages, were: the problem of reconciling religious faith with hard scientific fact; a denunciation of the ruthlessness of war; and an exploration of mob rule, analysing the psychology of mass religious or political hysteria. When his plays are staged today, they still grip audiences in an emotional vice.

SOCRATES 469-399 BC

SAVED FROM THE MISTS OF TIME

The career of Socrates stands as a watershed in Western thought. No written work of his survives, and his ideas were recorded only after his death, by the historian Xenophon (c.435-354 BC), who had little grasp of philosophy, and by the philosopher Plato, who at first used Socrates as a dramatic figure in his dialogues, but increasingly as a mouthpiece for his own theories.

TEST BY DEBATE

What is known about Socrates, and is consistently expressed in a large number of passing references to him, as well as in Plato and Xenophon, is that he insisted on testing every kind of belief and assumption by reasoned debate. Partly because of its philosophical legacy, 5th-century BC Athens used to be regarded as a supremely rational society, so much so that indulgent modern historians have been prepared to overlook some of its less attractive features – such as its dependence on slavery and aggressive wars. It is clear, though, that Athenian religion and culture had strongly irrational elements – indeed, without them the great literature of the time, the plays of Aeschylus, Sophocles and Euripides, could not have been conceived. Socrates stands out against this strain of irrationality.

Socrates' fame spread rapidly after his death. This Roman fresco of him dates from the 1st century AD.

REFUSING TO CONFORM

The temper of Socrates was closer to that of another genius of the period, Thucydides, the first great historian, who charted the course of the Peloponnesian War which ended after 30 years with the defeat of Athens by Sparta and her allies in 404 BC. This war polarized Athenian society between democratic and oligarchic factions, many of which employed thinkers and orators, usually called 'sophists', as propagandists for their views.

Socrates deplored the shallow views of such men, but his enemies may well have seen him as being just like them. He was accused and condemned for corrupting the city's youth and introducing new gods in 399 BC, probably because some of his friends and pupils had been part of the brutal regime of the 'Thirty Tyrants', which had ended only three years before. Socrates would not put on a show of conformity to the new government. Clearly, Socrates was also a man of great personal courage. He served in three military campaigns as a foot soldier, and he blazed a trail of the mind for future Western philosophy. The root of his argument was his assertion that every assumption must be tested and interrogated by reason.

EDUCATION IN ATHENS

What sort of education did an Athenian youth acquire? Only boys of noble birth were given a formal education. From an early age these boys were sent each day to a school which taught them reading, arithmetic and music. They then transferred to a gymnasium where they were trained in wrestling, boxing and throwing the discus and javelin. To the Athenian aristocrats, a perfect body was as important as the development of the mind. 'A sound mind in a healthy body' – which has been passed down to us in the Latin motto 'Mens sana in corpore sano' – was their ideal.

ENERGY

Socrates obtained the usual education for a noble Athenian youth, but he also studied geometry and astronomy. His early physical education stood him in good stead and as late as his 48th year he served in military campaigns in the wars of Athens against Sparta. He distinguished himself by his bravery, physical vigour and total indifference to heat, cold and fatigue.

MASTERMIND GROUP IN THE MAKING

The oracle at Delphi hailed Socrates as 'The wisest man in the world'. He left no written body of work but his pronouncements were recorded by Plato, who in 387 BC founded the Academy in Athens where Aristotle was to become a pupil. We can, therefore, see a direct line of intellectual inheritance from Socrates to Plato to Aristotle.

CONDEMNED FOR WANTING TO KNOW

It is a sign of the degeneration of Athenian government, a result of the war against Sparta, that Socrates was arrested and charged for disseminating knowledge. The precise accusation levelled against him by the 'democratic' Athenian government in 399 BC was that he was 'an evildoer and a person showing curiosity, searching into things under the earth and above the heaven and teaching all this to others'. Could this seriously be a charge against an individual in the once-glorious Athenian state? For most of the 5th century BC, the Athenians had been the main supporters of the search for knowledge, yet here they were, after the disastrous war against Sparta, condemning one of their fellow free citizens for precisely that endeavour.

SOCRATIC QUESTIONS

As recorded in Plato's *Crito* and *Phaedo*,

'Socrates spent his last days in intellectual conversation with his friends, discussing also the immortality of the soul'. For Socrates, virtue represented knowledge and knowledge was to be found by the dialectical technique of argument and counter-argument. Socrates would madden his critics and enemies. He would feign total ignorance and, with celebrated (so-called Socratic) irony, pose a simple question – such as, 'What is courage or piety or virtue?' From the replies he received, he would create self-contradictory conclusions and thus force the thinking process to start again. His actual aim was to assist those who were seeking knowledge while exposing those whose knowledge was superficial, or whose wisdom was shallow. His intellectual goal was to discover, through ceaseless questioning, what was actually true. Every new idea, as well as every hallowed political or religious belief, was subjected to close scrutiny. He questioned everything and such challenges attracted an immense following among young, aristocratic Athenians. One of Socrates' targets in his questioning process was the very democracy of Athens which he believed had allowed the city to fall into a disastrous war against Sparta through a series of irresponsible decisions. It seems, therefore, likely that the charge that Socrates was dangerously in pursuit of knowledge was simply a cloak to pinion him for his criticism of the government of the Athenian state.

FACING FEARS

Socrates was condemned by a majority of either six, or 60 (depending on which account one believes), from a jury of 500. He was given the choice of contemplating a fine for his crime, 'blasphemy against the state religion', as well as being too enquiring, but he refused even to consider this course. This was interpreted as a sign of insolence by the judges, and he was ultimately obliged to drink hemlock – a form of poison. Socrates could have escaped, but he refused to disobey the law. He drank the hemlock and thus committed judicially sanctioned suicide.

STILL ASKING

Socrates' final defence against the charges of the Athenian judges is recorded in Plato's *Apology*. Socrates speculates that, while he is the victim of judicial assassination by the authorities in Athens, he will go to the Afterlife, there to meet the great heroes of antiquity, which he anticipates with great pleasure.

SOCRATIC IRONY

Socrates says, 'Above all I shall then be able to continue my search into true and false knowledge as in this world, so also in the next. I shall find out who is wise and who pretends to be wise and is not. What would not a man give, oh my judges, to be able to examine the leader of the great Trojan expedition or numberless others. What infinite delight would there be in conversing with them and asking them questions. In another world they do not put a man to death for asking questions, assuredly not.' Socratic irony indeed, and consistent to the last!

PLATO *c.428-c.348* BC
MASTER GENIUS GROUP (OF TWO!)

Socrates thus stands as an early and heroic victim of political intolerance. Plato, the son of distinguished Athenians, in his long career, clearly took with him much he had learned from Socrates, especially his rational questioning method, or he would not have projected his own evolving ideas on to his teacher. But Plato also developed a distinctive idealistic philosophy, according to which ideal disembodied forms lie behind and shape the material world. In his *Republic*, Plato theorizes that states will only be well ruled when philosophers monopolize political power as kings, an anti-democratic doctrine which has found predictable admirers. Finally, Plato also founded a formal school, the Academy, to propagate his ideas. In all these ways he probably grew away from the non-conformist, politically uncommitted and unambitious figure of Socrates. Their relationship forms one of the most striking instances of creative collaboration between geniuses ever recorded.

GRANDFATHER OF PHILOSOPHY

Plato, simply because he left a large body of works (over 30 dialogues of varying length), exercised far more influence on later ages than any of his predecessors. Many different thinkers, from ancient times onwards, were Neoplatonists who adopted Plato's central idea that the world of experience is only a dim reflection of ideal forms. The famous image in his *Republic* is that of men sitting in a cave, with their backs to the entrance, only able to experience shadows projected on to the wall before their eyes, and unable to turn around to the light itself. Some of these theories passed to the Middle Ages in Christianized form, especially in Boethius's *Consolation of Philosophy*, written in the 6th century.

Hypatia's belief in Plato's philosophy contributed to her death in Alexandria.

Almost all of Plato's original texts were only recovered and studied in the 15th century. Since then they have served as a starting point and inspiration for almost all idealistic thinking. In fact Plato, pupil of Socrates, founder of the Athens Academy, and teacher of Aristotle, set the agenda for Western philosophy from the 15th century on. A. N. Whitehead, the 20th-century British philosopher, summed up Plato's influence: *'The safest general characterization of the European philosophical tradition is that it consists of a series of footnotes to Plato.'*

FEMALE INSPIRATION

However, Plato also influenced great thinkers, apart from Aristotle, well before the 15th century. Hypatia, who lived *c.*375-415, is one example. Her life and death dramatically represent the conflict between the followers of the old pagan philosophers and the new Christian thinkers in the early centuries after the death of Christ. Her terrible death at the hands of a Christian mob symbolized the struggle that was taking place to monopolize human interpretation of the cosmos. The little that we know of Hypatia suggests that she must have had a remarkable intellect and personality and, like Sappho, she was not content to be a passive observer of genius.

As is the case with so many gifted daughters, Hypatia was undoubtedly inspired by the work of her father, Theon, the mathematician. She taught astronomy with distinction in her home city of Alexandria, where she was a member of the Neoplatonic school, lecturing on the works of Plato and Aristotle. She was highly regarded by contemporaries for her learning and her skills as a teacher, and her home became a salon for a circle of powerful and learned Alexandrians. This led to her downfall, for she was torn to pieces by an enraged mob, urged on by monks who opposed the pagan philosophies that she had so publicly and successfully espoused.

Widely regarded as the most influential teacher in Alexandria, of either sex, Hypatia's lectures, which also embraced mechanics, attracted students from all parts of the Greek-speaking world, including Constantinople, the new capital of the Roman Empire.

ARISTOTLE 384-322 BC
MASTERMIND GROUP

Socrates taught Plato; Plato taught Aristotle – 'The master of the men who know' according to

Dante; and Aristotle taught Alexander the Great, who became an example to the world. Aristotle's work summarized the knowledge of 5th-century Athens. The dominant mind of his own era, he was the tutor and inspiration of Alexander the Great, and he fuelled alike the intellectual endeavours of Islam and Christianity in the Middle Ages. Much medieval intellectual effort was devoted to the interpretation of Aristotle's work, newly discovered through Arabic commentaries. However, what Aristotle said was, for the scholars of the Middle Ages, less important than the fact that he had said it, and the way he set his ideas out.

THE TRAGIC FLAW

The irony behind the immense intellectual investment in the rediscovery and reinterpretation of Aristotle during the Middle Ages, by both Christian and Islamic scholars, can be exemplified by Averroës' treatment of tragedy. Aristotle based his theory of tragedy on the plays of Sophocles in particular. When Averroës (see page 94) came to write his commentaries on Aristotle, he was operating with a translation of a translation (the tragedy, as a dramatic form, was unknown to Islam). What impressed subsequent generations of scholars was not the intrinsic meaning of Aristotle's work, but his impressive attempt to categorize all human knowledge.

LEARNING FROM PLATO

Aristotle was born at Stagira, near northern Salonica. His father Nichomachus was court physician to King Amyntas II of Macedonia, who was Alexander the Great's grandfather. In 367 BC, Aristotle entered Plato's Academy in Athens, where he studied politics, law, mathematics, astronomy and rhetoric. He became deeply attached to Plato. On his death, Aristotle described Plato as *'the man whom it is not lawful for bad men even to praise'.*

SYNAPSE CITY

In the year 347 BC, Aristotle was *given* the town of Assus by the local ruler Hermias to transform it into an intellectual centre. By 344 BC Aristotle was studying natural history and marine biology and in 342 BC he was invited by King Philip of Macedon to become tutor to the future Alexander the Great, who was then 13 years old. Aristotle spent seven years teaching Alexander politics, rhetoric and Homer. Aristotle, in fact, prepared an edition of Homer especially for his

pupil's use, and Alexander kept it by his side for the rest of his life, even when on campaign. When Alexander left for Persia, he took a legion of scientists with him to collect materials and specimens to furnish Aristotle with material for his research.

WALKING TO KNOWLEDGE

In 336 BC, Aristotle returned to Athens, where he founded the Lyceum, which was known as the Peripatetic School, because he used to talk to his students while walking in the gardens. This was an organized institution for 'the cult of the Muses', and many of Aristotle's writings that have come down to us are, in fact, the notes of lectures he delivered here.

THEORY OF EVERYTHING

Aristotle's notes consist of a grand categorization, or codification, of knowledge. Among the topics he covers are a catalogue of lists of victors from the Olympic Games, a chronology of Athenian drama, a collection of 158 separate Greek constitutions, and works on logic, metaphysics, the soul, physics, memory, meteorology, biology, politics, rhetoric. In his well-known work *The Poetics*, he analyses the nature of tragedy and comedy. Aristotle's thinking was based on reality and observation, on the collection of data from earth. The intellectual forebear of both Plato and Aristotle was Socrates who argued that the highest moral standards were not those of society, but those set by each individual's conscience.

THROUGH THE AGES

Aristotle was the first to work out the theory of reasoning, and this has survived to the present day as 'deductive logic'. According to Aristotle's *Poetics*, tragedy emphasizes plot. The hero is a great figure with a tragic flaw which propels him to disaster. This eventually leads to catharsis – the purging of harmful emotions – about which scholars have argued to the present day.

Aristotle's influence on the Middle Ages was immense. His works almost singlehandedly brought about a renaissance of thought and intellectual endeavour. Only Aristotle's work on logic was known in the original to the European scholars in the Dark Ages. The rest became known through Arabic translations, which in

Aristotle and Plato talk as they walk in this detail from Raphael's School of Athens *(see page 128).*

their turn were retranslated into Latin. A later parallel, in terms of an intellectual boost from the past, was the rediscovery of Euclid's mathematical book *The Elements*. When it was finally translated from Arabic into Latin in 1482, the effect on European consciousness was immediate.

Aristotle originally trained as a doctor and he brought to his philosophy a tremendous respect for solid facts. It is the colossal codification of this information which made such an immense impression on Europe, helping to dispel a period of myths, mysticism and superstition. Here, at last, was a man with his feet on the ground, a man whom people could trust – and to whom people would refer for millennia.

ALEXANDER THE GREAT 356-323 BC

THE TWIN DESIRES

Alexander, King of Macedonia, was driven by two overwhelming imperatives, the desire to conquer the world and the desire to amass all knowledge – in other words, heroism and insatiable curiosity. On his campaigns to achieve the first goal, he was accompanied by teams of scientists, constantly sending back research material for Aristotle in Greece, fuelling his investigations into the nature of the planet.

HOMER AND ARISTOTLE

These twin imperatives can be symbolized, first by Homer, who wrote of the hero (Achilles), in *The Iliad*, and secondly by Aristotle, Alexander's personal tutor and the man who cultivated in him the ideals of achieving all knowledge. For Alexander, the siege of Troy represented his personal drive to conquer the entire Asian conti-

At the height of his power, Alexander's empire extended into the countries shown below.

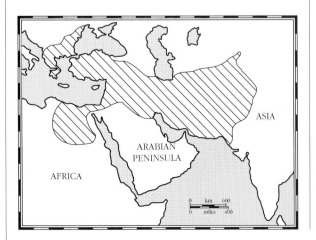

Determination and courage are captured on this relief of Alexander, a great leader.

nent. He carried a copy of Homer's *Iliad* and *Odyssey* with him at all times on his campaigns.

CREATIVITY

Alexander set the pattern and goal with which all future conquerors of the world could compare their own achievements. It is said that at the age of 40, Julius Caesar saw a statue of Alexander and burst into tears because he had not even started to control his world, whereas Alexander had already completed his conquest by the time he died at the age of 32. Alexander had extraordinary intelligence and an ability to reorganize or redefine the parameters of a problem so that he personally could solve it in a style which exerted the maximum public impact.

For instance, when he first met the great horse Bucephalus, nobody could tame or ride the horse. However, Alexander noticed that the horse was scared of its own shadow, so he held the horse and turned its face to the sun. Once the shadow had vanished, he mounted the horse and tamed it. Thereafter, Bucephalus carried him on all his campaigns.

MANAGING MEN

No leader will go far without the absolute loyalty and devotion of his followers. Alexander achieved this by establishing an extraordinary camaraderie with his men. He would share their deprivations with them, fight in the forefront of the battle, incur wounds himself, display his scars to his own troops, visit the soldiers after the battle and benevolently allow them to exaggerate about their own dangers and deeds of heroism during the struggle. They felt that he was one of them, and they would follow him to the ends of the earth – in fact they did.

COURAGE

What was the secret of his great success in battle? Alexander the Great invaded Persia and challenged the mighty Persian Empire, with its virtually unlimited resources, with a modestly sized Macedonian and Greek force. Yet the way he achieved decisive victories, such as the battle of Issus, which essentially broke the Persians' resistance, was by his tremendous personal courage and intellect. He had observed that the Persian king, Darius, although in charge of enormous manpower was not personally courageous. So Alexander, while maintaining a thin containing line of defensive infantry across the length of the front, directed the cutting edge of his army to attack directly against the Persian king. By charging personally against Darius, and driving the Persian king from the field, Alexander caused the demoralization and collapse of the entire Persian force, which retreated in confusion from the battlefield. This psychological insight and prominent display of personal courage was at the root of his genius in battle.

PERSISTENCE AND VISION

Let us briefly examine Alexander's conquest of Asia. In the year 334 BC, he crossed the Hellespont, the bridge between Greece and Asia, and marched into Persia. He won the battle of the River Granicus against Persian forces, making devastating use of the phalanx formation – ranks of spearmen in depth, creating a virtually impregnable porcupine of spearpoints on which the enemy always foundered. Then came the battle of Issus, where Darius personally was forced from the field. In the year 331 BC, Alexander founded the city of Alexandria in Egypt. He went on to found a further 12 cities, all named Alexandria. The name still persists in corrupted forms along Alexander's route of conquest, such as Iskenderun on the Turkish-Syrian border and the city of Kandahar in Afghanistan. In 331 BC, Alexander won a third decisive battle at Arbela and then took the great city of Babylon. This effectively terminated Persian resistance. In 329 BC, he defeated the Scythians and in 326 BC, he proceeded to his conquest of India. He only met serious opposition at one point, from the Indian king Porus, with his cohorts of elephants at the battle of the River Hydaspes, but he won that battle, too, and went on to found Greek colonies in India. At that point, his men, an army rarely larger than 40,000 troops, demanded to be allowed to go home. Over eight years, they would have marched at least 30,000 miles (20,000 kilometres) – an incredible distance.

STYLES OF CONQUEST

It is fascinating to compare Alexander with two other world rulers, Caesar and the first Chin Emperor of China. Alexander was insatiably curious, marching on to the ends of the earth, exploring, learning, understanding and conquering. Consolidation and centralization were the last things on his mind. Julius Caesar's ambition, on the other hand, was to reach and occupy Rome itself, the nerve centre, then to radiate lines of force outwards which would control the empire. The Chin Emperor devised a third and totally different strategy. He created a vast empire, set a boundary, the Great Wall of China, around it – but instead of operating from inside his capital, he constantly patrolled the interior lines of communication of that empire. He had no desire to thrust beyond it, as Alexander did.

CREATING FUTURE MASTERMINDS

Machiavelli, in *The Prince*, questioned how Alexander avoided insurrection in his newly conquered middle-eastern territories. The answer, most probably, is that Alexander sought assimilation rather than subjugation. He wanted to weld together the Hellenic and Oriental cultures he had brought into contact – not to humiliate the vanquished races.

Further, Alexander sought to enrich – intellectually – his new domains. Having founded the city of Alexandria in Egypt, it soon grew into a great port as well as a centre of culture and learning. It attracted writers and scientists from many other countries. This was encouraged, after Alexander's death, by his general, Ptolemy, who later became Ptolemy Soter I (died 283 BC) of Egypt.

Continuing Alexander's plans, King Ptolemy amassed a huge library at Alexandria, stocked with more than 500,000 books. It was a repository of the whole world's knowledge. Euclid studied there, as did Archimedes, and the astronomer, Ptolemy (AD 90-168). It was his astronomical system, which assumed that the earth is the centre of the universe and that the heavenly bodies revolve around it, which held sway in the European mind until the advent of Copernicus, some 13 centuries later.

VIE

Machiavelli records that Alexander chose Achilles, Homer's hero, from *The Iliad*, as his role model. The Italian poet Petrarch (1304-74) wrote:

*'Giunto Alessandro alla famosa tomba
del fero Achille, sospirando disse:
O fortunato, che si chiara tromba
trovasti, e chi di te si alto scrisse!'*

*'When Alexander reached the famous tomb
of fierce Achilles, sighing he said: – O happy
man, who found one so illustrious to trumpet your name and write so nobly of you for
posterity!'*

ALEXANDER'S CAPITAL

ALEXANDRIA – BEACON TO THE WORLD

Under the rule of the Ptolemies (which lasted from 323 BC to 30 BC) Alexandria in Egypt became the commercial and cultural centre of the civilized Western world. Most fittingly, a huge systematic body of knowledge was amassed in its library. In addition to this, the great Pharos Lighthouse, which was constructed there between 297 and 280 BC, was considered one of the Seven Wonders of the Ancient World. The Lighthouse was 460 ft (140 m) high with sides of 100 ft (30 m) each.

EXPLORATION AND CALCULATION

Alexandrian scientists calculated the magnitude of the earth, while Alexandrian ships travelled East and West on voyages of exploration. One such vessel is even recorded as having rounded northern Wales.

FLOOD OF WEALTH

When Alexander overthrew the Persian Empire, he gave away the Persian treasure hoards. The beneficiaries would have been his veteran troops, loyal commanders, and religious institutions. This gesture of regal generosity released vast wealth throughout the Hellenic world, but it also caused dramatic hyper-inflation. At the same time, the divine institutions, which had been particularly well endowed, now began to function as merchant banks to the public.

Euclid, teacher of geometry, contributed to Alexandria being a centre of learning.

CENTRE OF CIVILIZATION

Alexandria meanwhile, standing as it did at the epicentre of a gigantic trading network stretching from Ireland to India, with at least half a million inhabitants, became an irresistible magnet for scholars and intellects, drawn both by the wealth and its resources of learning, which included a university (the world's first!).

700,000 BOOKS

The Ptolemies were enthusiastic supporters of art and learning who invited Greek scholars to come to Alexandria at the state's expense. King Ptolemy I was the original biographer of Alexander the Great and his library grew from 500,000 to contain a massive 700,000 manuscripts.

MEASURING THE WORLD

Among the scientific community was the chief

librarian of Alexandria, Eratosthenes (276-194 BC). He calculated the earth's circumference by measuring the shadows of sticks and his answer was only 15% off the actual distance, which is 24,901 miles (40,075 km) at the Equator.

CIRCLING THE SUN

Another scientific denizen of Alexandria was the astronomer, Aristarchus, who flourished around 260 BC. He maintained that the earth moves around the sun, a theory completely rejected (even by Archimedes), until the days of Copernicus almost 2000 years later. The two greatest members of the Alexandrian community of learning, however, were Euclid and Archimedes himself.

EUCLID c.300 BC

Euclid was the founder of Alexandria's mathematical school where he was an inspirational teacher. His masterpiece is known as *The Elements*. Written in 13 books, it collects and codifies all of the considerable geometric wisdom which had been generated by different thinkers up to that time. *The Elements* is probably better known than any other book on geometry and is still in use today as a text book.

INTELLECTUAL SENSATION

Euclid's work was lost to Europe after the fall of the Western Roman Empire in the 5th century AD, but it was preserved in Arabic and created a sensation when first printed in a translation from Arabic into Latin in 1482. The printing was carried out by Erhard Ratdolt, whose version of Euclid's masterpiece broke ground in three ways. Apart from being the first printed edition of Euclid, it was also the first printed book to contain mathematical figures and drawings, and the first to use gold printing. In 500 years, over 1000 different editions have been published – a world record.

THE ORGANIZER OF KNOWLEDGE

Euclid's *Elements* became an instant classic, as can be seen from its extensive quotation in subsequent texts. The first book starts with sublime simplicity: '*A point is that which has no part – a line is breadthless length.*' It then proceeds with rigorous logic to a detailed examination of circles, triangles, squares and parallelograms. The final words of the last book repeat Euclid's refrain of conclusive proof, that most desirable quality which echoes throughout the entire work

– Quod Erat Demonstrandum – QED (which has been proved). According to Proclus, the 5th-century AD Greek philosopher: 'Euclid drew upon all his predecessors, he collected and perfected many of their theories and brought to incontrovertible demonstration, things which had only loosely been proved by his predecessors.'

ARCHIMEDES 287-212 BC

Archimedes was born into a noble and well-educated family in Syracuse, Sicily. The Greek historian Plutarch claimed that Archimedes was related to the ruler Hiero and his son Gelo (or Gelon), to whom Archimedes dedicated his 'Sand Reckoner'. This was an ambitious attempt to calculate the size of the universe. While the great minds that preceded him had focused their energies on the finite, it can be argued that Archimedes was the first to consider the infinite with relish. His father, Pheidias, was an astronomer, interested in the size of the sun and the moon and their distance from earth. (So often with geniuses, we observe this vital parental spark of intellectual ignition and impulse, bearing massive fruit in later life.) With his Sand Reckoner, Archimedes explained how you could estimate the universe's dimensions by first measuring the number of grains of sand in a small thimble; then how many thimbles would fit into a box; then how many boxes would fill a beach and so on.

MASTERMIND GROUP

Archimedes studied with the pupils of Euclid in Alexandria. While in Egypt, he invented a spiral pump to draw irrigation water from the Nile. He continued to maintain excellent relations with his fellow Alexandrian scientists, even when he returned to Syracuse after completing his studies and is known to have teased students with perplexing mathematical puzzles and problems. He dedicated his 'Method' to Eratosthenes and regularly communicated his discoveries – before publication – to Conon the mathematician, so that his conclusions could be verified and checked.

THE ENQUIRING MIND – ALL BRANCHES OF MATHEMATICS

Archimedes' investigations and research included arithmetic, astronomy, geometry, spheres, cylinders, conoids, spheroids and floating bodies. He alone of the ancient scientists contributed anything of real value to mechanics and hydrostatics; for example, he was the first to prove that a body immersed in liquid displaces an equal mass of that liquid.

MYTHS AND LEGEND

'*Eureka*' ('I have found it') is the word Archimedes supposedly called out as he ran home naked from the public baths, having suddenly grasped the water-displacement theory mentioned above. '*Give me a place to stand on and I can move the earth,*' is his other attributed aphorism, referring to his prowess with levers and pulleys in moving giant objects one-handed.

THE 'UNTIDY' GENIUS

Archimedes was said to have been untidy, unkempt and dishevelled, neglecting clothing and food while absorbed in his equations. He was even said to have been killed by a Roman legionary in 212 BC in the siege of Syracuse by the Romans, because he refused to attend the victorious General Marcellus until he had solved a certain problem. In that same siege, he is said to have invented all manner of defensive weaponry, including catapults, battering rams, cranes and burning glasses to ignite the Roman wooden ships at a distance.

THE ORGANIZED MIND

Three facts counteract these apocryphal stories.
1 Archimedes' written work is logically, cogently and forcefully argued and constructed. There is no trace whatsoever of scattiness or absence of mind. Read any page of Archimedes, and it becomes clear at once that a most lucid and well-ordered intelligence is at work.
2 Nowhere, in any of his texts, does Archimedes write a single word about levers and pulleys for use in giant engines of war. His comments on mechanical devices are all connected with water – for example, his astronomical machine composed of concentric glass spheres which, moved by water power, represented a world system. This was actually viewed by Cicero and described in his *Republic* but unfortunately the machine has now been lost.
3 Finally, it is well known that the city of Syracuse was aggressive well before Archimedes. Records survive of heavy battering rams, rock-throwing catapults and even a giant winch-powered mechanical crossbow, firing bolts 6 ft (2 m) long. This was invented the century before Archimedes was born.

The only part of the legend which may be true is Archimedes' death. After the fall of a besieged

Archimedes applied his enquiring mind to solve numerous problems by means of mathematics.

city, a riotous and uncontrolled sack and pillage was customary and Archimedes doubtless perished during this period of havoc. The Roman General Marcellus, leading the besieging forces, is said to have shown remorse at the death of the great scientist and arranged the funeral himself.

PARENT POWER

What can we learn from Archimedes, apart from studying his books? The answer seems to be, as is often the case with geniuses, that if the parents of a child actively foster intellectual values and the spirit of enquiry, the chances of that child developing its full intellectual potential are raised enormously. We also learn, from the experience of the city of Alexandria, how valuable the interaction of a cross-fertilization between a Mastermind Group can be in terms of expanding the individual potential for genius.

SUN TZU *c.*300 BC
THE ART OF WAR

At the same time as Alexander the Great was advancing towards the East with his army of Macedonians, Greeks and Persians, a Chinese general and thinker, Sun Tzu, was expounding his own philosophy of war. This was not centred on the thrusting dynamism of Alexandrine expansion, but on a Taoist search for balance and harmony. The teachings of Sun Tzu, as expressed in his book *The Art of War*, are a military homage to, and an extension of, the philosophy of Lao-Tzu and his Tao, or the Way.

LEARNING FROM NATURE
A powerful strain of Taoism, persisting vigorously until the present day, is its traditional emphasis on fighting and the martial arts. Taoists regularly perform combat-orientated exercises, which include astounding feats of swordsmanship and Tai Chi – a form of martial art. This is not simply because it keeps them physically fit and mentally alert, but also because it enables them to keep in tune with natural harmony, the rise and fall of rivers, the ebb and flow of the tides, and the motion of the planets. It has been observed that Taoist martial exercises are modelled on the study of the fighting tactics of animals – particularly circling movements, such as those of panthers and birds.

HARMONIOUS ACTION
It is disciples of Lao-Tzu who have composed the main Chinese military treatises, Sun Tzu's *The Art of War* being the most important of these. In it he advocates the seemingly paradoxical doctrine of Wu Wei, literally translated as non-action. In fact, his thinking is far more subtle. Wu Wei is rather the avoidance of all action which is out of harmony with the flow of the universe. Stated more positively, only take action that is in accordance with the harmony of nature. From this we can see the significance of martial exercises which are taken from the study of the unselfconscious movement of animals. Such martial exercises standardly include breathing techniques, which help to improve physical fitness and to guarantee longevity.

VICTORY THROUGH INTELLIGENCE
The three main tenets of Sun Tzu's *The Art of War* are: work with nature by dexterity and balance, not brute force; use intelligence to outwit the enemy; and, if possible, win by bluff and avoid fighting altogether. Many of the great commanders, whether consciously or instinctively, have followed these precepts in their victorious campaigns. For example, the Duke of Marlborough, whose chief skill lay in outmanoeuvring his enemy, only had to contest a physical engagement on very rare occasions.

ONLY FIGHT IF NECESSARY
Sun Tzu was the first to articulate this strategy clearly. One example from his book is the stratagem of the Empty City, which gives a perfect insight into his cast of thought. Sun Tzu relates the anecdote of a commander (believed to be himself), who virtually hypnotized the enemy force into believing an unguarded, indeed virtually deserted, fortress city was peopled with a vast, well-prepared and alert army. The ploy was to leave the gates wide open, while the commander himself sat in full public view on the city walls, relaxedly plucking at a musical instrument. The enemy force, far too small to contemplate an attack on such an apparently well-defended and self-confident citadel, promptly withdrew! This was a brilliant stroke. Had the general barred the gate and tried to defend, his lack of force would have spelt certain defeat. This method at least gave him a chance of survival.

MAO'S TEACHER
Just as Julius Caesar emulated Alexander the Great, and Napoleon consciously modelled himself on Alexander, Hannibal and Caesar, so the Chinese political and military leader Mao Tse Tung, during his campaigns of the 1930s and 1940s, closely studied Sun Tzu's *Art of War* and learned and profited from it.

UESHIBA – AIKIDO GENIUS
Earlier this century, the martial arts aspects of Taoism and of Sun Tzu were developed to an extraordinarily high degree by the Japanese thinker, poet and warrior, Morihei Ueshiba (1883-1969). Ueshiba, like Sun Tzu before him, gained personal practical experience of warfare in China and went on to catalogue and teach the combat lessons he had absorbed.

Ueshiba developed his ability to harmonize with nature to such an extent, and perfected his techniques of self-control and Wu Wei to such extraordinary pitch, that he was said to be able to defeat better-armed or physically more powerful or more numerous opponents, primarily by the exercise of an hypnotically charismatic strength of will. Stories abound of swordsmen being unable to strike even one blow against him, of gigantic Sumo wrestlers being paralysed by one prod of Ueshiba's forefinger, and of teams of rival martial artists literally bouncing off his invincible defence system, known as Aikido (the Way of Harmony). This is a method which, in fine Sun Tzu style, turns the attackers' energy against themselves.

Essentially, Aikido involves moving and breathing in harmony with the spirit, known as Ki' Chi, Prana or 'the force'. Ueshiba's particular genius was to develop a series of practical body movements and exercises that, as well as being a sophisticated method of self-defence, allow dedicated individuals to embody this non-violent philosophy, while becoming poised and physically fit. Ueshiba believed that *'True victory is self-victory'* and in his later years composed poem/songs ('doku') that reflected his philosophy. Before he died, Ueshiba had the satisfaction of knowing that Aikido had become the fastest-growing global martial art.

CH'IN SHI HUANGDI 259-210 BC

PLANS ON A SUPERHUMAN SCALE

Ch'in Shi Huangdi governed China from 246 BC. Assuming the title of The First Emperor, he greatly extended the Empire and completed the Great Wall of China. Legend has it that in 212 BC he ordered all books and historical documents burned. The fact that this cataclysmic act could even have been ascribed to Ch'in Shi Huangdi perfectly demonstrates his philosophy that the key to earthly rule was through the direction of men's minds.

Among the Emperor's many achievements, he conceived the vast and ambitious project of welding the disparate elements of China into one single realm. He truly created his own world, first by unifying China, then by building the Great Wall to exclude barbaric influences and finally, if the myth is true, by destroying previous history by burning all known records of it. He is said to have preserved the only surviving copies of those books in the Imperial Library for his own consultation. Since many Chinese texts predating 212 BC (including works by Lao-Tzu and Confucius) have survived, it may well be surmised that the so-called 'burning of the books' was no more than a metaphor used to describe Ch'in Shi Huangdi's draconian determination to mould and launch a new era.

Not content with creating his own world on earth, his plans for the afterlife were equally grandiloquent. For his final tomb, Ch'in Shi Huangdi created in astonishing detail a second realm, an underground kingdom he would rule in death as he had reigned on earth in life. His mausoleum was modelled on a map of the world, in which liquid mercury flowed through channels representing the Yellow and Yangtze Rivers. Man-made constellations of stars glittered down from the ceiling. The tomb was protected by crossbows triggered by intruders. His most spectacular and ambitious monument to the afterlife, however, lay in a life-size replica of the Imperial army in terracotta; more than 6000 men strong, it was deployed in serried ranks to protect him for eternity. Today, this terracotta army is one of the major tourist attractions in China. Amazingly, each face in the 6000-strong replica force represents a different, distinct individual from the Emperor's elite personal guard during his lifetime. It was not just a memorial to himself,

LEFT The First Ch'in Emperor's terracotta warriors, modelled on individuals who served in his army, were intended to provide protection for him in the Afterlife. It has recently been discovered that each warrior has been carved with a 'hidden' identifying mark.

RIGHT Publius Cornelius Scipio (237-183 BC), here extending his hand in a gesture of peace, was the Roman general who eventually forced a retreat upon the seemingly unstoppable Hannibal (shown with a faithful troop of elephants supporting him at the rear).

but an eternal monument to those who had served to protect him.

FACING FEARS

Ch'in Shi Huangdi was a lover of law and order, promulgating a philosophy known as legalism. He was an apostle of strong central power and hated the chaos of the warring states in which he had found China. He opposed each of these states, defeating them one by one and, at the end of the struggle, transplanted 120,000 former quarrelling noble families to his capital at Xian Yang where he had their weapons melted down and cast into bells and statues.

ENERGY AND DETAIL

Ch'in Shi Huangdi was determined to homogenize the entire spectrum of Chinese life. He brought about the standardization not only of Chinese written characters, weights and measures and the legal code, but he also standardized the gauge of wheeled vehicles, so that transport became possible over the entire Chinese Empire. In order to enforce all of these decrees, he toured tirelessly on personal inspection – often incognito.

IMAGINING THE 'IMPOSSIBLE'

Acting under Shi Huangdi's instructions, a million men completed the Great Wall of China in only seven years. It extended across the whole of China's northern frontier and is the only man-made object visible from the moon. It is 6760 miles (4200 km) long and stretches from the Yellow Sea in the east to the deserts of Turkestan in the west. Punctuating the length of the wall are towers 40 ft (12 m) high, set two arrow shots apart, so ensuring that any enemy was always within range of defending archers. The First Emperor's other great project concerned waterways. He constructed a 52 mile (32 km) long canal linking two Yangtze valley rivers which were flowing in opposite directions. This canal is still in use today; it ensured that 2000 continuous kilometres of inland waterway were available for civilian transport, military transfers and trade.

DESIRE AND LOYALTY

Ch'in Shi Huangdi could quite rightly be described as the man who redefined space and restarted time. He imagined earth's largest empire and dared to create it. Later generations of Chinese historians have depicted him in an unflattering way, but the 'official' history of his regime was written by functionaries of the Han Dynasty, Shi's enemies, who succeeded him in power. Their efforts have not diminished his achievement, which remains intact today: nothing less than the foundation of modern China and many of its cultural and academic traditions.

HANNIBAL 247-182 BC
THE MAN WHO NEARLY BROUGHT ROME TO ITS KNEES

Hannibal nearly defeated Rome. Had he succeeded, there would have been no Roman Empire, and later Roman poets and historians could not conceal their admiration for their inge-

nious and dangerous enemy. Livy devoted many books of his history of Rome to Hannibal, while the poet Juvenal wrote: *'Put Hannibal in the scales. How many pounds will that peerless General mark up today? This is a man for whom Africa was too small a continent, though it stretched from the surf-beaten shores of Morocco, East to the steamy Nile, to tribal Ethiopia and new elephants' habitats. Now Spain swelled his empire. Now he surmounts the Pyrenees, nature sits in his path, high alpine passes, blizzards of snow, but he splits the very rocks asunder, moves mountains with vinegar. Now Italy is his, yet still he forces on. We have accomplished nothing, he cries, until we have stormed the gates of Rome – until our Carthaginian standard is set in the city's heart.'*

PACHYDERMS FOR POSTERITY

Hannibal's name means 'Grace of the God Baal'. He was a soldier of Carthage, the growing empire that, in the 3rd century BC, was the main opposition in the Mediterranean to the equally expanding Roman Empire. He was the son of Hamilcar Barca, the Carthaginian general; when Hannibal was nine years old, his father made him swear eternal enmity to Rome. Hannibal served his military apprenticeship in campaigns in Spain against Rome. Then, in 218 BC, he crossed the Pyrenees, defeated the Gauls and traversed the Alps in just 15 days. This was an extraordinary achievement. His troops were accustomed to the warm African climate, and now they had to face appalling ice and snow. Not only did he march an army across the Alps – and thus non-plussed the Romans by appearing suddenly on the Italian plains with a massive force – but he also cajoled a troop of war elephants across those same mountains. The Romans had never encountered these ferocious animals before. They proved a most dangerous surprise weapon. Where rocky obstacles appeared on the crossing of the Alps, Hannibal legendarily melted them away by the application of acidic, sour wine, or, in the words of Juvenal, 'vinegar'. This shows imagination of the highest order, as well as enormous persistence, courage and determination.

VICTORY AND DEFEAT

Once in Italy, Hannibal's first great battle was fought in the plain at Trebbia, where the men of the Roman consular army were either cut to pieces or scattered in flight. His next victory was against the consul Flaminius, by Lake Trasimene,

where Hannibal inflicted another crushing defeat – the Roman army being totally annihilated. His third triumph came at Cannae, where Hannibal utterly destroyed yet another Roman army. After this incredible victory, though, the tide somehow turned against him. His miserly countrymen in Carthage refused to send him the necessary support and, as his veterans were greatly worn down by the strategy of attrition employed by Rome's new general, Quintus Fabius Maximus, Hannibal had no means of filling their places with adequate replacements. Meanwhile, the Romans could field army after army against him. However, through his long occupation of Italy, although he never had the resources to crush Fabius and storm Rome itself, Hannibal was never defeated.

Then, in 203 BC, the Romans amassed sufficient force to counter-attack against Carthage itself. Hannibal was called back and the next year, with an army of raw recruits, he faced the Roman general, Scipio, at the Battle of Zama. Hannibal suffered his first, and last, defeat and Carthage fell to the mercy of Rome. The second Punic War had ended in Rome's victory.

Hannibal went into exile to the court of Prusias, King of Bithynia, and when the Romans demanded his surrender, rather than give in he took poison and died at Libyssa. Ultimately, Hannibal had been defeated, not by any lack of his own genius, but by the refusal of the Carthaginian government to support him.

CHOOSING YOUR TACTICS

The tactics used by Hannibal at the Battle of Cannae exhibit extreme intelligence in a military situation and the battle has been studied in military classrooms for millennia afterwards. At least 50,000 Romans were slaughtered and 10,000 more taken prisoner. It was the most abject humiliation Rome had ever suffered.

Hannibal had conducted an in-depth study of standard Roman methods, and was therefore confident that his enemy would adhere to them. He faced 86,000 men, the largest army Rome had ever assembled. Hannibal's expectation was that they would lunge directly at the centre of his 50,000 troops. Hannibal, therefore, arranged his front in a long arch, with a deliberately weak centre. He placed his elite cavalry, backed up by columns of spearmen, on the flanks.

LEARNING TO LEARN

As anticipated, the Roman legions crashed into

Although he was the enemy, Hannibal was admired by the Romans for his tactics and determination.

Hannibal's centre which, predictably, gave way. Hannibal's crescent formation appeared at the point of collapse. As the Romans drove in deeper, they were suddenly surprised by Hannibal's cavalry, who closed in on both wings and at the rear, hemming the Romans in so tightly 'that they did not even have room to swing their swords'. Absolute slaughter was the outcome of this double envelopment. One might also compare this with the battle tactics of Suleyman in the Battle of Mohacs against the Hungarians in 1526. Suleyman had assuredly studied Hannibal closely, and applied the lessons 'magnificently'.

JULIUS CAESAR 100-44 BC
MODEL FOR EMPIRE

Caesar, essentially, founded the Roman Empire, although he never took the title of Emperor for himself. He ended the death throes of the Roman Republic and set the pattern for leadership of Rome by one man. He was a military leader of genius, an astute politician, and he recorded his exploits for posterity in a series of books about his campaigns. A powerful testament to his importance is that he bequeathed his own name as an eternal symbol of empire in the words 'Kaiser' and 'Czar'.

AMBITION

Caesar's ambitions were virtually without limit. He planned to control the known civilized world, and mould it in his own image. He was a brilliant propagandist and, like Alexander the Great before him, who served as his role model, and Nelson, Napoleon and Wellington in centuries to come, he took great pains to ensure the absolute loyalty and devotion of his own troops, usually by sharing their deprivations on campaign. An invaluable lesson for those who aspire to inspiring leadership, whether in the spheres of military or civil management.

ACQUIRING AN ARMY

After civil unrest in Rome in 60 BC Caesar, with 'rare tact and sagacity', reconciled Pompey and Crassus, the two leaders of the opposing factions – thus forming with them the first triumvirate, a trio that, temporarily at least, governed Rome as a team. Caesar's next ambition was to gain a province for himself. This would automatically and legitimately put him in command of a large and well-trained army. In 58 BC he marched into Gaul (essentially modern-day France) and for nine years conducted a series of brilliant campaigns, by which he conquered the country. In 55 and 54 BC Caesar was the first Roman commander to invade Britain, crossing the Thames and enforcing at least the nominal submission of the south-east of the island. Interestingly, Napoleon wrote an extremely detailed and well-researched account of this early invasion of Britain, complete with a detailed commentary on precise dates and locations.

On his return to Gaul in 52 BC, Caesar was faced with a rebellion of the Gauls. But, by his brilliant victory at the Battle of Alesia, he crushed the united rebel armies.

CROSSING THE RUBICON

Caesar at last found himself with a victorious and cohesive army in Gaul, utterly loyal to him and under his sole command. But at this moment, central government, now in the hands of Pom-

pey, a jealous ally-turned-rival, demanded his recall. In a powerful and decisive act, Caesar marched his forces across the River Rubicon, which separated his province from Italy proper. (Crossing the Rubicon has since become a symbol for a decisive act from which there is no turning back.) Within months, Caesar was master of Italy, and at the Battle of Pharsalia, on 9 August 48 BC, Caesar defeated Pompey's army and became master of Rome, as well as its empire.

LIP SERVICE

A subservient Rome now made him 'Father of the country', 'Imperator' (almost Emperor), dictator for life and Consul for 10 years. As if that were not enough, his person was declared sacred and the month Quintilis was renamed Julius (July) in his honour. Caesar had ambitious plans for Rome itself. He was in the process of revising the whole of Roman law, founding libraries, draining marshes and enlarging Rome's harbour when, on the ides (15th) of March 44 BC, he was brutally assassinated.

LEARNING

Caesar was a superb orator and, as a military historian, has never been surpassed for simplicity, directness and dignity. He also studied and employed mathematics, philology, law and

Julius Caesar not only had strong features. His physical fitness matched that of his troops.

architecture. It has been said of Caesar that he was tall, fair and well built and that his errors served only to educate him. He was an expert at turning bad fortune to his advantage. Cicero said of him, *'Do you know any man who, even if he concentrated on the art of oratory, to the exclusion of all else, can speak better than Caesar?'*

ENDURANCE AND SPEED

Before the campaign in Gaul, Caesar had had very little experience of military command. He had been a soldier himself, but he had not been in charge of an army. He had to learn 'on the hoof' as it were. The Roman historian Suetonius commented: 'Caesar was a most skilful swordsman and showed surprising powers of endurance. He always led his army, more often on foot than in the saddle, went bare headed in the sun and rain alike, and could travel for long distances at incredible speed taking very little luggage. [A lesson that Napoleon took very much to heart.] If Caesar reached an unfordable river he would either swim or propel himself across it on an inflated skin and he often arrived at his destination before the messengers, whom he had sent ahead to announce his approach.'

THE DIVINE CONFLICT

'LEARNING WITHOUT THOUGHT IS LABOUR LOST; THOUGHT WITHOUT LEARNING IS PERILOUS.'

CONFUCIUS (551-479 BC)

AS-SULI AD 854-946

CHESS – KING OF MIND SPORTS

Mind sports play a vital part in the lives of many geniuses and, of the various occidental mind sports, chess is the king. It is the one practised most widely and has the most well-documented and carefully written theory to back it up. A number of the geniuses have rated chess highly. Goethe called the game 'the touchstone of the intellect'. Haroun Al-Raschid, the Abbasyd Caliph of Islam (AD 786-809), the man idealized in the *Arabian Nights*, was the first of his dynasty to play chess. The 11th-century Byzantine Emperor, Alexius Comnenus, was allegedly playing chess when surprised by a murderous conspiracy, which being a good chess player he managed to escape! The Aladdin of the fairy tale was, in real life, a chess player, a lawyer from Samarkand in the court of Tamburlaine. Tamburlaine himself loved to play chess and named his son Shah Rukh, since Tamburlaine was moving a Rook at the time the birth was announced. Another genius, Benjamin Franklin, was an enthusiastic chess player – indeed the first chess publication in America was Franklin's *Morals of Chess* which appeared in 1786. Chess was mentioned by Shakespeare, Goethe, Leibniz and Einstein. Ivan the Terrible, Queen Elizabeth I, Catherine the Great and Napoleon all played chess.

A CRADLE FOR GENIUS

However, the first Chess Grandmaster, the first mental sportsman, the first genius of mind sports, was the Baghdad chess player As-Suli. It is difficult for Western audiences to grasp that Baghdad, As-Suli's home city, was once the world capital of chess; indeed it was *the* capital of the world for some time from the 9th century onwards. Baghdad was founded in AD 762 by the Caliph Al-Mansour, who employed 100,000 men to build it. This circular city, with a diameter of 8655 ft (2638 m) and surrounded by a rampart of no fewer than 360 towers, almost immediately

proved to be too small for the burgeoning population. By the time of the Caliph Haroun Al-Raschid, Baghdad had expanded, taking in quarters for commerce and artisans, and by AD 814 it was the world's largest city. The stupendous growth of Baghdad was a most astonishing global phenomenon. By 814 it covered an area approximately 40 sq miles (100 km²) – the equivalent of modern-day Paris within the outer boulevards. Baghdad was the dominant city of the world and As-Suli was the multi-talented mind sportsman, poet, politician, and Chess Grandmaster who exemplified the pre-eminent culture of Baghdad at that time. Baghdad dwarfed all other world cities, and in terms of culture, art, scientific investigation and chess, it was the most convincing and powerful testament to the astonishing force of Islam.

THEORY AND ANALYSIS

In the 9th and 10th centuries chess was known in the Arabic tongue as *Shatranj*, and Baghdad was to *Shatranj* what Moscow became to the modern game – the world capital of chess. Baghdad was a cultured flourishing centre packed with Chess Grandmasters and chess theoreticians, who wrote volume after volume about critical positions and chess opening theory. The main differences between *Shatranj* and chess as we now know it, which was developed during the Renaissance in the 15th century, was that in the old game of *Shatranj*, a win could be achieved by taking all of your opponent's pieces, apart from his King. You did not need to force checkmate. The Queen – known as the Visier – was a comparatively helpless piece, only able to move one square diagonally in each direction, whereas today it is the most powerful piece on the chess board.

THE FIRST MIND SPORTSMAN

Like the reigning modern World Chess Champion, Garry Kasparov, As-Suli came from an area bordering the Caspian Sea and, as a young man, he travelled to the capital to become the chess favourite of the political leader of his day, the Caliph Al-Muktafi. But in AD 940 As-Suli uttered an indiscreet political comment, and had to flee from Baghdad. He died soon afterwards in Basra at the grand old age of 92.

THE CHESS PUZZLE WHICH DEFIED SOLUTION FOR 1000 YEARS

A chess genius lives on in his published studies and puzzles. As-Suli set one puzzle which he described as: 'Old, very old and extremely difficult to solve. Nobody could solve it or say whether it was a draw or win. In fact there is no man on earth who can solve it if I, As-Suli, have not shown him the solution'. This was his proud boast and it held good until only very recently, when modern Grandmasters armed with computers finally cracked the puzzle.

VERSATILITY

As-Suli was the strongest player of his time, a composer of chess puzzles, and the author of the first book describing a systematic way of playing *Shatranj*. For more than 600 years after his death, the highest praise an Arab could bestow on a chess player was to say that he played like As-Suli – he won every chess match that he has known to have contested. As-Suli was a resident at the court of the Caliph where his reputation was that of an excellent conversationalist with immense encyclopedic knowledge. He owned an enormous library, and wrote many history books as well as his two text books on chess. He was also a great teacher of the game – the next great Arabic player of *Shatranj*, Al-Lajlaj, was one of his pupils.

SYMBOL OF INTELLIGENCE

As-Suli can be seen as a symbol of the great Islamic culture that flourished in Baghdad, possessing great qualities of mind, thought and intellect at a time when Europe itself was plunged in the Dark Ages and much of the world was in chaos. His was a pinnacle of sophistication and culture not to be attained by others for many centuries.

AVERROËS (IBN RUSHD) 1126-1198

RENOWN THROUGH THE CENTURIES

Averroës, the most famous of the Arabian philosophers, and author of a medical system repeatedly reprinted in the West, was born at Cordoba, the son of a Kadi. He himself became a successful magistrate and religious leader in Cordoba, Seville and Morocco. He has achieved the distinction of being cited by several of the geniuses in this book. In Dante's *Inferno*, the Moslem philosopher Avicenna, Averroës and Saladin, the epitome of Islamic chivalry in the medieval Crusades, were numbered among the virtuous heathens who were allowed to suffer only moderate punishment in the first circle of hell.

THE RESCUE OF KNOWLEDGE

Borges, the 20th-century genius of literature, also mentioned Averroës in his book *Labyrinths* in the short story *Averroës' Search*. According to Borges, Averroës regarded his monumental work, which would justify him in the eyes of men, to be his commentary on Aristotle: 'This Greek fountainhead of all philosophy had been bestowed upon men to teach them all that could be known. To interpret his works, as the ulema [Islamic theologians] interpret the Koran, was Averroës' arduous purpose. Few things more beautiful are recorded in history than this Arab physician's dedication to the thoughts of a man separated from him by 14 centuries. To the intrinsic difficulties we should add that Averroës, ignorant of Syriac and Greek, was working with the translation of a translation.'

MISSIONARY FOR THE MIND

In his ambition for posterity, though, Averroës succeeded magnificently. It was, in fact, Averroës' labours which brought Aristotle into common currency in Western Europe, translated into Latin from Averroës' own Arabic. Just as As-Suli was a representative of the great Islamic culture of Baghdad, so Averroës was the leading representative of Islam's cultural and military expansion into Spain. Averroës was a tireless and acute commentator on the writings of Aristotle and hence was known as 'The Expositor', expounding the Koran according to Aristotle, and thus founding a Moslem philosophy of religion. He profoundly influenced many of the great scholastics in Western Europe, including Thomas Aquinas who, like the majority of other scholastic theologians, had no knowledge of Greek or Hebrew. The sole conduit by which he could grasp Aristotle was through the Latin translation of Averroës' commentary. Unwittingly, therefore, Averroës had an enormous impact on the intellectual development of Christianity in the 13th century.

AVERROIS·

Averroës provided a valuable link between Aristotle and later theologians like Aquinas.

BANNED BY THE POPE

But of course, Aristotle, as interpreted by a Moslem, would not have been acceptable to a Christian like Aquinas. Indeed, at the beginning of the year 1269, Aquinas hurried to Paris where a conflict over Aristotle was coming to a climax. Aquinas's activity largely consisted of attacking the Latin Averroists of the Faculty of Arts at the University of Paris, who were presenting an interpretation of Aristotle which appeared to be incompatible with Christianity.

STOKING THE FLAMES OF THOUGHT

Averroës propelled the teachings of Aristotle into the Christian environment. But then the Christians, ironically, had to fight against the Islamic interpretation of the great Greek's work. Nevertheless, at the basis of Western science, which began in the 13th century with Thomas Aquinas, the man who united the philosophy of Aristotle with the doctrines of Christianity, we can see that scientific impetus fuelled by Averroës, Islamic thinker, religious leader, philosopher, magistrate, commentator, medical doctor and seeker after knowledge.

RELIGIOUS INFLUENCE

Another influence on the West in the Middle Ages was Jewish thought. Jewish communities within Europe were regarded with suspicion which often spilled over into hostility, as in the massacre of Jews in York in 1190, or their eventual expulsion from England in 1290. Converts, though, were generally welcome. The one-time Spanish Jew Peter Alfonsi ended his career at the court of King Henry I of England (1100-35), probably as the royal physician. Outside Christendom, other Jewish thinkers often wrote in Arabic and had the same role as Arab writers in transmitting classical texts to the West.

GREAT THINKER

Like Averroës, the greatest Jewish thinker, Moses Maimonides (1135-1204) was born in Cordoba, though he spent his life from the 1150s onwards

in Egypt. His main work, the *Guide for the Perplexed*, set out to show that Aristotle's works could be compatible with Jewish monotheism, and therefore rehearsed arguments useful also to Christians who, like Aquinas, wished to absorb ancient philosophy into their views of the world. Written in Arabic, the *Guide* was translated into Hebrew and then (by 1240) into Latin. Both Averroës and Maimonides exerted influence that reflected their genius for sensing the similarities and parallels between very different systems of thought and belief.

GENGHIS KHAN 1162-1227
VISION

Genghis Khan, the Mongol warlord, welded together into a cohesive fighting force all the ill-disciplined bands of scattered nomadic shepherds that made up the Mongol race. In so doing, he created the greatest land empire that the world had ever seen, covering almost the entire land mass of Asia. Genghis Khan's successors

ABOVE The great medieval Jewish thinker, Maimonides, shared much with his contemporary Arabian philosopher, Averroës. Both their studies of Aristotle had a profound influence on later philosophers and theologians.

RIGHT Some people have been surprised that we have included the Mongolian warlord Genghis Khan (shown here in a 16th-century woodcut) among the geniuses in our Hall of Fame. While even Arab scholars like Sir John Glubb (Glubb Pasha) find it difficult to explain some of Khan's reported massacres, he must be admired for his vision which he pursued with a single-minded determination.

would reign over China, under the splendid Kublai Khan, the first emperor of the Yuan dynasty. His followers would also come to rule vast tracts of Russia, and, in the guise of the Moghul emperors, Genghis Khan's distant descendants would establish the mightiest empire in India.

EARLY REJECTION

Genghis Khan was originally named Temujin by his father, after a rival chieftain whom he had defeated. He spent his early years exiled by his clan, subsisting in abject poverty, and even experienced slavery when he was forced by captors to wear a collar around his neck. For a time, he lived with his family in the harsh region of the upper Onon river on the central Asian plateau, 'subsisting only on a diet of berries and small creatures, such as marmots and dormice'. Just 50 years later, the Mongols had carved out for themselves the most extensive realm on the planet. The driving force for this was the military genius, inspiration and iron discipline of Temujin. He fought his way out of obscurity, gradually conquering neighbouring tribes and establishing a reputation as a chieftain until, finally, he was given the title Genghis Khan, Lord of the Earth.

SELF-BELIEF

What was the secret of Genghis Khan's success? In the first place, it was his powerful and overriding vision to unite the Mongol tribes. He realized that the Mongols could be fused into a lethal weapon, but he first had to overcome their legendary lack of discipline, their tendency to become intoxicated and be diverted from the main aim by orgies and debauch, and he had to submerge their fierce inter-tribal rivalries. He needed vision, persistence and an almost mystical belief in himself to achieve this.

MASTERMIND MODEL

By all accounts, he was an imposing physical specimen, with immense charismatic attraction – not just for his contemporaries, but for ages to come. Indeed, Genghis Khan served as the mastermind role model for oriental conquerors, such as his own grandson, Kublai Khan, Tamburlaine and Babur, the first emperor of the Moghul dynasty in India.

INNOVATION

Genghis Khan's two central innovations were in military technology and psychological warfare.

The first involved the development of mobile cavalry archers. The second one was more profound, and had far-reaching consequences for future ages; this was terror, directed against opponents to weaken their resistance in preparation for the physical annihilation to follow. Genghis Khan was a pioneer of pyschological terror as a branch of war.

MOBILITY AND FIREPOWER

Let us first examine the particular military arm, which Genghis Khan came to make his own. The twin key ingredients to the devastating impact of his mounted archers were mobility and fire power. In battle, every Mongol warrior carried two bows – one for shooting at short range and the other, with a capacity of over 985 ft (300 m), was for firing at a distant opponent. Every quiver could contain as many as 60 arrows, some of which were armour piercing. The essence was the Mongol warriors' ability to fire at the gallop, while standing in the stirrup. Mongol cavalry advanced in huge separate columns, often kilometres apart. They were co-ordinated by a sophisticated signalling system of flags, smoke and burning torches. In combat, a gigantic camel-mounted kettle drum was used to sound the charge, while a yak-tail banner waved to signal Genghis Khan's orders. These columns were independent, highly trained, with iron discipline and capable of operating in concert or as separate units. If an enemy engaged one Mongol column successfully, it was almost inevitable that, during the battle, a further Mongol column would move into the attack. Napoleon used exactly the same system of columnar interdependence.

TRAINING FOR COMMAND

Genghis Khan also had a personal bodyguard of 10,000 elite warriors. Each was trained to such a pitch of perfection, both physically and intellectually, that at any point in the battle, any one of them could have taken command if necessary.

PSYCHOLOGICAL WARFARE

Genghis Khan's innovations in pyschological warfare were designed to cause terror in his opponents and thus undermine resistance. Apart from sending spies in advance to spread panic and despair among populations that were about to be attacked, Genghis Khan used cities that he had captured as examples of terror to weaken the resolve of future opponents. For example,

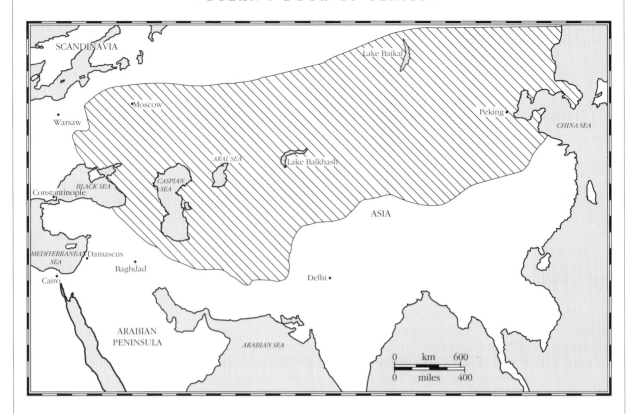

Genghis Khan and later his sons created an extensive Mongol Empire.

whenever a city which had resisted him was finally taken, the inhabitants were standardly marshalled outside the walls for massacre. The city was then looted, demolished and burned. A few days after the initial sack, Genghis Khan would regularly send a detachment of cavalry with orders to surprise the ruined town at dawn and kill any survivors. Faced with the fore-knowledge that this was their fate, many cities would surrender without a shot being fired. Of course, this was precisely what Genghis Khan wanted. Whenever possible, he would also try to persuade his opponents to join his movement through reasoned argument, rewarding their leaders with positions of power.

INSPIRING LOYALTY

In terms of religion Genghis Khan was a Shamanist or Animist, believing in a great num-ber of single spirits, though he worshipped just one single supreme deity, in the form of the blue sky. Perhaps this form of worship explains his widespread conquests: he simply followed God. Although he was a ruthless fighter, he was also capable of winning tremendous devotion, which is absolutely necessary if you wish to become

and remain a great commander. One can see this kind of loyalty being fostered by other great commanders, such as Alexander the Great, Napoleon, Nelson and Wellington. One of Genghis Khan's soldiers said, '*Genghis Khan will take the coat off his back and give it away. He keeps his men obedient, but he sees that they are well fed.*'

Genghis Khan's army was extremely well organized, divided into units of 10, 100, 1000 and 10,000, and consisted solely of cavalry. Apart from the bow, every man was extraordinarily well equipped with an axe, a sword and a lance, and protected by breast and back plates and a helmet made of leather, hardened with lacquer. In order to provide fresh food for his troops, flocks of animals accompanied the horde.

ORGANIZATION

Genghis Khan said, '*Men can pray to God equally well anywhere in the world,*' and he tried to conquer the whole world known to him at that time. But Genghis Khan was not simply a warrior and conqueror, he was also a skilful administrator and ruler. He organized an empire stretching from the Black Sea to the Pacific Ocean into states, which significantly outlasted the transience which usually characterized the span of Asiatic principalities of his day.

ST THOMAS AQUINAS 1225-1274

FORBIDDEN TO LEARN – BY FORCE

Aquinas was born the son of a count, in the castle of Rocca Secca near Aquino, a small town within Roman Naples, in 1225. He was educated by the Benedictine monks of Monte Casino and at the University of Naples. From an early age he displayed a desire to enter holy orders and, although opposed by his family, in 1243 he joined the Dominicans. At this point his less spiritually inclined brothers carried him off by force, keeping him a prisoner for two years. Ultimately, Aquinas escaped, went to France and became a pupil of the Dominican Professor, Albertus Magnus (Albert the Great), first in Paris and subsequently in Cologne.

THE 'DUMB OX'

In 1248 Aquinas, hitherto reviled as a 'dumb ox' by his contemporaries, became a teacher himself and began to publish his commentaries on Aristotle. In 1252 he transferred to Paris and, in spite of being briefly condemned for his views by the local bishop, he obtained great distinction as a philosophic theologian.

One contemporary described Aquinas as, 'tall, erect, large and well-built with a complexion like ripe wheat and whose head early grew bald'. Whatever his appearance, his deep contemplative devotion at prayer was matched by an intense power of concentration and an ability to dictate to four secretaries at once.

In 1258 Aquinas was summoned by the Pope to teach in Rome. He came to enjoy the highest respect throughout the Church, even though, like all the other scholastic theologians, he had no knowledge of source languages such as Greek or Hebrew and was equally ignorant of history. However, his writings display an intellectual power of the highest order and he was the first among 13th-century metaphysicians to stress the importance of sense perception and the experimental foundation of human knowledge.

THE STRUGGLE FOR ARISTOTLE

The long-range mental battle between Averroës, the Arabic philosopher, and Thomas Aquinas, the key architect of Western Christianity, is an excellent symbol for the divine conflict in this medieval period, with both of them struggling over the legacy of the great Greek philosopher, Aristotle. Yet the irony is that Aquinas had initially come to understand Aristotle through Arabic translations and through the commentaries on Aristotle which Averroës himself had written.

THE POWER OF THOUGHT

Why was Aristotle so important both to the Arabs and to Western Christianity? The rediscovery of Aristotle's vast codification of knowledge and his detailed assertions as to the nature of the cosmos were an inspiration to the medieval mind. Nothing else of such scope and grandeur in the realm of the intellect existed at that time. There was an urgent need to incorporate this unparalleled body of learning into religion. Averroës undertook this task for Islam. Aquinas, in his *Summa Theologica*, set himself the same goal for Christianity – seeking a triumphant fusion of reason and logic with faith. His was the first attempt at a complete theological system and it retains substantial authority in the Roman Catholic Church to this day.

In the *Summa*, Aquinas postulates a God inhabiting a realm beyond space and time, to whom he attributes a set of well-defined qualities, including perfection, omnipotence and omniscience. He then argues logically for their necessity and consistency in the style of geometrical theorems. The book also follows the standard pattern of medieval debate, with questions divided into objections, each of which is answered by a response.

The *Summa* is superbly rational, as can be seen from the sections in the first part: Treatise on God, Treatise on the Trinity, Treatise on the Creation, Treatise on the Angels, Treatise on the World of the Six Days, Treatise on Man and Treatise on the Divine Government. There is no mystic revelation here, just the exercise of logic, as with his reasonable treatment of sex – a subject often handled with hysteria by early Christian writers: 'Pleasure taken in thinking about sexual sin, if it is useful for preaching or discussing morals, or some such purpose, is no sin at all'.

The writing career of Aquinas came to an abrupt end on 6 December 1273; while saying Mass that morning, he fell into a trance. Thereafter, he never wrote or dictated again. Urged to complete the unfinished *Summa Theologica*, he answered: 'I can do no more. Such things have been revealed to me, that all I have written seems as chaff and I now await the end of my life.' Within three months, he was dead. It is a huge paradox that the man who had spent his entire life constructing a logical definition of the works of God was suddenly overwhelmed by a mystical revelatory experience. In the unfinished

Summa, Aquinas had reached the chapter Last Things. Perhaps, logically, he could go no further via the route of reason and so switched to intuition to grasp God.

DANTE ALIGHIERI 1265-1321

STUDENT, WARRIOR AND POLITICIAN

Dante Alighieri was described by Boccaccio, his first biographer, as 'the singular splendour of the Italian race'. Born the son of a lawyer in Florence in May 1265, he was baptized 'Durante', which became shortened to Dante. As a student, Dante devoured every type of knowledge – philosophy, theology, science (particularly astronomy), and the Classics. His ability to concentrate was intense. He once became immersed in a book

St Thomas Aquinas in Glory by Francesco Traini (1321-63) also includes Plato, Aristotle and Averroës.

outside an apothecary's shop and read on for six hours, standing in the street, quite unaware of a riotous carnival taking place all around him.

Best-known as a poet, Dante did not just sing of brave deeds in the abstract – he was himself a soldier and an active politician. Then, in a typical twist of political fortune, Dante, on an embassy to the Pope in 1302, was suddenly banished from Florence and condemned to be burnt at the stake if ever captured. This harsh edict, reinforced in 1311 and 1315, was backed up by Charles de Valois, brother of the King of France.

Dante's own estimate of his political acumen was: *'I have three gifts which might hamper the career of a professional politician – an unaccommodating temper, a blistering tongue and an indecent superfluity of brains!'*

After his exile, Dante travelled widely throughout Italy – Verona, possibly Tuscany – and he even made visits to Paris. He ended his days in Ravenna, where he remained until his death on 14 September 1321.

Dante was also extraordinarily prolific in creating a family, in spite of his travels and travails. He fathered seven children – his only daughter, Beatrice, became a nun. Clearly she is named after the great love of his early life, 'Beatrice', the subject of his first poem *Vita Nuova* (*New Life*).

CREATING HEAVEN AND HELL

Dante fashioned the most devastatingly effective and enduring weapon to be deployed in the

Dante in Exile *by Domenico Peterlini (1822-91) is in the Pitti Palace, Florence (Dante's exiled city).*

mental battlefield of the Divine Conflict. In a move which foreshadowed Michelangelo's *Last Judgement* in the Sistine Chapel centuries later, he created his own Heaven and Hell, and personally dispensed salvation or damnation, as he saw fit. This he did in his greatest, most enduring and most celebrated poem – the immense *Divina Commedia* (*Divine Comedy*).

The poem is a vision of Hell, Purgatory and Paradise – giving an encyclopaedic view of the highest culture and knowledge of the age drawn from all topics – philosophy, history, classical literature, physical science and moral theology – and expressed in the most sublime and exquisite poetry. Dante chose to write in Italian rather than Latin, thus making his native language respectable for the highest poetic aspirations. Indeed, the *Divine Comedy* has given rise to a vast literature – only the Bible and Homer exceed it in the extent of subsequent writing which it has inspired. Dante's classification of types of sin is based on Aristotle, but the theological structure of the *Divine Comedy* owes

much to Dante's near contemporary, Thomas Aquinas.

THE PERSISTENCE OF MEMORY

In *The Divine Comedy* Dante first visits the Inferno, choosing a symbolic guide from Classical literature to accompany him on his journey through Hell. This guide is the Latin/Roman poet from the Augustan period, Virgil. Dante chose well – Virgil was in the direct tradition of epic poets, stretching right back to Homer. The *Divine Comedy* is in fact a religious and a Christian epic in its own right. The keynote of the epics of Classical times – Homer's *Odyssey, Iliad* and Virgil's *Aenid*, was that the beat of the meter, the repetition of key phrases and the force of the verse, helped them to be memorized, declaimed and to maintain their value in perpetuity. If that is what Dante intended, he surely succeeded – the style and matter of Dante's *Inferno* has made it live vividly until today.

FACING FEARS – WEARING EXILE AS A BADGE OF HONOUR

From Dante, we learn the art of memory – how to render one's creation memorable forever. Also we learn about recovery from adversity, political rejection, exile, banishment and a sentence of death, reminding us of the *fatwa* passed on the 20th-century writer, Salman Rushdie, by the Ayatollah in Iran. Yet Dante did not hide himself away – he boldly travelled through Italy, remaining a public person and writing forcefully and powerfully until he died, constructing a savage critique of those whom he considered his enemies, personal, political and religious. He was a man of courage; clearly, having served as a soldier on active duty, he was highly active physically, prepared to take political and personal risks and to assume responsibility for his deeds. He suffered both depression and despair in his time, yet transmuted this experience into the pure gold of his poetry. Even in translation, the opening lines of his *Inferno* are brilliantly memorable: *'Just half way through this journey of our life, I reawoke to find myself inside a dark wood, way off course, the right road lost.'* Then, as he enters the Inferno, he comes up with more immortal words: *'Abandon all hope ye who enter here.'*

Dante's description of Hell mobilizes all the senses and conduits of perception in a grand orchestration of terror. Frightful tastes and smells, baleful sights, extreme physical pain, bodily torment, screeching, harpy-like sounds and psychological degradation. And what benighted wretch does Dante pinion in the nethermost circle of Hell? As one might expect from such a champion in the divine conflict, at the bottom of the pit Dante places Satan, gnawing perpetually on the spirit of Judas Iscariot, the betrayer of Jesus Christ. Fittingly, perhaps, Dante completed his Paradiso, the third and final part of the *Divine Comedy*, just a few months before his death.

THEORIST AND PHILOSOPHER

The final work, which thrusts Dante into the realms of philosophy, is *De Monarchia* (*Of the Monarchy*), which he wrote in Latin. It places Dante on the same level as Confucius, Machiavelli and other theorists of government like Plato. In it Dante expounds the theory of a divinely intended government of the world by a universal emperor, acting in harmony with a universal Pope (shades of Confucius here). The thrust of his argument is that a concord could be achieved by a civil government, owing responsibility to a populace which responds in like manner – a theory which many have considered in subsequent generations.

JOHN ZIZKA 1370-1424

Our account of the era of Divine Conflict closes with the Holy Wars in Bohemia, the modern Czech Republic, at the start of the 15th century.

NEW IDEAS

For some time, there had been stirrings of discontent against the prevailing dogma of the Roman Catholic Church. This dissatisfaction centred on the sacrament of the Eucharist. In this rite, only the celebrant priest was permitted to drink the holy wine, which represented Christ's redeeming blood. But the lay Christian flock of Bohemia also aspired to taste this sacred draught. One brave man who had preached the new way, Jan Hus (born 1369), was burnt at the stake for heresy at the Council of Constance in 1415, when the Papacy and the Holy Roman Empire joined forces to stamp out such dangerous new ideas.

However, this particular new idea stoutly resisted suppression. Within four years of the burning of Jan Hus, Hussite armies were raging across Bohemia, defying both the power of the Empire and the numerous crusades launched by the Pope to crush them.

LOVE OF THE TASK

The Hussite cohorts were led by a remarkable man, the general John Zizka. He was educated at court in aristocratic style before taking up a military career. Indeed, Zizka seemed irresistibly drawn to whichever corner of Europe was currently involved in the heaviest fighting. He fought for the Teutonic Knights against the Poles, for the Austrians against the Turks, and for the English, under Henry V, at the Battle of Agincourt against the French in 1415.

INTER-PERSONAL INTELLIGENCE

Zizka's achievements, after the revolt broke out at Prague on 30 July 1419, were truly extraordinary. He consistently had to face better-equipped professional troops, far superior in numbers to his own, with what amounted to little more than untrained peasant bands armed only with simple farming implements, and almost no cavalry. Yet, time after time, Zizka blasted the Imperial and Papal legions from the field. When the war started, Zizka was already blind in one eye. (Nelson suffered from the same handicap.) But Zizka's handicap helped make him an inspiration to his men, for whom a wounded officer meant one who had proved himself willing to share in their own dangers.

In 1421, with just 4000 men, Zizka defeated the 40,000 troops of the Emperor Sigismund and captured Prague. He established the stronghold of Mount Tabor as his base, and subsequently his forces became known as 'Taborites'.

TURNING ADVERSITY TO ADVANTAGE

In 1421, at the siege of Raby, Zizka was blinded in his second eye. To most people, sudden blindness would become an overwhelming handicap, or a reason for early retirement! But Zizka persisted. Within one week, despite suffering from a heavy infection, he had recovered sufficiently to lead his army to further victories over the forces of the Emperor and the Pope.

A MAP IN THE MIND

For Zizka to continue as a general when blind indicated both a colossal degree of mental organization and a fantastic mental picture of terrain, a well as total recall of his battlefield layout. During this period, Zizka did not just operate as commander-in-chief – he also effectively ran the Hussite government. No human opponent could defeat him; in 1424, however, he died of the plague while besieging Przibislav.

Zizka's blindness did not prevent him from being a brilliant general.

INDOMITABLE SPIRITUAL INTELLIGENCE

Zizka was undoubtedly a military genius. During the course of his campaigns, he invented a primitive form of tank well before Leonardo. This was an armoured peasant wagon, mounted with an early form of light artillery, and it proved particularly effective against the medieval massed cavalry tactics of the imperial Knights.

His early tanks rolled forwards en masse in groups of several hundred, virtually eliminating the armoured knight from central European battlefields. The accompanying noise and smoke were often sufficient of themselves to discourage and unnerve the opposition. Even more impressive was the fact that Zizka was regularly outnumbered by at least 10-1. His victories have become legends in Czech history.

INSPIRATION

Some of the geniuses in this book are relatively unknown. Zizka is one of them, a man whose achievements, in terms of persistence and determination, deserve to be heralded. To all who find themselves in a seemingly terminal negative spiral, Zizka should be an inspiration.

REDRAWING THE COSMOS

'ONE MUST TREAT THESE PEOPLE OF EXTRAORDINARY GENIUS AS IF
THEY WERE CELESTIAL SPIRITS AND NOT LIKE BEASTS OF BURDEN.'
COSIMO DE MEDICI (1389-1464)

ENTERING THE RENAISSANCE

GENIUS ATTRACTS GENIUS

We have come to the threshold of a sensationally fruitful period in history for the flowering of human genius. But before embarking on our investigation of this most remarkable phase in the unfolding of genius, it is worth considering a central question. Is there such a thing as a climate, or environment, of genius? If there is, do stability or chaos – whether political, social or military – play any dominant role in determining that climate? Indeed, various periods do stand out for their intellectual richness – for example, 5th-century BC Athens, the Renaissance in Italy and, as we shall see, Elizabethan England.

STABILITY AND CHAOS

During the 5th century BC, Athens enjoyed a period – after the Persian Wars – of great peace and stability, which all too soon degenerated into the chaos of the Peloponnesian War. Yet a remarkable incidence of genius continued unabated, with Aeschylus, Sophocles, Euripides, Socrates, Plato, Phidias, Aristotle and so on. Elizabethan England – with Shakespeare, and Elizabeth herself, to name but two – was a time of comparative stability. Protestantism was established as the state religion, and foreign threats, such as the Spanish Armada, were warded off with relative ease.

Let us now compare this with the Italy of the 1400s and 1500s. True, for much of the 1400s, Florence was relatively stable, yet Italy itself, in the days of Leonardo and Michelangelo, was chaotic and in turmoil. Life was characterized by warring city states, foreign invasions from the

French and Spanish, religious upheaval and the sack of Rome in 1527. Yet all this seemed, paradoxically, to act as a stimulus to creativity, rather than a serious check on it.

WEALTH OF GENIUS

Perhaps a key common factor in all three cases is a sudden access to a great surplus of wealth. A partial, but important, effect of such wealth is that it may filter down to those of relatively humble birth, who are thus given the opportunity to release their own potential. Athens, indeed, became rich as a city, following tribute received after the successful conduct of the Persian Wars. Meanwhile, religious and state stability in Elizabethan England, combined with vigorous exploration and foreign trade, made the country wealthy after its previous long and impoverishing entanglement with foreign and civil wars. Finally, Rome could rely on the concentrated wealth of the Papacy, while Florence had its trade.

PLAGUE AS CATALYST

Indeed, the situation in Italy is, perhaps, the most

The Ideal City *by an unknown artist in the school of Piero della Francesca is an excellent example of the use of perspective.*

fascinating of all. One intriguing theory is that the ravages of the Black Death (bubonic plague) of the 1350s may have destroyed whole populations, but it left gold and assets untouched. Florence, the cradle of the Renaissance, had a population of 100,000 in 1347, but it was reduced so dramatically by the plague that, even by 1500, its numbers had only revived to 50,000. The result was that the existing assets and gold were concentrated in the hands of fewer people, and this sudden surplus may have helped to finance the dramatic artistic flowering of the 1400s. It appears that while a genius can survive in any environment or period, social mobility, the free flow of wealth and being in the company of other geniuses are stimulating factors.

A further effect of the blanket annihilation brought about by the Black Death may have been a widespread desire by the wealth owners to cheat mortality and to ensure the survival of their identity. An additional factor in the artistic flowering of the 1400s may have been the need for a divine 'insurance policy'. Decorating a baptistry, panel or font, commissioning a sculpture with a biblical theme or, on a civic level, erecting the dome on a cathedral, which had lain unfinished for 100 years, could have been seen as a way of currying divine favour and warding off the retribution of a further deadly disease.

All these factors may well have combined to give the decisive impetus to the explosion of Italian genius in the 15th century.

RETURN OF THE ARTIST

For the two millennnia between Phidias, and Brunelleschi and his introduction of perspective, the artist – whether painter, sculptor or architect – was an anonymous craftsman, dedicating his work to the glory of God, not to that of human individuals. But, from the 1400s, people began seriously to explore both physical and artistic space. They wanted to discover their place in the cosmos and to know, quite literally, where they stood. In that sense, the new drive for perspective can be seen as a symbol for a burgeoning spatial intelligence and awareness. This led, at the end of the 1400s, to Columbus's discovery of a new world, and then to Copernicus's redefinition of the place of the earth itself in creation.

FEET ON THE GROUND

The most startling characteristic of medieval painting, paralleling the soaring architectural spires of Gothic cathedrals, had been (apart from the absence of any apparent perspectival ordering) the lack of contact between the ground and the feet of those depicted. The characters seemed to be reaching upwards towards God, floating almost like angels ethereally in space, and not rooted on terra firma. From Brunelleschi onwards, however, and increasingly during the 1400s and especially in Florence, humans, even though the themes remained essentially biblical or religious, are depicted within a definite space and in a clear context. Masaccio (1401-28), for example, was the first to paint figures with their feet firmly planted on the ground. When a student, Michelangelo himself made a point of copying Masaccio's work regularly.

FILIPPO BRUNELLESCHI 1377-1446

MASTERMINDS IN PERSPECTIVE

Perspective was developed by a Mastermind Group of four – namely, Brunelleschi the architect, Donatello the sculptor, Masaccio the painter and Alberti the theoretician, ideologue and formulaic law-giver of the group. Perspective became a new symbol for the secularization of art; in other words, art in the 1400s ceased to be a servant of the Church and started to glorify mankind.

SINGLE POINT PERSPECTIVE

The perspective initially employed was an exaggeratedly rigorous and artificial construct – an ordered structure of a strictly classical nature. People and objects were perceived with the vision of a single, highly focused eye, not the broader, more chaotic realism of normal double-eyed sight. Such geometric perspective is now known as 'single point' or 'single eye' perspective, directed unerringly at the vanishing point of infinity, as parallel lines appear to meet towards the centre of the work of art.

INDIVIDUAL IMPORTANCE

It was the experiments of Brunelleschi which launched the new perspective, while Alberti was the man who scientifically codified the geometric formulas of perspective. These made it possible for other artists to follow where the original Mastermind Group of four had led the way. This new order and proportion in art derived in part from the contemporary accent on Humanism – the study of man and man's works, and placing man's space, not God's, at the centre of all things. It automatically assigned new powers to the artist, who became an arbiter of person and space, and a celebrity with his work much sought after. Indeed, like Leonardo or Michelangelo, he graduated towards becoming a towering hero of superhuman capacity. 'Renaissance Man' was suddenly capable of anything! Meanwhile, the artist, by making the spectator of the painting part of the picture itself and the representative of the point of view on which the perspective depends, thus confirmed the individual's position of central importance in the world. The viewer of a perspectival painting is automatically drawn into it, and thus made to feel significant.

THE RISE OF THE MIDDLE CLASSES

At this time, the funding patrons of hero artists were no longer just the Church, but powerful princes such as the Medici and *condottieri* (mercenary military leaders) and, above all, the newly wealthy commercial guilds. This demonstrated not only the rise of the middle classes, but also their fierce and newly awoken desire to perpetuate their identities and values through artistic creation.

MEASUREMENT AS ART

Numeracy was absolutely vital to such a merchant class – especially in Florence, which was busy founding the first modern economy, based not simply on trade, but also on banking and insurance. Florence, with its wealth and power at the start of the 15th century, can justly be compared with the splendours of 5th-century BC Athens. To Florentine merchants, bankers and commercial men, accurate measurement, both in weight and geometry, was their lifeblood and this arithmetical realism is reflected in their preferred art.

PERSPECTIVE AND SECULARIZATION

As we have seen, single-point perspective is the visual manifestation of a shift towards secularization. As the 15th century dawned, the power of the Church was under question, and this resulted in a break with medieval ideology. The move towards modern consciousness had begun.

Expressions of independence were occurring in Florence, where, for some time, members of the educated middle class had increasingly based their studies on Classical antiquity and Arabic innovations in mathematics, as well as direct observation. From this awakened curiosity came a stampede to study natural science, mathematics, mechanics and optics as separate disciplines.

FREEDOM TO EXPERIMENT

We have observed that a particular quality of genius is to free avenues of thought and that the new general sense of freedom was first expressed in visual terms by Brunelleschi, Donatello (1386-1466), Masaccio and Alberti. Brunelleschi trained in Florence, as a goldsmith and sculptor. He made a trip to Rome with Donatello to study antique sculpture and in his work on the walls of the Florence Baptistry is credited with being the first artist to demonstrate the perspectival representation of space. This innovation was speedily assimilated by both Donatello and Masaccio. Brunelleschi then applied those concepts to architectural space, developing ways in which his buildings could be experienced in full from a single view point. Brunelleschi devoted the end of his life to architecture, and was responsible for the dome of Florence Cathedral, the designs for which he produced in 1417. The building was begun in 1296 and by 1417 it lacked only the dome. Measured diametrically, Brunelleschi's dome is the largest in the world and it served as the model for Michelangelo's work on St Peter's in Rome. It was, indeed, a difficult piece of engineering to span the vast cathedral with a dome, but its Gothic elongation perfectly expressed the soaring spirit of innovation that gripped Florence in the early 15th century.

SYNAESTHESIA – MATHEMATICS – ASTRONOMY – MUSIC – ARCHITECTURE

Brunelleschi's training in mathematics, and his friendship with one of Florence's leading mathematical theorists and astronomers, Paolo Toscanelli (who also encouraged Christopher Columbus), gave Brunelleschi the background he needed for his invention of perspective and to elaborate on his system of proportions. Brunelleschi's dome for Florence Cathedral was carefully designed to rise in fixed mathematical intervals. This ingenious use of proportion deeply impressed the musician Guillaume Dufay (c.1400-74, French composer and singer in the Papal Choir at Rome), who actually adapted mathematical ratios on which the dome's construction is based into a piece of choral music! Brunelleschi's architecture was made up of circles, squares, hemispheres and cubes, all in carefully articulated proportion, and was based on the theory that man is the measure of all things.

DRAWING THE SPECTATOR INTO THE PICTURE

Following Brunelleschi's innovations in the use of perspective, perfect representation of spatial illusion in painting was achieved by Masaccio in the Brancacci Chapel in the Church of Santa Maria del Carmine in Florence. This fresco was to become the model for artists of the later Renaissance – even Michelangelo came to learn the new principles of *chiaroscuro* (light and dark) from it. Masaccio's masterpiece relates the story of The Tribute Money – a seldom-told episode in the life of Christ, which refers to the need to pay taxes to the Romans. Masaccio unfolds the narrative in the traditional medieval fashion but places Christ and the Apostles in the recognizable landscape of the Arno valley in which Florence was situated. With Masaccio's painting, onlookers could, for the first time, take their places imaginatively within a painted story. The use of perspective invited each spectator to join in the debate about taxation.

LEON BATTISTA ALBERTI 1404-1472

It was left to the theoretician of the Mastermind Group of four to express the complicated geometric equation of single-eye perspective. Leon Battista Alberti (1404-72) – an aristocrat. Humanist, poet and scholar, architect and art theorist, engineer, mathematician, cartographer and cryptographer, Alberti is the prototype of the Renaissance 'universal man'. He was at the vanguard of almost every major development in the cultural life of early Renaissance Italy and has been subsequently admired for his many talents. In both his intellectual and artistic pursuits, Alberti struck a balance between theory and practice. He was also extremely fit and apparently could jump over his fellow athletes from a standing position with his feet together.

Alberti was born in Genoa the illegitimate son of an exiled Florentine, and did not return to Florence until 1428, having been educated in Padua and Bologna and subsequently employed by the Papal civil service. Once in Florence, he quickly became part of the group surrounding Brunelleschi, who probably encouraged the writing of Alberti's book, *Della Pittura* (*On Painting*), which he dedicated to Brunelleschi and which was published in 1436. Alberti wrote in Latin, using arguments based on rhetoric, thus giving painting, for the first time, the intellectual respectability that previously had been reserved for literature. In *Della Pittura*, Alberti laid down guidelines for prospective artists, instructing them to study geometry, astronomy, science, composition (both visual and verbal) and the laws of perspective. The book soon became an important influence on other painters and their patrons. Alberti followed this with *De Statura* (*On Sculpture*) in 1450.

In his later years, Alberti devoted his talents to architecture, collaborating with Pope Nicholas V, who restored St Peter's and the Vatican. Finally, the discovery of fragments of a treatise on architecture by Vitruvius (the 1st-century Roman architect) prompted Alberti to write his 10 books *De Re Aedificatoria* (*On Architecture*), published in 1452. Alberti here identified beauty with harmony and codified Brunelleschi's experiments with perspective. This masterpeice led to a great architectural revolution in the world.

JOHANNES GENSFLEISCH GUTENBERG 1400-1468

MASS PRODUCTION OF KNOWLEDGE

Although the Chinese had been aware of printing since AD 730, it had made little impact there. Perhaps the difficulties with their complex pictogrammatic alphabet discouraged them from exploiting the process to its full. In contrast, the staggering success of Gutenberg in pioneering printing in the West gave Europe a technological lead which endured for centuries. Gutenberg's invention of a moveable-type printing press can

be compared to the development of computers and artificial intelligence in the 20th century.

Gutenberg was born in Mainz, of a noble family. Between 1430 and 1444, he was in Strasbourg, working as a goldsmith, and it was here that he began experimenting with printing. By 1448 he had entered into a partnership with Johannes Fust, who financed Gutenberg's press.

Before Gutenberg's time, books had to be elaborately copied by hand. Indeed, only 50,000 completed book manuscripts, produced in Europe during the 15th century, still survive. After Gutenberg, however, there was a colossal explosion in the number of printed works. Naturally, this fuelled the accessibility of Classical authors and the Bible, as well as the sudden explosion of ideas and learning. This put Europe at an immense advantage over other parts of the world where printing had not taken root.

THE FLOODGATES OF KNOWLEDGE BURST OPEN

The following statistic reveals the power and impact of printing. In 1456, there were fewer than 60 copies made of the Gutenberg Bible, Europe's first printed book. By the year 1500, 35,000 different editions of books had been printed, amounting to 15 million copies – an incredible leap.

LEFT Along with Leonardo, Alberti was one of the most brilliant figures of Renaissance Italy who seems to have been able to turn his hand to anything. Good looking and athletic, his physical stamina matched his intellectual capabilities.

RIGHT Gutenberg was a genius who invented a printing press by combining several existing (but different) processes. The result of his innovative work was to revolutionize learning in Europe and increase the potential learning power of anyone who could read.

INVENTION AND FLEXIBILITY – COMBINING DISPARATE ELEMENTS

Gutenberg's revolutionary printing method cleverly combined several known, but separate, processes. He employed individual letters cast in metal, a technique borrowed from the already tried and tested method of producing gold coins by stamping metal in a die. The letters were composed in blocks of type of one or two pages. These were printed using a newly developed metal adhesive oil-based ink and a press cunningly adapted from those used by papermakers.

In terms of the power conferred by printing, consider the number of new printing centres which were established during the 15th century. Those in western Europe numbered 1000, and they were spread over 250 separate towns and cities; but in the east of Europe, the whole of the Ottoman Empire and Africa combined, only one printing centre was established in Constantinople (Istanbul) in 1488.

RED RUM – A FORMULA FOR SUCCESS

Sadly however – and this is where a contrast can be drawn with William Gates in the 20th century, whose promulgation of computer software is the modern equivalent of the widening of frontiers by printing in the 15th century – Gutenberg was not a competent businessman. His partnership with Johannes Fust ended with Fust securing a verdict against Gutenberg for money he had advanced. Fust then took over Gutenberg's printing business, carrying on the concern with the assistance of one Peter Schoffer.

The lesson we learn from Gutenberg is a qualified one. The man was clearly a genius – inventing a method, combined from a number of apparently unrelated processes, which transformed the world almost overnight. Unfortunately, in spite of his colossal genius in this respect, his failure to back that up with even moderate business acumen meant that he failed to profit from his magnificent invention as he

When he invented his printing press, Gutenberg laid the foundations for the proof that information, knowledge and learning ultimately lead to power and wealth. Once books could be mass-produced by means of his press, there was obviously a dramatic increase in the number of readers who now had more immediate access to a new source of knowledge.

should have done. Instead, the mantle of book-printing passed to Manutius in Venice and Caxton in London.

There is a principle at work here – we call it the Red Rum Principle (see page 43). However hard one tries, however ingenious one is, one has to put the finishing touches to conclude the masterpiece and derive the maximum benefit. Just when the victory seems won, that is the moment to concentrate, to try hardest and check all possible angles for defects. Gutenberg undoubtedly deserves his place among the great geniuses. With the Red Rum Principle in operation, he might perhaps have profited from it personally to the same extent that others have benefited from his great invention.

CHRISTOPHER COLUMBUS 1451-1506
NEW WORLD DEVELOPMENTS
Columbus, whose name means 'the dove, bearer of Christ', discovered the New World for Spain in

1492. The 15th century is normally termed the Renaissance, with its recovery of ancient Classical knowledge. But that age was also characterized by a new imperative towards fresh ideas in all areas of human endeavour. Take chess, for example. During the 15th century, the surprisingly rapid process had been initiated whereby the game emerged from its slow, tortuous Arabic form, as practised by As-Suli; suddenly, castling was introduced, pawns gained the privilege of moving two squares forward at their first turn, and the Queen was transformed at a stroke from a waddling cripple (the Arabic 'Vizier') to a unit of devastating ferocity.

SYMBOLS OF DISTANCE
If chess is truly a game of warfare, then the increased firepower of the Queen surely mirrors the contemporary introduction of artillery as a long-range means of destroying the opposition in the sphere of battlefield technology. These

sudden developments in the game reflect the overall 15th-century dynamic. The increasingly urgent perception of distance, space and perspective which distinguished that period. Indeed, perspective in art, the telescope and the microscope were parallel developments.

Controlling the Centre

Columbus not only discovered the New World, he also exported European ideas and ideals there – including chess. At a stroke, Columbus's discovery suddenly placed Spain in a perfect position to become a centre for world communication – placed at the junction of the European mainland with trade routes south towards Africa, and now facing the vast new vista across the Atlantic Ocean.

Humble Origins

Columbus was born in Genoa, the son of a wool comber. At first he was expected to take up the same trade, but at the age of 14 he went to sea, fought against Tunisian galleys and, around 1470, was shipwrecked off Cape St Vincent. He reached the shores of Portugal by surviving on a wooden plank. By 1474 he had already conceived the idea of sailing to India by travelling westwards, and he was encouraged in this by Toscanelli, an astronomer from Florence.

Amassing Subject Knowledge – Everything Connects

Meanwhile, Columbus gathered vital experience in his intended profession of becoming a great navigator. He sailed to Iceland, the Cape Verde Islands and Sierra Leone. In 1485, he applied for a patron to finance his intended expedition westwards, in order to reach the East. He approached John II of Portugal, Henry VII of England and the Catholic Queen Isabella of Castile. Over a period of seven years, he was frequently rebuffed; those who had the power to decide whether money was to be spent on such ventures were often traditionally inclined churchmen, emotionally opposed to the notion that the earth might be round. Eventually, in April 1492, King Ferdinand and Queen Isabella of the newly united Spain gave him the green light and, on Friday 3 August 1492, Columbus sailed in command of the *Santa Maria*, the *Pinta* and the *Nina* – three small ships with just 120 explorers on board – his avowed intention to cross the Atlantic Ocean and reach the rich trade of the East by that method.

Persistence

By Friday 12 October, land was sighted after just over two months of continuous sailing. The land he discovered included an island in what came to be known as the Bahamas, and Cuba and Hispaniola – now known as Haiti. Columbus then set out on the return voyage, arriving back in Spain on 15 March 1493, where he was received with the highest honours.

Intuition and Auto Suggestion

It is said that Columbus underestimated the size of the globe before he set out and believed he was en route to Cipangu (Japan), not the New World. Nevertheless, he had the determination, vision, and belief in his own new theory of the world, and the power to convert those in a position of authority to share and back that vision and his single-minded purpose.

'To Boldly Go'

Columbus indeed had the courage 'to boldly go'

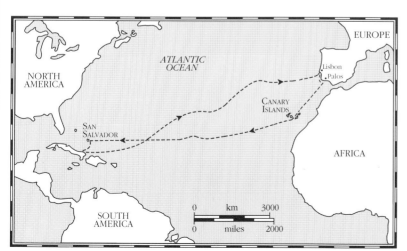

Intrepid explorer Christopher Columbus was the first to plunge out and forward across a vast ocean with uncharted waters. Whereas previous explorers had followed the coastline when they ventured out to sea, Columbus sailed across the Atlantic in 1492-3 even though he did not know what, if anything, lay ahead.

where no one had gone before. It is an irony that the continent he discovered – America – was not named after him. It was, in fact, named after a later explorer, born in Florence in the same year as Christopher Columbus, namely Amerigo Vespucci.

AVOIDING THE COASTLINE!
What truly distinguishes Columbus from all previous maritime explorers is that he did not follow the coastline. Previous seafarers had all sought to travel in correspondence with established continental contours. Not Columbus! He additionally handled his nervous crews so well that they reached their destination, and his trailblazing exploitation of the then-unknown trade winds ensured that he could return safely home.

Although there has been recent speculation about Columbus's character and the way that he treated slaves and native inhabitants, no one can deny his genius, determination and bravery in exploring the uncharted seas.

LEONARDO DA VINCI 1452-1519
Leonardo da Vinci is one of the world's most famous artists, and the greatest artistic tourist attraction is his *Mona Lisa* (painted *c*.1504) in the Louvre in Paris. For Leonardo, though, art was by no means separate from any other facet of his complex life.

He was born in 1452, the illegitimate son of a notary and a peasant girl in the small town of Vinci. Throughout his life, his desire for knowledge and new discoveries was insatiable; he wanted to know and record everything. In fact, he frequently signed himself 'Disciple of Experience'. His eye was sure and his observations bordered on the miraculous. In his *Codex on the Flight of Birds*, he recorded details which remained unconfirmed until high-speed photography proved him right!

EVERYTHING CONNECTS
Like Brunelleschi and Alberti before him, he was fascinated by all aspects of intellectual activity. In his day, he was the leading thinker in numerous arenas of knowledge, from acoustics and aquanautics to meteorology and physiology. One can speak of Leonardo the engineer, specializing in hydraulics, early attempts at flying machines, and military science; of Leonardo the natural scientist, with an interest in botany, geology, geography and anatomy; and of Leonardo the artist. Added to this were his skills in making and play-

ABOVE Queen Isabella and Columbus by Henry Nelson O'Neill (1817-80).

ing musical instruments, his spontaneous compositions of music and songs, his fame as a jester and teller of tales, and his renown for excelling at whatever he applied himself to. His enthusiasm for experimentation was limitless.

Leonardo believed that all disciplines are interrelated, and for him the final authority was the human eye – he maintained that no activity is nobler than sight.

REINVENTING NOTE-TAKING
Thousands of pages of notes by him survive. Much of it was written in left-handed mirror-writing, either in notebooks or on separate sheets. Every page contains spectacular insights into his chosen subject matter, and he often addressed questions that were impossible to answer until the 20th century.

EARLY WORK
Leonardo began his professional career in the workshop of Andrea del Verrocchio (1435-88), a

RIGHT Leonardo da Vinci's view of himself remains with us in his famous self-portrait.

goldsmith, painter and sculptor, in Florence. Leonardo's distinctive hand is first identified in one of the Angels in a painting of the Baptism of Christ, otherwise painted by Verrochio. The attribution was due to the treatment of the Angel's head, particularly the curling hair. This shows the analogies Leonardo made between all living things, particularly water. The blonde curls are similar to the eddying pools of water that recur in his notebooks, even at this early date.

LIGHT AND DARK

Leonardo's first Florentine masterpiece was the *Adoration of the Magi*, commissioned in 1481 and abandoned, unfinished, when he departed for Milan in 1482. Many drawings for this picture survive which show him experimenting with light and dark. His notebooks confirm this and describe the importance of having a controlled light source. Leonardo warns against drawing or painting faces in the direct sunlight, reminding the reader of the beauty of figures and faces seen in half light. To produce such light in the studio, he advises painting the walls black and stretching a sheet of linen over the courtyard, so that the model will be lit with soft diffused light, with no sharp shadows to break up the forms. His theories about light seem to imply that, for him, darkness precedes light, and in his paintings form and colour have to compete with encroaching darkness. This was going against contemporary Florentine fashion, which was in favour of bright, light colour.

MOVE TO MILAN

Leonardo travelled extensively in his life, moving from Florence to the court of Milan in 1482-3. In his confident letter of application to the Milanese Duke Ludovico Sforza, Leonardo stresses his ability as a military engineer and sculptor and offers to create an equestrian statue of the Duke's father. Almost as an afterthought, he mentions his skill at painting. While in Milan he painted *The Virgin of the Rocks* – we have two versions.

EQUESTRIAN ENTHUSIAST

Sadly, nothing remains of the legendary Sforza

It has been possible to build Leonardo's flying machine, and other devices, from his notes.

monument but Leonardo's wonderful drawings. It was constructed originally in clay, but the Duke could not spare the bronze for the cast, as he was embarking upon his unsuccessful war with France. The swiftly triumphant French troops then used the clay horse for target practice! Leonardo's superb drawings display a figure on a rearing horse, and such dynamism would not be repeated until Bernini created his equestrian figure of Louis XIV in the 17th century.

An accomplished horseman, Leonardo kept his own stables, and it was known that he trained his horses with great patience, understanding and kindness. He was not only fascinated by the anatomy of creatures, but was compassionate towards them as well. If he passed markets where caged birds were being sold, Leonardo often used to pay the vendor the appropriate price, and then open the cages so that the birds could fly to freedom.

THE *LAST SUPPER*

Although in a sadly damaged state, the greatest work to survive from the time Leonardo spent in Milan is his *Last Supper*. Painted in 1495-6 for the refectory of Santa Maria dell Grazie, Leonardo's new technique was unsuited to fresco (painting on walls), so he experimented with a kind of oil tempera, the exact composition of which is still unknown. In the damp climate of Milan, the work had begun to deteriorate even before Leonardo's death. Recently, however, it has been carefully restored.

The psychological tension of this great ruined masterpiece is still unsurpassed. Leonardo has moved painting away from the mathematically perfect, with perspectival, illusionistic space, developed with such excitement in the quattrocento (1400s). The state of affairs in Italy had changed after the French invasion of 1495. It was now clear that a divided Italy would remain impotent. Despite Machiavelli and others, it was only a matter of time before the Italian states, with the exception of the Venetian republic, would be overwhelmed by foreign forces. The High Renaissance, in both Florence and Rome, has to be understood as an extension of images of human grandeur which, in reality, were doomed. Contrasted with the perspectival invitation to the spectator of Masaccio, in the refectory at Santa Maria there is nowhere that one can stand and enter imaginatively into the mythical space of the *Last Supper*. The painting is a projection of an ideal world. We have entered the High Renaissance.

EVEN MORE ENERGY

Leonardo returned to Florence in 1501, where he was commissioned by the Republic to paint *The Battle of Anghiari*, in celebration of a Florentine victory, for the council chamber of the town hall (now the Palazzo Vecchio). It was intended to complement Michelangelo's *Battle of Cascina* (both have been destroyed). For the *Battle of Anghiari*, we do have Rubens' copy of a copy and some wonderful drawings to help us to reconstruct the centre of the composition. This shows Leonardo creating a furious, dynamic engagement of four horsemen battling for the standard of the Republic with such ferocity that the action remains as a prime example for all other subsequent battle pictures.

Two easel pictures remain from this period, the *Mona Lisa* (*c.*1504) and the *Madonna and St Anne* (*c.*1508-13). Leonardo took them to France with him and they are now to be found in the Louvre. Leonardo brought to both these paintings the monumentality he had created in the *Last Supper*.

VERSATILITY

Leonardo returned to Milan in 1506, where he painted little. Much of his time was occupied on another equestrian monument never executed, for Trivulzio, marshal for the King of France, whose armies had occupied Milan. The rest of his time was spent in scientific research, and particularly in anatomical drawings. It is believed that Leonardo dissected over 50 bodies to acquire his information. He climbed the neighbouring mountains, examining fossilized shells embedded in rocks, which caused him to question the theologically accepted date for the beginning of creation. His studies allowed him to devise methods of irrigation and water transportation. He drew relief maps, without benefit of surveying instruments. He also designed innovative machines for war (including an early

tank), and invented a machine for grinding concave mirrors, which resulted in a telescope built in 1509 (a century before Galileo). These various drawings were not published during his lifetime and the notes he left to his pupil, Francesco Melzi, disappeared until the latter's death.

Leonardo's notebooks – some of the most complete records of the human mind – are filled with minute details of natural phenomena.

HUMOUR AND EXPERIMENTATION

Leonardo enjoyed a joke, especially at the expense of pompous court life. When he arrived from Milan at the Papal court of Leo X in 1513, Pope Leo gave him apartments in the Belvedere, from which he would emerge (so contemporary reports insist), with exquisite but useless objects that he had made. These included a pair of skin wings, mounted with golden wires on a live lizard, which then marched about frightening the courtiers like a little dragon.

As in virtually all other areas, Leonardo was nearly five centuries ahead of his time in the field of cooking. For instance, he liked to serve tiny portions of delicacies, beautifully arranged on exquisitely carved shapes. It is comforting to know that like all geniuses and all good learners, Leonardo occasionally made mistakes – and he made some exceptional ones when invited to be head chef at the court of Ludovico. The devices he designed to increase efficiency in the kitchen, which included sprinkler systems, all went disastrously wrong. Added to this, the cooks did not expect to have to carve as well as cook the vegetables, so Leonardo recruited artist and sculptor friends to perform the task, bringing the number of people in the kitchens, which usually accommodated 20, close to a very crowded 200!

RESILIENCE

Leonardo has unjustly been accused in some quarters of being pathologically incapable of completing his work. This is, however, most unfair as it was common in 15th-century Italy for artistic commissions to remain unfinished. (Michelangelo, for example, also left many incomplete works.) The environment at that time was one of social fragmentation, internecine war, and fortunes suddenly made and just as swiftly lost. Funding from patrons for planned masterpieces often evaporated overnight and Leonardo had to live with such circumstances and, constantly reconstructing his life, he made the brilliant best of them that he could.

IMPARTING WISDOM

Towards the end of his life, Leonardo accepted an invitation from Francis I to spend his remaining years in Cloux, a little chateau provided by the French king which was conveniently near Amboise (his residence). Here Leonardo could perform his final function, to impart his accumulated wisdom in conversation with the king himself. Leonardo died in Cloux in 1519 and the pictures that remained in his possession passed to the French crown, and thus to the Louvre.

As well as his notebooks and works of art, Leonardo bequeathed four principles for the development of genius, which physiologists and brain researchers have recently 'discovered' for themselves:

1 Study the science of art.
2 Study the art of science.
3 Learn how to see. [Develop *all* your senses, especially sight.]
4 Study all the above in the light of the continuing knowledge that everything connects, in some way, to everything else.

Throughout his life, Leonardo approached the vastness and minutiae of the universe with an insatiable curiosity, a lust to probe all its secrets, and the Utopian dream of transmitting to others the knowledge that he gained.

DESIDERIUS ERASMUS 1466-1537
FLEXIBILITY

As major players of the Renaissance, such as Columbus, Magellan and Copernicus, began to redraw the cosmos, others, such as the Dutch priest Erasmus, redefined the position of humankind within that cosmic order. Erasmus was a humanist, scholar and thinker who challenged the authority of the Roman Catholic Church to shift the intellectual centre of gravity and give human beings greater importance. This meant sweeping away the symbolic, challenging old ideas about the nature of the universe, replacing blind dogma with real experimentation and addressing life as it was really led.

COURAGE

Erasmus was a man of immense courage. At a time when heretics and opponents of the Church were regularly burnt at the stake, he wrote a series of books criticizing the superstitions of the Catholic clergy. He also published studies of both the Old and the New Testaments to give people a better understanding of what the Bible actually said. He put people before the dictates

Erasmus sat for this portrait by his fellow countryman Quentin Matsys (c. 1466-1531).

of the Church – at the time a shocking and revolutionary idea.

It is fascinating to observe the extent to which early personal experience may have determined the later bent of Erasmus's theological and humanist thinking. In his youth he attended the school of the Brothers of the Common Life at Deventer. When his parents died, his guardian insisted that he enter a monastery and Erasmus spent six years in the Augustinian college of Stein near Gouda. It was almost certainly this direct personal experience of the ways of Catholic monks that in later life turned Erasmus into one of their most relentless critics.

SPREADING EDUCATION

Erasmus, in fact, acquired a very well-rounded education. From 1509 to 1514 he resided chiefly at Cambridge, England, where he acted as Professor of Divinity and Professor of Greek. Thereafter he returned to the continent and became an itinerant scholar, residing alternately in Basle, Switzerland, and England. His main work, *Colloquia*, was published in 1519. In the boldness, vigour and courage with which it attacks the abuses of the Church, it can be seen as a preparation for the revolutionary work of Luther and the Reformation, which finally and definitively challenged the Catholic Church in Europe. In 1516, Erasmus published his annotated New Testament. In all his publications of biblical works, Erasmus's aim was to introduce a more rational conception of Christian doctrine and to free men's minds from the frivolous, pedantic methods of the scholastic theologians – people who could calculate how many angels might dance on the head of a pin.

COMMITMENT

Erasmus possessed supreme common sense. He stands as a cultivated man, one who was appalled at the vagaries and pedantry of theology, the subject known then as the Queen of Science. He wanted to rescue theology from the clergy and to expose the abuses of the Church – such as indulgences by which the Church sold pardons for sins. Erasmus also achieved more than any other single person in advancing a revival of learning throughout Europe. He seized knowledge, capturing it from the arcane mysteries of the Catholic Church, and made the Bible accessible to common men. His genius resides in his desire to make the arcane comprehensible and in having the courage to challenge the established order (in this case the Catholic Church), when it sought to monopolize knowledge and comprehension.

TRUTH

The *Colloquia* might be Erasmus's masterpiece, but his best-known work is the satire *Encomium Moriae* (*The Praise of Folly*), published in 1509. Why was it so necessary to attack the Catholic Church? At that time it had become entrenched and fixed in its views and it had created a dogma which was blocking the advancement of science. Just how dangerous this was is apparent if you consider Galileo, born around 30 years after Erasmus died. When Galileo's scientific truths were challenged by the Church, the Church won. It was in fact several centuries before the Catholic Church finally recanted and agreed that Galileo was right about the way in which the universe was constructed. With this kind of giant obstruction stifling the advancement of knowledge, one can see why it was vital that Erasmus should challenge that monopoly of knowledge, break it down and prepare for the Reformation.

The extent to which Erasmus's challenge to dogma and mental absolutism was necessary is demonstrated by two (numbers 1 and 13) of the Spiritual Exercises prescribed by Saint Ignatius Loyola (1491-1556), Erasmus's contemporary and also the founding General of the Jesuit movement:

'The following rules are to be observed in order that we may hold the opinions that we should hold in the Church Militant:

1. We should put away completely our own opinion and keep our mind ready and eager to give our entire obedience to our Holy Mother, the Hierarchical Church . . .

13. To arrive at complete certainty, this is the attitude of mind we should maintain: I will believe that the white object I see is black, if that should be the decision of the Hierarchical Church . . .'

Some opponent Erasmus had to face!

The Protestant Reformers, on the other hand, were far more friendly towards the new science and that vital redrawing of the cosmos which reflects the physical truth of the universe.

Erasmus was the scholar chiefly responsible for introducing new learning into northern Europe. He wrote theological treatises, social criticism and satire and made a pioneering Latin translation of the New Testament from the original Greek. It was his work which provided the ammunition for those who criticized the Church's control of areas over which it had no scriptural authority. Among the excesses he attacked were philandering and corruption among the clergy. He gave only qualified support to Martin Luther. Although he criticized the Roman Catholic Church, he did not want to overturn it. He said: '*I laid a hen's egg, but Luther hatched a bird of quite a different species.*' Unsurprisingly, all of Erasmus's works, including his observations on Latin grammar, were among the first to be banned by the Papacy.

NICCOLO MACHIAVELLI 1469-1527

Machiavelli is the most celebrated theorist of government, state craft and political science. He appears briefly (as the character Machevill) in Christopher Marlowe's play *The Jew of Malta*. Shakespeare also cited him, in *Henry VI Part III*. In contrast with Confucius and Dante – two idealists in the theory of government – Machiavelli was a realist, and therein lies his genius.

Much lip service is paid to the teachings of liberal idealism, but when the gloves come off,

Although he wrote many works, Machiavelli is best known for his masterpiece The Prince.

those in authority have regularly demonstrated that they are all good students of Machiavelli at heart. Machiavelli's basic message is to demonstrate by example how rulers can establish and maintain authority.

INSIGHT

It is, however, essential to realize that Machiavelli did not necessarily approve of or applaud the ruthless measures he described to achieve the above goal. The task he set himself was to record accurately and faithfully, and then subject to intense analytic scrutiny, those measures which lead either to success or to failure.

He did this in the same way as an objective, detached scientific observer might survey a cluster of particularly fascinating microbes through a powerful and revealing microscope. And once Machiavelli had detected the truth of any situation, he did not hesitate to publish his conclusions, however unpalatable they might appear.

TRUTH

This urge to describe how politics is really conducted has led, in some quarters, to a quite unjustifiable condemnation of Machiavelli's writing as diabolical. Indeed, 'Old Nick', a reference to Machiavelli's forename, has come to signify the Devil himself. As an example of the unparalleled precision with which he pinpoints the psychology of government, consider these quotations from his book *The Prince*. Machiavelli's very concise volume shows how princes – in other words, any persons or parties who have attained state power – do not rule necessarily for the benefit of the populace, but to keep themselves in control.

'*Every prince would like to be both loved and feared, but it is far more effective to be feared than loved, if you cannot be both.*'

'*Nothing brings a prince more prestige than great campaigns and striking demonstrations of his ability.*'

SUBJECT KNOWLEDGE

Machiavelli cut through to the heart of *realpolitik* statecraft and explained things as they 'really were'. There is no cloudy idealism in his writings – they are based on a profound study of history and on his first-hand experience of Renaissance Italy and its politics.

Machiavelli held prominent state office himself. In 1498 he became Government Secretary of Florence – a post he occupied until the fall of the Republic in 1512. The Medici family had been autocrats in Florence before the Republic was established. Upon their return in 1513, Machiavelli was exiled, never to hold public office again.

During his period of influence, Machiavelli had been employed as an emissary to the King of France, the Holy Roman Emperor, Maximilian and Cesare Borgia. His career evinces distinct parallels with those of Dante and Confucius, both of whom published theories of government, and both of whom, having held high office, were exiled. Ironically, Dante had also been expelled from Florence two centuries before Machiavelli.

THE SCIENCE OF POLITICS

Machiavelli wrote seven books on the art of war and one comedy, *Mandragola*, a masterpiece of ribald comic art full of mordant humour and riotous obscenity. Nevertheless, his enduring legacy is *The Prince*. His observations are based on history and contemporary Italian political leaders, especially Cesare Borgia, whom Machiavelli clearly admired. Cesare's subsequent detractors have blackened his reputation, but among those whom he governed he was considered 'a just prince, upright and severe'. Machiavelli had harboured hopes that Cesare might live up to his illustrious forename and reunite Italy. But the potential new Caesar's career was cut short by an early death.

In 1588, the year of the Spanish Armada, Christopher Marlowe summed up, through his character Machevill, the popular view of Machiavelli's political insight (Peter's chair refers to the Papacy).

'*I . . . weigh not men, and therefore not men's words.*
Admir'd I am of those that hate me most.
Though some speak openly against my books,
Yet will they read me, and thereby attain
To Peter's chair; and, when they cast me off,
Are poison'd by my climbing followers.
I count religion but a childish toy,
And hold there is no sin but ignorance.
Many will talk of title to a crown:
What right had Caesar to the empery?
Might first made Kings, and laws were then most sure,
When, like the Draco's, they were writ in blood.'

Prologue from *The Jew of Malta*

MACHIAVELLI STATES THE VIE PRINCIPLE

It would be wrong, though, to assume that the lessons to be drawn from *The Prince* are exclusively heartless and cynical. Machiavelli also found plenty to admire in the rulers he observed – not only in the aspirations of Cesare Borgia, but also in the style of heroes of antiquity. Indeed, Machiavelli's procedure in *The Prince* was substantially the same as ours in this book. He provided examples of heroes, statesmen and governors from both past and present. He then drew general precepts from their particular achievements. This is the VIE principle (Veneration, Inspiration, Emulation) in action!

Machiavelli actually describes how he would dress up in his official state robes in the privacy of his own study. He would then transport himself in his imagination back into the courts and palaces of great men of antiquity and pose them questions. In order to record their answers for posterity, he wrote *The Prince*:

'Study the actions of illustrious men, to see how they have borne themselves; examine the causes of their victories and defeats, so as to imitate the former and avoid the latter. Above all, do as illustrious men do, who take as their example, those who have been praised and famous before them, and whose achievements and deeds still live in the memory, as it is said Alexander the Great imitated Achilles and Caesar imitated Alexander!'

NICOLAS COPERNICUS 1473-1543

Copernicus, the arch re-drawer of the cosmos, is known as the founder of modern astronomy. He was born at Torun in Poland, his uncle, the Prince Bishop of Ermeland, being responsible for his education. Copernicus travelled widely – in fact it almost seemed as if he was hunting down knowledge all over Europe, relentlessly seeking out the best possible universities in order to discover the subjects that they taught most expertly, so that he might increase his learning.

VERSATILITY

His initial studies included mathematics, optics, perspective, church law, Greek and Latin. He absorbed these at the universities of Cracow and Bologna. In 1497 he was appointed canon of Frauenburg, the cathedral city of Ermeland. Significantly, though, Copernicus never definitively took holy orders; in fact, throughout his life he steered clear of the religious conflicts of the Protestant Reformation and the Catholic counter-Reformation.

Continuing his eager hunt for knowledge across Europe, in 1501 he studied medicine at Padua. In 1503 he became a doctor of canon law at Ferrara, and in 1512 he was in Frauenberg, where he had settled down studying the stars. At Frauenberg, Copernicus gradually took over from his uncle, the Prince Bishop, becoming Military Governor, judge, physician and reformer of the coinage. His medical skills were so renowned that he was always in demand from the rich and, conversely, always at the service of the poor.

ICONOCLASM

Copernicus's major book, *The Revolution of the Heavenly Spheres*, promulgated the heliocentric view of the cosmos. In Latin, his great work was called *De Revolutionibus Orbium Coelestium*. The whole thrust of this amazing volume was to prove, from his observation, that the earth travels around the sun, not vice versa. He completed the book in 1530, but delayed publishing it. In 1542, Copernicus was seized with apoplexy; on 24 May, 1543, he touched the first printed copy of his work. He died on that very same day.

PATIENCE

Through patiently cultivating relations with the Church, Copernicus succeeded in avoiding the sort of opprobrium which other revolutionary astronomers succeeded in pulling down on their heads (Galileo, for example, springs to mind). Copernicus treated the Church with enormous tact, although he knew his theories about the heliocentric nature of the cosmos to be correct. He in no way wished to upset the Church or to damage his relations with the ecclesiastical authorities. This, perhaps, explains his 12-year delay in putting his book into print.

THE EARTH MOVED

Let us try to imagine the seismic shock waves

Copernicus, huntsman of knowledge, thought that the sun is at the centre of the universe.

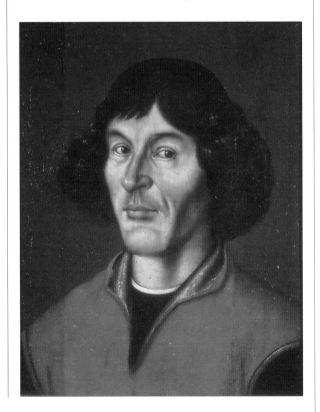

The planets circle the sun in this 16th-century chart of the Copernican solar system.

which emanated at the time from Copernicus's discovery. Even now, when we talk of the sun rising, we in fact mean that the earth is spinning! It is difficult to overcome the evidence of our eyes and to rid ourselves of that long-ingrained geocentric terminology.

COURAGE

The revelation that the earth moves around the sun and rotates on its own axis has led, in some quarters, to something more extreme than mere terminological inexactitude. It has resulted in what is referred to as 'post-Copernican depression'. To certain dogmatically orthodox religious minds, the assertion that the earth may not be at the centre of all things seems almost an obliteration of faith, a denial of the possibility of reli-

gious belief itself. Yet Copernicus had the immense courage to face up to this question and asserted that the earth, rather than being at the precise epicentre of God's creation, might be nothing more than a piece of rock, ceaselessly revolving in empty space around a star which, in itself, is of no special significance.

When Galileo upheld the scientific facts almost a century after Copernicus, he was condemned by the Papal Inquisition. In fact, it was not until October 1992 that the Vatican officially conceded, at long last, that Galileo had not offended against Catholic belief.

INSPIRATION TO OTHERS

Johannes Kepler (1571-1630) correctly refined and advanced the Copernican theory (which still held that the heavenly bodies moved in pure circles) by proving instead that their motion was in elongated circles, namely ellipses. In 1601,

Kepler was appointed Imperial Mathematician, astronomer and astrologer, to the Holy Roman Empire, based in Prague and Vienna.

CREATIVE INTELLIGENCE

It is a prime objective of genius to *derestrict the type of reasoning which is open*. Kepler's main work was entitled *The Harmony of the World*. In it, as can be seen from certain chapter headings, he postulates the most remarkable poetical and musical insights into his scientific measurement of the Heavens, namely:

'Musical Modes or Tones have somehow been expressed in the Extreme Planetary Movements.'

'The Universal Harmonies of all six Planets may exist like Common Musical Counterpoint.'

'In the Celestial Concords, which planet sings soprano, which alto, which tenor and which bass.'

(*Harmony of the World*, Book 5, Sections 6, 7, and 8).

As we have seen from Brunelleschi, whose architectural calculations were turned into music by Dufay, the relationship between artistic harmony and exact scientific measurement is extremely close.

MICHELANGELO 1475-1564

Michelangelo Buonarroti was 23 years younger than Leonardo da Vinci, but he already had a reputation when Leonardo returned to Florence from Milan in 1501. It was to be Michelangelo, rather than Leonardo, who dominated the 16th century. Michelangelo was deeply religious, and a committed Florentine republican. As his sonnets show, he was extremely sensitive to human suffering; his subject was always the life of the human soul, expressed through the human body.

LIBERATING THE FIGURE

Born in Caprese, a little hill town of which his father was governor, Michelangelo was sent to a nurse in Settignano, a village of stone cutters. He always said his love of stone came from the nurse's milk. Always a carver, rather than a modeller, like Donatello, in one poem he talks of 'liberating the figure from the stone' – he used to cut inwards to reveal a shape.

PERSISTENCE

Michelangelo came from minor nobility, pretentious, but penniless, and he experienced difficulty in becoming an artist, because it was considered a career unworthy of a 'gentleman'. As a young boy, he was regularly beaten by his father and uncle when he took drawings home because they despised art. Nevertheless, he was allowed to continue his artistic studies and finally entered Domenico de Ghirlandaio's studio in 1488. Here, he learned the ancient Tuscan wall-painting fresco technique which he later used on the Sistine ceiling. Michelangelo always claimed that he taught himself to carve. Tradition, however, says he studied with Bertoldo, who had been Donatello's assistant and was in charge of Lorenzo de Medici's collection of antique sculpture. Bertoldo ran a free studio in the garden of the Medici Palace. It was here that Michelangelo carved the small marble relief known as the *Madonna of the Stairs* (1489-92). It was the only time that Michelangelo used Donatello's carving technique known as '*rilevio schiacciato*' (shallow relief).

SENSUAL INTELLIGENCE

Michelangelo was in Rome in 1496, where he carved the Bacchus for a rich Roman named Jacopo Galli. The sensuality of this figure was to resurface later in the nudes on the Sistine ceiling. In 1498, Michelangelo accepted the commission for the *Pietà* for St Peter's, ordered by a French cardinal. Here Michelangelo initiated the practice he adhered to for the rest of his life, going himself to the quarries at Carrara to choose the marble. This group – the first to be carved with such delicacy and refinement – remains the most popular of Michelangelo's early work, and is certainly the most finished. It is the only statue Michelangelo signed (the signature is located on the strap that crosses the Virgin's breast).

SYMBOL OF HUMANITY

Michelangelo returned to Florence in 1501, where he began to work on his gigantic masterpiece *David*, which was originally intended for the buttress of the cathedral. It was made from a spoiled marble block that had been left in the open since 1460, when it had been abandoned by Agostino di Duccio. The block determined the size of the finished statue, which is 14 ft (4.3 m) high. Upon its completion in 1504, the Florentines decided that *David* deserved to be put in a more important position than the cathedral buttress and so they placed it next to the principal entrance to the Palazzo Vecchio where, in full public view, it became a symbol for the Florentine Republic itself.

known, and that only from a copy. The original cartoon became a kind of template for the next generation of artists, who finally destroyed it with over-tracing.

PAPAL MASTERMIND GROUP

Michelangelo was next called to Rome by Pope Julius II (whose pontificate had begun two years earlier). Julius, Michelangelo, Raphael and Bramante together created the High Renaissance in Rome, much as Donatello, Brunelleschi, Alberti and Masaccio had jointly launched perspective years before. Bramante was summoned from Milan to begin work on St Peter's. Michelangelo was called from Florence to work on Julius's tomb (this commission, which started with such expectation, dragged on for 40 years and was never resolved). After a brief interval when Michelangelo fled to Florence after arguments with Pope Julius over the tomb, he was recalled by the Pope to fresco the Sistine Chapel vault. This Michelangelo began in 1508.

COMMITMENT

The complicated narrative of the ceiling painting, which describes episodes of the Creation, was probably decided upon by the Papal council. The eastern half of the ceiling was completed in 1510 and the western half two years later. In all, 300 figures were executed. The sheer physical exertion of this task was monumental. For years, Michelangelo had to paint virtually doubled over and upside down. His physical resilience must have been enormous to accomplish the work, which he describes as bodily torment in his poems of the time:

> *I've got myself a goitre from the strain*
> *As water gives the cats in Lombardy.*
> *Or maybe it's in some other country.*
> *My stomach's pushed by force beneath my*
>   *chin,*
> *My beard towards heaven, and my brain,*
> *I feel, is shoved upon my nape,*
> *And my breast is like a harpy*
> *And the brush, ever over my face,*
> *Makes a rich pavement for its droppings.'*

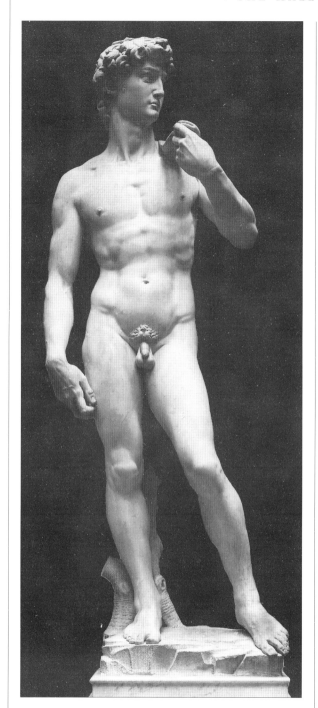

Michelangelo's David *drew admiration and acclaim from the citizens of Florence.*

PUPILS VIE WITH MASTER

After this success, Michelangelo was commissioned by the Republic to paint the *Battle of Cascina*, to complement Leonardo's *Battle of Anghiari*, on which Leonardo had been working for a year. In the event, nothing but the cartoon was completed, of which only the centre is

Michelangelo considered sculpture 'the supreme art' and himself no painter. Despite this, on completion the vault of the Sistine Chapel was immediately recognized as a supreme work of art. From that time on, Michelangelo was regarded as the greatest living artist, although he was then only 37.

LAST JUDGEMENT

From 1533 Michelangelo was in Rome, where he received the commission for *The Last Judgement* from Pope Clement VII (Medici), who died in 1534 and was succeeded by a Farnese Pope Paul III. *The Last Judgement* fresco was completed in 1541. Michelangelo destroyed two lunettes of his Sistine ceiling for the sake of the composition, which is a terrible evocation of retribution. Michelangelo has represented a unified scene of whirling bodies. Generally, the figures are unclothed, rising from their grave and gathering round the central Christ before sinking down towards Hell. The nudity was shocking to the counter-reformation and Michelangelo's pupil, Daniele da Volterra, later had to paint drapery over the genitals. In *The Last Judgement*, Christ is seen as the awesome judge of mankind, and among the Apostles, Bartholomew, who had been flayed alive, sits holding his tattered flesh. The face is a self-portrait of Michelangelo, revealing, as do his poems, the artist's sense of guilt and inadequacy.

STRIVING UNTIL THE END

While he was in Rome, he also became chief architect of St Peter's (amazingly starting work on it when he was 71), and designed the magnificent dome which still dominates the city. Michelangelo was rarely satisfied with his work, and frequently destroyed it, considering it not the best that he could achieve. He did not give up, however, and spent his final years in an accelerating creative burst, continuing to integrate sculpture, painting and architecture, into a unified whole. He even adopted as his personal emblem three interwoven circles, to show the interdependence of these arts.

Only a few days before his death in 1564 – the year that Shakespeare and Galileo were born – Michelangelo began to work again on a *Pietà* which he had begun 10 years earlier and sounds like he was enjoying it. In his last confession, he said, '*I regret . . . that I die as I am beginning to understand the alphabet of my profession.*'

For many, Michelangelo has become the archetype of the genius: a dedicated, passionate and single-minded visionary.

FERDINAND MAGELLAN 1480-1521

What more superb icon could there be for the redrawing of the cosmos than the first man to circumnavigate the globe? Magellan was born near Villa Real, Portugal, in 1480. He served in the East Indies and was lamed for life in action in Morocco. He then offered his services to Spain and laid before the Emperor Charles V the plan for reaching the Moluccas, the trade and spice islands, by sailing west and not east – as had been customary.

The Emperor, a man of some vision himself, agreed and Magellan duly sailed from the port of Seville on 10 August 1519, with five ships. He coasted Patagonia, off the very southernmost tip of South America, and threaded the straits, which now bear his name, between 21 October and 28 November 1520. At all times he had to exercise utmost caution in not infringing Portuguese colonial territory, for the Portuguese would have regarded him as a traitor for selling his services to the rival Spanish.

Having rounded Cape Horn, Magellan then reached the ocean, which he named the Pacific. Tragically, he was killed in the Philippine Islands, but his flagship, *The Victoria*, was brought safely to Spain on 6 September 1522. The voyage had lasted a full three years – and completed the first circumnavigation of the earth.

FAITH

Magellan's career shows enormous physical courage, tremendous vision and determination to carry out a vast project. Navigators before him had sailed east from both Spain and Portugal (the primary nautical powers at that time) to India. They had sailed west to America, but no one had ever dared to sail west in order to reach east and then return home by continuing along that same circular route. He had perfect faith that the world was round, a view by no means universally accepted at that time, and he possessed equally perfect faith that he would be successful.

MASTERMIND GROUP

Magellan built on the achievements of others, including Gomez in 1469-75, Bartholomeu Diaz in 1487-8 and Vasco da Gama in 1497. These were all Portuguese navigators who had sailed eastwards. Magellan also advanced on the achievements of the Spaniards, and those in the employment of Spain, who had travelled westwards. These included Christopher Columbus in 1492, Amerigo Vespucci in 1499 and Cortés, who had conquered Mexico in 1519. What an illustrious group of mastermind role models!

A detail from Michelangelo's magnificent fresco on the Sistine Chapel ceiling.

MEMORY AND INFORMATION

Ferdinand Magellan's circumnavigation of the world produced not just a new passage to the Indies and their wealth and spices, but also a wealth of new information. Wonderful accounts of the voyage were brought back by all the survivors, but principally by the Italian chronicler, Antonio Pigafetta, who had specifically requested to join the venture in order to record its exploits for posterity. Of course, the new European invention by Gutenberg of printing made it possible for such information to be rapidly disseminated throughout the civilized world – and it was!

FLIGHTS OF FANCY

Throughout the voyage, Magellan and his crews encountered many wonders and seeming miracles – cannibals, people who were apparently giants, huge sharks, flying fish, naked natives, great riches, spices – all these things baffled and amazed listeners on the survivors' return. They also overcame the most frightening difficulties – mutinies, loss of stores, near starvation, appalling weather and vast distances. It was a matchless feat of endurance – 98 days and 13,000 miles just to cross the Pacific, an ocean the true size of which had never been envisaged. At one point the crews were reduced to eating penguins, and the weather was a torment – months of storms, blinding rain and squalls so violent that the long masts of the ships dipped into the ocean. Time and again the vessels were on the verge of capsizing while the crews frantically stood armed with axes to chop down the masts. All sails were struck and the fleet was at the mercy of the gales under bare poles. Most of the crews despaired of ever surviving.

PERSISTENCE AND COMMITMENT

What lessons can we learn from Magellan? Primarily, one of enormous persistence – what greater exploratory persistence can there be, than, for the very first time, to circumnavigate the globe itself? Magellan set sail in old leaky ships – not the best galleons of the time, but ones that were considered expendable for such a dangerous voyage. Magellan went as far as it was humanly possible to go at that time. He believed in himself and he set forth in full confidence that he could achieve his goal. It is one of the sad ironies of history that, although the voyage itself

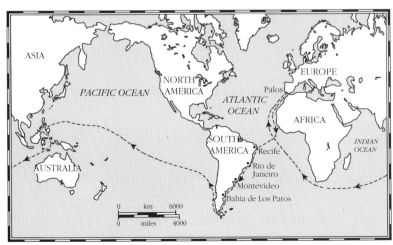

ABOVE *Although he did not live to make it home, Magellan is credited with being the first man to circumnavigate the world. He also discovered and gave his name to the narrow passage which links the Atlantic and Pacific Oceans (the Strait of Magellan).*

LEFT *This map shows the route of Magellan's epic three-year west-east voyage around the world.*

was a huge success, and the circumnavigation completed, Magellan himself did not live to see the final triumph.

MAGELLAN OR THE MOON?

The first circumnavigation of the globe might be compared with the first space flight to the moon in 1969. However, there are many differences, and these, strangely, are in favour of the circumnavigation. For a start, Magellan was furnished with third-rate vessels. His backers were most reluctant to risk top-quality ships on such an enterprise. Secondly, he was setting forth without communications – there was no way to stay in touch with headquarters in Spain while he was under way. So they had no idea what he was doing at any given moment and he could not ask for help or reinforcements if he needed them. Thirdly, he set out to cross an ocean, without knowing its extent or, indeed, whether it was infinite! It was a leap in the dark and Magellan had only his faith and rudimentary calculations as to how great the ocean would turn out to be.

Compare this with the voyage to the moon in 1969: the best quality materials and the greatest resources the planet had available were invested in the lunar enterprise. There was constant contact with earth, the distances were known in advance. There were even instantaneous pictures from the moon landing. Although the moon shot was, in many ways, technically far more difficult, there was far less an element of 'plunging into the unknown'. It was more of a scientific exercise and a brilliant technological feat, and it lacks that spark of the unpredictable, which characterized Ferdinand Magellan's exploit.

RAPHAEL 1483-1520

Raphael was an artist fascinated by genius and drawn inexorably to it in others. He revered Leonardo and Michelangelo, and his own most celebrated picture, *The School of Athens*, pays homage to the great minds of antiquity – Plato, Aristotle, Socrates, Pythagoras, Euclid and Ptolemy – as well as the Moslem thinker Averroës and the seven philosophical arts, namely: geometry, grammar, rhetoric, dialectic, music, arithmetic and astronomy.

CRADLE OF EDUCATION

Raphael Santi was born in Urbino and probably lived there until adolescence. Urbino, at that time, was the most civilized court in Italy. Frederico Montefeltre (1422-82) was made duke of Urbino in 1474; he was a soldier, ruling over his poor mountainous land and supporting it by his activities as a mercenary, or *Condottiere*. But he was also a cultivated scholar who built an enchanting palace high upon a crag. There, other princes sent their sons to be educated, both in the art of warfare and in civilized behaviour.

ACQUIRING SUBJECT KNOWLEDGE

Raphael is next heard of in the studio of Perugino, an Umbrian painter with an extremely busy workshop. From Perugino, the young Raphael took the delicate blonde colour, the low eye level and the tranquil landscape that Perugino repeats on innumerable occasions in the sweetly pious altarpieces that he created and that were so much in demand. It was in Perugino's workshop that Raphael learned how to control his assistants. This was to prove an invaluable lesson during his heavy production schedule in Rome.

IN THE FOOTSTEPS OF GENIUS

Probably some time in 1505, Raphael moved to Florence, where he found a ready market. Appetites for pictures had been stimulated by Leonardo and Michelangelo, whose works were becoming increasingly unavailable. So Raphael suddenly became very busy. In three years he painted, in addition to major works, 17 Madonnas and Holy Families for Florentine patrons. These works still survive, and are all harmonious and serene. A great number of beautiful drawings also remain, which show Raphael working with seemingly unstressed ease to create the ideas for the finished panel pictures.

In 1508, Raphael arrived in Rome while Michelangelo was working on the first part of the Sistine ceiling. Pope Julius II immediately engaged Raphael to work on the stanze (rooms) in the Vatican. The first to be painted was the Stanze della Segnatura (the room in which the Pope signed the most important documents). It was here that Raphael created, between 1509 and 1511, the first example of High Renaissance classicism: *The Disputation (Disputà) over the Sacrament of Christ's Blood*.

SPATIAL INTELLIGENCE

In this Raphael extends the dome-shaped composition of his *Marriage of the Virgin* into an airy space composed of clouds and figures. The painting describes the complete Doctrine of the Eucharist: the *Disputà* is not an argument, it represents a developing divine debate, and as such is an allegory of theological intelligence.

Facing the *Disputà* is *The School of Athens*, now universally recognized, with its receding arches, as the perfect perspectival culmination of High Renaissance space and harmony. It is made up of a group of philosophers from classical antiquity – all, like the theologians in the *Disputà*, seen in furious debate. In the centre, engaged in absorbed conversation, walk Plato and Aristotle, the former pointing to heaven and the latter indicating the earth in an oratorical gesture (the detail of this is shown on page 81).

In the foreground are grouped the famous philosophers from antiquity, and off to the side sits a single figure in the left foreground, wearing the clothes of a 16th-century stone cutter. This is usually accepted to be a portrait of Michelangelo. It was generally believed that, before painting *The School of Athens*, Raphael was permitted by Bramante (the architect for St Peter's in Rome) to see the first half of Michelangelo's Sistine Chapel ceiling, when the scaffolding was being erected in the western half. Certainly there is new vigour in Raphael's figures. He has consciously placed his own likeness behind the allegorical figure of 'geometry', vital to artists for rendering perspective accurately.

The new interest in monumentality causes the classic poise to give way to an almost baroque movement and a greater emphasis on drama in the next series of Vatican rooms: the Stanza d'Eliodoro (1511-14). The subject matter of the rooms generally refers to incidents in the history of the Church which had some relevance to circumstances in Raphael's time.

INFLUENCING REMBRANDT

In 1513, Julius II died and was succeeded by Leo X, who continued to support Raphael and who appears in the final dramatic fresco in the Stanza, the Expulsion of Attila the Hun by the fifth-century Pope Leo III. Again, this may refer to a near contemporary event, when Louis XII of France almost took the city in the summer of 1511. For the old Pope, Julius, Raphael painted a final picture, the *Sistine Madonna*, the first picture he painted on canvas. It has always been assumed that it was intended as a funeral image. It is certainly a magnificent portrait of the Pope and one of Raphael's supreme creations. Rembrandt later tried to buy Raphaels in Amsterdam, never forgot his compositions, and often did variants upon them for his own work.

ENERGY AND PRODUCTIVITY

Upon Bramante's death in 1514, Raphael inherited the post of papal architect, whose task was to continue the construction of St Peter's. He was now showered with commissions for Madonnas, portraits, frescoes and mosaics, as well as a commission for a third Stanza, the Stanza dell 'Incendio, plus the commission to decorate the loggie built by Bramante in the Vatican. He was also responsible for directing the building of a palace for Cardinal Guilio Medici and an enchanting little palace for the rich banker Agostino Chigi, which was later called the Farnesina (because it was bought by the Farnese family). This building is a perfect evocation of ancient Rome. Next he was appointed the first superintendent of antiquities, and given full power over all excavations in the papal dominions. One of his most important projects was a map of ancient Rome, with all of its major monuments carefully traced and identified, thus laying the foundations for modern archaeology.

COMPETING WITH MICHELANGELO

In 1515-16, Raphael was asked to produce 10 full-scale colour cartoons for tapestries to be woven in Flanders for the Sistine Chapel. They would complete the iconographic cycle, begun under the Quattrocento artist who had depicted in the ceiling the Lives of Christ and Moses, and Michelangelo who had extended the cycle to include the Ancestors of Christ, the prophets, the sibyls who had foretold the coming of Christ, as well as scenes from Genesis. Raphael's contribution brought it all to a triumphant climax, with the Acts of the Apostles in the tapestries helping to create a brilliant overall theme. This stretched from the infinite in the ceiling, down to the zone of men who, although born mortal, had become sacred through their behaviour. Raphael must have been aware that he and his workshop were now competing intellectually with Michelangelo, the most magnificent of the Renaissance painters. Together, they produced a figural composition that covered an area of 1200 sq ft (111 m²), all in the language and grand scale of the High Renaissance. The magnificent architecture, and the densely packed narrative, caused this work to become the most influential of Raphael's career. Constantly copied in the centuries to come (engravings were made from it almost immediately), it became the single work of art which did more to spread Renaissance ideas to the rest of Europe than any other.

COMBINING CHRISTIANITY WITH ANTIQUITY

Raphael died, during a bout of plague in Rome, after a short illness on Good Friday 1520. He was only 37, and with him passed the briefly-held conviction that the noblest ideas of classical antiquity and the highest aspirations of Christianity could coexist in harmony.

Raphael brilliantly foreshortened the pointed hand in his Self-portrait with a Friend.

TITIAN 1488-1576

The troubles that beset the rest of Italy in the 16th century did not reach Venice. So the equilibrium associated with the High Renaissance lingered on in the republic of St Mark (sometimes called the Serenissima). The city's position in the middle of a lagoon protected Venice from her enemies – indeed, Venice was never sacked, nor invaded. Consequently, very few works by Titian were inspired by anger, fear or war. This is not surprising, however, as great genius and great art tend to be generated by an urge to discover and a compelling individual vision.

MASTERMIND CO-OPERATION

Until his death Giovanni Bellini (c.1430-1516) dominated Venetian art. He had two brilliant students: Giorgione (c.1478-1511), who died young, and Titian, who lived to a great age.

Titziano Vecellio (Titian) was born in Cadore, a village in the mountains above Venice. He became a successful professional, achieving all his objectives and accumulating great wealth. He also raised the status of the artist in the commerce-minded Venetian republic from that of a tradesman to a powerful member of the Venetian elite. He organized a hugely successful workshop and made conscious use of publicity, becoming a partner with Pietro Aretino (1492-1557), poet and writer, whom he twice painted and who acted as his sales agent.

In his personal and professional life, he lived according to the highest virtues. He married a young girl from his birthplace in 1525, who bore him two sons named Orazio and Pomponio. After his wife's death in 1530, it is reported that Titian was most distressed – he never remarried, so devoted was he to her.

EARLY SUCCESS

When Bellini died, Titian succeeded him as official painter to the Venetian Republic. His most important early work is the *Assumption of the Virgin*, a huge altarpiece over 20 ft (6 m) high, painted in 1516-18 for the Frari church in Venice. The Frari Virgin was a totally original concept which changed for ever altarpieces in Venice. The Madonna, soaring into heaven, creates a scene of cosmic jubilation, leaving the earth filled with sturdy, gesticulating disciples. Titian restricted himself to a few dominant, dramatic hues and the result is a composition of grand simplicity and strong tonal contrasts. The work was an immediate success and confirmed Titian's reputation. He next worked on his first commission outside Venice: three dazzling pictures for Alfonzo d'Este, Duke of Ferrara. These are now scattered to different continents, but they must have created a remarkable synergy when placed together. They were intended for the duke's private study, to complete a cycle of pictures with subjects taken from classical antiquity.

FREEDOM OF EXPRESSION

The first painted was the *Festival of Venus*, the second the *Bacchanal of the Andrians* and the third *Bacchus and Ariadne*. In all these paintings, Titian reaches a new freedom of figural and colouristic brilliance. They are filled with a joyful sensuality and display a new freedom of brushstroke, unlike anything seen before. Contemporaries tell how he used to build up his pictures in oil over a reddish ground to communicate warmth to all of the colours, often leaving them for months before reapplying glazes – a method he continued to use throughout his life – and frequently painting with his fingers instead of a brush.

SPATIAL INTELLIGENCE

In his more public religious work, Titian developed a monumental composition device. He used his favourite diagonal/triangular method to break from the more symmetrical Renaissance composition, the traditional 'Sacra Conversazione' type first elaborated by Donatello. This new style first appeared in the Pesaro altarpiece, also destined for the church of the Frari, which was unveiled in 1526 to general admiration! The diagonal emphasis first influenced Veronese, and then the Baroque in the next century.

Titian's portraiture in the 1520s entered a phase of dignity and reserve and introduced to the genre the idea of the poetic young man. A good example is the *Man with the Glove* (1523). The simple triangular relationship of hands and face function within a colour scheme that is restricted to black, white and flesh tones, and it all adds to the gentle romantic melancholy of the image. It was originally owned by Frederico II Gonzaga, the son of Isabella d'Este and one of the greatest art collectors of the Renaissance. In about 1525 Titian painted the duke's portrait, which was seen by the Holy Roman Emperor, Charles V, when he visited Mantua in 1530. He agreed to sit for Titian and in 1533 sat again for Titian in Bologna. The resulting painting, *Charles V with a Hound*, was a new departure for Titian – the full-length portrait. The format was a German invention that had been used by Cranach (1472-1553) as early as 1514, but it was new to Italy. The Emperor was pleased with the result and Titian was consequently knighted and appointed Court Painter in recognition of this.

In 1547, Titian was summoned to Augsburg (he had to cross the Alps in winter at the age of 60), where he stayed for a year and painted two more portraits. The most influential depicted the Emperor on horseback, which commemorated his victory at the Battle of Mühlberg. It became the exemplar for all subsequent royal equestrian portraits. For Titian, it meant the consolidation of a long and fruitful association with Charles V and, later, his son Philip II (whose subtle full-length portrait he painted on his second trip to Augsburg in 1551).

BODY INTELLIGENCE

It is for the Pope's nephew, Cardinal Alessandro Farnese, that Titian now painted a new and staggering triple masterpiece, the first of three versions of Danae, the mortal who was visited by Zeus, the King of Gods, in the form of a shower of gold. This one was a gift to the cardinal, in gratitude for bringing Titian to Rome. In the variant that Titian later painted for Philip II, he removed the cupid from the right of the picture, replacing her with a greedy servant who holds out her apron to try to catch some of the coins. Titian used the contrast of avarice, as expressed by the old woman, to the open rapture and acceptance of Danae, lying waiting for love. In 1553 Titian sent to Philip his *Venus and Adonis*, explaining the pose in an accompanying letter: 'Since I had already painted a Venus for you, shown reclining and seen from the front, I had decided to send you a view of her from behind, to set opposite the other one in your private chamber, and so make a fine scene.' In 1556, Charles V abdicated in favour of his son Philip, who moved the court to Spain. Titian continued to work for him, producing a number of sacred pictures, as well as some of his greatest mythological subjects, mainly of nudes that are thinly disguised as goddesses.

VERSATILITY AND STYLE

Titian returned to his native Venice in 1551, where for the 25 years until his death his productivity accelerated in quantity and creativity, breaking new boundaries and setting standards for all portraitists who were to follow.

In the 1560s, Titian split his output into two groups, giving his workshop orders to replicate his most popular pictures, which were continually being sought by collectors; he himself continued to work on new themes that interested him, producing work that was not always intended for sale. He returned often to Cadore to look after his business interests, which included selling timber from the Dolomites to the Venice Military Arsenal.

In his late work Titian created even thicker, denser handling of oil paint, in which the colours darken and the subject matter shows an increasing tendency to violence. One gets the impression that Titian had by this time come to believe that evil will dominate good.

Titian kept up his contacts with the court of Spain, while frequently complaining of delays over payment (he was the most famous and expensive painter in Europe). His late self-portrait shows a melancholy old man, wearing the gold chain that was a gift from Charles V. The light coming from the left shines on the forehead. He wears a black cap and a simple heavy black coat. The portrait is chest length, and we see only the gnarled right hand, clenched on the brush. Now in his 80s, Titian's private life had been darkened by his fears for Venice, engaged in ceaseless wars with the Turks. There had also been a fire in the Palazzo Ducale which had destroyed many of his pictures.

Nevertheless, Titian's technique broadened even further. He was now painting without any evidence of first drawing the subject. Titian had been influenced by Greek and Roman excavations and by his giant contemporaries, Leonardo da Vinci, Raphael and Michelangelo. Yet he forged his own individual style and is thought of as the Founder of Modern Art by many. In the firmament of the Renaissance universe, the art theorist Giovanni Lomazzo in 1990 declared Titian 'the sun amidst small stars, not only among the Italians but all the painters of the world'.

SULEYMAN THE MAGNIFICENT
1494-1566

Suleyman, the greatest of the Turkish Sultans, was a contemporary of Henry VIII, Elizabeth I, Czar Ivan the Terrible of Russia and the Holy Roman Emperor, Charles V. The son of Sultan Selim I, he came to the sultanate in 1520. He added to his father's dominions by conquering Belgrade, Budapest, Rhodes, Baghdad, Aden and Algiers. He also fought a war with Venice and his fleets dominated the Mediterranean.

The walls of the old city of Jerusalem, which still survive, were built during his reign; at that time, the Holy Land was firmly in Moslem Turkish hands. Amazingly active until his 70th year,

Perseus and Andromeda (1554-56) is one of many paintings which Titian based on a mythological theme.

Suleyman died during the siege of the city of Szigeth, or Szigetvar, in his war against Austria.

THE RULER AND MAN

Suleyman was a great patron of the arts. He wrote poetry and had the intelligence to employ Sinan (see page 134) to build such architectural masterpieces as the mosques dedicated to himself and to members of his family in Constantinople, or Istanbul as it had then become.

Suleyman pushed the realm of the Ottoman Turks to its greatest extent, reformed the laws of his empire and left Istanbul in a state more beautiful than it had been for many centuries. The city became a monument, both to aesthetics and to the Moslem religion, of which Suleyman saw himself as the supreme representative on earth. In portraits, he is often portrayed in an exaggeratedly large turban, but in the Ottoman Empire, the size of a turban denoted its wearer's rank, and its colour, his religion: white for Moslems, yellow for Jews and blue for Christians.

In his personal life, Suleyman was devoted to his chief consort, known to the world as Roxelana, who had been chosen as if by fate to match his own talents. The Ottomans called her 'Hurrem' (The Smiling One). She was captured in a raid on Russia and sold as a slave in Istanbul, where Suleyman spotted her and immediately fell in love. She herself was a paragon of the intellect, using her new-found wealth and status to endow numerous mosques.

CONQUEST AND TOLERANCE

It is extraordinary, when one considers that the Christian Byzantine empire – the last relic of the Eastern Roman empire – had only collapsed to the Ottoman Turks in 1453, that a mere 70 years later Suleyman had established perhaps the most stable and powerful realm on earth at that time. During his reign, the Turkish Moslem armies even reached the gates of Vienna – although they did not actually conquer that city. Suleyman himself was the grandson of Mehmed the Conqueror (Fatih), the Sultan who had taken Constantinople for the Turks in 1453, and he planned to continue that tradition of conquest against Christendom. His aim was not so much to convert Christian Kingdoms to Islam, but to insist that they regarded him as their suzerain.

Constantinople itself had been founded in the year AD 324 by the Roman Emperor Constantine the Great. The city fell to the Ottomans in 1453, and by the time of Suleyman it had a population totalling half a million inhabitants. Of these, 60 per cent were Moslems and the rest Jews or Greek Orthodox Christian. Suleyman presided in his capital over a multi-racial, multi-ethnic, multi-religious community, but he experienced no serious difficulties. He exhibited a wise degree of tolerance of personal religious conviction. His mosque-building programme was not just a religious gesture. The mosques were also centres of education, as well as being colleges, hospitals, shops, public kitchens and gardens, thus catering for the social and physical health of the inhabitants of the capital.

EVERYTHING CONNECTS

Suleyman's systems of laws earned him the Turkish name 'Kanuni', which means 'The Law Giver'. The Kanun were additional rules and regulations required beyond the teachings of the Koran to regularize life in Moslem territories. As Sultan, Suleyman personally drew up new civil and criminal codes that covered not just land and taxes, but also military rights and privileges, prices, wages, health regulations and compensation for injuries. The implementation of this system meant that, for the very first time, a uniform system of justice operated throughout the Turkish Empire.

Suleyman will be remembered as a military commander, a codifier of the law, and a faithful husband – at a time when the pleasures of the harem were more common – a patron of the arts, an organizer and administrator, all on a grand and, indeed, imperial scale. His empire spanned three continents – Africa, Europe and Asia – and artistic monuments of great splendour commemorated the superb achievements of his reign. His versatility was immense and, like Alexander the Great and Elizabeth I, once he was given the chance to rule he seized it with both hands.

INNOVATION

Suleyman also distinguished himself as a military commander. He made brilliant new use of the Janissaries – the term is a Westernization of the Turkish Yeni Ceri (New Force) – and he honed his artillery to perfection. The Janissaries were the Sultan's praetorian guard. All promotions within this elite force were according to merit, a common feature also with Alexander, Caesar, Napoleon, Nelson and Wellington. Amazingly, the troops that composed the Janissaries were recruited as slaves from young Christian boys in subject Balkan states. This was known as the Devshirme (Gathering). These boys (Sinan was one) were taken as slaves to Istanbul, converted to Islam and then given a fierce military training. They became the first standing army in Europe and were superbly well-provisioned. The psychological justification was that, by taking slaves at an early age, who were free from family and local allegiances, they would show loyalty to the Sultan and to the Sultan alone.

SUBJECT KNOWLEDGE

The campaign in Hungary in 1526, where Suleyman personally commanded the Ottoman army, shows just how devastating the Janissaries, combined with the imaginative use of artillery, could be. Suleyman's objective was to take Budapest. At the Battle of Mohacs, on the Hungarian plains, Suleyman revealed his military genius. It was said by the Turks that he led his armies from Istanbul 12 times, and 12 times was victorious. The Battle of Mohacs lasted the incredibly short time of only two hours. At first, the Hungarian army charged and shattered the Turkish front line. The Hungarians plunged on, but, as they did so, Suleyman's Turks opened up their ranks to reveal 300 cannon and thousands of musketeers, invisible until that decisive moment. The musketeers and the artillery opened fire at point-blank range, the Hungarians were annihilated and their King Louis drowned while trying to escape from the rout. The victory was complete. (Compare Hannibal's victory at Cannae, on which Mohacs was a variation.)

Suleyman was termed by his contemporaries as Sultan of Sultans, King of Kings, Distributor of Crowns to the Princes of the World and the Shadow of God on Earth. He fully lived up to that grandiloquent description.

SINAN 1491-1588

ENERGY AND PRODUCTIVITY

Sinan was the imperial architect and the prime mover in the architectural glorification of Istanbul, the capital of the Ottoman Empire, which had been ordained by Suleyman the Magnificent. Dominating the city was Suleyman's great masterpiece – the Suleymaniye Mosque. This was the heart of a great complex of hospitals, schools, medical and theological colleges, public soup kitchens, wash places and gardens that catered for the body as well as the soul.

Originally, Sinan was a Christian, but he was enslaved, converted to Islam and trained to fight with the Sultan's forces, which he joined in 1521. On military campaigns in Hungary, Austria and Iraq, he learned how to build bridges and fortifications. In 1538, at the age of 47, he was given charge of Suleyman's imperial building programme. The enormous scale of this task demanded all the discipline and qualities of flexibility he had learned from his military campaigns. For over 50 years as imperial architect he designed and oversaw the construction of 500 new buildings – showing energy, dedication and innovation within the traditional 'mosque' format. In his soaring architecture, he expressed the imperial grandeur and aspirations of Istanbul and the Ottoman Empire.

COMBINING DISPARATE ELEMENTS

The secret of Sinan's brilliant success was his combining of the Moslem tradition of architecture with that of the Christian Byzantine tradition. Indeed, there is a quite striking outward similarity between Greek Orthodox churches and Turkish minarets of this time. The larger mosques were showered with cascades of domes of different sizes, vaulting arches and as many as six slender minarets towering up to 330 ft (70m) into the sky.

VIE

He worked unceasingly until his death in 1588 at the age of 97. In his greatest architectural designs

Suleyman the Magnificent, the greatest ruler of the Ottoman Empire, is shown wearing an oversize turban which indicates his status.

he adapted existing Byzantine and Islamic styles, but ultimately produced something altogether new. When Sultan Mehmed the Conqueror (Fatih) took Constantinople in 1453, one of his first acts was to convert the Emperor Justinian's Great Orthodox Christian Cathedral of Hagia Sophia into an Islamic mosque. This became the first imperial mosque in Constantinople. So impressed was the Sultan with Hagia Sophia that it formed the initial design basis for all subsequent mosques in Istanbul.

The interior hallmark of a Sinan mosque was a centralized organization of absolute space, unhindered by pillars or columns and covered by a soaring dome. To the Christian eye, tutored in perspective, the ability to enter the place of worship from any direction implied a lack of organization, but to Islamic perception this was a symbol that the kingdom of heaven could be entered at any point.

Sinan saw the size and architectural brilliance of the Christian Hagia Sophia cathedral as his lifelong challenge. His ambition was to equal its beauty and surpass its dimensions. He finally achieved his aim in his 80s with the Selimiye Mosque at Edirne. As he wrote in his memoirs: *'Christians say that they have defeated the Muslims because no dome has been built in the Islamic world which can rival the dome of Hagia Sophia. I determined to erect such a Mosque!'*

VERSATILITY AND HUMILITY

Sinan was an architect of genius in a dynamic new empire that expanded into Africa, Asia and Europe. He could be seen as a true man of the Renaissance, and as a true redrawer of the cosmos, working at the very same time as Michelangelo was putting the finishing touches to St Peter's in Rome. Sinan's output included mosques, palaces, mausoleums, tombs, hospitals, schools, caravanserai, aqueducts and baths. As he himself said: 'With time, each edifice became, with the help of Allah and thanks to the generosity and benevolence of the state, the very image of the world in lands ruled by the Ottoman dynasty.'

PERSISTENCE AND DURABILITY

As a sign of the enormous energy displayed by Sinan, his architecture does not just appear in Istanbul, but adorns almost all the provinces of the Ottoman Empire – Greece, Bulgaria, Hungary as well as the cities of Mecca, Medina, Jerusalem, Damascus, Basra and Baghdad. Most of his structures are still standing and in good repair after more than three centuries of constant use – which proves the excellent design, materials and quality that he invested in them. Sinan was a supremely skilful architect.

FOCUS

Considering that St Peter's Cathedral in Rome took 160 years from Bramante to Bernini to complete, and that Sir Christopher Wren worked for 40 years on St Paul's Cathedral in London, then the completion of the Istanbul Suleymaniye mosque in just seven years demonstrates both the wealth of the Ottoman Empire and the speed and efficiency with which Sinan was able to perform his duty.

MASTERMIND GROUP

The Ottoman Empire had, in fact, invited Michelangelo and Leonardo da Vinci to Istanbul to construct a bridge over the Bosphorus (the Golden Horn), but both declined. In Sinan, the Ottoman Empire finally found its own Leonardo da Vinci and Michelangelo.

ELIZABETH I 1533-1603

WOMAN RULING A MAN'S WORLD

The first Queen Elizabeth of England shines by the fact that she not only entered and survived the predominantly masculine political world of the 16th century, but also ultimately ruled and governed it. Elizabeth I presided over the most remarkable flourishing of English culture in the military, scientific and artistic spheres. She had the intelligence to surround herself with the greatest brains of the day, transformed herself into an icon and symbol of English success, and her masterstroke was that, by tremendous self-control, she avoided romantic entanglements. Marrying a man who might overshadow her on the throne was the fate that befell Mary, Queen of Scots, Elizabeth's cousin. If Elizabeth's goal was to maintain power, and it was, then childbirth was also probably the single most serious health hazard of the age. By this enormous self-restraint she succeeded in staying on the English throne from 1558 to 1603.

She left England in a far better state than it had been for centuries beforehand, united, calm, at peace, prosperous and with the immense scientific and literary tradition bequeathed by Francis Bacon, William Shakespeare, Marlowe, Spenser and many others. She also left an England proud of its achievement at having overcome the threat from Spain, embodied by the successful victory over the Spanish Armada of 1588.

THE VIRGIN QUEEN

Elizabeth planned to remain an inspiration to the nation as a whole, so a further ingenious element in her decision to remain a virgin was that she avoided irrevocable favouritism to any one party or group of interests. She was the daughter of the first Protestant king, Henry VIII, and the people needed a new symbol to revere. This role had been filled under Catholicism by the Virgin Mary but the new Queen, deliberately and as a matter of policy, became seen as the embodiment of English pride and national aspirations. She had her pictorial image distributed as widely as possible to impact on the consciousness of her subjects. The majesty and glory of her person, combined with the wisdom and foresight of her government and her own inspired direction, were officially extolled in paintings, statues, music, literature, poetry and song. An example of this was that during the 1590s, the Queen's Privy Council ordered any picture depicting her in old age to be destroyed!

Queen Elizabeth rose to become the foremost Protestant ruler of Europe, but en route she had to negotiate a minefield in her personal and political life. Her mother, Anne Boleyn, had been executed. Before Elizabeth came to the throne, her elder brother, Edward VI, and her elder sister, Mary I, both succeeded to power and both had died. It was extremely fortunate for Elizabeth that she reached the crown at all in view of her mother's disgrace and her own initial distance from the succession. Indeed, Elizabeth was twice declared 'illegitimate', first by her father and then by her sister, which, if upheld, would have disqualified her from the throne.

Not all those given the opportunity to become a monarch are equal to the task. Elizabeth was, and more so. Once Queen, she had to surmount perpetual Roman Catholic plots and, above all, excommunication by the Pope in Rome. Catholics were incessantly in conflict with Protestants throughout the 16th century. Protestant Reformation, Catholic counter-reformation, and religious wars were the order of the day. The Pope's edict was backed by the military force of the fanatical Catholic King Philip of Spain and his 1588 Armada, but Elizabeth faced up to these threats and emerged triumphant.

What made Elizabeth's early life even more difficult to negotiate was that, though her father, Henry VIII, and her elder brother, Edward VI, were Protestant, her elder sister Mary, who directly preceded her on the English throne, was a devout Catholic – one who made a habit of burning at the stake those Protestants who would not recant. Elizabeth had to protect herself from snares that lay about her in her early life – such as the dangers of being accused of treason and heresy. There was no rule in the 16th century that potential heirs to thrones could not be executed – they often were.

THE ADVANCEMENT OF LEARNING

Elizabeth, as she had carefully planned, indeed proved an inspiration to her country, and the

Nicholas Hilliard (1547-1619) was an outstanding miniaturist who painted a number of portraits of Elizabeth I. He originally trained as a jeweller, and in recognition of his talent the Queen appointed him Court Miniaturist and Goldsmith.

expansion of England in the spheres of political and commercial greatness was accompanied by corresponding growth in the realms of the intellect. The second half of Elizabeth's reign – a period of 20 years – was more fertile in great literary names than the two whole preceding centuries. The excitement of the long religious wars, the sudden opening up of the hitherto dark places of the world by great explorers such as Raleigh and Drake, and the free spirit of individual enquiry which accompanied the growth of Protestantism, all combined to stir up and develop the minds of men and women of the day. The greatest English dramatist, William Shakespeare (born 1564), and the philosopher, Sir Francis Bacon (born 1561), were both children of Elizabeth's long struggle with Spain. Both had watched the final crisis of the Armada in their early manhood.

Edmund Spenser (*c*.1552-99) showed even more clearly the spirit of the times. His lengthy epic *The Faerie Queene* (1590) was inspired by the enthusiasm of the struggles of England and recounts the great glories of Elizabeth. When we add Christopher Marlowe, writer of *The Jew of Malta, Tamburlaine the Great, Dr Faustus* and *Edward II*, never before or since has England produced, in just a few short years, such a pantheon of giant literary names. This period could, indeed, be well compared with the Athens of the 5th century BC.

INTUITION

One of Elizabeth's supreme talents was dealing directly with men. She retained two superb advisors, Robert Cecil (Lord Burleigh) and Sir Francis Walsingham, and there was no greater instance of her personal ingenuity than her management of her fractious parliament. The parliament of 1601 was raging against so-called monopolies, grants under the Royal Seal permitting individuals to be the sole vendors and manufacturers of certain articles of trade. Sensing parliament's resolute and hostile mood, Elizabeth came in person to the House of Commons and addressed the members, at length and so cleverly that she persuaded them that she was as much opposed to monopolies as they were themselves. She won enormous support from them when she announced, of her own initiative and with all the inspiration of a genius, that all monopolies were to be withdrawn and declared illegal. Eighteen months after this magnificent scene, Elizabeth died in her 71st year.

INSPIRATION

Elizabeth was adored by her subjects and well deserved it. She had led England through 45 troublesome years, left her subjects prosperous and contented, and personally received the credit for all the progress and prosperity of her reign. The nation, in centuries to come, would cry for a renewal of the days of Good Queen Bess. Historians invariably speak of the 'Elizabethan Age' – and rightly so, when considering the evils which a less capable or ingenious sovereign (such as Charles I, half a century later, who provoked Civil War with his parliament) might have brought upon England in that time of great storm and stress.

FOCUS

What do we learn from Elizabeth? In addition to caution, prudence and patience, she must ultimately be admired for having an unshakable belief in her own self and ability. She navigated a perilous path through the pitfalls and snares of first heresy and treachery, then politics and war, guiding her nation with a single-minded determination to glory and success.

GALILEO GALILEI 1564-1642
PERCEPTION

Galileo's contribution to the history of science and culture is two-fold: first the inherent value of his observations and theories, second the circumstances of his condemnation by the Roman Catholic Inquisition in 1616 and 1633 and his reaction to it. He was born in Pisa in 1564, the year of Shakespeare's birth and Michelangelo's death. The son of a musician who conducted practical experiments into musical pitch and proportions, Galileo began his serious studies in the 1580s, and by 1589 was Professor of Mathematics at the University of Pisa. It was there, in the *campanile,* the famous leaning (bell) tower, that he conducted his historic demonstration that heavier and lighter objects both fall to the ground at the same speed. His claim was that only air resistance could make some objects, such as a feather or a parachute, fall more slowly, not the mass of the objects themselves. Accordingly, everything would fall at the same speed in a vacuum; even in air, streamlined objects would differ very little in their rate of descent. His achievement was not just to measure and experiment, which others could also do, but to perceive the true general principle of constant acceleration. His experiment shattered the long-held Aristotelian belief that heavy objects fall faster than lighter ones.

This was also when the 'Legend of the Lamp' was born. Apparently, Galileo was daydreaming in church one day, while watching the chandeliers gently sway to and fro. Like Archimedes in the bath, he had a 'Eureka!' experience, when he realized that no matter how long the range of the lamp's swing, it always required the same time to complete an oscillation. Galileo later developed this discovery into the law of the pendulum, its application to time-keeping and the development of the pendulum clock.

PERSISTENCE AND INGENUITY

Along with Galileo's insight went persistence and ingenuity. Faced with apparent contradictions between theory and practice, he did not fall back on the view of his philosophical opponents that pure mathematics and practical physics were quite different subjects; instead he struggled on to build links between them, confident that mathematical principles lay behind the appearance of all things.

In 1592 he was promoted to a better post at Padua and applied his methods more widely – especially to astronomy, moving from practice (making his own improved telescope in 1609) to theory. By 1610, when he discovered sun-spots and the moons of Jupiter, he was ready to defend publicly what he had believed privately since the 1590s: the theory of Nicolas Copernicus (1473-1543) that the planets orbited not the earth, but the sun. Galileo also turned his telescope towards the Milky Way, and was the first to recognize that it consists of millions of stars and is not just a hazy pattern. A few months before he went blind, Galileo discovered the moon's diurnal and monthly movements from side to side. He continued to pursue his interests and theories with a passion, even after his blindness.

TRUTH AND FAITH

So far, Galileo's work had been treated with great respect, and so he seems to have been taken aback by the papal instruction in 1616 that he should no longer teach Copernican views. He accepted the instruction, and powerful patrons made sure he was not further persecuted. That was until the publication of his *Dialogue Concerning the Two Chief Systems of the World, Ptolemaic and Copernican* in 1632, for which the Inquisition put him on trial for breaking the ban of 1616. Even then, though, his imprisonment was commuted to house arrest.

Galileo published his discoveries about the solar system and Jupiter in 1610.

Galileo was not, therefore, quite the martyr he is sometimes portrayed to be. He seems to have retained his faith in religion and even the Church, blaming individuals and his philosophical opponents for twisting the ecclesiastical procedures against him. Nevertheless, his condemnation has had great symbolic value for later generations. It was his defence of his views, as well as the views themselves, which led a modern scientist of such eminence as Stephen Hawking (*b.* 1942) to claim that '*Galileo, perhaps more than any other single person, was responsible for the birth of modern science*'. Galileo's genius was one of faith as well as scientific observation, faith that the truth of the evidence would ultimately prevail.

WILLIAM SHAKESPEARE 1564-1616

'What a piece of work is a man! How noble in reason! how infinite in faculty! in form and moving how express and admirable! in action how like an angel! in apprehension how like a god!

the beauty of the world! the paragon of animals!'
(*Hamlet* II.ii)

And what a man of work was Shakespeare! In the relatively short period of his working life he wrote 36 plays – or 37, taking into account Pericles, which is generally accepted as written by him. The 36 were published in the first folio in 1623 by two of Shakespeare's partners, John Heminges and Henry Condell. This kind of tribute was unusual and without it we would lack many of the plays, as only 18 had been published separately by 1616.

In the 1590s, Shakespeare wrote a cycle of 154 sonnets of exquisite quality, first printed in 1609. Many subsequent writers and scholars consider that he perfected the art. In 1593-4, he also produced two long poems, *Venus and Adonis* and *The Rape of Lucrece.*

Shakespeare's works are generally agreed to be the greatest single achievement in English, or even in world, literature. His plays have been translated into at least 50 languages – more than any other playwright; they have been performed in widely varying interpretations, and have become the measuring stick against which all subsequent drama has been compared. In addition, Shakespeare is by far the most quoted writer in the history of the human race. In the *Oxford Dictionary of Quotations* which contains almost 20,000 quotations, a staggering 65 pages (about 10% of the book) are devoted to him.

CRAFTSMAN OF WORDS

A mark of Shakespeare's genius was his ability to transform the nature of theatre, and to become simultaneously the greatest writer of tragedies and comedies, often combining the two masterfully, allowing each to 'feed' off the other. Whereas Greek tragedy had dealt with matters on a heroic scale, Shakespeare approached subjects from an intensely human angle, thus making his plays more tragic, more heroic and more comic. He saw life as theatre, theatre as life. As he succinctly put it in *As You Like It* (II.vii):

All the world's a stage,
And all the men and women merely players:
They have their exits and their entrances;
And one man in his time plays many parts . . .

His works, as no others do, range over the whole panoply of human activities and emotions, covering issues from birth, love, lust, deceit, hope and despair, intrigue and murder.

Shakespeare deployed a vast vocabulary to accomplish his aims. To put this into perspective, the average person uses, in total, slightly fewer than 1000 words when writing; slightly over 1000 words in general conversation, and has a 'recognition vocabulary' of approximately 5000 words. Shakespeare, *in his writing alone*, used a greater vocabulary than any English writer has ever done – an extraordinary *25,000 words*. The extent of vocabulary, and the ability to see relationships between words is one of the major factors in measuring intelligence – and Shakespeare's was one of the highest (and deepest) that has ever been known. He used this intelligence to acquire an all-encompassing knowledge of Classical literature, law, Latin, French, politics, science, sociology, psychology, history, sports, music, mathematics and the arts – all of which he draws on in his plays.

THE PROCESS OF GENIUS

There are thus many difficulties in the way of anyone who tries to study the nature of Shakespeare's genius. Did he write effortlessly, never blotting out a line, as one later story would suggest? It seems unlikely, and the texts of the plays do contain evidence of revisions, though perhaps this is because they were adapted for revivals and new performances. Was he a self-

This miniature by Nicholas Hilliard is thought to be a portrait of Shakespeare.

taught genius, brought up with 'small Latin and less Greek', as the dramatist Ben Jonson put it? This seems unlikely too, although this type of comment accords with Shakespeare being the son of a provincial tradesman from Stratford-upon-Avon and a professional 'player' who had not gentrified himself by attending university.

A QUESTION OF IDENTITY

Shakespeare's life is poorly documented and many aspects of it are unknown. Nothing survives in his own handwriting except six 'signatures' (three on his will of 1616), but they appear to be in four different hands and none is definitely his – it was, however, not unusual for such documents to survive in copies. There have been persistent claims that the Shakespeare canon could not have been written by the William Shakespeare of Stratford-upon-Avon, whose birthday is celebrated on St George's Day. In academic circles debate still rages about who Shakespeare really was, this ultimate of geniuses having created, perhaps, one of the greatest plays/detective stories ever – the hunt for the Great Writer.

Candidates for the title have included three other contemporary writers: Edward De Vere,

Shakespeare's plays were performed in a theatre with an open roof.

Earl of Oxford (1550-1604), who was a young aristocrat renowned for his wit and many talents; Sir Francis Bacon (1561-1626); and Christopher Marlowe (1564-93). However, the leading candidate remains the Shakespeare from Stratford, about whom there is remarkably, and mysteriously little verifiable information, other than the fact that he has been accepted by most as the author of the plays.

SPIRIT OF THE AGE

Whoever the 'real' Shakespeare was, he has inspired more universal praise than any other writer, and perhaps more than any other genius. The true mystery remains the achievement of his genius and how it can be linked with the real but dimly recorded figure of William Shakespeare. What can be said is that Shakespeare was uniquely fortunate in living when he did, and that it took a writer of genius to exploit the ideas and influences available to him. He flourished in an age of great poets and a formative stage in the development of the English language, as witness the verse of Marlowe and others, or the King James Bible of 1611. Shakespeare lived in an England which was becoming securely Protestant, but in which the religious clashes of the earlier 16th century still influenced people's minds. The threat of Catholic conspiracies and foreign invasions, as in the Spanish Armada of 1588, led the English to take a passionate and committed view of their own history. Popular culture was poised between superstition and the beginnings of rationalism: a world of witchcraft persecutions in which the supernatural could be humorous (as in *A Midsummer Night's Dream*) but which also possessed real power (as in *Macbeth*).

THE ALCHEMY OF GENIUS

Finally, Shakespeare had, in the theatre of his day (which he played a major part in developing) a perfect instrument for reaching a wide audience, from the noble and learned to the enthusiastic London crowd. The theatre of Shakespeare's mind transmuted the teeming life of Elizabethan London into the enduring gold of the plays, even if the alchemical process involved remains one of the greatest mysteries in the history of human genius. It is, indeed, an extraordinary coincidence that three of the greatest bodies of work in the Greek, Indian and English cultures should have been ascribed to authors (Homer, Vyasa, Shakespeare) of whom we know virtually nothing for certain!

SEARCHING FOR PATTERNS

'I DO NOT KNOW WHAT I MAY APPEAR TO THE WORLD, BUT TO MYSELF I
SEEM TO HAVE BEEN ONLY A BOY PLAYING ON THE SEA-SHORE, AND
DIVERTING MYSELF IN NOW AND THEN FINDING A SMOOTHER PEBBLE
OR A PRETTIER SHELL THAN ORDINARY, WHILST THE GREAT OCEAN OF
TRUTH LAY ALL UNDISCOVERED BEFORE ME.'
SIR ISAAC NEWTON (1642-1727)

RENÉ DESCARTES 1596-1650
BREAKING FREE

With Descartes we witness a brilliant mind breaking free from the constraints of the old philosophy. By the process of 'Cartesian doubt' he argued that anything that cannot be proved must be doubted. Like Sir Francis Bacon, Descartes swept away the unenlightened acceptance of traditional knowledge and ushered in new patterns

Queen Christina of Sweden listening to Descartes lecturing on philosophy.

of learning and human thinking. He based his philosophy on the premise 'cogito ergo sum' – 'I think, therefore I am'. Although there is a logical flaw in this argument – that it cannot be proved to be true – it placed man and his rational thoughts at the heart of the cosmos. Descartes developed his philosophy by arguing that there was a dualism of mind and matter which were separate entities and could not influence each other. He outlined these ideas in his two most influential works, *Discourse on Method* (1637) and *Meditations* (1642).

HERESIES

Descartes, however, was concerned by the hostility of the Catholic Church to modern science, as revealed by the condemnations of Galileo in 1616 and 1633 for teaching the Copernican hypothesis of the rotation of the earth. Despite his emphasis on the centrality of the human thought process, Descartes was very careful to find a place within his philosophical system for God as an absolute, perfect being. Also, he never published his great book *Le Monde*; he claimed this contained two heresies: his belief in the rotation of the earth and his belief that the universe was infinite.

MATHEMATICAL PATTERNS

Descartes came from a wealthy French family and received a superb education at a Jesuit school. He studied law at Poitiers, but never practised. Instead, he travelled widely through Europe in the pursuit of knowledge (which he could afford to do) and in 1628 settled in Holland where he concentrated on his writing.

Although he is best known as a philosopher, and is often referred to as the father of modern philosophy, his genius also extended to the realms of mathematics and astronomy. Importantly, he was the inventor of co-ordinate geometry, but his explanation that the movement of the heavenly bodies was caused by vortices was less enduring and was superseded by Newton's theory of gravitation. Descartes' death was hastened by the strict regime he undertook when invited to tutor Queen Christina of Sweden in philosophy. The queen could only grant her mentor an audience at five a.m., and so Descartes was forced to abandon his regular habit of waking late and working in bed until midday. Already weakened in health, he struggled vainly with the unfamiliar routine and within months had succumbed to fatal illness.

REMBRANDT VAN RIJN 1606-1669

'No artist ever combined more delicate skill with more energy and power. His treatment of mankind is full of human sympathy. His special study was old age.'

DUTCH TREAT – WEALTH CREATION AND GENIUS

The great success story of the 17th century is the emergence of Holland as an independent country with its own empire in America and the Indies. The defeat of the more powerful Spain gave the Dutch a pride in their achievement and a prosperity which was shared by a large proportion of the population. Holland had become a world empire in the space of only two generations. Her economic power stretched from New Amsterdam (later rechristened New York) to Van Diemen's Land, later to be known as Tasmania, to the Far East. All the power and the tremendous wealth was sucked back into the cramped space of Holland and to a relatively small population of about two million. By 17th-century standards, the Dutch people were well fed, since the great ports of Rotterdam and Amsterdam were situated in a pivotal position for control of the Baltic grain trade. There the Dutch built massive granaries in which to store rye, corn and wheat. Consequently, Holland did not suffer from the constant food shortages that plagued the rest of Europe, so was saved the threat of civil riots.

BRAIN FOOD – THE BENEFITS OF NUTRITION

Dutch citizens enjoyed an excellent diet: good amounts of protein from fish, most of them ate some meat and there was also a plentiful supply of vegetables and imported exotic fruit and spices. It was a stable population, predominantly urban and surprisingly literate, with what seems to have been a great appreciation of art.

THE HUNGER FOR ART

It was in Amsterdam that the real art market developed. John Evelyn, the English diarist, commented upon the proliferation of objects, prints and works of art he saw in the market place when he visited Rotterdam in 1641. One theory for the explosion of new art in Holland during the 17th century was that the fanatically Puritan Iconoclastic Movement had destroyed all the Catholic Church art, thus creating an aesthetic vacuum. At the centre of this world stood the burgher, a citizen who was aware of his obligations to society and concerned that the poor should be fed and decently housed. This sense of civic responsibility created the world depicted by the extraordinary talent which emerged – artists of calibre such as Vermeer, Frans Hals, de Hooch, Ruisdael and Rembrandt.

LEARNING THE TRADE

Born in 1606 in Leiden, Rembrandt Harmensz van Rijn was the eighth child of a miller. His parents were typical of the mixture of religions that coexisted in 17th-century Holland. His mother was Catholic and his father a Calvinist. Economically his family were also typical: middle class of middling income, comfortable enough to afford Rembrandt's education. He obviously showed early academic talent, because he was the only one of the children to attend the local Latin school, where he studied the Classics, Geography, History and Mathematics. Later he enrolled at the University of Leiden.

His artistic mentor was Pieter Lastman (1583-1633) of Amsterdam, a painter only remembered today as Rembrandt's teacher, but highly esteemed in his own time. Lastman had been in Italy in 1603-7 where he encountered the new realism of Caravaggio, and it was through Lastman that Rembrandt learned the method of using just one strong light source, thus adding to the dramatic intensity of the depicted scene. Rembrandt had already begun to etch, the one aspect of his craft he did not share with his pupils. The *tenebroso* (light and dark) that we associate with his painting was developed simultaneously with the etchings. He returned to Leiden after six months and set up as an independent painter, taking his first two students, Gerrit Dou and Isaac Jouderville. Rembrandt's success was immediate. Constant Huygens, the humanist writer and secretary to Prince Frederick Hendrik of Orange, praises his work and was responsible for the prince commissioning from Rembrandt seven paintings on the Passion in 1632. Rembrandt was not paid as much as demanded for the commission, which took a considerable amount of time. In a letter to Constant Huygens, written in 1639, Rembrandt apologizes for the delay in delivery of *The Entombment* and *The Resurrection*: 'In these two pictures, the greatest and the most natural emotion and animation have been observed, which is also the principal reason why they have been so long in the making.' Perhaps because of this unsatisfactory transaction with a patron, Rembrandt decided to work for the open market.

BODY INTELLIGENCE
At much the same time as the beginning of his association with the prince, Rembrandt signed a business contract with an Amsterdam painter and dealer, Hendrik Uylenburgh, who ran a form of painter-workshop. Rembrandt set up (with his students) a partnership with Uylenburgh and, investing both talent and money, produced portraits and small historical paintings for the mar-

ket. This was the time of his greatest prosperity. He moved to Amsterdam, where he gained his first important commission, *The Anatomy Lesson of Dr Tulp* (1632). The picture was very well received and marks the beginning of Rembrandt's most fashionable period.

ADMIRING RAPHAEL
In 1634, Rembrandt married Uylenburgh's cousin Saskia, the daughter of a burgher who brought with her a considerable dowry. In 1635, their first son was born, but he only survived two months. The couple then had two daughters who also did not survive. Finally, in 1641, their son Titus was born. They were then living in a grand house, now the Rembrandt House in Jodenbreestraat. He also had a large studio, where he taught many students in a nearby sugar-refinery (Ferdinand Bol was among his pupils). Some enchanting paintings of Saskia survive and, as it was his happiest and most financially secure time, he was a familiar figure at the auction house. Amsterdam was the centre of the art market and it was here that Rembrandt saw the work of the great Renaissance masters. In 1639, Raphael's portrait of Castiglione was auctioned and Rembrandt tried to buy it. When he failed, he did a quick drawing from it, giving the portrait his own features. He later based two of his own self-portraits upon this work.

INNOVATION REJECTED
Saskia died in 1642 when she was not quite 30, the same year that Rembrandt completed his most famous painting, *The Night Watch*. This canvas portrays the militia company of Frans Banning Cocq, who was to become mayor of Amsterdam, and so belonged to the top echelon of the governing élite. Most of the others in the picture were not from the same social class, but they were by no means poor – each paid 100 guilders a copy for the painting.

Rembrandt's bold innovation was to transform a group portrait into a dramatically animated crowd. It has considerably darkened over time, and recent cleaning has not managed to restore any real semblance of natural light. It was this darkened state which caused it to be called 'The Night Watch', although the event actually took place in daylight. The painting was probably commissioned to commemorate a parade held in honour of a state visit made by Marie Medici, dowager Queen of France, in 1638. The movement of the two officers is the decisive factor for

Rembrandt's Self-portrait with Hat and Gold Chain
(1633) is in the Louvre.

the composition, as all the lines of the pikes and the muskets repeat the major diagonals of the design and the variety of movement is carried as far as it can be without interrupting the dominant forward thrust of the two major figures. The symphonic tide of colour flickers in the irrational lighting – the strongest is the lemon yellow of the uniform of the lieutenant and the captain's scarlet sash. Contemporary scholarship has revealed that the red was achieved with an expensive glaze, so the importance of the captain is expressed by the materials that – literally – decorate his sombre black costume. The criticisms from the men who paid equal amounts for this work are legendary. Since some figures are so far sunk in shadow that they become difficult to identify, perhaps it was inevitable that Rembrandt would lose his popularity as a portrait painter after this.

INDIVIDUALITY

In 1654, Hendrickje Stoffels who had joined the house as a maidservant, was summoned before the magistrates. She was five months pregnant, and was accused of living with Rembrandt as a whore. Rembrandt's personal behaviour suggests a character unwilling to conform to the conventions of his time, which may help to explain the individuality we sense in his work, particularly in the self-portraits. No other artist has recorded himself with such penetrating honesty: begun when he was a very young man, probably to teach himself to describe emotions expressively, by the middle years his self-portraits had become a record which described his time of confidence, and the late, infinitely moving, depictions of old age that he painted have never been surpassed.

ADVERSITY TO ADVANTAGE

Rembrandt was bankrupted in 1656 and over the next two years he experienced the liquidation of all his assets, including his fine house. So he, Titus, Hendrickje and Cornelia moved to the Jewish quarter on the Rozengracht, and it was at this point that Rembrandt began one of the most active periods of his painting life. Titus and Hendrickje set up an art dealership in which they themselves employed Rembrandt, so he was relieved of any further business responsibilities.

WORKING FOR POSTERITY

Hendrickje died in 1663 and was buried in a rented grave in Westerkerk. She was followed by Titus who, having just married, died in 1668 and

was buried in the same church. It was probably in the next year, that of his own death, that Rembrandt painted *The Return of the Prodigal Son*, now in St Petersburg. The story deals with the love of an earthly father, and in this painting Rembrandt made his personal grief universal.

Rembrandt was an empathetic, uncompromising, diligent and indefatigable man – in fact, this last quality used to exhaust many who knew him. As his life progressed, his energy seemed to increase and he was an ardent teacher with a large school of enthusiastic pupils. He was active until the end of his life, continuing to break new ground in the depiction of light and shadow, detail and colour intensities.

He was the first artist to understand that it is only ourselves that we truly know, and thus he was not the inventor, but the discoverer of the individual state. Unwilling to work for patrons, he was dependent on the market, and finally, when his supreme masterpiece, *The Night Watch*, was fatally underestimated by the Amsterdam Burghers, the market failed him. His individual genius has since been recognized. In 1817, for instance, the essayist William Hazlitt wrote: '*Rembrandt might have been said to have created a style of his own, which he also perfected.*'

JOHN MILTON 1608-1674
EPIC WRITER

Milton, like Homer before and Borges after, was a blind seer. Using the epic form hallowed by Homer, Virgil and Dante, he sought his own grand reconciliation between the Classical and Christian universes and, in so doing, set himself the lofty ambition of justifying God's way to men. In particular, he sought to explain why, according to devout Christian cosmology, man had been hunted forth from paradise and why God had allowed the fall of Adam and Eve to occur. Milton achieved this goal in his masterwork *Paradise Lost* (completed in 1665 and published in 1667):

Of Man's first disobedience, and the fruit
Of that forbidden tree, whose mortal taste
Brought death into the world, and all our woe,
With loss of Eden . . .

Along with his direct contemporary Spinoza, he can be considered one of the ultimate seekers for patterns in creation. In the opening lines of *Paradise Lost*, Milton wrote:

What in me is dark
Illumine, what is low raise and support;

That to the height of this great argument
I may assert eternal Providence,
And justify the ways of God to men.

SUBJECT KNOWLEDGE

Milton was born in Bread Street, London, and at the age of 17 went to study at Cambridge University. At first he was intended for the Church. He was a precocious composer of verse, even at Cambridge, where he acquired an extensive grounding in Latin, Greek and Italian. Having completed his studies, he embarked on a grand European tour, making a special point of visiting Galileo who, according to Milton, had 'grown old, a prisoner to the Inquisition, for thinking in astronomy, otherwise than the Franciscan or Dominican licensers thought'.

TAKING RISKS

Milton was rapidly becoming a spokesman for personal liberty at a time when this was not a fashionable point of view. He wrote a pamphlet urging the freedom to divorce if couples were incompatible – which was extremely unpopular. When he was threatened with prosecution for issuing a pamphlet without having it cleared by the censors, he promptly produced a new pamphlet insisting on the right to freedom of speech.

In the English Civil War, Milton became a powerful supporter of the Cromwellian party against Charles I. After the war, he was rewarded for his efforts by being made Latin Secretary to the Council of State – a post he held until 1660. He also vigorously defended Cromwell's Commonwealth in a massive series of further pamphlets many of which (written in Latin) were intended for the European market, thus making Milton the international spokesman of the 'English revolution'. His defence of freedom of speech and the liberty of printing is still quoted today, while his Tractate on Education is a brilliant exposition of the Renaissance ideals for forming young minds. No wonder that Milton – who was totally blind from the mid-1650s onwards – has been described as the 'champion of the revolution'.

However, at the death of Cromwell, the demise of the Commonwealth and the restoration of King Charles II in 1660, Milton retired into private life where he was left alone.

COMMITMENT

Milton's composition of *Paradise Lost* and *Samson Agonistes* – his greatest works – when he was completely blind, could be compared with blind Homer, blind Borges and, perhaps the most apt comparison of all, with the deaf Beethoven, who composed his most marvellous symphonies towards the end of his life.

INNOVATION

For the 12 books of *Paradise Lost*, Milton cultivated his own distinctive style – both in terms of language and content. He recalibrated the English language according to Latinate parameters, and he treated Christian heaven as a battlefield on the plains before Classical Troy. The plot is simple: Satan, the rebel Angel Lucifer, revolts against God and is cast out of heaven after a series of thunderous battles and hurled into the pit of hell.

In the first two books, Satan and his associate devils and demons plot as to how they can revenge themselves on the Almighty. Over the course of the remaining 10 books, the plot unravels. It involves the voyage of Satan to God's new creation, earth, to tempt Adam and Eve and to cause them to sin against God the Father and so have them cast out of their earthly paradise as he, Satan, and his diabolical colleagues had been exiled from heaven itself.

CREATIVITY

The language Milton created in this epic poem is extraordinarily rich and full of the most dense and complex imagery. It is absolutely unique and it makes *Paradise Lost* the greatest single extended poem in English literature.

BENEDICT DE SPINOZA 1632-1677
THE MIGHTY 'MUST'

Spinoza, the ultimate seeker after patterns, believed that it is largely impossible that events should be other than they are. He wrote that 'Things could not have been brought into being by God in any manner or in any order different, from that which has in fact obtained.' He was a determinist, philosopher and theologian. Yet, although he was an extraordinarily complicated thinker, he was a remarkably simple human being, born in Amsterdam into a Jewish émigré family who had come from Spain and Portugal. They were obliged to pretend to be Christians but secretly remained loyal to Judaism.

A RECEPTIVE MIND

Spinoza showed an early interest in optics, the new astronomy and the philosophy of Descartes,

A true literary genius, blindness did not prevent Milton from writing poetry.

which did not make him popular in the synagogue. By the age of 24 he was clearly a professed rebel in his own community, and so was formally excommunicated from Jewish society. Thereafter he made his living grinding and polishing lenses. In 1660 he published his *Short Treatise on God, Man and his Well-being* and his *Short Treatise on the Correction of Understanding*. In the opening passage of the latter, he outlines his aim of discovering '*A true good capable of imparting itself by which alone the mind could be affected to the exclusion of all else. A joy continuous and supreme to all eternity.*' Spinoza was evidently a confirmed and incurable optimist. He was also keen to protect his own freedom – in 1673 he declined the post of Professor of Philosophy at Heidelberg, in order to retain his independence.

FAITH

His masterpiece was *The Ethics* (in Latin *Ethica*) published posthumously in 1677. It is a metaphysical system of extraordinary rigour developed mathematically from axioms, theorems and definitions. The basic question is: 'God or nature?'. Spinoza believed that everything must

happen according to a logical necessity and that nothing corresponds to ordinary notions of free will. Human beings are limited, in so far as our passions make us subject to outside causes, and we are only free in so far as we act in accordance with God's will. Spinoza's search for patterns was absolute. His answer was that God and nature are identical. He saw the physical universe as an attribute of God, rather than created by God – a dangerous view to hold at the time.

FACING FEARS

Although a simple artisan in appearance, Spinoza was a deep, profound and devastating thinker, possessed with extraordinary personal clarity and conviction in the correctness of his own views. He was also a man of great physical courage, who endangered his own life by protesting against the murder of Jan and Cornelius De Witt. These two brothers had sided with the French against the ruling Dutch House of Orange and King William III during the French/Dutch wars. Cornelius De Witt, accused of conspiring against William's life, was imprisoned and tortured. When Jan visited him in prison, the two were attacked by the mob and torn to pieces.

Like Milton, Spinoza was not afraid to publish his views.

One sees here a reflection of the way in which Spinoza was excommunicated from his own personal community, the Judaic synagogue in Amsterdam. He refused to accept what the majority dictated and always thought clearly, concisely and precisely along his own lines, searching for the patterns which he believed to be inevitable – those that governed life and the universe. Perhaps what stands out most clearly about Spinoza's genius was his absolute rejection of any authority that told him what to think. When, in 1665, Spinoza began the composition of his theological political treatise, he wrote: *The liberty of philosophizing and of saying what we think cannot be destroyed unless the peace and piety of the state itself is therewith also destroyed.* However, condemnations of his treatise were many and furious and his theological, political work was frequently denounced as 'forged in Hell by a renegade Jew and the devil'.

Spinoza died in 1677 of consumption aggravated by his breathing in the glass dust created by his lens-grinding activities. Just 44 when he died, this tenacious mental warrior left a small library, his clothes, a little furniture, some finished lenses and his manuscripts – all of which were published the same year by his friends.

SUPPORTER OF THE TRUTH

What lessons can be derived from Spinoza? He believed that a definite process can be observed in the unfolding of human potential throughout the ages. This process is man's constant struggle to be able to think and speak the truth freely in the face of opposition from a strict prevailing dogma that is frequently imposed by the state or by religion, both of which tend to exhibit a natural preference for conformism.

In this belief, Spinoza was one with Socrates, Copernicus, Galileo, Milton – even Chaplin. They belong to different states and different religions, but the pattern of struggle is the same. If preordained, ready-made categories of thought and belief are to be the sole ones permitted, how can progress be made and how can the iconoclasm of genius ever manifest itself? Spinoza teaches us that such mental absolutism must not be tolerated, either by complicity or silence, if true results are to be achieved.

CHRISTOPHER WREN 1632-1723

A MIRACLE MAN

In his inaugural oration as Professor of Geometry at Gresham College, London, in 1662 Isaac Barrow (1630-77) declared that it was an open question whether Wren 'was most to be commended for the divine felicity of his genius or for the sweet humanity of his disposition – formerly, as a boy, a prodigy; now, as man, a miracle, nay, even something superhuman!' At the time, Wren – still only 30 – was just about to start on his career as an architect. It is for his buildings, including the new St Paul's Cathedral, that Wren is deservedly famous, but as Barrow's words indicate, he had already established himself as one of the foremost English scientists, second only to Newton.

PRODIGY

Wren was truly a prodigy. He left Westminster School at the age of 14 and worked as an anatomist's assistant to Sir Charles Scarburgh (1616-94) and as a Latin translator before going to Oxford University at the age of 16 or 17. Here Wren joined a circle of philosophers and scientists, many of whom would, along with Wren, later found the Royal Society, the oldest scientific society in Great Britain. In 1657, at the age of 25, Wren was made Professor of Astronomy at Gresham College and in 1661 he was appointed Savilian Professor of Astronomy at Oxford, a chair which he held until 1673. The plans he laid down there for long-term weather forecasting were not realized for 300 years.

MASTERMIND GROUP

The existence of a group of talented members of the Royal Society such as Wren, Newton and Sir Robert Boyle (1627-91) created an ambience in which experimentation could flourish in late Stuart Britain. In this atmosphere of creativity, Wren produced a wealth of papers and ideas which he communicated to his fellow scientists. These included a demonstration of the transfusion of blood between two dogs, inspired by the discoveries of William Harvey (1578-1657), which had appeared in Wren's treatise of 1628 *De Motu Cordis et Sanguinis in Animalibus* (On the Motion of the Heart and Blood in Animals). Wren also produced treatises on optics, especially telescopes, and observations on the laws of motion.

MATHEMATICAL PATTERNS

Wren was intensely curious and dedicated, nearly always approaching problems through visual means (he had taught himself art in his youth). It is, however, as an architect that Wren's

Sir Christopher Wren is best known as the architect of St Paul's Cathedral.

eye for mathematical patterns was most accessibly demonstrated to the public at large. Among his earliest designs were the Sheldonian Theatre in Oxford and Trinity College Library in Cambridge; he also rebuilt part of Hampton Court Palace. After the Great Fire destroyed the heart of London in 1666, Wren submitted a plan for a redesigned city on a mathematical plan with broad avenues that would have made the capital city the envy of Europe. This was not adopted, but he was chosen as architect for St Paul's Cathedral. Work on this massive building started in 1675 and was not completed until 1710. It is fitting that Wren's plain monument in the crypt of St Paul's declares *Si monumentum requiris, circumspice* ('If you would see his monument look around'). Wren also rebuilt 52 of the churches destroyed by the Great Fire and for more than 300 years his designs have dominated the skyline of London. The magnitude of his achievement is aptly summarized in the words of his friend and colleague Robert Hooke: '*I must affirm, that since the time of Archimedes there scarce ever has met in one man, in so great perfection, such a mechanical hand, and so philosophical a mind.*'

SIR ISAAC NEWTON 1642-1727

'Nature and Nature's laws lay hid in night.
God said, Let Newton be! and all was light.'

This encomium by Alexander Pope underlines a significant point about the career of Isaac Newton. He was not an isolated genius working on the fringes of contemporary orthodoxy, but a man who received huge recognition in his own lifetime. He became a Member of Parliament, President of the Royal Society, was given lucrative offices as warden and master of the royal mint in the 1690s (which he found much more congenial than teaching at Cambridge), and was knighted in 1705. Though he is often referred to as 'the first scientist to be knighted', the award was not a disinterested one – it reflected as much as anything else Newton's skill at operating the political and patronage system of his day. All the same, his giant scientific reputation, extending far beyond those who actually read his works, arose from the manner in which he addressed and solved problems which most worried his contemporaries. As Pope pithily expressed it, Newton was thought to have demonstrated that the universe was rational, that its principles could be discovered, and that they were entirely compatible with creation by a benevolent deity.

LOGICAL GENIUS
But if Newton gave his contemporaries the conclusions and proof that they wanted, and for which other thinkers were also searching, he succeeded in so doing because of a genius for logical thought and because of the sheer range of his vision and interests.

The exact order in which Newton made his discoveries is not definite, and is not helped by his involvement in an acrimonious dispute with the German philosopher Gottfried Leibniz (1646-

1716) over who first discovered mathematical calculus. But it does seem that, in his early 20s (roughly between 1664 and 1666), Newton had already conceived three major breakthroughs: the way in which white light decomposed into the colours of the spectrum; the calculus; and above all a theory of gravitation which could link Galileo's conclusions about the movement of objects near the earth with the observed movement of heavenly bodies – a universal law of motion. Until this time, mathematicians had dealt with the world as if it were static, whereas Newton knew that the world was in constant motion. The calculus system subsequently provided the basis for the majority of work and progress in modern mathematics and science.

PERSISTENCE AND DEVELOPMENT
Newton can thus be seen as a genius from the beginning of his career. By 1669 he was already Lucasian Professor of Mathematics at Cambridge, a title he retained until 1701 (currently held by Stephen Hawking). But he was also a monument of persistence and continual development over a long life. His early insights of the 1660s were tentatively formulated and incomplete, though the central theories of gravitation were eventually published in *On Motion* (1684) and *The Mathematical Principles of Natural Philosophy* (1687). By 1789 the 1687 *Principia* had appeared in 40 English editions, as well as 17 in French and 11 in the original Latin.

ACHIEVEMENT
Modern research on Newton's manuscripts and books has shown that, despite his success, he continued to wrestle with the implications of his ideas all his life; he was a much more complicated figure than Pope's reassuring dealer in certainties. He was unscrupulous and devious in undermining his opponents. Like many great thinkers, Newton had unorthodox religious views which he kept quiet for fear of being regarded a heretic. He spent much of his career conducting experiments in alchemy, as well as (in modern terms) 'orthodox' science. And finally, although Newton was content to show *how* gravity worked and leave its *cause* to the intervention of God, later thinkers used his ideas to justify deism (a non-intervening creator) or even atheism. The genius of Newton's scientific achievement grew out of his beliefs, but it could not be confined within them indefinitely.

One of the greatest gifts that Newton donated

PHILOSOPHIÆ
NATURALIS
PRINCIPIA
MATHEMATICA.

Autore JS. NEWTON, Trin. Coll. Cantab. Soc. Matheseos Professore Lucasiano, & Societatis Regalis Sodali.

IMPRIMATUR.
S. PEPYS, Reg. Soc. PRÆSES.
Julii 5. 1686.

LONDINI,

Jussu Societatis Regiæ ac Typis Josephi Streater. Prostat apud plures Bibliopolas. Anno MDCLXXXVII.

ABOVE This is the frontispiece of Newton's Mathematical Principles of Natural Philosophy. He wrote it in Latin and it was not translated into English until after his death.

LEFT Newton's early investigations into how glass and sunbeams can create rainbows eventually led to his invention of the first reflecting telescope.

to humanity was that for the first time, based on his laws, the motions and future positions of the solar system and the stars could be predicted. The intellectual and physical leap from the earth into the universe was no longer a dream; it was a beckoning reality.

GOTTFRIED WILHELM LEIBNIZ
1646-1716
VERSATILITY AND CREATIVITY

Leibniz was a multi-faceted and prodigious intellect who stated: '*I strongly approve of rational games for they serve to perfect the art of thinking.*' Like many geniuses, he put his mind to many subjects and was a philosopher, theologian, mathematician, military planner, theorist of legal education, historian, scientist, librarian, mining engineer and a reformer of the German coinage. He bubbled over with ideas.

In 1666, Leibniz was refused a doctorate at Leipzig University, where his father was already established as Professor of Moral Philosophy, because he was considered to be too young. Fortunately, the University of Altdorf stepped in to offer both a doctorate and professorship to the precociously talented youth.

In 1672, Leibniz went to Paris where he devised a plan for a French invasion of Egypt which he presented to the Sun King, Louis XIV. Louis did not implement it, but Napoleon did – in 1798! While in France, Leibniz also invented a calculating machine which was so impressive that it led to his election as a Fellow of the Royal Society when he visited London in 1673. In 1676 Leibniz met Spinoza in Amsterdam, where they discussed Spinoza's *Ethics*. From there, Leibniz proceeded to Hanover, where he became the Chief Librarian and worked on a plan for reconciling the Protestant and Catholic Churches. He then founded the Academy of Sciences in Berlin,

A philosopher and mathematician, Leibniz always came up with new ideas.

of which he became the first president. He also wrote profusely on a massively divergent series of topics – only a fraction of these were published in his lifetime.

CONTROVERSY

We have observed that geniuses tend to be attracted to each other, and that absolute genius attracts absolutely. However, in one notorious instance involving Leibniz and Sir Isaac Newton, the two geniuses became embroiled in a bitter dispute. Yet a third genius, Professor Stephen Hawking, describes the fracas thus: 'Both Leibniz and Newton had independently developed a branch of mathematics, called calculus, which underlines most of modern physics. Although we now know that Newton discovered calculus years before Leibniz, he published his work much later. A major row ensued over who had been the first, with scientists vigorously defending both contenders.'

What is the current verdict of science as to the respective claims to priority? Newton is now considered the first inventor, but a greater debt is owed to Leibniz for the superior facility and completeness of his method, as well as its more advanced notation, which helped Continental mathematicians to make advances beyond that of English mathematicians throughout the 18th century. However, it is universally accepted that the two discoveries were separate. The global intellectual climate of the time may, in any case, have been ripe for just such an advance. We now know, for example, that at the very same time as Newton and Leibniz were engaged in their controversy, the Japanese scholar Kowa Seki had also, quite independently, invented the differential calculus, as well as elaborating a procedure for computing the number π!

OPTIMISTIC THEORY OF EVERYTHING

Like Spinoza, Leibniz devoted immense effort to seeking out a universal pattern in the cosmos. He reached a similar conclusion to Spinoza's, though by different methods – namely that God, a supremely rational, omnipotent, omniscient and perfect being must, of necessity, have created the best and, therefore, only possible world. It would be irrational for God to have done anything less. Therefore, we are here because we have to be! Leibniz's unashamedly optimistic cosmic and theological conclusions were viciously parodied by the French satirist, Voltaire (1694-1778), in *Candide* (published in the late 1750s). In it, Leibniz is caricatured as Doctor Pangloss, saying: '*All is for the best in this best of all possible worlds.*' Voltaire pours scorn on the notion by cataloguing various ills of the world, such as earthquakes, rape, slaughter, and so on. Optimism has always been an easy target.

THE PATTERN OF THE UNIVERSE EMERGES

Certainly Leibniz, a true optimist, believed in a pre-established universal harmony providing a rational basis for all creation, one with which God, having created it, could not interfere. Leibniz based his conclusions on a complicated hierarchy of what he termed 'Monads'. These were infinite and indivisible substances, the highest of which was God himself. In the course of his argument, Leibniz took a theological swipe at Newton, who believed that the universe was only saved from gravitational disintegration by perpetual miracle. Leibniz wrote: 'Mr Newton and his followers have an extremely odd opinion of the work of God. According to them, God has to wind up his watch from time to time, otherwise it would cease to go. He lacks sufficient foresight to make it a perpetual motion. According to my view, the same force and vigour goes on existing in the world always.' Of course,

Bach's manuscripts are relatively neat compared with those of other musicians.

erized data bank of information. Leibniz's point was that if one has accumulated all knowledge, then argument, discussion and controversy are abolished. Knowledge replaces them.

USING KNOWLEDGE

Leibniz's philosophy is complicated and, indeed, open to satirical thrusts, as Voltaire demonstrated. What remains, though, is a picture of a mind relentlessly active, applying itself with great energy to a wide range of problems, both theoretical and practical. Leibniz was fiercely optimistic and believed in the ultimate harmony of the universe and in the possibility of codifying all knowledge, and therefore being able to utilize it. This is a colossal vision – not merely global, but penetrating into the entire future of humankind. In the modern computer age, Leibniz's vision is no longer beyond the bounds of possibility.

JOHANN SEBASTIAN BACH
1685-1750
TIRELESS PRODUCTIVITY

J. S. Bach's output is extraordinary in both its quality and quantity. Some of his greatest works were even temporarily forgotten and only came to be revived again after the 1820s. Many musical styles, from jazz to Walt Disney, have adapted Bach's creations, but his own distinctive character always shines through.

Bach was a tireless worker. During the late 1720s, for example, he wrote, rehearsed and conducted a substantial new choral piece every week for his church in Leipzig, besides holding several other services, supervising a school and fulfilling larger commissions. He was also supremely adaptable, switching from secular to spiritual compositions and back again; he was never tied down to one form.

Throughout his musical career Bach maintained a prodigious rate of musical production, composing, in addition to many other pieces: 200 Cantatas; 48 Preludes and Fugues; 20 Concertos; six Sonatas for violin and six solo suites for 'cello. Among his most enduring works are the six Brandenburg concertos, the Christmas Oratorio, the Goldberg Variations, the Toccata and Fugue in D minor and two monumental choral works – the St Matthew Passion and the Mass in B minor.

For the study of genius, Bach's career has a special relevance to the 'nature and nurture' debate. Although Bach was orphaned by the age

the gravitational stability of the universe is today well understood.

GOD AND SCIENCE

The English astronomer, mathematician and philosopher Sir Fred Hoyle (born 1915) has made an interesting observation which can now be applied to both Newton and Leibniz: 'I have always thought it curious that while most scientists claim to eschew religion, it actually dominates their thoughts more than it does the clergy.'

A UNIVERSAL LANGUAGE

Ultimately, Leibniz postulated a universal language to incorporate all existing knowledge, which would render argument obsolete and displace it by a process of calculation. In essence, Leibniz seemed to be striving in his philosophy towards the conceptualization of a vast comput-

of 10, he was very much influenced by his family's tradition of pursuing musical careers. His elder brother, Johann Christian (1671-1721), the organist at Ohrdurf, took care of the young orphan and taught him how to play the organ and the clavier, but he forbade his charge the use of his library. Such was Johann Sebastian's dedication to music that he secretly removed the books he wanted and copied them by moonlight, in order to circumvent the ban. Bach studied Latin, arithmetic, history, Greek, Hebrew, philosophy and rhetoric at school, where – like many other geniuses – his performance was only average, though he usually managed to come somewhere in the top half of his class.

Between the 16th century and the 1840s the Bach family produced at least 70 musicians, drawn from every generation. This was probably a triumph of tradition and education more than of genetic inheritance. There was, after all, only one genius, and five or six talented composers who achieved contemporary reputations (including three of Johann Sebastian's own sons – he had 20 children by two wives). It did mean, however, that his musical talent was naturally encouraged and admired. The majority of the Bach family were nearly all undistinguished performers, simply plying the family trade. Bach himself is modestly said to have told his pupils that *'anyone who works as hard as I did will do as well'*, but they cannot have believed him, any more than do modern critics.

AMBITION
Bach was extremely ambitious in terms of making a career from his talents. By the time he was 19, he had established himself as a competent singer, violinist, composer and organist. In 1705 he was given a month's leave from his post as organist at Arnstadt to travel to hear the virtuoso organist, Buxtehude (*c.*1637-1707) at Lübeck. The story goes that Bach travelled the 500-mile round trip on foot. He was certainly absent for much longer than a month, to the fury of his employers at Arnstadt.

While his musical upbringing gave Bach his start, the Protestant Work Ethic enabled him to absorb and reshape a rich inheritance of ideas. In his musical legacy we can see the mathematical patterns of music transformed by genius into the great beauty of polyphony.

MUSICAL RECOGNITION
Despite his obvious talents, Bach was not fully appreciated by all his contemporaries, and like Newton, Lincoln and Cézanne, Bach had to wait until the later years of his life, and to posterity, for his full genius to be recognized. His work is unquestionably one of the cornerstones in the history of music, and had a profound influence on Mozart and Beethoven. His compositions have been described as universal, encyclopaedic, and apparently simple but subtly concealing an enormous complexity and great depth. The mastery of his music still inspires other creative artists; the conceptual and philological problems he set still intrigue scholars, and the technical difficulty of performing his exceptionally complex works remains one of the most exciting challenges and accomplishments of performers.

MASTER OF COUNTERPOINT
Paul Collins, the concert violinist, described Bach as 'infernally clever'. This cleverness and brilliance is demonstrated in his unparalleled mastery of counterpoint. His music for soprano, alto, tenor and bass often contained four inversions, and transmuted time. As Leonardo da Vinci was able, with either hand, to write back-to-front, upside-down, and in mirror image, so Bach would compose pieces which contained simultaneously, inversion, retrograde and retrograde inversion statements of the same melodic line. Many modern music students have said that Bach's scores are some of the most fascinating to study and that his brilliance and talent can only be fully appreciated after close analysis of the music. Bach was also an innovator, creating new themes and variations, and taking standard forms to new heights. His other great contribution to music was that he combined the current musical forms from Europe, especially the Italian, French and German, and synthesized them all in grand musical designs.

REVIVAL
In his later years Bach continued to compose prolifically, became a teacher to an increasing number of devoted students, and was active as a conductor. Like Homer, Galileo and Borges, he endured a period of blindness shortly before his death. His works went into relative obscurity until the early 1800s, when, with the help of Robert Schumann and Felix Mendelssohn, they were collected, published and performed. This revival has continued to grow in strength to the current day.

THE SPIRIT OF REVOLUTION

'I REJOICE THAT AMERICA HAS RESISTED. THREE MILLIONS OF PEOPLE,
SO DEAD TO ALL THE FEELINGS OF LIBERTY, AS VOLUNTARILY TO SUBMIT
TO BE SLAVES, WOULD HAVE BEEN FIT TO MAKE SLAVES OF THE REST.'
WILLIAM PITT, EARL OF CHATHAM (1708-78)

BENJAMIN FRANKLIN (1706-1790) AND THOMAS JEFFERSON (1743-1826)

ARCHITECTS OF AMERICAN INDEPENDENCE

The men who came together in the last quarter of the 18th century to create a new nation were an extraordinary group. We shall soon encounter George Washington, the military leader of the American Revolution which gained Independence from the British Crown, and who also became the first President of the United States.

MASTERMIND GROUP

Washington was supported in this grand endeavour, which led ultimately to the creation of the most prosperous and freedom-conscious nation the earth had ever witnessed, by two towering intellects. Benjamin Franklin was a journalist, scientific experimenter and man of reason, who turned to politics when necessity dictated. Thomas Jefferson trained as a lawyer – indeed he became a brilliant advocate – but his main gift was a lucid cast of mind, capable of the concise, yet ringing, prose which would consolidate and enshrine the liberty of the new nation. Together, these men took on the might of Great Britain, one of the world's foremost naval and military powers of the day.

OLYMPIAN VERSATILITY

Franklin's achievements are so varied as to beggar credibility. The youngest son and 15th child of a family of 17, he was born in Boston, where at the age of 12 he was apprenticed to his printer brother, James. He had started a newspaper, the *New England Courant*, in 1709, and Franklin both printed and wrote for it. Franklin's formal education had ended when he was only 10, but that did not stunt his desire for learning. For instance, he devised a series of mental training games that were to serve him for the rest of his life. These included making notes on essays in *The Spectator*, and then rewriting the essays

'He snatched the lightning from the skies and the sceptres from tyrants' is a fitting epitaph for Franklin.

based on his notes and memory. He also converted essays into poetry and then back into prose and embarked on a massive training programme to improve his vocabulary.

Franklin continued with the occupation of printer in Philadelphia (the City of Brotherly Love) and London, which he visited in 1724 at the age of 18. In 1729, aged just 23, Franklin bought the *Pennsylvania Gazette*. These achievements are amazing for one so young and suggest that Franklin was possessed of enormous energy and was fiercely imbued with the spirit of individual enterprise. He also founded *Poor Richard's Almanac*, in which he regularly advised readers on how to be successful.

FROM POLITICS TO ELECTRICITY

Franklin entered politics, and at the same time conducted his famous experiment in electricity, which earned him election as a Fellow of the Royal Society in London. He proved that lightning and electricity are identical and demonstrated the distinction between positive and negative charges. He invented the lightning conductor to protect buildings, bi-focal glasses and an efficient stove. He also charted both the routes of storms over North America and the course of the Gulf Stream.

CHESS AS METAPHOR FOR LIFE

Benjamin Franklin wrote and published the first American book on chess. In his autobiography, he explains how useful the playing of chess was in his life, but his most frequently quoted writings about chess come from a piece entitled *The Morals of Chess*, published in Philadelphia in 1786. In it, he likens the game to life itself: 'The game of chess is not merely an idle amusement; several, very valuable policies of the mind, useful in the course of human life, are to be acquired

BELOW Many have noticed a striking similarity between Thomas Jefferson and the 42nd President, William Jefferson Clinton.

ABOVE The Declaration of Independence was signed on 4 July 1776.

and strengthened by it, so as to become ready on all occasions. For life is a kind of chess, in which we have often points to gain, and competitors or adversaries to contend with, and in which there is a vast variety of good and ill-events, that are, in some degree, the effect of prudence or the want of it.'

IMPORTING ARMS – EXPORTING REVOLUTION

Franklin's skills as a foreign emissary were extensive and successful – no doubt because he found it easy to get on with people. (Incidentally, he had a strong sexual drive and was greatly attracted by and attractive to the opposite sex; he eventually enjoyed a long and happy marriage.) Working in London, Franklin devised all manner of ingenious ideas to prevent the split between the British Crown and the American colonies. But once the break became irreversible, he travelled as a plenipotentiary to Paris to obtain French support for the insurgent colonists in their war of independence. In this objective, he was supremely successful and in 1778 the French began to export arms and troops to North America to aid the colonists. Meanwhile, Franklin had exported egalitarian notions of freedom and brotherly love to Paris. He was therefore partly responsible for the causes of the French Revolution of 1789 and for establishing the notions of 'Liberté', 'Egalité' and 'Fraternité' whereby the French themselves overthrew their own form of despotism.

INDEPENDENCE AND ESTABLISHMENT

On 3 September 1783, the peace treaty which guaranteed the Independence of America was signed with Great Britain. Thereafter, Franklin was elected three times President of Pennsylvania state, and was also a delegate to the convention which framed the constitution of the USA. He was responsible for establishing a civic fire and police force, a hospital and the Academy of Philadelphia from which grew the University of Pennsylvania. Franklin remained active until he died, when there was international mourning.

FROM ENLIGHTENMENT TO REVOLUTION

At the commencement of hostilities, Benjamin Franklin had formed part of the committee which drew up the Declaration of Independence, dated 4 July 1776. The committee included John Adams, Roger Sherman, Robert Livingstone, Benjamin Franklin and Thomas Jefferson, and it is Jefferson's name that has been appended to the official version.

Jefferson, the chief draftsman of the document, was 33 when he came from Virginia to imbue the declaration with the egalitarian and humanitarian ideals of enlightenment philosophy. After considerable debate by Congress, the Declaration of Independence was adopted with just one major change. (Although Jefferson was a slave owner himself, he had included a denunciation of slavery in the original declaration.) Congress, however, decided to remove this out of deference to the delegates from the Southern States, where society and industry were still largely founded on slave labour.

VERBAL INTELLIGENCE – MEMORY

Thomas Jefferson's prose was clear, lucid and brief, his words utterly memorable and appropriate to the occasion: 'We hold these truths to be self-evident, that all men are created equal, that they are endowed by their creator with certain inalienable rights. That among these are life, liberty and the pursuit of happiness. That to secure these rights, governments are instituted among men, deriving their just powers from the consent of the governed. That, whenever any form of government becomes destructive of these ends, it is the right of the people to alter and abolish it.'

WE THE PEOPLE

The Declaration of Independence bore Jefferson's name. The Articles of Confederation and Perpetual Union between the founding states of New Hampshire, Massachusetts Bay, Rhode Island and Providence Plantations, Connecticut, New York, New Jersey, Pennsylvania, Delaware, Maryland, Virginia, North Carolina, South Carolina and Georgia, bore the signature of George Washington. As, indeed, did the first constitution of the United States of America, dated 17 September 1787. The opening words of this are immortal: 'We, the people of the United States, in order to form a more perfect union, establish justice, insure domestic tranquillity, provide for the common defense, promote the general welfare, and secure the blessings of liberty to ourselves and our posterity, do ordain and establish this Constitution for the United States of America.'

ASSEMBLY OF DEMI-GODS

The convention to establish this constitution took place in Philadelphia in 1787. In the words of Jefferson himself, the men who gathered in Philadelphia were 'an assembly of demi-gods'. Their problem was to balance the rights of the individual against the need for effective central government. The solution to this was enshrined in the United States Constitution.

JEFFERSON THE MAN

In 1801 Jefferson was chosen as the third President of the United States. He was to become the personal hero of the 35th President, J. F. Kennedy, and of the 42nd President, Bill Clinton, who has said:

'*What is most amazing about Jefferson was his ability to pursue not only his ambitious public agenda but also his personal interests. Jefferson did so many things – he invented gadgets, designed homes, rode a horse daily well into his 70s . . .*'

Jefferson was indeed a man of many talents and accomplishments. A consummate politician and lawyer, he was also a philosopher, meteorologist, archaeologist, architect and mathematician. Added to this, he had a remarkable memory, which helped him to become fluent in six languages as well as English, and wrote over 18,000 letters.

Whereas Franklin had been born into a relatively poor family, Jefferson came into a large inheritance when he was in his early teens, which he acknowledged was a great help in establishing him in business and politics. Like Franklin, Jefferson was also a passionate admirer of the opposite sex, which led him to considerable intellectual turmoil, particularly when he tried to seduce a neighbour's wife. He married in 1772 and was devastated when his wife died 10 years later, giving birth to their sixth child. Later, while travelling in Europe, he fell in love and corresponded with Maria Cosway, an English artist and musician.

From 1784 to 1789, Jefferson (like Franklin) served as a diplomat in France before returning to become President. He was subsequently re-elected, by a large majority, for his next presidential term. Jefferson helped to found the University of Virginia, and one of the main achievements of his second term of Presidency was the prohibition of the slave trade. However, the United States had to wait for a further half century and Abraham Lincoln before slavery was finally and effectively abolished, and yet another century after that before Martin Luther King finally and conclusively established civil rights for all black Americans. Nevertheless, Thomas Jefferson, the writer of the Declaration of Independence and the first major opponent of slavery in the US, was the man who laid the foundations for the achievements of Abraham Lincoln and Martin Luther King and the granting of civil rights to the entire population of the American continent.

WILLIAM PITT THE ELDER, FIRST EARL OF CHATHAM 1708-1778

PLANNING EARTH'S FUTURE

It was during the mid-18th century, in the worldwide colonial battles between England, France and Spain, that the future cultural and linguistic pattern of the planet was, to a very large extent, determined. William Pitt the Elder, First Earl of Chatham, the most brilliant statesman of the period, realized that these battles between the European nations were of decisive importance to the future direction of the world. He was absolutely determined and resolute that the English language and English culture would emerge triumphant from this worldwide struggle. It was on the plains of North America and in Canada that this battle was primarily fought and where Pitt won his major victories.

BRIDGING THE ATLANTIC

Not only was Pitt resolved to beat France and Spain in the colonial wars, he was also determined to maintain the ties between the burgeoning states of America and the motherland of Great Britain. In 1764 the British parliament had passed a measure known as the Sugar Act which imposed a tax on every imported gallon of molasses into the States of Northern America. It was not a tax over which the Americans had any influence or any say; it was merely imposed by the British central government, and it infuriated the American colonists. The American polymath, Benjamin Franklin, journeyed to London to suggest a brilliant and imaginative alternative – the creation of a native American bank which would make loans to the American colonists and pay the wages of British troops (for this was the reason for the tax in the first place) with the interest. His proposal was ignored by the British parliament and a year later the British government passed the detested Stamp Act, imposing a tax on all legal documents, newspapers and playing cards in Northern America.

GLOBAL VISION

In 1766, Franklin again appeared before the House of Commons in London. This time he had given up on the suggestion of the American bank. He merely argued that the British parliament had no right to tax subjects who were not represented. Further, he warned that any attempt to enforce the Stamp Act would lead to a rebellion. Interestingly, among Franklin's supporters was William Pitt, the politician who had masterminded Britain's victory in the Seven Years' War from 1756 to 1763. Eight days after Pitt's representations and his desperate attempts to keep Britain and America together, the British parliament withdrew the Stamp Act. The American colonists rejoiced but this rejoicing was premature. On 4 March 1766, the British parliament passed a new act asserting its right to impose laws on the colonies. This led, within 10 years, to the American War of Independence. Pitt's vision of keeping America and Britain together had been thwarted by small minds. He, in stark contrast, had been a man of vision. What was that vision and how was it implemented?

ARMY – POLITICS – ORATORY

Pitt was born in Cornwall in 1708, educated at Eton and Trinity College, Oxford, and enrolled briefly in the army in 1731. He came from a political family and in 1735 he entered parliament for what was then the family borough of Old Sarum. He was a brilliant orator with an imposing figure and a magnificent voice and rapidly rose through government. In 1756, he became Secretary of State, though his role was essentially that of Prime Minister. He immediately carried out his plans of proceeding with a war against France, Britain's chief colonial rival. He raised a militia, and strengthened naval power. (At one point he had to resign, but the populace demanded his reinstatement.) His war policy was characterized by tremendous vigour, wisdom and brilliant success. French armies were defeated by Britain and her allies in India, Africa, Canada and Europe, while British fleets swept the French ships from almost every sea. When Pitt resigned in 1761, the object of the war in North America had been gained – the French had been defeated and the British language and culture had been established as the dominant future force in North American and Canadian life.

Pitt himself was a steadfast parliamentarian; although racked by illness and exhausted in his old age, he still insisted on speaking in the House of Lords, where he died on 11 May 1778, falling into the arms of friends as he concluded a speech. He was honoured with a public funeral, a statue in Westminster Abbey and a pension of £4000 per year for his descendants.

CONQUERING A NEW WORLD IN THE OLD

Pitt was a global player on a grand scale who expressed the aspirations of the entire British nation by exporting their culture, trade and ideas around the planet. The opening of 1758 began a succession of victories all over the world which justified the claims of Pitt to be the restorer of the greatness of Britain. Everywhere he put new vigour into the struggle against France by placing young generals, chosen by himself, at the head of his expeditions and by raising loans for war expenses with a profusion which appalled more timid financiers. Part of this wealth was lavished on the King of Prussia, Frederick the Great, whose aid was invaluable in decoying the forces of France. Pitt proudly announced, 'I am conquering Canada on the plains of Germany.' This was his reproach to those who criticized him for the vast subsidies which he sent to Frederick. Pitt's epigram came true, for the reinforcements which were absolutely necessary if France was to retain her American possessions were being sent instead across the Rhine to join in the great

European struggle against Frederick. Pitt was working to a glorious end, a global policy to ensure British supremacy. It may seem from the fact that America did in fact break with Great Britain in the American War of Independence that Pitt had failed. However, the links he had forged in the Seven Years' War, whereby Britain became the dominant cultural force in North America, persist to this day. That was Pitt's vision.

HONESTY – FORESIGHT – LEADERSHIP

What do we learn from Pitt? First, vision – vision spanning centuries and supported by persistence, honesty, faith and courage. He was the only British politician of that period who was perceived by the populace at large to be free from personal, financial and moral corruption. That honesty stood him in good stead and guaranteed his position in the government. Using that position, unlike so many politicians who can see no further than the next election, Pitt stood for a global and historical vision which, as a result of his untiring efforts, ultimately came true.

GEORGE WASHINGTON 1732-1799

Washington was Commander-in-Chief of the American forces in the War of Independence and went on to be elected the first President of the United States.

SUBJECT KNOWLEDGE

Tall and with an imposing figure, he possessed great physical presence. In his youth he had learned the use of arms and studied the art of war. In 1759 he married well and, combined with his own inheritance, this made him one of the wealthiest men in the land and a successful farmer. According to witnesses at that time, he displayed great generosity and frequently entertained guests at his open house.

When the quarrel between England and the colonial Americans broke out, Washington initially favoured peaceful measures. Soon, however, he realized that nothing except force would secure his countrymen their rights. He represented Virginia in the first and second Continental Congresses of 1774 and 1775 and immediately took a leading role. He was not a great speaker nor a great writer, even though he did leave 14 volumes of writings when he died. He did, though, excel in common sense and the

William Pitt by the fashionable portrait painter John Hoppner (c.1758-1810).

management of affairs and men. Having fought in the colonial wars against France – on the British side – he was the one American soldier of national reputation. Inevitably, he was the natural choice to become Commander-in-Chief of the new American army.

INSPIRING LOYALTY

The American army which Washington took over was extraordinary – poorly armed and consisting of barely disciplined farmers, fur trappers, mechanics, scouts and amateur soldiers. Yet Washington, a dignified, well-dressed country gentleman, took command of this motley crew and forged them into an effective fighting force. This compares with Genghis Khan's disciplining of the divided Mongolian tribes to fuse them into a deadly military weapon.

As the War of American Independence raged across the land, Washington's army experienced varied fortunes. They besieged a well-armed, professional British force in Boston and forced their evacuation. Names such as Concord and Bunker Hill redound to Washington's credit as victories but, in New York, he was forced to retreat and suffered defeats at Brandywine and Germantown. These, though, were counterbalanced by victories which were achieved at Trenton and Princeton in 1777.

PERSISTENCE – IT'S NOT OVER TILL IT'S OVER

However, Washington's main achievement was to hold the revolutionary army together through the winter of 1778 at Valley Forge. Hostilities had ceased during the winter, but the cold was bitter, supplies vanishingly small, and his army was in danger of total disintegration. But by dint of his forceful personality, he maintained the cohesion of his troops and they lived to fight on. Washington's strategy, essentially, was a Fabian one – a delaying strategy, much in the same vein as that of Quintus Fabius Maximus, the so-called 'delayer' who defended Rome against Hannibal in the second Punic War by attrition, or of the Duke of Wellington at the Battle of Waterloo. In both cases, the strategy was to hold the enemy at bay until reinforcements could arrive. In Washington's case, the reinforcements were the French!

In 1778, the new American Republic sealed an alliance with France and, with the assistance of French troops, Washington managed to force the defeat and surrender of the British under General Cornwallis at Yorktown in 1781. This victory effectively ended the War of Independence in America's favour.

VISION

Eight years later, Washington was chosen as first Chief Magistrate, President, of the new American republic. At the outset of his government, Washington sought – as one might expect – to enlist in support of his new government the ablest men in the country, whether they had approved or disapproved of the precise form of the new constitution. Washington retired from the Presidency in 1797, and died at his estate Mount Vernon on the Potomac River on 14 December 1799. In his honour, the capital of the United States bears his name.

JOHANN WOLFGANG VON GOETHE
1749-1832
HIGHEST IQ

'Voilà un homme' (What a man!) is how the Emperor Napoleon described Goethe at their meeting at Erfurt in 1808. Goethe's achievements are multifarious. He has been described as 'the prince of the mind' and also as the man with the highest IQ and the largest vocabulary in history. He was a poet, man of action, dramatist, a scien-

BELOW Goethe had a vast vocabulary of 50,000 words (twice that of Shakespeare).

ABOVE Washington, like many military geniuses, inspired his troops in battle.

tist who was fascinated by optics, plants and minerals, a statesman, sage, novelist and theatrical producer. In 1784, he discovered a bone in the human body, hitherto unknown to science – the intermaxillary bone in the jaw. For decades Goethe *was* European literature!

LIMITLESS SEARCH FOR KNOWLEDGE

Goethe's work fuelled the sense of national identity that Germany began to experience towards the end of the 18th century and the beginning of the 19th, with works such as *Götz von Berlichingen* (1771). (This was a play, incidentally, in which Goethe described chess as the mind game 'par excellence', the 'touchstone of the intellect'.) Goethe's novel *Werther* (1774), with the romantic suicide of the young hero, swept Europe. Then there was his play *Egmont* (1788), a stirring tale of the liberation of the Netherlands from the Spanish empire, the plot of which Beethoven drew on to construct his own *Egmont,* an overture of liberation. Goethe is best known, however, for his masterpiece *Faust*, which he began in 1775. He spent many years revising the text, publishing the first part in 1808 and the second in 1832. Goethe himself, when it was finally published, was immediately seen as a legendary Faustian figure, with a limitless thirst for knowledge and investigation.

STRIVING

The theme of *Faust*, which involves alchemy, mysticism, love, death, suicide, Classical learning and ultimately salvation, represents Goethe's central theory: '*Whoever strives throughout life, that person can be saved*' (in German: 'Wer immer strebend sich bemüht den können wir erlösen!'). Goethe deeply admired Napoleon, whom he saw as an exemplar of this eternal type of striving, and Napoleon returned the compliment. He kept Goethe's novel *Werther* in his campaign library and claimed to have read it seven times.

IMMENSE PHYSICALITY

In his later life, Goethe came to be seen by his admirers as almost an aloof Olympian figure, but this would be to deny one of the great realities of the man. Throughout his full and long life, Goethe perpetually fell in love with attractive young women, who at times inspired his work and at others distracted him from it. Following his appointment as a court official in 1776, he held a state post for many decades and enjoyed court life. His employer, the Duke of Weimar, said famously of him: 'Goethe could drink terribly, he could match the best.'

MORE LIGHT

Contemporary sources often provide the best descriptions. In 1807, a court official wrote of Goethe: 'He is tall of stature and gives an impression of slimness. The colour of his face is dark, almost like night. There is a certain hardness in his features, which are, however, very alive. His eyes retain a hidden beam of light, shining the moment he smiles. I have seen him glow with warmth and heard the seething of the riches within. I have recognized the lion by his claws.' An inspirational figure indeed, both in appearance and in his work. In fact, it was Goethe's essay on nature which inspired Sigmund Freud to take up the study of medicine. Goethe's last words, appropriately, have been reported widely as 'Mehr licht', meaning 'more light!'.

THEORY OF GOETHENDIPITY

Goethe is one of the central figures in this book, not only for his great intelligence and his enormous achievements, but also for the following quotation, which is an essential key to the development and unleashing of one's personal genius: '*Until one is committed there is hesitancy, a chance to draw back. Always ineffectiveness concerning all acts of initiative and creation. There is one elementary proof – the ignorance of which kills countless ideas and splendid plans. This is, that the moment one definitely commits oneself, then providence moves too. All sorts of things occur to help one, that would never otherwise have occurred. A whole stream of events issues from the decision, raising in one's favour all manner of unforeseen incidents and material assistance, which no man could have dreamed would have come his way. Whatever you can do or dream you can, begin it. Boldness has genius, power and magic in it, begin it now.*'

This is the central text of our Goethendipity Principle, which is explained in more detail on page 45. It states that if you have a plan or a dream, you must act on it. You must resolve yourself to carry it out. Once that resolve has been taken, events will move in your favour. It is serendipity with plan, vision and intention. This is the most valuable lesson to be learned from Goethe and perhaps the single most important lesson to be derived from this book.

WOLFGANG AMADEUS MOZART
1756-1791

MEMORY

Ask any musician to rank the leading composers and Mozart will regularly emerge at the top of the list. The facts of his extraordinary life are well known. Mozart was composing and performing in public at the age of six, he had perfect pitch and after just one visit to a concert he could write down from memory all the music played in it. He could compose vast operatic and orchestral scores in his head; then commit them to paper without making a single correction or error. His skills in rearranging music were legendary. For example, he once wrote a minuet, threw its different sections into a hat, shuffled them around and in whichever order they came back out of the hat, the minuet still played perfectly.

MASTERPIECES AND STUDY

His masterpieces included an entire canon of symphonies, chamber music and operas, such as *The Marriage of Figaro* (1786), *Don Giovanni* (1787), *Cosi fan tutte* (1790) and *The Magic Flute* (1791). A seemingly endless series of masterpieces flowed from his brain – indeed, he left more than 600 compositions.

Mozart made his first professional tour of Europe when he was six years old. He was the youngest son of Leopold Mozart, Kapellmeister (Concert Master) to the Archbishop of Salzburg, where Mozart was born. One can see here the

Mozart at the clavichord by Joseph-Siffrede Duplessis (1725-1802).

Part of Mozart's original score for Requiem K. 626 (written in 1791).

influence of the father on the son – Mozart's genius was nurtured and trained by his father who was also a professional musician. Fortunately, Leopold found in the young Wolfgang a most receptive and ingenious student.

THE RIGHT NUMBER OF NOTES!

In 1781, Mozart settled in Vienna, also as Concert Master to the Archbishop of Salzburg. But he quarrelled famously with his patron. When the Archbishop criticized one of Mozart's pieces by saying: 'Too many notes, my dear Mozart, too many notes!' Mozart replied witheringly: 'Sir, neither too few nor too many. There are exactly as many notes as there should be.'

HARMONY

Finally, in 1787, Mozart was appointed as Chamber Musician to the Emperor Joseph II. During his life, however, he never, whether through jealousy or opposition to his radical new style of music, received the recognition for his genius that fell to him after his death. It has been said of Mozart that he left 'no branch of music unenriched by his genius. Gifted, with an inexhaustible vein of the richest, purest melody, he surpassed all Italians on their chosen ground, while his strict training in the German tradition placed at his service wonderful resources of harmony and instrumentation.' Of his 41 symphonies, the pre-eminent are the C major, known as the Jupiter, the G minor and the E flat.

POSITIVE ATTITUDE

However, what is less well known about Mozart is that his work has given rise to two theories

closely connected with the unleashing of one's own personal genius. The first we call 'Amadeity' – based on Mozart's name, Amadeus – the parallels of which in this book are the Synergistic, Success, Red Rum, Goethendipity and VIE Brain Principles (see pages 42-45). All of these principles have been designed to assist in the unleashing of the reader's potential for genius.

It is increasingly apparent, from a study of Mozart's letters, that he was never depressed by setbacks. If it happened that very few people attended a concert, he still regarded it as a huge triumph. He may have been paid almost nothing for his endeavours, but he would still have been totally delighted with whatever he received. Whatever fate strew in his path, he put an unfailingly constructive and positive interpretation on the turn of events. This defensive shield of obliviousness to any disaster that might befall him helped him to survive in a difficult environment. This was Mozart's method of ensuring buoyancy of spirit, and it could be compared with the message promulgated by Lao-Tzu.

AMADEITY IN ACTION
'Mozart's inability to believe that he might be a failure, even when his concerts were a disaster, was an essential part of his genius, according to psychologists.' (*The Times*, 13 February 1993.) 'A new analysis of the composer's correspondence shows that he was almost pathologically optimistic. Failure or defeat were not part of his vocabulary and the idea that fate might be against him, even when he suffered a series of setbacks, was inconceivable.

'A study of about 600 of Mozart's surviving letters reveals his high optimism and exuberant self-confidence. An understanding of how people cope with negative events provides an important insight into their character. Optimistic people tend to attribute any setback they may suffer to external causes that are temporary and can be changed. Pessimistic people, on the other hand, appear helpless in the face of events and are more likely to blame themselves. In 1790, after giving a disastrous concert in Frankfurt, Mozart wrote to his wife, "My concert . . . was a splendid success from the point of view of honour and glory, but a failure as far as money was concerned. Unfortunately some Prince was giving a déjeuner and the Hessian troops were holding a grand manoeuvre. But . . . I was in such good form . . . they implored me to give another concert next Sunday."

INCREASING OPTIMISM
'Writing in *The Psychologist*, the journal of the British Psychological Society, Professor Andrew Steptoe, of St George's Hospital Medical School, says that towards the end of Mozart's short life, after he had suffered from the death of four children, serious illness and repeated professional and financial disasters, his optimism actually rose.' Similarly, Borges has related how he treated the loss of his sight as a window for new opportunities (*Seven Nights*).

MOZART INCREASES YOUR IQ!
Secondly, it has recently been demonstrated by Dr Gordon Shaw of the Physics Department of the University of California that listening to the complex harmonies of Mozart can in fact stimulate one's brain and increase one's IQ. Dr Shaw carried out tests on students who were playing Chess, and discovered that their brainwaves appeared to be making music. The natural patterns of their brains were similar to musical patterns. Dr Shaw himself has said that any great venture must start out with a dream, and his dream was to show that Mozart's music can increase IQ.

ABSTRACT REASONING
Dr Shaw, together with psychologist Frances Rauscher (an ex-professional cellist), also attempted to find out whether providing music training for young children could improve their spatial reasoning skills. The initial results were extremely positive. After three, six and nine months of lessons, the children's abstract reasoning showed great improvement.

Encouraged by these results, Shaw and Rauscher decided to analyse what happens to adults when they listen to music. They compared three listening states – Mozart's Sonata in D Major for two pianos, a relaxation tape and silence – and tested the subjects' spatial reasoning after each tape. Although the effects wore off, listening to Mozart raised their IQ scores by an average of nine points more than the other two tapes.

HIGHER BRAIN FUNCTIONS
What about other forms of music? Can listening to heavy rock, acid house or rap music have the same stimulating effect as Mozart? Shaw and Rauscher believe not, since these forms do not have the required structural and harmonic complexity. Shaw claims that we were born with

some of the structure already programmed into our brains. So there are already certain natural patterns that can be excited, and when we hear Mozart's music, it is pleasing to us because these natural patterns are being aroused in our brains while we listen.

The implications are clear. 'We need to be educated into classical music at an early stage, the earlier the better. In future, children will be given music lessons, not just for music's sake, which is not to say that it is not valid, but also because it enhances higher brain functions,' says Rauscher.

No doubt Mozart would have been delighted had he realized that 200 years after his death, his music would be used to increase the intelligence of his fellow human beings.

HORATIO NELSON 1758-1805

Nelson was the most successful fighting admiral in history. The oceans were his playground, the keys to his success were his own inspiration to his men, his personal courage, the training system he instituted, the rate of fire he succeeded in developing among his artillery crews and, above all, nutrition. Nelson realized that a properly nourished naval crew is a fighting-fit naval crew.

INSPIRING LOYALTY

Nelson shared a quality with other great military commanders – their ability to inspire intense loyalty and devotion among their troops. Usually, commanders such as Alexander or Caesar

At the Battle of Trafalgar, Nelson adopted an unorthodox naval strategy. His outnumbered ships sailed to the positions shown in grey, from where he achieved an outstanding victory.

achieved this by sharing the deprivations of their men and exposing themselves to the same hazards of battle. In this sense, Nelson succeeded brilliantly. However, he also had severe, highly visible wounds – the loss of one eye and one arm. There could be no more convincing proof of his 'sharing of hazards' than this, and it inspired his men to do their utmost.

COURAGE

From a very early age, Nelson's one overriding ambition was to go to sea. Also from an early age, he displayed tremendous personal courage, almost oblivious to any dangers which he might encounter. On an Arctic expedition in 1773, Nelson, then a 15-year-old coxswain, sneaked away from his ship to hunt a polar bear so that 'I might carry its skin to my father'. There is a painting which shows him swinging an empty musket at an enraged polar bear. Apparently the musket misfired and Nelson was in extreme danger from attack by this large carnivorous animal. Fortunately, a well-timed shot from the ship's cannon frightened the bear away.

PERSISTENCE

During the wars against Napoleon, Britain ultimately succeeded in establishing naval domination over the French, and this was due in great measure to Nelson's achievements. In a series of brilliant battles at Cape St Vincent, the Nile (after which he was given a peerage), Copenhagen and ultimately Trafalgar, Nelson virtually destroyed the French fleet.

INNOVATION

The Battle of Trafalgar in 1805 was Nelson's masterpiece. In those days it was conventional naval

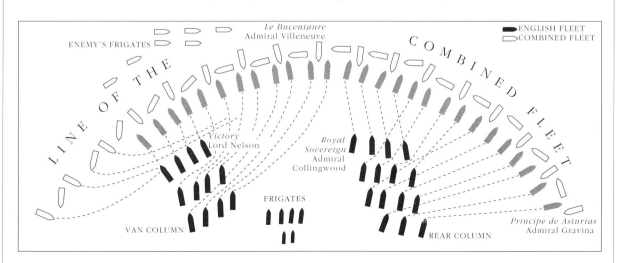

Viscount Horatio Nelson by portrait painter Sir William Beechey (1753-1839).

strategy, given the type of artillery available, for fleets to line up against each other and blast away with broadsides. At Trafalgar, Nelson observed that he did not have as many ships as the combined French and Spanish fleets. He also knew that his men were capable of firing up to 10 times faster than their opponents. This was because they had trained vigorously under his command for just such an eventuality. He resolved, therefore, to destroy the opposing fleets by sailing his ships directly at them in separate columns. This entailed the risk that he would not be able to engage his broadsides fully until a later stage in the battle, but it also produced a huge compensating advantage, given the superior rate of British firepower. Once the hostile ships were engaged piecemeal, the British battleships could then use their cannons on both sides – thus attacking double the number of French and Spanish vessels. The strategy succeeded brilliantly, although Nelson himself was killed by a stray musket ball at his moment of greatest triumph.

FITNESS – IN CORPORE SANO

What do we learn from Nelson? Personal courage, transmitted with electric force to his colleagues, including brilliantly inspirational messages flagged to his crews before battle; the value of unremitting training in order to reach a peak of perfection; and finally, the inestimable nutritional value of fresh food and vegetables. He knew his men had to be fit to extract the maximum from them – and he did!

NAPOLEON BONAPARTE 1769-1821

HUMOUR

Napoleon's minister Savary, his man in charge of censorship, once reported to the Emperor on new publications. He mentioned a three-volume work on Germany written by Madame de Stael, adding that he had read it and found nothing objectionable – the Emperor's name was not even mentioned. Napoleon retorted: 'A three-volume work, in which I am not mentioned. It must be banned immediately!' Strong evidence of a sense of humour by the great Emperor of the French who, at one time, was probably the most powerful person ever in the world.

GOETHE AND MERIT

Goethe knew and admired Napoleon and described his particular kind of genius as 'demoniac'. Goethe said: 'The demoniac is to be seen in its most terrible form when it is overwhelmingly manifested in some one individual. A titanic force emanates from him and he exercises incredible power over every creature, and even over the elements, and who can say how far his influence will extend. As more forces are combined against him, his opponents are still powerless. It is in vain for the more enlightened section of humanity to brand him as deceived or deceiver. The masses will be attracted by him. Rarely if ever, do his equals exist at the same time and nothing can overcome him, but the very universe against which he declared battle.' Words which might also apply to Alexander the Great and Genghis Khan.

A further feature that unites Napoleon with Alexander the Great and Genghis Khan was the fact that promotion within their armies was based on merit – one secret of their success.

EARLY REJECTION

As a young man, Napoleon was snubbed at college. He was not even French; he came from Corsica and French was not his first language. Rejected at school, he hurled himself into his personal studies and at one time he even tried to write novels. He had immense energy and an extraordinary eye for detail. In later life

Napoleon Crossing the Alps *by Jacques Louis David (1748-1825).*

Napoleon was an early speed reader, who used to shock his civil servants by thoroughly perusing documents of staggering size, with thousands of minute details, in a very short time and pointing out to the bureaucrats discrepancies of which even they had been unaware.

SUBJECT KNOWLEDGE

Napoleon's first revolutionary contribution to the art of war was to recognize the devastating force of the technical advantages in artillery that occurred towards the end of the 18th century. He also recognized the power of independent columns, moving as separate army corps of 40,000 men each and able to converge flexibly on any enemy. This was the strategy employed by Genghis Khan, one that had apparently been forgotten or overlooked by commanders since.

APPLICATION OF KNOWLEDGE

Like Julius Caesar and Suleyman before him, Napoleon was also a law giver, creating the Code Napoleon to standardize and modernize the French legal system. Essentially, this was still in force until it was rescinded and replaced by more modern laws on 1 March 1994! As a military commander, Napoleon was pre-eminent. In the space of just 10 years, he smashed the empires of Austria, Prussia and Russia. He was the French revolution incarnate, winning victories which have gone down in history, such as Marengo, Austerlitz, Wagram, Jena and Ulm.

MASTERMIND GROUP

It has been said that Napoleon's greatest assets were his mathematical mind, phenomenal memory, boundless energy and prolific imagination. He sought immortality through conquest, saying: *'Space we can recover, time never.'*

Napoleon had heroes as his mastermind group. As he said: 'Peruse again and again, the campaigns of Hannibal, Caesar and Alexander. This is the only means of becoming a great captain and acquiring the secret of the art of war.' Like Caesar he valued speed and mobility, and drove his officers to their physical limits. Napoleon also ensured the loyalty of his troops by being seen among them – sharing their deprivations, marching with them and even, at times, appearing in threadbare clothes while his own marshalls were dressed in finery.

SELF BELIEF

He projected a careful mix of the grand and the common, utilizing every means of propaganda, press, war bulletins, pageantry and the charisma of his own legend. His eventual downfall was occasioned by his decision in 1812 to invade Russia – biting off more than he could chew. As one critic said: *'It was amazing: Although Napoleon's common sense amounted to genius, he never quite knew where the possible left off.'* Julius Caesar hoped to take control by radiating power from the nerve centre of Rome, the first Chin emperor built his boundaries and patrolled them ceaselessly without going beyond them, while Alexander the Great wished to conquer for ever. In trying to emulate Alexander and the Alexandrian mode of conquest, Napoleon, in the final analysis, took one step too far.

THE DUKE OF WELLINGTON, ARTHUR WELLESLEY 1769-1852

The Duke of Wellington has entered history as Britain's most brilliant military commander. He won the Peninsular Campaign in Spain against France during the Napoleonic Wars; he rose to become Commander-in-Chief of the British armies and he defeated Napoleon at the Battle of Waterloo in 1815. Having completed a glorious military career, in which he never lost a battle and had beaten the best in the world, he went on to twice become British Prime Minister. Towards the middle of the 19th century, he evolved into the revered elder statesman who guided the young Queen Victoria, as Britain's empire expanded to become the largest on earth.

FLEXIBILITY – AT THE RIGHT TIMES

Wellington is known not just for his exploits in the political and military spheres but also for the force and brevity of his aphoristic wit. Once Queen Victoria complained to him about young couples making love in the Royal Parks and asked how much it would cost to put an end to it. After careful thought, he replied, 'Half a Crown, Ma'am.' His royal questioner promptly abandoned the plan, which would have proved most unpopular with her subjects. At the great London Exhibition of 1851, which displayed the imperial trade and self-confidence of Queen Victoria's reign, the organizers came to him for advice: 'Duke, the Crystal Palace is infested with sparrows which make a terrible noise and are defiling the hall with their droppings. How do we get rid of them?' After careful thought, the Duke replied with just one word: 'Sparrowhawks'.

Known as the Iron Duke, as a result of both the physical hardships he endured in his military life and also his inflexible resolve in battle, he had started his distinguished career in campaigns in India in the late 18th century. A young officer in the British army was due to go to India in the 1840s and before leaving he went to see the Duke for some tips about life in the subcontinent. Wellington reflected and then said after some more careful thought: 'Tell the young man to take plenty of good light claret with him. You can't trust the water in India.'

The Duke's style of government was tinged by his military experiences. When he held his first cabinet meeting as Prime Minister he was alarmed at the way politicians behaved. He confided to a close aide after the meeting: 'It's amaz-

Wellesley became Duke of Wellington a year before the Battle of Waterloo.

ing. I gave them all their orders and they wanted to stay behind and discuss them.'

TRUTH AND PLANNING

As a General, the Duke of Wellington was the most successful and ingenious land commander that Britain has ever seen. His credo was always to avoid loss of his own troops and the men admired and trusted him for this. Usually fighting at inferior odds, against well-equipped, mobile and superior numbers of the Napoleonic armies in the Spanish campaign during the Peninsular War, Wellington's standard tactic was to locate a powerful position, line up his troops in deep defence and then wait for the French onslaught. Time and again French marshals, such as Massena, Ney and Marmont, the greatest military talents that Napoleon's army could boast, found their advancing tides of men broken against Wellington's defensive formations.

A typical Wellington victory came about due to the fortifications he erected at Torres Vedras in Portugal in 1810. He lured a gigantic French army to the extremity of the Peninsula, where they anticipated sweeping Wellington's forces into the sea. But they suddenly found themselves confronted by an impregnable series of trenches and ramparts which the Duke had meticulously and in great secrecy prepared well in advance. The French army was obliged to encamp in an area where the supplies, resources and food were rapidly dwindling. Eventually, forced to admit defeat, they retreated and it was the Duke who swept down and finally drove the French conclusively from Spain.

COURAGE

Wellington's greatest triumph, though, came with the Battle of Waterloo in 1815. There he faced the spirit incarnate of the French revolution itself, Napoleon Bonaparte – the man most widely regarded as the greatest military genius in history – the victor of Austerlitz, Wagram, Marengo and so many other resounding names. As always, Wellington suffered from a numerical inferiority in the battle and his army was a desperate concoction of British, Hanoverian, German and Dutch troops. Nevertheless, he drew up his forces at Waterloo in his normal deep defence, concealing and protecting his men just behind the brow of a hill (his standard tactic). For an entire day Napoleon threw battalion after battalion of cavalry, the young guard, the old guard and the veterans of his imperial campaigns, against the Duke's lines. Wellington, by his constant encouragement and personal inspiration, riding between the lines of his men on his horse Copenhagen, forming squares of infantry at appropriate moments, counterattacking when necessary, drove Napoleon back and ultimately defeated him.

POSITIVE ATTITUDE

What can we learn from the Iron Duke? He was not a dashing commander and he was not someone who launched into unnecessary attacks. But he emerged victorious from every military engagement in which he was ever involved, achieving this by careful and intelligent choice of terrain, caution, long-range planning and anticipating the moves and counter-moves of all of his opponents at the right time. If one lesson can be drawn from his immense military record it is that of persistence, determination and courage under fire, never giving up, always coming back and extracting the absolute maximum from slender resources. He once described the French army as a 'gloriously caparisoned leather saddle' and the British army as 'a piece of rope held together by string'. Invariably, the Duke succeeded in making that piece of rope victorious. However dangerous or precarious his situation, he looked for the positive signs and the positive elements which could combine to his advantage and to frustrate his enemy.

LUDWIG VAN BEETHOVEN 1770-1827
ODE TO FREEDOM

Throughout his life, Beethoven, the great Viennese composer, fought for three freedoms. The first was freedom from tyranny and censorship. This is manifested by his angry decision to tear out the dedication of his third symphony, *Eroica,* when Napoleon (the original dedicatee), crowned himself Emperor in 1804. Beethoven's battle for freedom on this level is further shown by his music to *Egmont,* Goethe's play of political liberation that depicts the Dutch struggle to throw off the yoke of their Spanish masters. Beethoven's single opera, *Fidelio,* also treats the theme of triumph against political, military and intellectual oppression. Finally, Beethoven's commitment to freedom from tyranny is specifically shown by his choice of Schiller's poetry to crown his own supreme masterwork, the 9th symphony.

ARTISTIC FREEDOM AND INNOVATION

Beethoven also sought freedom of artistic expression by breaking away from the patterns established by his own teacher, Haydn (1732-1809), and by Mozart. For example, Beethoven's turbulent, questing, creative spirit and his desire to bend music to his own will rather than utilizing ready-made, traditional classical forms, led him to expand considerably the length of his symphonies in comparison to the old masters. Beethoven even introduced a choral finale to his 9th symphony, an innovation not repeated for almost a century until Gustav Mahler wrote his 8th symphony, the Symphony of 1000.

TIME AND ART

Beethoven was also a pioneer in the use of the recently invented mechanical timing device, the metronome, writing: 'I look upon the invention of the metronome as a welcome means of assuring the performance of my compositions everywhere, in the tempi conceived by me, which, to

my regret, have so often been misunderstood.' Here we observe once again the intertwining of the scientific and the mathematical with the creative and artistic, a relationship established by Phidias, Brunelleschi, Dufay and Leonardo.

TURNING ADVERSITY INTO ADVANTAGE

Beethoven finally sought to liberate his spirit from encroaching deafness – a terrible fate for a composer. As his deafness increased, he became more isolated and wrote to a friend that he felt he would be happier if he married. In his Will to his brothers, Beethoven gave his disability as the main reason for what some described as anti-social behaviour and his withdrawal from society. As early as 1802, in the poignant *Heiligenstadt Testament,* Beethoven describes his dreadful predicament. His heroic determination to continue composing music, even after such a blow, places Beethoven in the same league as other geniuses who have transcended extreme physical handicaps – for example, Milton, Borges and Hawking. Indeed, Beethoven's most sublime compositions, seven of his nine symphonies, as well as the Kreutzer Sonata (described as 'dazzlingly difficult'), the Diabelli variations, the Archduke Trio and Beethoven's superb string quartets were all composed after Beethoven became aware of the onset of his malady. From then on, Beethoven increasingly had to rely 'On the ethereal instruments of his inner ear', as Ben Zander of the Boston Philharmonic has movingly put it.

BEETHOVEN'S 9TH AND SCHILLER

The opening of Beethoven's 9th symphony in D minor (opus 125), of 1823, represents the awakening of the primordial forces of the universe. The symphony proceeds to the grand affirmation of the choral finale, 'His suns fly across the glorious landscape of the heavens . . .'. This final movement is based on the *Ode to Joy,* by the German poet, Friedrich Schiller (1759-1805).

As a youth, Schiller had been forcibly drafted into the army by the Duke of Württemberg and forbidden to write! But Schiller escaped, going on to become a passionate advocate of personal freedom, a friend and colleague of Goethe, and also Germany's leading writer of historical dramas. His masterpiece in poetic form is the *Ode to Joy,* of around 1787, while his stage masterpiece is the blank verse dramatic trilogy *Wallenstein* (1796-99). Drawing heavily on Shakespeare, Schiller demonstrates in these plays

Ludwig van
Beethoven
Fidelio

BREITKOPF & HÄRTEL
LEIPZIG

ABOVE *This is the frontispiece from* Fidelio, *Beethoven's only opera which he completed in 1814. The story is of a faithful wife who saves her husband from execution.*

LEFT *Many portraits of Beethoven survive. In this idealized interpretation by Joseph Carl Stieler, he is composing a Mass. At the time of the painting (1819-20), Beethoven was profoundly deaf.*

how entrenched formalism, tradition and the sheer inertia of that which has been sanctioned by custom and usage can, on occasion, conspire to defeat the bold, revolutionary new idea which might change the world for the better.

THE ODE TO JOY

It is a little known fact that Schiller's *Ode to Joy* (in German, *Freude*) was originally written as the *Ode to Freedom* (in German, *Freiheit*). But the tyrannical censorship at that time refused to allow a hymn to freedom to appear in print. Schiller therefore substituted another similar two-syllable German word, beginning with 'F', that would satisfactorily approximate to his metre and his meaning. Schiller's readers, of course, knew that they should understand 'Freedom' wherever 'Joy' appeared. Consider the opening lines of the *Ode* which Beethoven now took up for his 9th symphony. The words are: 'Joy, joy, joy. Beauteous godly spark, daughter of Elysium, drunk with fire. Oh heavenly one, we come into your sacred shrine, your magic once again unites that which fashion sternly parted. All men are made brothers where your gentle wing abides.' Now consider this passage again with *freedom* substituted for *joy*. It makes considerably more sense and is also more inspiring.

INFLUENCE

Beethoven exerted enormous influence upon the Romantic composers and interpreters who followed him, and his 9th symphony fired their imagination more than any other piece of music. It has been described as 'a radiating point for all subsequent experiments for enlarging the time-scale of music. No later composer has escaped its influence.'

HARNESSING THE PLANET

*'GENIUS IS ONE PER CENT INSPIRATION AND NINETY-NINE PER CENT
PERSPIRATION.'*
THOMAS EDISON (1847-1931)

GEORGE STEPHENSON 1781-1848

PERFECT CONFIDENCE

'His courage and perfect confidence in his work
and judgement were shown by his venturing
with his trial safety lamps into parts of the mine
purposely rendered dangerous. The services that
he rendered to the well-being of mankind by his
invention of steam locomotion and railways
place him among the world's greatest benefac-
tors.' This assessment of Stephenson from the
Dictionary of National Biography perfectly cap-
tures the essence of the man's strength of character and foresight.

The son of a colliery fireman, Stephenson
joined his father as his assistant at the age of 14,
and in his 18th year began to learn to read and
write at a night school. His inventive powers
were first displayed in his designing a safety
lamp for miners, but a fierce argument developed between Stephenson and Sir Humphry
Davy, who brought out the Davy lamp at almost
the same time, as to who should take the credit
for the equipment (Davy triumphed).

MASTERMIND GROUP

Stephenson also became interested in the problems of haulage in the coal mines. In 1814 he
demonstrated a steam locomotive that could pull
a load of 30 tonnes up an incline of 1 in 450 at
four miles an hour. Stephenson was able to build
on the work of earlier engineers, who had envisioned the potential of steam power. By 1698
Thomas Newcomen (1663-1729) had invented
the atmospheric steam engine, used for pumping
water out of mines, while in 1769 the Scottish
engineer James Watt (1736-1819) had patented
his 'watt' steam engine. (Watt first coined the
term 'horsepower', but the watt, as a unit of
energy [for example, the '100-watt' lightbulb],
was simply named after him, not used by him.)
Both Stephenson and Watt learned much about
the use of steam when they were called upon
to mend one of Newcomen's machines.

*Stephenson applied his genius to improving
steam locomotives.*

Stephenson was also influenced by Richard
Trevithick (1771-1833), who in 1801 completed
the first steam carriage to convey passengers,
although this engine encountered problems
which Trevithick never successfully overcame.

MECHANICAL GENIUS

In 1815 Stephenson patented an improved version of his steam engine. In 1822 he was
appointed engineer to the Stockton and
Darlington railway and the first locomotive carrying passengers and goods ran on that line on
27 September 1825. He was subsequently
employed on the Liverpool and Manchester line
and ultimately designed the *Rocket*, which made
its trial trip in a contest against three other locomotives in 1829. Stephenson's mechanical genius
triumphed, as his locomotive was the only one
ready on time and covered 12 miles in 53 min-

utes. The opening of the line in 1830 was attended by the Prime Minister, the Duke of Wellington, and other notables. Stephenson continued to develop the steam engine and worked on nearly every railway scheme in England. In 1847 he became President of the Institution of Mechanical Engineers, which he had founded that year in Birmingham.

MICHAEL FARADAY 1791-1867

'All this is a dream. Still, examine it by a few experiments. Nothing is too wonderful to be true, if it be consistent with the laws of nature.'

Faraday's *Notebook*

For around 5000 years, civilization had relied for its motive power on the horse, the ox, or human muscle – either voluntary or enslaved. Then, in the space of just over a century, steam, electric and nuclear power were all discovered. Michael Faraday was the man who was chiefly responsible for harnessing the power of electricity for the good of humanity.

CURRENCY OF FAME

Just as the face of George Washington adorns the American dollar bill, so Michael Faraday is another of the great minds in this book whose image is to be found on a unit of currency. In his case, Faraday's likeness appears on the English 20-pound note.

HONOURING ATHENE

Faraday was the foremost experimentalist and natural philosopher of the first half of the 19th century. Among his distinctions was to be appointed the first Secretary of the Athenaeum Club in London – a gathering of scientists and thinkers which, to this day, boasts one of the greatest assemblages of Nobel Prize winners in the world. As we have seen, this type of society was also popular in 5th-century Athens. The foundation of the Athenaeum Club as a homage to Athens and its patron deity, Athene, is yet another clear case of the magnetism exerted by genius over other great minds.

STUDY AND COMMITMENT

Faraday was celebrated for his public lectures, dominated by his imposing appearance and his expansive physical gestures. Queen Victoria's Consort, Prince Albert, for example, was an enthusiastic member of his audiences. Faraday came from humble origins. Born a blacksmith's

son, at Newington Butts, London, on 22 September 1791, Faraday was later apprenticed to a book-binder. He studied science in all of his spare moments, however, poring over borrowed volumes of the *Encyclopaedia Britannica* by candlelight. In 1813, in response to Faraday's persistent entreaties, Sir Humphry Davy engaged him as an assistant at the Royal Institution. Sir Humphry himself was a celebrated chemist, whose own father had been a woodcarver from Truro in Cornwall.

LAUGHING MATTER

It is extraordinary that, in 1813, in vigorous and single-minded pursuit of their studies, both Sir Humphry Davy and Faraday visited France, even though there was a war raging between France and England at the time. The two British scientists crossed the Channel to investigate Davy's new theory of volcanic action and, surprisingly, they were received with the greatest distinction by the French scientific fraternity. Perhaps this trip appealed to Sir Humphry's sense of humour – after all, he was the first person to use laughing gas!

INQUISITIVENESS – NOT INQUISITION!

After conducting experiments which led to the condensation of gases into liquids by pressure (*Liquefaction of Gases*, 1823), Faraday succeeded to Davy's chair of chemistry at the Royal Institution in 1827. There followed a tour de force of scientific investigation, experimentation and publication. Among the subjects he covered were: the preparation of lungs for diving, the ventilation of lighthouse lamps, lectures on mental education, vaporization, the improvement of optical glass, acoustics, light and conservation of force. His Christmas lectures at the Royal Institution charmed and attracted all classes of students – including royalty.

His speciality, though, was the annual children's lecture. He loved children and his favourite topic was to explain how a candle was made, what occurred during combustion and what had happened to the candle at the end of the process. Children adored him in return. But his *magnum opus* was the series of experimental researches on electricity. Between 1821 and 1831, Faraday essentially discovered the secret of how to make electricity flow. Modern power stations, and hence electricity in industry and the home, owe their existence to his brilliant work during this period.

ELECTRICITY

It is important to understand that, in Faraday's time, electricity as we understand it now had simply not been discovered. Through his experiments Faraday convincingly demonstrated that electrical fields did exist and that they could propagate themselves through empty space. His development of the electro-magnetic field is one of the cornerstones of modern physics.

MASTERMIND GROUP

Faraday corresponded vigorously on scientific matters with Brunel and Ampère. André Ampère (1775-1836) was the French mathematician and physicist who first devised techniques for measuring electricity. Certainly, Faraday was not an isolated phenomenon in the scientific world of his day. The invention of the battery by the Italian scientist, Alessandro Volta (1745-1827), was enormously helpful in Faraday's discoveries, (Faraday had to make his own batteries painstakingly by hand). Similarly, the first indication of a link between electricity and magnetism which was shown by the Danish physicist, Hans Christian Oersted, greatly contributed to Faraday's findings. Nevertheless, it was Faraday who built the first generator in 1831 and it was Faraday's work which laid the foundations for the modern electricity industry.

MASTERMIND GROUP OF ONE

Sir Humphry Davy encouraged Faraday, gave him opportunities and, by his own lectures and brilliant investigations, provided a role model, a hero for Faraday to study, emulate and surpass. One vital lesson to be learned from this book is the importance of establishing a personal pantheon of heroes, geniuses and great minds who can be analysed, whose methods can be dissected and whose route to success can be followed. The relationship between Sir Humphry Davy and Michael Faraday, in spite of their occasional disagreements and jealousies at unimportant junctures, admirably illustrates one of our main theories for unleashing your own genius potential – namely, the construction of a Mastermind Group to inspire you.

A 'real Mastermind Group' would be a set of heroes with whom one was in personal contact. An 'internal Mastermind Group' would consist of role models who appear in literature, myth or history, but whom one had not actually met. Thus Homer and Achilles formed part of Alexander the Great's 'internal Mastermind Group', whereas Aristotle was part of his 'real Mastermind Group'. As far as Faraday was concerned, Sir Humphry Davy was, perhaps, in a 'real Mastermind Group' all of his own.

HUMILITY

Faraday's chief inspiration was the hunt for new knowledge. Having declined honours, titles and proffered wealth, Faraday was, in 1858, given a house in Hampton Court by the government. In 1862 he advocated the use of electromagnetic light in lighthouses. With shipping so important to the British economy, lighthouses were vital. A devout Christian for all of his life, he died at Hampton Court on 25 August 1867.

SUPREME SCIENTIFIC COMMUNICATOR

Dr Frank James of the Royal Institution, Faraday's distinguished biographer, provides his own summary of Faraday's achievement:

'All his professional scientific life was spent in the Royal Institution, then as now in London's Albemarle Street. His discoveries in chemistry and physics changed our perceptions of the world both intellectually and practically . . . His invention of the electric motor, transformer and dynamo effectively founded electrical engineering. His theoretical interpretations of these devices, together with his discoveries of the liquefaction of gases, the laws of electro-chemistry and his development of field theory challenged the prevailing Newtonian view of the world and paved the way for the work of Einstein.

'Furthermore, Faraday was universally acknowledged as the supreme scientific communicator between 1830 and 1860. His lectures allowed scientific knowledge to be widely disseminated and were one of the chief vehicles that made science such an integral part of Victorian culture.'

THE FUTURE

It is fascinating to speculate, given the types of previously untapped energy uncovered in the past two centuries, whether some Faraday of the 21st century might not yet still discover the hidden key to a colossal new source of environment-friendly power, hitherto unimagined.

ISAMBARD KINGDOM BRUNEL
1806-1859
INSPIRATION AND PERSEVERANCE

Brunel's genius lay in his mathematical flair and

Above A deputation to Faraday requesting him to accept the presidency by Edward Armitage (1817-96).

Left Brunel did not just supervise but frequently worked on his constructions.

his innovations in railway traction and steam navigation. He was inspired by the achievements of his father, the French-born Sir Marc Isambard Brunel (1769-1849), who escaped the French Revolution and became chief engineer of New York City before settling in England. The younger Brunel showed his talents at an early age and at 14 was sent to be educated in Paris. At the age of 17 he joined his father's office and worked on the tunnel underneath the River Thames from Rotherhithe to Wapping. On one occasion he worked continuously in the tunnel for 96 hours taking only snatches of sleep, and on another heroically prevented a workman from drowning. Brunel invented a giant boring machine (on which the machine used to dig out the Channel Tunnel was based).

MATHEMATICAL CERTAINTY

One of Brunel's earliest independent designs was the Clifton suspension bridge in Bristol, which was declared the most mathematically correct of all the plans tendered. In 1833 he was appointed engineer to the Great Western Railway, for which he designed viaducts, tunnels and bridges, but his great fame rested on his construction of ocean-going steam ships which were larger than any previously built. These included the *Great Western* in 1838, which measured 236 ft (72 m) in length and 35 ft (10.5 m) in breadth and had a displacement of 2300 tonnes. She was the first steam ship employed in regular service between England and America and was able to make the voyage in the then-record time of 15 days. Brunel also designed the *Great Eastern* – the largest sea vessel of its day and a marvel of Victorian technology. Sadly, the launch of the *Great Eastern* (incidentally, Brunel devised the slipways down which launchings took place) coincided with a deterioration in his health and he died 10 days later, a wealthy man. This brilliant engineer, who through his career was physically strong and often adopted a hands-on approach to his projects, single-handedly developed many of the transport systems and communication networks which contributed to making Britain a foremost world power.

JOHN STUART MILL 1806-1873

RIGOROUS EDUCATION

John Stuart Mill, politician, philosopher and logician, was entirely educated by his father, the Scottish historian James Mill, who set his son a remarkable system of education. This included learning Greek at the age of three and Latin at the age of eight. By the time he was 14 Mill had studied logic, political economy, history, literature and mathematics. He later said that his education had been designed to stimulate his powers of thought and not to cram his mind.

Mill was raised as an agnostic and in his autobiography described himself as one of the few people in England who had not thrown off religious belief, but had 'never had it'. He firmly believed that his own education demonstrated that children could benefit from more rigorous training at an early age.

INFLUENCED BY BENTHAM

In 1823, Mill founded the Utilitarian Society. Much of his work was in fact a development of the philosophy advocated by Jeremy Bentham (1748-1832), a lawyer and leading utilitarian philosopher. Bentham proposed an amazing range of reforms, many of which were later adopted. These included the reform of the representative system in the British Parliament, the abolition of transportation of convicted criminals from Britain to Australia, penal reform and religious toleration. He also predicted the formation of the United Nations by advocating an international assembly responsible for maintaining perpetual peace through disarmament. Bentham's basic premise was that actions could be judged to be morally right or wrong according to whether they maximized pleasure or minimized pain. He applied this test of utility to all areas of human society – law, education and ethics – and he was an enemy to vagueness of thought, legal fictions and specious argument.

BREADTH OF THOUGHT

Mill's writings display an astonishing breadth of philosophical and political thought that still has a continuing influence today. He was a staunch defender of freedom of liberty, thought and

Jeremy Bentham founded University College, London. His embalmed body (which he bequeathed to research) is still displayed there to the public.

Apparently John Stuart Mill considered that the rigorous education he received gave him an advantage over others.

speech, and among his most influential works was *On Liberty* (1859), in which he argued that society had no more right to silence the individual than the individual had to silence all other men. Mill considered utilitarianism too narrow and in his *Utilitarianism* (1863) redefined it as 'the greatest happiness of the greatest number'. Mill entered parliament as the member for Westminster in 1865 and spoke in favour of female suffrage, a theme which he expanded in his *The Subjection of Women* (1869). His most influential work of philosophy was his *System of Logic* (1843), which was the foundation of modern inductive logic by which a general principle is derived from particular examples and which owed much to the experimental scientific methods of the philosopher and politician Sir Francis Bacon (1561-1626).

CHARLES DARWIN 1809-1882
ICONOCLASM

Charles Darwin has gone down in the history of science as the discoverer of the theory of evolution by natural selection. He was born in Shrewsbury, studied medicine at Edinburgh University and then went to Christ's College, Cambridge, where he had originally planned to enter the Church.

TACT

Once there, however, he developed a serious interest in biological studies. In later life, although his theories were to shatter the Biblical Creation myth forever, he did not enjoy humiliating those with religious conviction. For this reason, although the implications were already clear, he stayed away from explicit comment on the ascent of man in his book *The Origin of Species* – that comment was to come in later works.

FIVE-YEAR MISSION

After Cambridge, Darwin became a naturalist on HMS *Beagle* in 1831, accompanying that ship on a scientific survey of the South American waters. This was to become a five-year mission which took him to Brazil, Montevideo, Buenos Aires, Patagonia, Chile, the Galapagos Islands, Tahiti and New Zealand and throughout the voyage Darwin painstakingly wrote up his detailed observations on flora, fauna and geology. These stood him in excellent stead – in fact, the varied nature of the comparative information he gathered proved vital for his future investigations and the development of his theories.

SUBJECT KNOWLEDGE

The publications derived from his lengthy expeditions, published after his return, made Darwin's scientific reputation, and in 1839 he was elected a fellow of the Royal Society. Three years later he removed himself to Downe in Kent and became almost a country gentleman, devoting himself to his garden, looking after pigeons and rearing birds. Here he gained more valuable preparatory knowledge concerning variation and interbreeding for his later work on the transmutation of species. In fact, Darwin was to continue gathering notes for a further 16 years. However, like Copernicus, he was reticent in publishing his theories for fear of offending the religious community of the day. Nevertheless, in 1858, a letter from the Welsh naturalist Alfred Wallace (1823-1913), foreshadowing the theory of natural selection, precipitated Darwin into publishing *The Origin of Species by Means of Natural Selection or the Preservation of Favoured Races in the Struggle for Life,* which appeared in 1859.

At first Darwin hesitated to publish his most devastating conclusions – that human beings are, in fact, monkey-like creatures, ultimately descended from primeval ooze. However, this was a conclusion to be utterly vindicated, if

proof were, in fact, still needed by Crick and Watson's discovery of DNA in the 1950s. Although Darwin's theories appeared to contradict revealed religion, a grateful nation gave him a superb burial in Westminster Abbey.

OPPOSITION

As was to be expected, *The Origin of Species* and Darwin's later work *The Descent of Man* (1871) met with violent, fierce and malicious opposition and criticism from those with entrenched views. Darwin had a powerful way of expressing himself. For example, in *The Descent of Man*, he refers to man's immediate ancestor, biologically speaking, as 'a hairy quadruped, furnished with a tail and pointed ears, probably arboreal in its habits'. He coined the phrase '*struggle for existence*' and the most famous of all, '*survival of the fittest*', yet he always retained a child-like sense of wonder at the complexity of the natural world. 'A larval cirripede with six pairs of beautifully

LEFT Although Darwin's health was always fragile, he lived to the age of 73.

BELOW Mary Anning excavated dinosaur skeletons with great success.

constructed natatory legs, a pair of magnificent compound eyes and extremely complex antennae.' Just relish the joy and delight in that sentence, doubtless describing what, to most eyes, would just have seemed a revolting bug!

Perhaps the greatest irony was the verdict of Darwin's father when he was a young student – 'You care for nothing but shooting, dogs and rat catching and you will be a disgrace to yourself and all your family.' Most families would wish for a disgrace like Charles Darwin.

EVOLVING INTEREST

Massive interest in Darwin's *Theory of Evolution* was fuelled to a large extent by the excitement caused by the discovery, during the earlier half of the 19th century, of the remains of giant dinosaur bones by Mary Anning (1799-1847). At a time when the leading palaeontologists – such as Professor Sir Richard Owen, who founded the London Natural History Museum – were regularly misconstructing fossil remains, Mary Anning's achievements in unearthing perfect dinosaur specimens were unparalleled.

LEARNING TO SEE WHAT IS THERE

Mary Anning was perfect in her reconstructions. She was born in Lyme Regis in 1799, the daughter of a carpenter. Her father died in 1810 and left her, at the age of 11, to make her own way in the world. This she did with an extraordinary degree of success. She knew that the cliffs around Lyme Regis were rich in fossil specimens, so she set about learning how to identify the most promising potential seams and how to extract the fossils with maximum expertise and in the best possible condition.

In 1811, just 12 years old, Mary Anning discovered and successfully excavated the fossil skeleton of a complete Ichthyosaurus from a local cliff. She also discovered the first complete Plesiosaurus and, in 1825, the very first Pterodactyl, the great flying reptile of the Jurassic/Cretaceous periods. An extraordinary hat trick!

SUBJECT KNOWLEDGE

At the time, contemporaries were quick to dismiss Mary Anning's ability to discover these skeletons as some freak of nature. Many alleged that she had been struck by lightning while a child and that the spark of electrical genius had imbued itself into her nervous system. Of course, this kind of legend is ridiculous. Her success was due to perseverance, knowledge and vision.

BREAKING THE CHAINS

*'WE CANNOT BE FREE MEN IF THIS IS, BY OUR NATIONAL CHOICE, TO BE
A LAND OF SLAVERY. THOSE WHO DENY FREEDOM TO OTHERS DESERVE
IT NOT FOR THEMSELVES.'*
ABRAHAM LINCOLN

ABRAHAM LINCOLN 1809-1865

'I would rather be assassinated on the spot than give up the great promise embodied in the Declaration of Independence and the Constitution, that in due time, the weights should be lifted from the shoulders of all men and that all should have an equal chance.'

(Abraham Lincoln, 1861).

A great orator, Lincoln frequently captured the hearts of his listeners.

CHAIN-BREAKER EXTRAORDINAIRE

Lincoln was born in Kentucky into extreme poverty. Indeed, his birthplace was a log cabin of rudimentary construction. Yet he rose to become the President of a nation that would soon become the most wealthy and powerful the planet had ever seen; and he did so by dint of his own passion for freedom, honesty, oratorical skill and intense personal conviction that the institution of slavery in the southern states of the American Union was an evil which had to be eradicated.

STUDYING LAW

In 1831, Lincoln moved to New Salem, Illinois, where he worked as a local storekeeper, surveyor and postmaster. He was also studying to acquire his law degree – which in 1836 he did. Developing an interest in politics, Lincoln's speeches became celebrated for their fire and personal vision. In 1847 he was elected to Congress and in 1855 and 1858 he ran unsuccessfully for the US Senate; but, nothing daunted, he persevered and aimed for the very top. In 1860 he was elected 16th President of the United States. He represented the Republican party, mobilized to oppose slavery (his anti-slavery stance was already well known).

Soon after Lincoln's elevation to the Presidency, the Southern States left the Union, declaring themselves an independent confederacy. Then they also declared war on the Northern States by launching a pre-emptive strike on the military outpost of Fort Sumter on 12 April 1861.

OLYMPIAN INTELLIGENCE

On 22 September 1862, after one and a half years of a futile civil conflict between north and south which saw neither side gaining any decisive advantage, Lincoln enacted his first masterstroke, the Proclamation that officially emancipated the slaves in all the states of America. Suddenly, the southern Black population was seriously motivated to support the North. Some slaves fled to the North, where many of them enlisted in the Northern armies and turned on their erstwhile masters.

INTERPERSONAL INTELLIGENCE

Tall, craggy, gaunt and bearded and with his customary stove pipe hat, Lincoln launched his second masterstroke in Gettysburg in 1863. The Gettysburg Address, delivered on the field of a most bloody battle, restored flagging morale in the North, where people had been appalled by the slaughter and waste of resources. It required all of Lincoln's oratorical skill to express his near mystical belief in the sanctity of the union of the two warring sides.

Lincoln began his speech with these immortal words: 'Four score and seven years ago, our fathers brought forth on this continent, a new nation. Conceived in liberty and dedicated to the proposition that all men are created equal. Now we are engaged in a great civil war, testing whether that nation, or any nation so conceived and so dedicated can long endure. We are met on a great battlefield of that war. We have come to dedicate a portion of that field, as a final resting place for those who here gave their lives, that that nation might live. It is altogether fitting and proper that we should do this.' His speech concluded with the equally immortal words: 'That we here, highly resolve, that these dead shall not have died in vain. That this nation, under God, shall have a new birth of freedom and that government of the people, by the people, for the people, shall not perish from the earth.' Lincoln was reportedly displeased with his performance, but the world judged it differently.

FINAL MASTERSTROKE

Lincoln's third and final masterstroke came in 1864 with the appointment of General Ulysses S. Grant (whom he described as a fighter) as Commander-in-Chief of the Northern armies, with General William Tecumseh Sherman as his deputy. These two ruthless commanders realized that only by an unremitting war of attrition and by bringing the struggle directly to the civilian population of the South, could the balance of power be decisively shifted. The objectives of Grant and Sherman were swiftly achieved, with Sherman's advance on the city of Atlanta and Grant's victories at the Battles of Rapidan, The Wilderness, Petersburg and Richmond.

DYING FOR HIS PRINCIPLES

Lincoln's reward for his efforts was assassination by a fanatical supporter of the South – John Wilkes Booth – on 14 April 1865, in Ford's Theater, Washington.

VISION FOR THE FUTURE OF THE WORLD

It has been said of Lincoln that he was 'fair and direct in speech and action, steadfast in principle, sympathetic and charitable, a man of strict morality, abstemious, and familiar with the Bible, but not a professed member of any church. His fame is established as the saviour of his country and the liberator of a race.'

CHARLES DICKENS 1812-1870

ENERGY AND PRODUCTIVITY

Charles Dickens is known as the greatest writer of the realistic novel in the 19th century. He was a man who lived powerfully in the actuality of the present and was also a most potent social campaigner and reformer. He had seemingly boundless mental and physical energy. He composed 14 full-length novels, several novellas, numberless pieces of political and social journalism, travel writings, plays, biographies, a children's history of England (Dickens loved children and fathered 10 of his own). He was also an enthusiastic amateur actor.

TRUTH

One of the things that lent Charles Dickens a ferocious edge of realism and insight into the social conditions of his day was the incarceration of his father John and his entire family in the Marshalsea Debtors' Prison, when his father could not meet the family debts. In fact much of his novel *Little Dorrit* (1855-57) is set in Marshalsea Prison. This experience gave Charles Dickens' social conscience and his power of expressing it the keenest possible bite.

PASSION

Dickens was not just a writer – he was also a public performer, reading his work aloud to an audience, often at Royal Command. His performances were so impassioned they may well have shortened his life. He was warned by his doctor not to declaim the scene from *Oliver Twist* (1837-9) in which Nancy is murdered, because he invested it with so much emotion and effort.

Eyewitness accounts relate that strong men fainted in the audience when Dickens read this scene. Another account of his writing methods is

For all his bubbling life and comic touch, the central message of Dickens – a genius whose writing has conquered the world with its wit and wisdom – is that poverty and ignorance are the most deadly threats to the future of civilization and in order to survive we must eradicate them.

VISION

In addition to *Little Dorrit* and *Oliver Twist*, Dickens' works include *The Pickwick Papers* (1836-7), *Nicholas Nickleby* (1838-9), *The Old Curiosity Shop* (1840-1), *Domby and Son* (1846-8), *David Copperfield* (1849-50), *Bleak House* (1852-3), *Hard Times* (1854), *Great Expectations* (1860-1), and *Our Mutual Friend* (1864-5). Perhaps the most popular of all is *A Christmas Carol* (1843). Dickens virtually invented Christmas. Before his time it was not unusual, both in the United States and Great Britain, for office or factory staff to work on Christmas Day. After Dickens had written his novel, Christmas became a universally acknowledged holiday and employers, instead of extracting the last ounce from their work force, often gave them free turkeys and the day off. Dickens himself gave a moral boost to the whole of Western civilization. The world will be perpetually a better place for him, even though his message and clarion warning about ignorance is as vital now as it was 100 years ago, if not more so.

GIUSEPPE VERDI 1813-1901

VERSATILITY

Verdi is the towering figure in world opera. Active in Italy throughout virtually the whole of the 19th century, he was closely identified with the aspirations of the Italian people for freedom from the Austro-Hungarian Empire. Verdi was not just a writer of operas and great music; he was also a politician, a deputy in the Italian parliament and a Senator, yet his origins were humble. He rose to great heights after many early rejections. The grand themes of his operas, often taking Shakespeare (he kept the complete works beside his bed for inspiration) or the Bible as his raw material, were honed and tempered by bitter personal experiences of riot, revolution, death and personal tragedy. Yet Verdi lived to a grand old age, dying at the age of 88, universally and justly revered.

ENERGY

Verdi is one of the few undisputed great opera composers. His most popular works remain at

Scrooge's Third Visitor, from Dickens' much-loved A Christmas Carol.

supplied by his daughter Mamie, who was once permitted to lie on a day bed in his study while Dickens was composing. According to her, Dickens wrote feverishly and then 'jumped from his chair and rushed to a mirror which hung near'; in it she could see the reflection of some extraordinary facial contortions which he was making. He returned rapidly to his desk, wrote furiously for a few moments and then went again to the mirror. The facial pantomime was resumed and then, turning toward his daughter but evidently not seeing her, he began talking rapidly in a low voice. This shows the enormous physical effort which Dickens put into not just his performances on stage, but also the actual composition of his work.

Dickens captured the very texture of the world in which he lived. The moral message of his stories pushed to the forefront the plight of the poor, the impoverished – the classes which were left behind by the explosion of wealth in 19th-century industrial Britain.

*Verdi painted by the Italian portraitist
Giovanni Boldini (1842-1931).*

the very centre of the repertory of the leading
opera houses in the world. For half a century he
dominated Italian opera, and his work was identified with the revolutionary movement which
strove for the reunification of Italy. As he
achieved greater maturity with his masterpieces,
he never stopped developing as a composer and
the two works of his old age, *Othello* (1887) and
Falstaff (1893), are magnificent achievements in
the fields of both tragic and comic opera.

The themes of Verdi's operas are ambition,

love, jealousy, greed, loyalty envy and heroism – all especially powerful when imbued with the force of his music.

REJECTED BY THE CONSERVATOIRE

Verdi's early years were a struggle against poverty, and when he was only 13 months old, Russian soldiers marching through Italy during the dying throes of the Napoleonic Wars looted the little village Le Roncole where he had been born. Women and children sheltering in the local church were massacred but Verdi and his mother escaped the slaughter by hiding in the church's bell tower. Verdi's musical education came from Provesi, the organist of Busseto Cathedral. His promise was subsidized by local admirers and he was sent to Milan to study. But there he was rejected by the conservatoire. More tragedy followed when, during the period 1839-40, his wife and his children died. Yet he emerged from this great loss with renewed vigour and force.

COMMITMENT

Nabucco, performed in Milan in 1842, was his first major success and from then on his career was one continuous triumph. There followed *Rigoletto* in 1851, *Il Trovatore* in 1853, and *La Traviata* also in 1853 – all supreme works in the operatic canon. They immediately established Verdi's unshakable position as the leading Italian operatic composer of his day.

Widely recognized as the pinnacle of his career up to that point was *Aida*. It had been commissioned for the opening of the new opera house in Cairo, built in celebration of the newly constructed Suez Canal. In fact, though, the opera's premiere was delayed until 1871 because of the onset of the Franco-Prussian War. From 1873 until 1887 Verdi was in retirement, before emerging once again to write *Othello* in 1887 and *Falstaff* in 1893 – both having their triumphant premiere at La Scala in Milan.

DESIRE

In his youth Verdi was an enthusiastic nationalist supporter of the patriotic forces in Italy, which wished to unify the country and expel the Austro-Hungarian oppressors. Verdi's first great opera, *Nabucco,* expressed that nationalist fervour in sparkling fashion. The opera deals with the oppression of the Hebrews by the Assyrians under their king, Nabucco. In this opera the Hebrews were in a sense the central character – a people enslaved and in exile – and, of course,

the Italian nationalists obviously identified with them and with songs such as *O Mia Patria si bella e perduta*.

Nabucco was not the only one of Verdi's operas which provoked demonstrations and riots against the Austrian oppressors and he became a symbol of the Italian resistance, not least because his name was also an acronym that suggested the name of the king to all those present who were in on the secret. When the audiences chanted 'Viva Verdi', the V-E-R-D-I spelt out the name Victor Emmanuel Re de Italia, (Victor Emmanuel King of Italy). What a superb way to support the nationalist aspirations and break the chains of a foreign oppressor by using one's name, one of the most popular in the country, as a nationalist freedom-fighting code.

PERSISTENCE

What lessons can be drawn from Verdi? In his early years he was almost killed by foreign soldiers – but escaped through his mother's intelligence. In his personal and musical life, he was rejected by official bodies such as the conservatoire, yet by believing in himself, he persisted and fought through.

At the age of 80, Verdi produced perhaps his greatest triumph, *Falstaff,* and in doing so showed that genius has no age limit. He was a deeper, more profound and more brilliant man at the close of his career than he had been at the beginning.

GEORGE ELIOT 1819-1880
CHRONICLER OF THE RIGHT TO VOTE

George Eliot (which is the nom de plume that Mary Ann Evans decided to adopt) has often been described as 'The English Tolstoy'. When her novel *Middlemarch* (1871-2) was screened on UK television in 1994 it attracted immense press comment and record viewing figures. In it, Eliot penetratingly evoked British middle-class life in the mid-19th century, a time when ancient and creaking parliamentary and government institutions were being swept away and when voting inequalities in Britain were at long last beginning to be eradicated. It was a time of reform – a movement which Eliot had wholeheartedly endorsed. She herself had lived through an election riot at Nuneaton in 1832, the year of the great Reform Bill, and she sympathized strongly with those elements of British society who had previously been denied the right to vote.

Eliot's linguistic skills easily surpassed those of many male contemporaries.

LINGUISTIC INTELLIGENCE

Mary Evans was educated in the strict evangelical Christian faith by her father. She was also an avid student of music and of languages – namely French, Latin, German and Italian. In 1842 she abandoned Christianity, much to the chagrin of her father, and translated her first book from German, David Friedrich Strauss's *The Life of Christ, Critically Examined*, which claimed that the New Testament should be viewed as myth. She went on to translate (from German) *The Essence of Christianity*, by the philosopher Ludwig Feuerbach (1804-72) which claims that Christianity is an illusion, and then she translated, from the Latin, Spinoza's *Ethics*.

VENERATING GOETHE

Evans became Assistant Editor of the *Westminster Review* in 1851. Three years later, she travelled with the love of her life, George Henry Lewes (journalist, philosopher and scientist), on a three-month pilgrimage to Goethe's home town of Weimar, where Lewes was preparing his own masterpiece, *The Life of Goethe*. Like many others, George Eliot appears to have taken Goethe as a role model.

She was also much attracted to Renaissance Italy, and in 1862 she published *Romola*, her historical novel about the Republic of Florence at the end of the 1400s. This novel earned her £17,000, an immense sum at a time when it was possible for a single person to live comfortably on £100 per year.

SPEED READER

Eliot studied Florence first hand and read and absorbed 40 books per month about the city. In fact, George Eliot is a well-documented and important example of a long-term speed reader with near 100% retention who used the potentially vast benefits of this skill for practical purposes.

VERBAL INTELLIGENCE

Her first published book as 'George Eliot', *Scenes of Clerical Life,* came when she was nearly 40. There followed, among other writings: *Adam Bede* in 1859 (eight printings in its first year alone!), *The Mill on the Floss* (1860), *Silas Marner* (1861) and her masterpiece, *Middlemarch*. It is a novel of realism, full of the depth and texture of English county life – landed gentry, officers from the army, bankers, debt, crime, medicine, commerce – all pervaded by the powerful undercurrent of political, social and scientific change. Her perceptive eye for detail enhanced her skilful grasp of language. The critic and writer Henry James (1843-1916) wrote: '*George Eliot lived in the intelligence a freer, larger life, than probably had ever been the portion of any woman.*'

JOSEPH LISTER 1827-1912

COMMITMENT

The English surgeon Joseph Lister was a man showered with honours during his lifetime because of his single, crucial discovery in the field of medicine – the principles of infection. His introduction in the 1860s of the antiseptic system completely revolutionized modern surgery. Without Lister's detection of the microbes which threaten life during surgery, and his method of eradicating such microbes (thus making surgery safe, rather than a hazardous gamble), modern medicine would not exist.

FROM ARTS TO MEDICINE

Lister was the second son of the microscopist Joseph Jackson Lister, himself a Fellow of the Royal Society. Lister graduated at London University in Arts in 1847 and in Medicine in 1852.

In the same year he became a Fellow of the Royal College of Surgeons and successfully lectured on surgery at Edinburgh before becoming Regius Professor of Surgery at Glasgow, Professor of Clinical Surgery in Edinburgh in 1869, Professor of Clinical Surgery at King's College Hospital, London (1877-83), and finally the highest accolade – President of the Royal Society in 1895. Like many of the geniuses in this book, Lister was an extremely accomplished speaker and he delivered his lectures to a captivated audience.

Lister's work included important observations on the coagulation of blood, but it was his introduction of the antiseptic system which made his name. In recognition of this he was made a Baronet in 1883, a Baron in 1897 and received the Order of Merit in 1902. If there is one man in the 19th century who could claim to have freed ordinary people from the shackles of disease, Lister was that man.

LEARNING FROM MISTAKES
Amazingly, until Lister, doctors and surgeons did not wash or sterilize either their hands or their medical instruments before operating on a patient. Lister noticed with alarm that a large number of patients were dying from deadly infections following the operations that were meant to cure them. Instead of following, by rote, the nostrums of his colleagues and assuming that the operation was 'good for the patient', Lister worked out that infection through bacteria (invisible organisms) could be the cause of the deaths. In order to counteract this, in 1865 he started to spray carbolic acid continuously over the operating area from a special pump during operations. This effectively destroyed bacteria in the operating room and the result was a dramatic drop in the number of fatalities following surgical operations. Events had proved Lister right.

OPPOSING COMPLACENCY
The lesson to be learned from Lister when seeking to solve one's own problems is that if a situation is unsatisfactory, it must be changed, not passively tolerated. It is a question of actually addressing the situation in one's own mind and then searching for a solution experimentally in order to apply it. Lister saw that surgery that was intended to cure patients was, in fact, killing them. He was not content, as others had been, to let this 'natural' order of affairs proceed unopposed. He sought actively with persistence and determination until he found the hidden cause of the problem and could then eradicate it. This was in line with the general 19th-century view of freeing mankind from the chains which bound it to a barbaric past.

Lister himself was a superb physical specimen who died at the ripe old age of 85. Throughout his life he was a fighter against apathy, complacency, ignorance and prejudice. Fittingly, he was rewarded with honours for his many achievements by a grateful nation during his lifetime.

ANDREW CARNEGIE 1835-1918
Many men have risen from nothing to become exceedingly rich. What marks out Andrew Carnegie, however, was his philosophy of wealth and his practical measures for the disposal of the vast fortune he had personally earned. Born in Dunfermline, Scotland, in 1835, Carnegie emigrated in 1848 to the city of Pittsburgh in the United States. Here he started at the bottom of the career ladder, first as a factory worker, then a telegraph messenger boy, next as a railway clerk, until he had, by energetic application in these various positions, amassed sufficient funds to make investments of his own. He put his savings into oil lands, and ultimately into the business which was to grow into the largest American iron and steel works.

FLEXIBILITY
Carnegie saw the American Civil War as an opportunity for himself, but his first success was to avoid being gunned down in the carnage. In 1863, President Abraham Lincoln had issued the first federal draft, in order to raise 300,000 fresh troops for the Union. All men of between 20 and 45 years of age were subject to the call-up, with a three-year term of service. Carnegie, not exempt by reason of his Scottish descent, legally evaded the draft by paying for a substitute to take his place. This was perfectly acceptable at the time. Even Lincoln himself, though no one expected the over-age President to take up arms personally, provided a legal substitute for his own military service.

ENERGY
Carnegie then turned his head to increasing his incipient fortune, by selling supplies to the Northern armies. By the close of hostilities, and with the North's victory, Carnegie's combination of dedicated hard work, enterprise, judicious savings, shrewd investment and logistical operations had left him well-placed to exploit the new

Andrew Carnegie was a self-made, very wealthy tycoon with a difference. His philosophy was such that he gave away vast amounts of his personal fortune to educational establishments abroad as well to those in his home country, America. He also sent extravagant copies of Carnegie Diplodocus skeletons to various leaders of European countries.

post-war commercial environment, often described as the American 'Gilded Age'. The Civil War, of course, had left its mark, especially in the victorious North, on the style, speed and scale of economic development, which substantially accelerated.

PROPELLED BY FAITH

By now a steel tycoon, Carnegie's business methods were characterized by his extreme faith in social Darwinism, the belief that the survival of the fittest was an appropriate maxim for commercial, as well as natural, evolution.

Carnegie became the arch capitalist and industrialist, who saw entrepreneurial competition – weeding out the weakest elements of industrial society to ensure that the strongest survive – as being a positive benefit for humanity. Indeed,

Carnegie elevated his new capitalist ethic into a virtual law of nature.

DESIRE TO WIN

Carnegie's principles embodied a ruthless race against any competition and an insatiable demand for higher production, with efficiency seen as the ultimate goal. Nevertheless, he regarded himself as merely the custodian of his wealth, not its owner, and he derived immense pleasure from the creative redistribution of his fortune.

CONSCIOUSLY STIMULATING VENERATION, INSPIRATION AND EMULATION

Carnegie expounded his theories in two books, *Triumphant Democracy* and the *Gospel of Wealth*. In the latter, he advocated a wise disposal of wealth to stimulate others to strive as he had done. Carnegie also commissioned Napoleon Hill to research the principles of success they had discussed, which were published in *Think and Grow Rich* – one of the most successful self-improvement books ever written, with worldwide sales of over 20,000,000. Carnegie was convinced that studying the brain was a key to success. As Hill wrote: 'Man with all of his boasted culture and education understands little or nothing of the intangible force (the greatest of all the intangibles) of thought. He knows but little concerning the physical brain and its vast network of intricate machinery through which the power of thought is translated into its material equivalent, but he is now entering an age which will yield enlightenment on the subject.'

ENDOWMENTS FOR EDUCATION
In 1901, at the age of 66, Carnegie retired. Having sold his company to the US Steel Corporation, he was a multimillionaire many times over. Carnegie himself returned to Scotland to live in a castle. Meanwhile, he had distributed around $350,000,000, or about £70,000,000 at the exchange rate of the day, to education, public libraries, Scottish and American universities and his own Carnegie Institution in Pittsburgh and Washington.

BLACK AND WHITE
The industrial landscape Carnegie helped to create, and from which his vast fortune derived, was both grandiose and menacing. Photographic records of his Pittsburgh steel plants reveal endless stacks of chimneys, belching forth black smoke in what resembles nothing more than a blasted industrial moonscape. At Carnegie's Homestead steelworks in Pennsylvania, the largest in America, the plant owned its own railway and steamships to bring in supplies of coal and iron ore. Immigrant labourers worked 12 hours a day, seven days a week; any strikes were suppressed and Union activity was crushed out of existence. Nevertheless, when Carnegie gave away his fortune, a substantial portion of it went towards pension funds for his former workers.

OLYMPIAN INTELLIGENCE
Carnegie's brand of capitalism was all-embracing and ruthless. It should be noted, though, that it also fuelled education on a massive scale, gave opportunities to those who would otherwise have been hopelessly handicapped, and helped transform the USA into an international advocate for democracy, with the financial and military muscle to back up its own beliefs. In that sense, Carnegie and other capitalists of his ilk laid vital foundations for America's global opposition to the forces of totalitarianism and fascism in the 20th century.

THINKING BIG
As befits a man with supreme faith in social Darwinism, Carnegie also exhibited tremendous fascination with natural evolution. In 1899 and 1900, he personally sponsored expeditions to search for the remains of dinosaurs. From this fascination with extinct monsters, Carnegie developed the world's strangest, and certainly largest, visiting card! In 1900 the first example of a skeleton of a fossil Diplodocus had been discovered in Wyoming. This find was named Diplodocus Carnegie in the sponsor's honour. At 87 ft (26.5 m) the Diplodocus was by far the largest-ever land animal to have roamed the earth. Relative to its size, however, the Diplodocus had one of the smallest brains known. In essence, its immense body was directed by a minute central control.

MEMORY IMPACT
Carnegie had plaster casts of his Diplodocus skeleton made, at the cost of $30,000 (about £6000) each – an immense sum at that time. He personally arranged for these replica skeletons to be created, shipped and presented to crowned heads and elected presidents around the world and donated to their leading national museums. King Edward VII received one, and it can still be seen in London's Natural History Museum. Another recipient of Carnegie's Diplodocus visiting card was Kaiser Wilhelm in Berlin, as was the President of the French Republic in Paris, while other skeletons went to Vienna, Bologna, La Plata in Argentina and Mexico City.

It is no wonder, given the impetus from Carnegie, that the Diplodocus skeleton is the most impressive exhibit in many of the world's finest museums. It is also a permanent ongoing memorial to the memory of Andrew Carnegie: the industrialist and educationalist who probably gave away the largest fortune in history for pedagogic purposes.

PAUL CÉZANNE 1839-1906
MASTERMINDS OF IMPRESSIONISM
Cézanne developed his mature style of painting in virtual isolation. As a young man he had stud-

ied Latin and Greek and, urged to do so by his father, he reluctantly agreed to read law at the University of Aix-en-Provence, an attempt he abandoned in 1861. His father, a banker in Aix, finally gave him a small allowance to enable him to go to Paris to study art. Cézanne enrolled at the Académie Suisse, where he met Pissarro, Monet, Renoir and the Mastermind Group who were to become the main exponents of Impressionism.

PARIS OF THE SECOND EMPIRE

When Cézanne arrived from Aix to join his childhood friend Emile Zola in Paris in 1861, he came to a city in ferment. Since 1853, when Baron Haussmann was given the job of remodelling the old medieval Paris by the Emperor Napoleon III, great wide thoroughfares had been driven through old neighbourhoods, destroying the narrow cobbled streets which were thought to house subversives. The emperor had come to power in a *coup d'état*; as he was always expecting another insurrection, the city was planned to facilitate control. Huge new railway terminals were also being built and they had to be accommodated. The Gare Lazare was redesigned and enlarged and surrounded by an entirely new district to house the prosperous bourgeoisie. Displaying intense pride in the new city, the first French International Fair had opened in 1855 in the Champs-Elysees.

ARTISTIC REVOLUTION

It was at this fair that the avant-garde first made its appearance. In answer to the criticisms of the artists who had been rejected by the official exhibition, and backed by a sympathetic press, Napoleon agreed that there should be a Salon of 'refused' pictures, next to the official one, so that the public could decide between the two. Manet's *Déjeuner sur l'Herbe* (1863), inspired by Titian's *Fête Champêtre*, became the notorious subject of outraged propriety at this event and so, for the official art establishment, Manet became demonized as a leader of dissident artists. At the same time, a liberalization of the laws regulating theatres led in turn to a rapid expansion of café concerts and the vaudeville and artists, particularly Degas and Manet, found new subject matter for their work in this aspect of Parisian life. But the official Salon, the only place where a reputation could be made, continually rejected their work, preferring instead to show popular, non-controversial artists.

PUPIL OF PISSARRO

In 1870, France went to war with Prussia and was defeated. The Parisian artists scattered: Monet and Pissarro to London and Cézanne to L'Estaque, a small village on the Mediterranean. There he hid, along with his secret mistress, in order to avoid the draft. They then moved back to Paris, where their son Paul was born in 1872. Cézanne was dependent upon his dominant father for subsistence, so the birth remained a secret. After the birth, they all moved with Pissarro to Pontoise, where Cézanne and Pissarro painted landscapes together in the open air. This experience of painting alongside Pissarro caused Cézanne's colours to lighten. Pissarro constantly said that one should have no other master but nature, a lesson Cézanne never forgot (he later described himself as 'pupil of Pissarro').

BIRTH OF IMPRESSIONISM

In 1874, the first group show for the Impressionists was held in the studio of the photographer, Nadar. Degas was the organizing leader, but Manet would not participate and indeed did not do so for all the eight subsequent shows. Called La Société anonyme by its 29 participants, it was rechristened (derisively) by a critic in the popular newspaper, *Charivari*, as 'The Exhibition of Impressionists'; the name stuck. All the artists were vilified, but none more than Cézanne. He had exhibited three pictures, two of which were in his early dark-palette style and the third in the lighter-palette style he had discovered with Pissarro. This was *La maison du pendu* (1872-3) which, although still heavily painted, has the strong construction lines and the confident spatial organization which determines Cézanne's mature style.

NEW COLOURS – BREAKING THE MOULD

For the third Impressionist exhibition in 1877, Cézanne painted the portrait of Chocquet, to whom he had been introduced by Renoir. The public found it bewildering. Cézanne had painted the seated Chocquet with strong colours, using blue-green reflections on the hair, blue touches on the beard and red and yellow tones on the skin. All this colour disconcerted a public that was accustomed to overall flesh-tones. He received aggressive reviews and was apparently so disappointed by this setback that he decided to work alone and not participate in the group's shows again. Each year, he continued to submit work to the official Salon, and each year was rejected.

TRUTH

When his father died in 1886, Cézanne suddenly became a rich man. But there was little change in his lifestyle. He continued to paint every day, gradually refining the experience he referred to as 'sensation', which seemed to mean the actual experience the painter felt for the landscape, as much as his attempt to make an accurate copy of it. The paint became thinner and the colours brighter, as Cézanne strove, over and over, to register the exact nuance he felt when in front of the object. Scrupulously honest while recording his 'sensation', he transferred to his canvas colours exactly as he saw them. He worked in familiar places, registering in his resulting work the same intensity he was experiencing emotionally. In his work we see, for the first time, the complete process of painting a picture.

BREAK WITH ZOLA

Cézanne's personal life was as isolated as he had forced his working life to be. Indeed, locals who thought his work strange, regularly threw stones at him when he returned home from a day's painting in the open air. It seems that he was indifferent to his wife, and none of his friends liked her. She did, however, pose for him patiently (he required long hours from his sitters). His relationship with Zola came to an end when, in 1886, Zola published *L'Oeuvre,* a book, the major character of which is based upon Cézanne. In it, Zola speaks of the painter's failure in such a way that Cézanne realized the writer had always misunderstood his work. After a brief letter of acknowledgement for the copy Zola had sent him, a deeply-hurt Cézanne never communicated with the writer again.

MONT STE VICTOIRE

Cézanne's life now was one of daily work, in which he was always searching for a new motif. His brother-in-law had bought a house southwest of Aix, and so Cézanne could now paint his beloved Mont Ste Victoire from a different angle (he painted around 40 different versions of it).

Cézanne's paintings from this period have a tremendous richness of tone; the skies are not only blue, but also pale green, blue-grey, bright violet, brown and pink. As he later observed: 'there are no lines in nature, no shadows without colour . . . Pure drawing is an abstraction. Line

Cézanne's Bathers *evokes a world with humans and nature in harmony.*

and modelling do not count; drawing and outline are not distinct, since everything in nature has colour . . . by the very act of painting, the accuracy of tones gives simultaneously the light and shape of the object, and the more harmonious the colour, the more drawing becomes precise.'

EMULATING THE MASTERS

Whenever he was in Paris, Cézanne took advantage of the permission he had been given early in his career, to paint inside the Louvre. This practice, which he continued until the end of his life, enabled Cézanne to work while being constantly inspired by the great masters of the past, whose work surrounded him.

STILL LIFE – ATTENTION TO DETAIL

When he was not able to work in the open, Cézanne painted still lifes. He worked very slowly, spending hours on arranging the objects precisely on the plain kitchen table. Only when he was completely satisfied would he begin to paint. He was obliged to use paper flowers and artificial fruit, since real flowers wilted and fruit rotted long before the picture was finished. He took the same care in applying the paint, and is the first artist to show us the actual process of looking at an object.

SUDDEN FAME

By now, Cézanne was being discovered by the young generation. In 1888, the symbolist novelist Huysmans, convinced by Pissarro of Cézanne's value, wrote an article (later a chapter in his book, *Certains*) about the artist. In 1889 a painting by Cézanne appeared in the Paris World's Fair, at the insistence of Chocquet, who had refused to loan his own pictures unless Cézanne was included. At the end of the year the Belgian group of the XX approached Cézanne, and three of his pictures were hung in the Brussels Exhibition of 1890. More articles appeared, and a young dealer, Vollard, approached Cézanne because his pictures were commanding good prices at sales. He put on a successful one-man show of 150 pictures.

Cézanne was so used to indifference that he found this sudden attention overwhelming; he became even more solitary, withdrawing further. In 1899 Vollard bought everything in Cézanne's studio, and three of his works were hung at the centennial exhibition in Paris.

Cézanne then exhibited in the Indépendants in Paris and in Brussels again with the XX.

RECORDING THE WORLD

Cézanne carried on much as before, but his pictures changed. All the careful deliberate analysis of form of his middle period of isolation now gave way before an onrush of emotion. He could afford to relax, and it is in these last years that he painted his monumental canvases, one after another. In them, his beloved mountain, Ste Victoire, becomes nearer and nearer. Cézanne also rented a room in the courtyard of an abandoned château where he began a series of some of his most resolved and meditative late works.

CÉZANNE'S THEORIES

In 1904 Emile Bernard visited Cézanne at Aix and the two began to correspond. It is from these letters that Cézanne's theories became known, revolving around his central proposition: 'When the relationship of tones becomes harmonious and complete . . . the picture develops of its own accord.' In Cézanne's late work, the colour patches, from which Cubist analysis derives, are created by the parallel vertical brushstrokes that unite the canvas. These patches of colour underline the horizontal of the horizon, while the emphasis on the colour is as continuous on the surface of the painting as it is in the depth. Cézanne explained this to Bernard in a letter in 1904: 'Lines parallel to the horizon give breadth . . . but nature for us men is more depth than surface, thus the need to introduce vibrations of light, represented by the reds and yellows, with a sufficient amount of blueness to give the feeling of air.'

CÉZANNE'S BATHERS

Throughout his life Cézanne had worked on a series of bathing figures, sometimes of men alone, sometimes women – only rarely did he combine the two. For the female figures, he preferred to work from drawings or photographs of a model, rather than directly from the model herself. The male nudes seem to be an evocation of his remembered idyllic youth, swimming and sunning with his friends. There are some 200 examples of these bathing figures, on canvas and paper, in which Cézanne constantly re-explores the theme which has such a tradition in Western art. The culmination are his three large canvases of women bathing, all executed between 1900 and 1906.

FATHER OF CUBISM

Cézanne painted to the last. He died on 22

Alexander Graham Bell was the first to patent the telephone.

October 1906 after he had been working on a landscape near his studio and caught in a rainstorm.

Cézanne's legacy is immense. All of the succeeding movements of 20th-century art are indebted to him, none more so than Cubism, which has visually shaped this century. Cézanne's oeuvre consists of approximately 850 paintings, 650 watercolours, 1200 drawings and some prints. Few of his works can be dated with any accuracy, due to the solitude in which he worked and, because of his lack of recognition in his lifetime; fewer still are signed.

MAKING FEELINGS KNOWN

Cézanne's life was a difficult one, full of disappointments. He finally succeeded in uniting his emotional temperament with his intellectual rigour. Always finding it increasingly difficult to communicate with people, he withdrew more and more to nature, through which he endeavoured to describe to us his 'sensation'. His ulti-

mate conception of painting was of an art of rational intelligibility, while he considered the means of art as 'simply the means of making the public feel that we feel ourselves'.

ALEXANDER GRAHAM BELL
1847-1922

PATERNAL INFLUENCE

The inventor of the telephone, Alexander Graham Bell was greatly influenced by his father, Alexander Melville Bell, elocutionist and the inventor of 'visible speech', by which deaf people learned how to speak correctly by being shown the exact position of the vocal chords for each sound.

SPIRIT OF THE AGE

As a child, Alexander Graham Bell was largely taught by his family which encouraged his natural curiosity. He later studied at Edinburgh and London Universities, after which he accompanied his father to North America. In 1872 he became professor of vocal physiology at Boston University, where he devoted his energies to teaching deaf-mutes and spreading his father's system. He was deeply concerned about the deaf, and married one of his deaf students.

Bell also experimented with acoustic devices and transmitted the first telephone message, to his assistant, on 5 June 1875. He took out a patent for the telephone in 1876 and offered his rights to the Western Union Telegraph Company, which astonishingly turned it down. So Bell formed a company of his own, the Bell Telephone Company, and the commercial success of the telephone was ensured. The company was to develop into the largest private business corporation in the world. Bell was almost beaten in his moment of success by the American inventor, Elisha Gray, who patented a similar device hours after Bell's patent was received. That two men could be working on the same idea at the same time illustrates the fertile scientific atmosphere which existed in the last quarter of the 19th century.

THOMAS ALVA EDISON 1847-1931

INVENTIVE GENIUS

Edison was a genius of truly staggering imagination, and is often described as the greatest *inventive* genius of all time. He patented over 1000 different inventions, but his claim to fame rests particularly on his patents for the phonograph or gramophone (1877), and the incandescent light

bulb (1879). He also invented a carbon transmitter which developed Bell's work and improved the audibility of telephone messages; he developed a storage battery and found a way to improve film projectors.

CREATIVITY

Astonishingly, this hugely talented man had been expelled from formal schooling when he was 12 because his teacher thought that he was educationally subnormal and backward – a verdict that was also made by Einstein's teachers. So, having had almost no education, Edison started work as a newsboy on the Grand Trunk Railway and soon displayed the energy and creativeness that were to be the hallmarks of his career. He produced his own newspaper for distribution on the trains – the *Grand Trunk Herald* – the first newspaper ever printed on a train. Incidentally, it was in a newspaper interview that Edison was quoted as saying: 'Genius is one per cent inspiration and 99 per cent perspiration'. He certainly persisted with his inventions. He failed thousands of times before he found a way to convert electricity into light, but would not give up – saying to his friends that as he knew so many ways that did *not* work, he was closer to making a discovery than anyone else.

Thomas Edison holds the world record for the greatest number of inventions.

During the American Civil War (1861-5) he worked as a telegraph operator and invented an electric vote-recording machine, while in 1871 he designed a ticker-tape machine for use by the stock market. The proceeds from these inventions allowed him to set up his own laboratory, in much the same way that Renaissance painters founded Academies, with a group of employees, which was one of the world's earliest research and development plants. Those at the laboratory served as a Mastermind Group for Edison, inspiring him in his inventions.

Edison discovered that electric currents can flow over a space – wires do not have to connect – and he can be thought of as the founder of the modern electronics industry. Like Bell, he established a company which was eventually to become a giant in the business world (General Electric). Throughout his life, and particularly towards the end, he was hard of hearing, but in the same way that Beethoven ignored his deafness and Zizka disregarded his blindness, Edison did not let this become an obstacle. Instead, he dedicated himself to work with an extraordinary enthusiasm and great energy.

TAKING FLIGHT

'MEDIOCRITY KNOWS NOTHING HIGHER THAN ITSELF, BUT TALENT
INSTANTLY RECOGNIZES GENIUS.'
SIR ARTHUR CONAN DOYLE

IVAN PETROVICH PAVLOV
1849-1936

JOINING THE BRAIN CLUB

The Russian physiologist Pavlov was almost an exact contemporary of Sigmund Freud (1856-1939), yet his philosophy of the mind diverged sharply from that of the great Austrian thinker. Pavlov was a man of imposing physical stature who lived to the grand age of 87. Indeed, is it coincidental, or causal, that an intensive study of the workings of the brain has resulted in extreme longevity in several notable cases? We can cite that of Pavlov himself, Freud, who lived to be 83, Jung 86, and Ernest Jones, Freud's biographer and founder of the *International Journal of Psycho-analysis*, who reached 79. The exception is Freud's early disciple and the inventor of the inferiority complex, Alfred Adler, who only lived to be 67.

TRILLIONS OF NEURONS

Pavlov studied medicine at St Petersburg, was appointed professor there in 1891, awarded the Nobel Prize for Medicine in 1904, and became the Director of the Institute of Experimental Medicine in 1913. But it was from his study of 'conditioned' or 'acquired' reflexes that Pavlov made his reputation.

Rejecting analysis of subjective mental states, Pavlov insisted that each conditioned reflex is associated with a particular part of the brain's cortex. He claimed that the function of the brain was to couple neurons, or nerve cells (of which the brain contains 12 trillion), through synaptic junctions to produce such reflexes.

INSPIRATION AND EXPERIMENTATION

Pavlov's most enduring experiment is the one in which he demonstrated the conditioned reflexes of a dog. Pavlov used to feed a dog while simultaneously ringing a bell. Once the dog had become accustomed to this procedure, Pavlov showed that, when he merely rang the bell without producing any food, the dog would still salivate in anticipation of something to eat. Pavlov received criticism at the time and since for his experiments, with some people saying that they do not prove anything. His approach, however, was always investigative. After his findings with the conditioned dog, for instance, he simply said that further investigation was needed and did not suggest that every creature could be conditioned. His work formed the basis for all modern forms of experimental psychology and he was pivotal in changing the way in which the nature of intelligence, memory and learning have subsequently been investigated.

Pavlov's training and education took place at both theological and military colleges. In his professional career, he carried out important studies into digestion and conducted a deep investigation into animal physiology. He was renowned for his extraordinary energy and great enthusiasm. Professor Robert Thouless, author of *Straight and Crooked Thinking*, witnessed a lecture he gave at Cambridge University in the 1920s. Pavlov delighted and inspired his English-speaking audience – even though he had delivered it in Russian and the majority had not actually understood a word of what he was saying!

SIR ARTHUR CONAN DOYLE
1859-1930

DAYDREAMS INTO LITERATURE

Sportsman, doctor, historian and writer, Sir Arthur created one of the most enduring – indeed, legendary – characters in English literature: Sherlock Holmes, the brilliantly observational denizen of 221B Baker Street.

Conan Doyle was born of Irish parents in Edinburgh and educated partly in Great Britain and partly in Germany. He qualified as a medical doctor in Southsea, but the absence of both patients and revenue persuaded him, as he himself has related, to turn his daydreams into imaginative writings. The result was a true stroke of genius, the creation of the great detective and his honest, down-to-earth colleague and 'chronicler', Dr Watson.

INVENTING SKIING

In addition to his works of fiction, Conan Doyle was also a superb physical specimen and an avid boxer. In 1894 at Davos, Switzerland, he invented and subsequently popularized the concept of skiing as a sport. He also served as an army doctor in the war between England and the Boers of South Africa at the beginning of the 20th century, wrote a history of that war and was appointed official War Historian of the 1914-18 World War. His keen sense of justice involved him in two notorious cases of mistaken identity, those of Edaljee in 1903 and Oscar Slater in 1909. Conan Doyle personally, at his own expense, fought the courts on behalf of these two men, both total strangers to him, because he felt that they had been wrongfully convicted.

THE EXERCISE OF INTELLIGENCE

Conan Doyle was an idealist who believed in his country and 'fair play'. In his writings, women tend to be modest, charming, faithful, beautiful and in need of defence. Gentlemen are honest, altruistic, gallant and brilliant. But Conan Doyle's

Holmes was so popular that Sir Arthur was unable to let him die in a story.

Many of the Holmes detective stories were published in illustrated editions.

fertile brain also conjured up an opposing criminal class of extraordinary depravity and ingenuity, led by the diabolical and brilliant Professor Moriarty, Holmes's arch enemy.

MODERN MYTHS

The titles of the Sherlock Holmes stories are modern myths in themselves, recreated again and again for stage, radio and the large and small screens, with perhaps the best known being *The Hound of the Baskervilles* (1902). All the stories are full of the most engaging dialogue between Holmes and Watson, fiendishly ingenious plots and all the grand self-confidence of the late Victorian Empire.

Creation of atmosphere was Conan Doyle's speciality. London itself is pervaded by a sinister aura of swirling fog-bound menace, while the counties outside London are inhabited by dubious characters from the Imperial Colonies – India, Africa, Canada and Australia – who have racked up vast fortunes by illicit methods and are now hiding from fanatically murderous and duped ex-partners in crime.

SCIENCE FANTASY

Conan Doyle's other immortal character is the ebullient Professor Challenger, as brilliant in the realm of science as Holmes is in detection. Professor Challenger is the hero of *The Lost World* (1912), the progenitor of all subsequent fantasies that dinosaurs still live. *The Lost World* was made into a silent picture almost as soon as it was written.

THE PLEASURE PRINCIPLE

As well as being a consummate story-teller, Conan Doyle was also a huge optimist, who made pertinent observations on human nature through his fictional characters, including 'Mediocrity knows nothing higher than itself, but talent instantly recognizes genius' (*The Valley of Fear*). Amazingly, his great detective is so real for some readers, that people still write to Sherlock Holmes in Baker Street today.

MARIE CURIE 1867-1934
ACHIEVEMENT

The use of X-rays (discovered by German scientist Wilhelm Röntgen in 1895) and the development of nuclear physics owe much to the achievements of Marie Curie, who conducted the experiments necessary to find the atomic weight of radium. Curie holds the distinction of being the first woman to win a Nobel Prize and the only woman to have been awarded two Nobel Prizes for her scientific discoveries. (Only three men have ever been double Nobel Prize winners.) In 1903, Curie shared the prize for physics with her husband, Pierre Curie, and Henri Becquerel (1852-1908), an expert on fluorescent rays; in 1911, she won the prize for chemistry on her own (both the men had died by this time).

TEAMWORK

Curie was born in Poland and educated at the Sorbonne in Paris, where she met and married the physicist Pierre Curie in 1895. Together they researched the properties of magnetism and radioactivity. After her husband's death in a traffic accident in 1906, Marie was appointed to his chair of Physics at the Sorbonne, becoming the

Marie Curie and her husband Pierre at work in their laboratory. Although Marie seems to have been the driving force in the partnership, much of their research into radioactivity was a joint effort.

first female professor there. She published numerous papers and was responsible for isolating not only radium (with her husband), but also polonium, which she named after her native country Poland.

In 1934 Marie Curie died of leukaemia, caused most probably by selfless dedication to her work at a time when the dangers of radioactivity were not fully understood. Although she devoted her life to scientific research (in a man's world), by all accounts she was also a loving mother who appreciated the importance of a supportive family. The Curies' daughter, Eve, wrote a moving biography of her mother, *Madame Curie* (1935). The couple's other daughter, Irene, assisted her mother in her work and in 1935 won the Nobel Prize for Chemistry jointly with her husband, Jean Joliot.

WILBUR (1867-1912) AND ORVILLE (1871-1948) WRIGHT

OVERCOMING THE CHALLENGE

Throughout the ages, human flight has been the stuff of legends and conjecture. From the ancient Greek myth of Daedalus and Icarus, who flew with the aid of feathered wax wings, to the prototype flying machines sketched by Leonardo da Vinci, mankind has dreamed of flight. In 1783,

the Montgolfier brothers, Joseph (1740-1810) and Jacques (1745-99), were the first to realize the dream of manned flight, when they successfully launched a hot-air balloon. And it was another pair of brothers, the self-taught American Wrights, who developed the technology to build aircraft.

BROTHERLY PARTNERSHIP

The Wrights set up in business together making and repairing bicycles, which financed their great passion. From an early age they were interested in mechanical things but their great enthusiasm was for aeronautics. In 1899 they embarked on a lengthy series of experiments with gliders, making over 1000 flights between them. They worked together extremely well and concentrated on how to keep control of an aircraft in flight, whereas others were working on getting a machine airborne. They gradually broke down the various problems of powered flight by designing their own engine, propellers and wings, which they tested in wind tunnels. On 17 December 1903 they built and flew the

The Wright brothers (pictured here in 1908) built an aeroplane which flew!

Mahatma Gandhi achieved freedom for India without resorting to violence.

HUMOUR

Although they had to face opposition from sceptics, in 1908 the Wrights triumphantly unveiled their invention simultaneously in America and Europe. They patented their flying machine and in 1909 set up an aircraft production company, but it was not until the outbreak of the First World War that there was any real impetus from the governments of either side to develop aircraft technology. Neither of the Wright brothers married – they often quipped that they were both bachelors because they could not 'support a wife as well as an aeroplane'.

MOHANDÂS K. (MAHATMA) GANDHI
1869-1948
NON-VIOLENCE

Mahatma (the name means Great Soul) Gandhi's great achievement was the liberation of India from the British Empire which had ruled there since the 18th century. Without a doubt, the British involvement in India brought that country immense civilizing benefits. On the other hand, the aspirations of the Indian populace to be allowed finally to govern themselves after 200 years were indisputable, and it was Gandhi who brought about the realization of this dream. He did this, not by violent opposition to British Imperial rule, but by a systematic policy of avoiding bloodshed and by fasting, denying himself food in order to shame the violent into peaceful solutions. Non-violence became his credo, but it is a message which is still widely ignored today, in spite of his success. Most modern-day resistance movements, by resorting to terrorism to achieve their ends, simply inflame reciprocal vendetta situations and so exacerbate the conflict.

first powered aeroplane near Kitty Hawk, Carolina. On that momentous day Orville piloted the first and third flights and Wilbur piloted the second and fourth. On his first attempt Orville covered a distance of 120 ft (36.5 m) at a height of 8-12 ft (2-3.5 m) for 12 seconds. The fourth flight covered 852 ft (260 m). Their plane, the *Flyer I*, was later dubbed the *Kitty Hawk*. It weighed 750 lb (340 kg), had a wing span of 40 ft (12 m) and was powered by a 12-horsepower engine. The Wrights' success was partly due to the light engine, which weighed only 170 lb (770 kg) and was strong enough to drive the plane without weighing it down.

POSITIVE ATTITUDE

Nevertheless, Gandhi's appeal to peaceful methods – rather than violence – an emphasis on rationality and 'thinking out' the problem was colossal. Once, during the vicious partition confrontations in 1947 between Moslem Pakistan and Hindu India, Gandhi was approached by a distraught Hindu. His son had been killed by Moslems and in revenge he himself had killed a Moslem child. He came to Gandhi in despair asking what he should do. Gandhi considered for a while, then said: 'Go forth and find a Moslem child who has been orphaned by the riots. Take that Moslem child into your own Hindu home and raise him as your own son, but as a Moslem.' This is a fine example of Gandhi's philosophy.

PLANNING

The methods Gandhi chose to liberate India were perfectly suited to his opponent, the British Empire. He knew that his non-violent methods and fasting would be just the thing to strike a raw nerve with British public opinion and bring moral pressure upon their politicians.

FITNESS

Sadly, though, his final months were darkened by the continuing strife between Hindu and Moslem, and he was assassinated in Delhi on 30 January 1948 by a Hindu fanatic, just 10 days after another attempt on his life. Gandhi has been venerated as a moral teacher, a reformer who sought a new India free from the caste system, and a patriot who gave the Home Rule Movement in India a new quality of moral force.

Thin and attired in a simple cloth draped over his shoulder, Gandhi appeared physically fragile. But he was enormously resilient, enduring frequent bouts of fasting and long periods of imprisonment by the British. He always emerged from jail fitter and stronger than before.

COMMITMENT

Gandhi was born in Porbandar, India, in 1869 and studied law in London. In 1893 he gave up his Bombay legal practice, which had been worth £5000 a year (a vast sum at the time), to live on just £1 per week in South Africa, where he spent 21 years opposing that country's discriminatory legislation against Indians. In 1914 he returned to India and soon took the leading role in the Home Rule, or *Swaraj*, Movement. In due course he became the leader of the Congress organization. From 1920 onwards he organized campaigns of civil disobedience, always based on non-violent methods, and in 1930 he led a mass, 200-mile march to the sea to collect salt in a symbolic gesture against the government monopoly of that substance. The mere collection of salt may seem a strange way to start a revolution against a foreign power, but it had its effect. He was arrested, but soon released, and by the following year had negotiated a truce between the Indian Congress and the British government and was invited to a London conference to discuss Indian constitutional reforms.

FOCUS

Gandhi spent much of the Second World War in British jails in India. He was released in 1944 and in 1946 he negotiated with the British the new constitutional structure. In May 1947 came his greatest triumph – Britain's decision to grant India independence, which he described as 'The noblest act of the British nation'. Gandhi had achieved his goal; but even he, in spite of his saintly creed of non-violence, could not prevent the ongoing unrest between the Moslems (who eventually broke away to form Pakistan) and the Hindus. The atmosphere was rife with political, racial and religious problems which persist to this day.

If anyone had contributed to eradicating that tension and to freeing a nation without resorting to bloodshed, Gandhi was that man. His was a course of material renunciation and immense focus on one great goal, which he achieved – albeit at the cost of his own life.

MARIA MONTESSORI 1870-1952

BREAK WITH TRADITION

Maria Montessori established an education system which relies heavily on children's responses. Her work with mentally handicapped children led her to appreciate how the young human brain is stimulated by colours, shapes, textures and the relative size and weight of objects, and how all the senses must be appreciated. She soon realized that her programme could successfully be applied to all children, not just those with special needs, and she put her ideas into practice in schools which still bear her name internationally. She abandoned totally the traditional, rigid formulas for teaching reading, writing and arithmetic to young children aged from three to six and she encouraged instead free expression and self-discipline.

THE WILL TO ACHIEVE

On a personal level, she consistently came at the top of her class at school at a time when girls still had to battle to have their achievements recognized. Later, she displayed grit and determination to become the first woman in Italy to receive the degree of doctor of medicine, which she was awarded in 1894. She then taught at the psychiatric unit of the University of Rome, where she put her energies into child development, and was appointed director of Rome's Scuola Ortofrenica for retarded children in 1898. She was influenced by the work of earlier educationalists, such as the Swiss Johann Pestalozzi (1746-1827) and the German Friedrich Froebel (1782-1852), but she achieved startling successes with her own innovative regime, which included special learning equipment, apparatus and furni-

ture designed with children's needs in mind.

Montessori's achievements were so dramatic that she gave up her medical practice and her two positions at the university to concentrate on educating the disadvantaged slum children of Rome. Her first school opened in Rome in 1907 and the Montessori method spread rapidly throughout Italy and then to Switzerland, England and the United States. She even took it to India, where she conducted a lecture tour in Madras, Karachi, and Poona. Her educational methods have profoundly influenced the teaching of young children worldwide.

GUGLIELMO MARCONI 1874-1937
IMAGINATION AND CONVICTION
Marconi, the inventor of the radio, was born into a wealthy family and educated by private tutors

Montessori, aged 80, visited an English school where her methods were taught.

in Bologna, Italy. He had an agile mind and an ability to solve problems quickly. He was inspired by the work of Heinrich Hertz (1857-94), the German physicist who demonstrated the existence of radio waves. Marconi was convinced that these waves could be used to transmit messages over long distances without wires, and his earliest experiments with wireless technology were conducted in 1895 in his home town. Within a year of his first experiments he had invented a device which fulfilled his dream.

Marconi then emigrated to England, where in 1899 he transmitted signals across the English Channel to France. His new invention was so successful that in 1900 Marconi established his

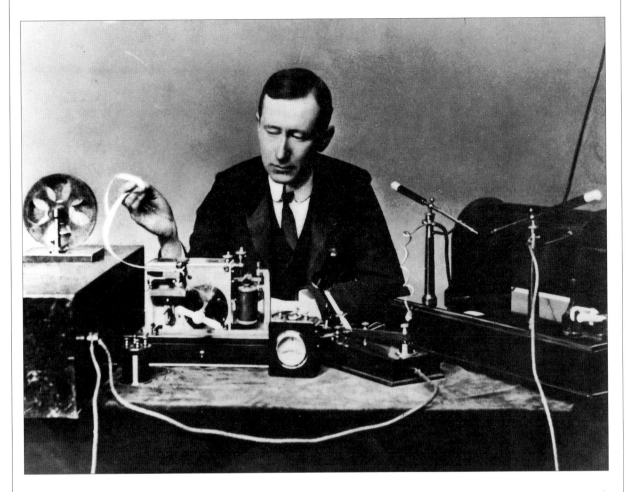

Marconi used similar equipment to this when he transmitted and received wireless signals over long distances.

Wireless Telegraph and Signal Company (later the Marconi Wireless Telegraph Company Limited) and established himself as a shrewd businessman as well as an inventor of genius. In 1901 he sent Morse code signals across the Atlantic from Cornwall to Newfoundland, and in 1910 he transmitted from Ireland to Argentina – over 6000 miles (9660 km).

IMMEDIATE IMPACT
The impact of Marconi's invention was immediate. He was asked to develop his system for the British and Italian governments and he was showered with honours by the King of Italy and the Czar of Russia. In 1909 he shared the Nobel Prize for Physics with the German physicist Karl Ferdinand Braun (1850-1918), who was working in a similar field. During the First World War Marconi was put in charge of the Italian wireless system and in 1929 he was made a Marchese and a senator. The following year he became President of the Italian Royal Academy.

TELEVISION
When Marconi died in 1937, he was given a state funeral in his home town of Bologna. That same year his company won a television contract with the British Broadcasting Company (BBC). A competitor for that same contract had been John Logie Baird (1888-1946), who had first researched the concept of television.

Baird had started his career studying electrical engineering in Glasgow. In 1926 his vision of producing moving images on a screen became reality when he demonstrated the world's first television. His 30-line mechanically scanned system was adopted only three years later by the BBC. Baird improved his invention and by 1936 was transmitting 240-line images, but Marconi-EMI were able to cap this with a more sophisticated 405-line system.

Together, Marconi and Baird revolutionized not only the communications industries, but also the leisure pursuits of the 20th century.

THE POWER OF THE NEW

'ENOUGH HAS BEEN DONE TO OVERTHROW THE CERTAINTY OF AGES,
AND TO REQUIRE A NEW PHILOSOPHY OF THE UNIVERSE, A PHILOSOPHY
THAT WILL SWEEP AWAY NEARLY ALL THAT HAS HITHERTO BEEN
ACCEPTED AS THE AXIOMATIC BASIS OF PHYSICAL THOUGHT.'
THE TIMES ON EINSTEIN, NOVEMBER 1919

CARL GUSTAV JUNG 1875-1961

Jung once said: *'All science is a function of the soul in which all knowledge is noted. The soul is the greatest of all cosmic miracles. It is the condition sine qua non of the world as an object. It is exceedingly astonishing that the Western world (apart from very rare exceptions) seems to have so little appreciation of this being so. A flood of external objects of cognizance has made the subject of all cognizance withdraw to the background – often to apparent non existence.'*

Jung popularized the concept of people being 'introvert' or extrovert'.

FLEXIBILITY

Whenever psychoanalysis and psychology are mentioned, Jung and Freud are continually bracketed together, as if their messages were identical. In fact, Sigmund Freud (1856-1939), who started his work before Jung, was the pioneer of psychoanalysis. His message tended to blame sex as being the underlying cause of almost every type of problem. Jung's insight into the human psyche, on the other hand, was richer and deeper, and in general he was less dogmatic in his judgements than Freud.

GENIUS ATTRACTS

Jung was a Swiss psychiatrist who studied medicine at Basle and worked under Bleuler at the Berg Holzli mental clinic in Zurich from 1900 to 1909. The Berg Holzli clinic was, in fact, the first institution outside Austria to adopt Freud's method of psychoanalysis. As with so many of the great minds, Freud had met with fierce opposition when he began his work.

ICONOCLASM

Jung began as a firm disciple of Freud and became one of his early allies. After the two men met in Vienna in 1907, Jung went on to become Freud's leading collaborator and was himself elected President of the International Psycho-Analytical Association – a post which he held from 1910 until 1914.

However, Freud appears to have had a particularly prickly character and was extremely intolerant of any kind of criticism. Jung's independent research made him increasingly sceptical of Freud's exclusively sexual definition of libido, and when Jung published the *Psychology of the Unconscious*, in 1911, an irretrievable break occurred in their relationship. From that point onwards, Jung developed his own theories separately from Freud and he termed his own research *Analytical Psychology*, so as to distinguish it from Freud's *Psychoanalysis*.

INNOVATION

The depth and range of Jung's perceptions were immense. He described psychological types – the extrovert and the introvert – and perhaps his best-known discovery is the exploration of the 'collective unconscious' with the archetypes – an impersonal layer of ideas, beliefs, patterns and pictures that underlie the personal unconscious. This is a concept which charts back to the Platonic ideals.

EVERYTHING CONNECTS

A contemporary Jungian psychotherapist (Liz Greene, quoted in *The Financial Times* of 19 February 1994) has expatiated on Jung's theory as follows: 'We still have a collective psyche. We are still plugged into a unified life which all human beings share. There is something which connects us. It lies behind mass movements and the appearance of the same mythologies in different parts of the world.'

POLYMATH

Jung was fascinated by the individual identity – the identity of the self. Most of his later work is devoted to this. The enormous scope of his ideas included: examinations of the dreams and drawings of patients; the symbolism of religion; myths; historical precedence; and even the realm of fables. He also brought modern physics into the equation.

Jung's studies were so wide ranging that they overspill the bounds of pure psychology. His main works were: *Psychic Energy* (1928); *Psychology and Religion* (1937); *Psychology and Alchemy* (1944); and *The Undiscovered Self* (1957). Jung has also influenced the realms of anthropology, religion, art, literature and history. It is reassuring to note that Jung, like Lister, was recognized fully in his lifetime, holding Professorships at Zurich University and Basle and being showered with academic honours during his life.

TO VIE WITH GOETHE

As a student, Freud was attracted to the theories of Charles Darwin, but it was the inspiration of Goethe which eventually impelled him to take up medicine as a career. '*It was upon hearing Goethe's beautiful essay on nature that I decided to become a medical student.*'

Freud studied in Vienna, Paris and Berlin, where he investigated the nervous systems of both animals and humans. He became fascinated

Freud reading (perhaps at speed?) A Summary of Psychoanalysis in 1938.

by the use of hypnosis to treat hysteria, by which the patient, while hypnotized, was requested to relate past incidents which could be of significance for a cure. In the 1880s, hysteria was regarded as a purely physical condition. Freud took the iconoclastic step of treating hysteria as a disorder of the mind or a psychological phenomenon.

THE INTERPRETATION OF DREAMS

Freud's advances as a specialist in nervous diseases was rapid. Once established in Vienna, he rejected hypnotism as a means of penetrating to the truth, replacing it first with so-called 'free association' and then the final and decisive step, analysis of the patient's dreams. Freud's seminal work *The Interpretation of Dreams* was published in 1900. No one since the pre-enlightenment astrologers, or the soothsayers and oracles of antiquity, had sought to place serious significance on dreams. Freud proposed to build an entire scientific edifice upon them, an edifice which further claimed to explain the mysteries of the human mind itself.

OPPOSITION AND RIDICULE FROM THE AUTHORITIES

Essentially, Freud founded psychoanalysis, but from the very beginning his new theories faced opposition and ridicule from the scientific and medical establishments. Indeed, even the few disciples Freud did gather around him, notably Jung and Adler, soon broke with the founding father of the group to promulgate their own theories of the mind.

PSYCHOANALYSING CIVILIZATION

Over the following decades, though, as Freud published a growing number of treatises on his ideas, acceptance inexorably escalated. Freud extended his individual psychological work, which embraced both the theories of the Ego and the Id and the Oedipus Complex, to wide-ranging psychoanalysis of entire cultures in books such as *Thoughts for the Times on War and Death* and *Civilisation and its Discontents*.

THE GOETHE PRIZE

In 1930, Freud was awarded the Goethe prize and given the freedom of the city of Vienna. He

Einstein's theories revolutionized thought about space and time.

must have considered this to be the ultimate accolade. His triumph, however, was to be short lived. Like many other Jewish intellectuals, such as Einstein, Freud was hounded out of the country by the Nazis. He died in England, but with the consolation that psychoanalysis, from once being regarded as a theory for the lunatic fringe of medicine, had now become a worldwide cult industry.

SHATTERING THE MOULD

What Freud achieved was to redefine investigation into the human mind in such a way that the pre-Freudian and post-Freudian mental landscapes employ utterly different vocabularies and frames of reference. Freud shattered all the moulds. He did not just find new answers to old questions, he completely and comprehensively rewrote the entire agenda, in a way that posterity has been unable to ignore.

ALBERT EINSTEIN 1879-1955

Einstein is a serious candidate for the supreme genius of all time. In just a few years, his brilliant insights entirely changed the way the universe is perceived, while his mighty equation, $E=MC^2$, was to make available both for creative and destructive purposes a source of energy of hitherto unimagined intensity – atomic power. Einstein's investigations ushered in the atomic age. For the very first time, human beings were actually placed in the position of understanding how the universe works, while simultaneously being given the terrifying capacity to annihilate their own world.

PRECOCIOUSLY DISRUPTIVE

Einstein has the reputation of having been a relative dunce at his school in Munich, but this is a misapprehension. Although precocious, he did not excel in those subjects taught by the Luitpold Gymnasium, where he was a pupil. Einstein was later to denounce their lessons as 'lies', and he was in fact expelled from the school on the grounds that he was a 'disruptive influence' on his fellow students. He had an enquiring mind and often used to daydream. When he applied himself to something that he really enjoyed doing he would excel.

He studied music as a boy and eventually became an accomplished violinist, playing for relaxation. One amusing story recounts how, while playing a duet with a professional violinist, Einstein missed a few notes and beats. This prompted his exasperated companion to ask 'What's the matter with you, Einstein? Can't you count?'

INSPIRED BY EUCLID AND MICHELANGELO AND DAYDREAMS

It is clear, though, that from an early age (he was fascinated by a compass at the age of five), Einstein was determined to probe the secrets and solve the riddle of the physical world. He was inspired by a book of Euclid's geometry and he made a particular point of studying Michelangelo's pictures. By the age of 16, Einstein had already written a scientific paper on the relationship between electricity, magnetism and the ether. He reported at the time that he came up with his theories by encouraging himself to play mind games, in which he allowed his imagination to run riot.

Einstein also reported that in one daydreaming session he had imagined riding on a sunbeam to the end of the universe. To his amazement, when he got to 'the end of the universe', he found he was back where he had started his 'journey', and thus concluded that the universe must be both finite and curved. In his paper, Einstein explored the question 'what would happen if one could follow a beam of light at the *speed* of light?' As a result, he discovered a paradox which, in scientific jargon, is 'a spatially oscillating electromagnetic field at rest'. In other words, in spite of moving at a vast speed, one would appear to have not moved at all.

ROLLER COASTER OF THE MIND

In 1895, Einstein joined the Swiss Federal Polytechnic School at Zurich, at an age two years below the standard age of enrolment. There Einstein studied under Professor Hermann Minkowski, the Russo-German mathematician, whose special interests were the theory of numbers, space and time. Einstein could not have found a teacher more in tune with his own predilections. Einstein took Swiss nationality in 1901, and in 1902 he was appointed Examiner at the Swiss Patent Office. From this point on, his achievements begin to take on the aspect of an intellectual roller coaster!

PLANCK'S QUANTUM THEORY

Einstein began to publish a steady stream of scientific papers on a number of problems in the field of physics. One concerned the quantum theory of Germany's greatest physicist, Max Planck (1858-1947), which held that energy changes or emissions occur in violent, abrupt instalments, packages or quanta. Planck himself was to become a Nobel Prize winner, President of the Berlin Science Academy and a member of the London Royal Society.

RELATIVITY

In 1905, Einstein applied Planck's quantum theory to light and published his revolutionary paper on Special Relativity. From 1909 onwards, the scientific world realized that a new Galileo or Newton was upon them, and showered Einstein with Professorships – for example, in Zurich, Prague and Berlin. In 1916, Einstein published his theory of General Relativity. Three years later, two British expeditions confirmed, through their observation of eclipses, that Einstein's theories were correct. The world of science was now in ferment, but excitement also gripped the world at large. As *The Times* of London wrote: 'The scientific conception of the fabric of the universe must be changed. It is confidently believed by the greatest experts that enough has been done to overthrow the certainty of ages, and to require a new philosophy of the universe. A philosophy that will sweep away nearly all that has hitherto been accepted as the axiomatic basis of physical thought. The ideals of Aristotle and Euclid and Newton, which are the basis of all our present conceptions, prove in fact not to correspond with what can be observed in the fabric of the universe. Space is merely a relation between two sets of data and an infinite number of times may coexist. Here and there, past and present, are relative not absolute and change according to the ordinates and coordinates selected. Observational science has in fact led back to the purest subjective idealism.'

E=MC² = ATOMIC ENERGY

Hitler's rise to power in the 1930s led to Einstein leaving Germany and establishing himself at Princeton in the United States, where he lived for 20 years. In September 1939 he wrote to President Roosevelt, advising him to start work on an atomic bomb project and warning of the dangers of a possible German initiative in this field. This was to lead directly to the Manhattan Project, on which Richard Feynman worked.

Einstein's equation, $E=MC^2$, where energy equals mass multiplied by the speed of light squared, demonstrates that a very small amount of mass is the equivalent of a vast amount of energy. By utilizing this theory, two German scientists, Otto Hahn and Fritz Strassman, were already engaged in 1938 in splitting the uranium atom. They were thus on the brink of unleashing untold energy for Germany. Fortunately though, Werner Heisenberg, Germany's top physicist during the 1940s, succeeded in leading the Nazi authorities down a blind alley and thus deflected them from concentrating on the creation of an atomic bomb.

POLITICS OR EQUATIONS

After the dropping of atomic bombs on Hiroshima and Nagasaki, and the subsequent cessation of global hostilities, Einstein (who had earlier written an anti-war book with Sigmund Freud, *Why War?* 1933), urged international control of all atomic weapons. Then, in common with Charlie Chaplin, Einstein also protested against the communist witch-hunt of Senator Joseph McCarthy's un-American Activities Committee in the early 1950s. In 1952, Einstein was offered the presidency of the newly created state of Israel, but declined to accept the honour, saying: '*Equations are more important to me, because politics are for the present, but an equation is something for eternity!*'

EVERYTHING CONNECTS

In his later years, he spent much of his time playing the violin, sailing and working for world peace. Recent research has confirmed that he was a 'ladies' man' which has upset a number of modern commentators, but as *The Times* reported: '*Great artists or thinkers mature through their work; it is thus that they define themselves, and it is thus that they are defined. Had Einstein been a solicitous husband, selfless father and well-adjusted family man, he would not have been able to be Einstein.*'

Examination of Einstein's brain after his death revealed that it contained 400% more glial cells per neurone than usual, which would have had the effect of boosting his power of association between seemingly disparate items way beyond the average. But whether this was the cause or effect of his genius, it is impossible to tell.

PABLO PICASSO 1881-1973

THE POWER OF THE NEW

In terms of passion, output and sheer, vibrant creativity, Picasso is the colossus – the supreme powerhouse of 20th-century art, in all its forms, and a great influence on those who followed.

THE CLIMATE OF CHANGE

The 20th century opened to an acceleration of scientific advance; everywhere, but particularly in science, a need was felt to express the optimism of the new century. Inroads were being made in all branches of science, but it was in physics that developments were occurring which would change our concept of the universe. New perceptions on the formulation of matter were being published; in 1900, Max Planck proposed the quantum theory of energy; in 1905, Albert Einstein published his first special theory of relativity, while in 1911 Ernest Rutherford announced his theory of the atom. Finally, in 1913, Niels Bohr applied the quantum theory to Rutherford's atomic theory, thus completing the equation. Gradually, non-scientists became aware that human beings were made from essentially the same substances as the rest of the planet, and it also became increasingly apparent that the world did not exist entirely for man's pleasure.

For their part, artists were seriously questioning their role in this changing society. The old certainties about space and time were fast disappearing.

CREATIVITY

In and around artists' studios there was talk of the 'fourth dimension'. Henri Bergson, a philosopher concerned with the nature of experience and of time, published *Creative Evolution* in 1906. He argued that change was the stuff of reality and that it is the creative urge that lies at the heart of evolution, not natural selection. Bergson's book was eagerly devoured by the avant-garde, who found his championing of creativity as life's driving force to be immeasurably more attractive than the slow workings of deep time, as identified by Darwin.

PICASSO'S COMPETITOR

Henri Matisse, later to become Picasso's main artistic competitor in France, had sprung to notoriety in 1905 with his painting of his wife, *The Woman with the Hat*. He was profoundly influenced by the philosophy of Bergson. The painting was bought by Leo Stein, an American who, along with his sister Gertrude, became one of the first patrons for advanced art. Stein later wrote of his initial bewilderment with the picture, of the apparently chaotic colours and brushwork on the face of the woman, which when looked at again, however, demonstrated intentional order.

LES FAUVES

The exhibition where Matisse first exhibited 'Woman' was held at the Salon d'Automne and it created such a scandal it was called 'Les Fauves' ('Savages') by a critic of a popular newspaper. This derogatory term was adopted as the name of the first incontestably modern art movement of the 20th century. Matisse, meanwhile, continued to simplify his work. He dismissed perspective and modelling, and found a balance between line and colour.

PICASSO AND EINSTEIN

At first, Picasso denied any relation between science and his work, but in 1956 he acknowledged it in the following statement: 'When I read a book on Einstein's physics, of which I understand nothing, it doesn't matter: that will make me understand something else.'

SPANISH ROOTS

Picasso was born in Spain and lived most of his life in Barcelona. He was 19 when he visited Paris for the first time. Academically trained (his father was a drawing master), he had already chosen to take the side of 'modernism' and was producing works in the fashionable Symbolist manner. These paintings of doomed solitary individuals eventually came to be identified as his blue period, which lasted from 1901 to 1904, when he made Paris his home.

Throughout his long life, though, he surrounded himself with other Spaniards and always remained emotionally committed to Spanish tradition. Spain and its Mediterranean legacy were an essential part of his various styles. But Picasso, who painted more than 40 variations of Velazquez's *Las Meninas*, never returned physically to Franco's Spain.

CUBISM

The developers of Cubism were Georges Braque (1882-1963) and Pablo Picasso. Cubism is undoubtedly the most important visual movement of the 20th century. For the first time in Western art, pictures were made on the principle that, in conception as well as appearance, the image need not be restricted to the object for which it stands. Artistic reality can be something other than the kind of visual image that the convention of Renaissance perspective had fixed as the true representation of an actual object in physical space. In the same way that Cézanne painted light and shade as he really saw it, Picasso and Braque painted portraits with their minds' eye, using a multiple perspective of how they saw a person rather than relying on the actual reality of sight.

ARTISTIC RELATIVITY

From 1907 on Picasso and Braque saw each other almost daily, and together they created the pictorial innovation of Cubism. The chosen subject matter was a simple still life, which usually consisted of bottles, glasses and almost always a musical instrument. The painting would be set out in planes which indicate, but do not define, the external and internal boundaries of the objects. The artist describes the objects from several different positions, so that the experience is of shifting instability, sometimes seeming to dissolve, sometimes to materialize. As Picasso said, 'I paint forms as I think them, not as I see them.'

ORVILLE AND WILBUR

Braque later said of his partnership with Picasso that they were like mountaineers roped together. Each took turns in leading while the other followed. This selfless interaction is best expressed by their nicknames for each other, 'Orville and Wilbur', after the American aviators.

One major innovation the two artists shared was collage. For some time Braque had added different substances to his pigment – sand, metal filings – which changed the surface of the work. Then Picasso, in 1912, created his first collage, *Still Life with a Cane Chair*. It was made by sticking a piece of oilcloth, onto which caning had been lithographed, to the surface of the canvas. Braque followed this with his first composition of pasted paper, in which pieces of wood-grained wallpaper were combined with charcoal drawing. Both artists followed this innovation with sculpted paper objects, of which only Picasso's have survived; Braque's sculptures disappeared when he joined the army in 1914. Picasso and he were separated for ever. Braque was severely wounded in 1916 and after he finally recovered in 1920, he spent the rest of his life refining his earlier Cubism. Picasso, a Spaniard, was exempt from the war. Relatively unaffected, he was able to work throughout the war years, and gradually evolved in other directions. Persuaded by Cocteau, he worked on designs for the Diaghilev Ballet, where his contribution, particularly with *Parade* (1917), revolutionized stage sets and introduced him to a wealthy and fashionable lifestyle, encouraged by his first wife Olga, one of Diaghilev's dancers.

Picasso was as fascinated by the animal form as he was by the human figure. In the words of Gertrude Stein, one of his first patrons, 'He walks in the light and a little ahead of himself, like Raphael.' Here he is 'riding' one of his plaster sculptures, The Goat, *at his house in Cannes in 1955.*

VERSATILITY AND PRODUCTIVITY

Always inventive and dynamic, Picasso's work in the 1920s again explored figurative art (doubtless because of his proximity to dancers), creating some of the most monumental figures, inspired by classical sculpture. Picasso alternated these with magisterial late-Cubist compositions, in which all colour has returned. In the late 1930s he reverted to sculpture with portraits of his new love (Marie-Thérèse), first modelled in plaster or clay, then turned into bronze. At the same time, he began to engrave the marvellous series of 40 etchings for *The Sculptor's Studio*, followed by the five plates of *The Rape* and the 15 plates of *The Minotaur*, all printed by the master engraver Roger Lacourière between 1930 and 1937. The group became known as The Vollard Suite.

INTENSITY OF EXPRESSION

The only time Picasso admits to using symbols is for his masterpiece *Guernica*. Civil war had broken out in Spain in 1936, Franco had invaded Spain and the Fascist governments of Germany and Italy had given him their support.

Picasso had promised the Republican government that he would contribute something to the Spanish pavilion at the International Exposition to be held in Paris in the summer of 1937. On 28 April, the Nazi Condor Legion (sent to Spain to aid Franco) bombed Guernica, a town sacred to the Basques. The bombing was timed for an hour when the maximum number of people would be in the streets. Picasso immediately reacted to the news and his first sketches were made by 1 May, when the huge canvas, measuring 25 ft 8 in by 11 ft 6 in (351 × 782 cm), was stretched. He stripped the story to its simplest tragic elements, abandoning colour for black, white and grey. Nothing separates us from the women screaming in horror as death rains from the sky. The noble horse is struck down and the bull is a force of darkness. In 1953, Picasso said: 'The bull represents brutality, the horse the people . . . it is allegoric.'

IDEAS AND EMOTIONS

After the war Picasso lived mainly in the south of France, continuing to create with ever greater

intensity. When he discovered the pottery town of Vallauris, he became interested in working with the local potters, thus revolutionizing ceramic sculpture. He died in 1973, having bestrode the 20th century like a colossus. Every artist has been affected by him, by his dynamic energy, his singleness of purpose and, most of all, his inventive imagination.

No other artist excelled Picasso in his inexhaustible transformations of human and animal forms. He was never an abstract artist, always believing 'There is no abstract art. You must always start with something. Afterwards you can

Picasso's Les Demoiselles d'Avignon *(1907) which he called 'the brothel picture' considerably influenced other artists.*

remove all traces of reality. There's no danger then, anyway, because the idea of the object will have left an indelible mark. That is what started the artist off, excited his ideas, and stirred up his emotions. Ideas and emotions will in the end be prisoners in his work. Whatever they do, they can't escape from the picture. They form an integral part of it, even when their presence is no longer discernible' (1935).

IGOR STRAVINSKY 1882-1971

ICONOCLASM

The Czech-born Gustav Mahler (1860-1911) and Stravinsky are undoubtedly the two greatest composers of the 20th century, but Stravinsky scores over Mahler in the enormous variety and range of his musical compositions. Stravinsky was born in St Petersburg in 1882. At first he studied law, but then turned to musical composition, studying under the famous Russian composer Rimsky-Korsakov (1844-1908). It was when Stravinsky joined the Diaghilev Ballet that he achieved instant fame with music which encapsulated the ardour of Russian legend, of fairytales expressing love, but which also possessed a menacing overtone of threatening despotism.

PINPOINTING DESPOTISM

In 1910, Stravinsky wrote music for *The Firebird* ballet and then in 1911 he wrote a second ballet, *Petrushka*, which finally established a glittering international reputation for him. Originally, *The Firebird* had been intended 'as a purely orchestral piece, characterized by harmonic warfare between solo piano and the orchestra'. Diaghilev suggested that it should be transformed into a ballet puppet drama, expressing the eternal triangle of love under the eye of a despotic puppet master.

TAKING RISKS

Stravinsky's masterpiece, however, was *The Rite of Spring* (1913). It has been described as deliberately violent, chaotic music portraying primitive emotions and infringing every rule of harmony – yet somehow achieving a strange stylistic unity. There followed *The Soldier's Tale* (1918) – in which, appropriately enough, the devil seizes the soul of the soldier. Stravinsky's further works included *Pulchinella* (1920), *Apollo Musagetes* (1928), the *Symphony of Psalms* (1930), the *Symphony in C Major* (1940) and *Agon* (1957) – which used Schoenberg's atonal system.

Stravinsky settled in France in 1934 and moved to the United States in 1945. In addition to his feats as an innovative composer, he was a poet and also a dedicated weightlifter (proud of his body), with great strength and physical vigour. As befits the greatest composer of the 20th century, when he died he was given a magnificent state funeral in Venice.

POWER AND COURAGE

The premiere of *The Rite of Spring – Le Sacre du Printemps –* was at the Théâtre des Champs-Elysées on 29 March 1913, and it aroused bitter opposition. As one eyewitness said: 'Stravinsky tells us he wants to portray the surge of Spring, but this is not the usual Spring sung by poets with its breezes, its birdsong, its pale skies and tender greens. Here is nothing but the harsh struggle of growth, the panic terror from the rising of the sap, the fearful regrouping of the souls, Spring seen from inside with its violence, its spasms and its fissures. We seem to be watching a drama through a microscope.'

Another eyewitness that evening in Paris wrote: 'I look back with delight at the uproar of that evening. I knew already that the music of this ballet outstripped in violence and in dangerous experiment anything that had gone before. I also knew that the choreography had necessitated an incredible amount of work and that Nijinsky, the great ballet dancer, who had become a choreographer, had shown a terrible determination during the countless and arduous rehearsals, had even one day at the theatre, lost

A ballet costume by Leon Bakst (1866-1924) for Stravinsky's Firebird.

his temper to such an extent while teaching the ballet to the company, that he had literally nearly hit the ceiling of the rehearsal room. But I was expecting neither so great a work of art nor such a scandal.'

MARCEL DUCHAMP 1887-1968

Marcel Duchamp demonstrated that anything is possible in art. His influence on the art of the second half of the 20th century has been greater than that of any other artist.

FRATERNAL MASTERMIND GROUP

He was born near Rouen in 1887 into a solid mid-dle-class background. His father was a notary who had six children. Marcel was the youngest of three brothers, who all became artists; Raymond Duchamp Villon (1871-1918), the eldest, was a sculptor; Jacques Villon (1875-1963) was a painter. The three brothers, particularly Jacques, were very much part of the contentious art world of 1910. Living in Puteaux, a suburb of Paris, they became the centre of a group of artists who painted in a Cubist manner and exhibited under the name Section d'Or from 1912 to 1914.

REJECTED BY THE REJECTS!

Marcel Duchamp first gained notoriety when his picture, *Nude Descending a Staircase*, was rejected by the *Independents* in 1912. The paint-ing describes movement, and especially the mechanistic aspect of movement. Two promi-nent sequences of dotted lines in the centre of the canvas seem to be graphs of the torso's twist-ing rhythm and demonstrate Duchamp's desire to translate natural forms into energy. He despised what he called 'retinal' pictures, and later said, *'I wanted to put painting once again at the service of the mind'*. *Nude* was the sensation of the Armory Show held in New York in 1913, after which it was to become the most celebrated 'modern' painting in the western hemisphere.

THE LARGE GLASS

In 1912, Duchamp visited Munich for two months, and it was at this point that he began the work that was to take him out of painting alto-gether – the first drawings for the complex and enigmatic work which was to occupy him for the next 10 years, *The Bride Stripped Bare by Her Bachelors, Even*, sometimes called *The Large Glass*. Upon his return to Paris, Duchamp spent a great deal of time with the wealthy Cuban artist, Francis Picabia (1879-1953). They were joined by the poet and critic, Apollinaire. Picabia's wife later wrote that the three of them, with their 'forays of demoralization, pursued the disintegration of the concept of art.'

READY-MADES

In 1913 Duchamp began the 'ready-mades', per-haps the most baffling of all his creations. In 1934, André Breton, the French essayist and poet (1896-1966), defined them as *'Manufactured objects promoted to the dignity of objects of art through the choice of the artist'*. According to Duchamp, their importance is that they have no aesthetic value whatsoever, and function as a derisive comment on all art traditions and dog-mas. The first was *Bicycle Wheel*, put together in 1913. Duchamp claimed that he simply took a bicycle wheel and mounted it upside down on a kitchen stool, where, with a touch of the hand, he set it spinning. 'It just came about as a plea-sure,' he said. The next, *The Bottle Rack*, received no intervention from the artist's hand at all. Duchamp simply bought a galvanized iron rack used for drying bottles and signed it, thus demol-ishing the concept of art and codified beauty. (These works all exist only as replicas; the ori-ginals, which Duchamp turned out for his own pleasure, have all been either lost or destroyed.)

CHANCE OPERATIONS

Duchamp, while experimenting with these ideas, was working as a librarian, which gave him enough money to live on and also removed him intellectually from the 'art-world'. His critical fac-ulties led him to a similar distrust of scientific the-ory. His brothers were fascinated by geometry, as the title of their group, Section d'Or, suggests. Perhaps because of this atmosphere, Duchamp next began to question standard units of mea-surement, as a result of which he invented his own. From a height of one metre, he dropped a thread, one metre in length, upon a canvas. Having fixed it where it lay with varnish, he placed a sheet of glass over it for protection, then repeated the process twice. He then cut three wooden 'rulers' from these patterns, placed them inside a box, and called the result 'Standard Stops'. This was the first example of Duchamp's fascination with the idea of chance, which would be the single most important element in the development of Surrealism. Most of these ideas of Duchamp's were related to *The Large Glass*, which he later claimed to have essentially worked out before 1915.

THE FOUNTAIN

The First World War had ended for ever the optimism of the early years of the 20th century. Because of a weak heart, Duchamp was declared unfit to serve. He accepted an invitation from one of the organizers of the Armory Show to visit America, and in 1915 arrived in New York, where his reputation as the painter of *Nude* had preceded him. He was immediately caught up in the sophisticated world of Walter Arensberg. Duchamp began to work on *Glass* in a studio paid for by Arensberg, who was to have the finished sculpture in return. Duchamp next began to create his American *ready-mades*. He later said that he had deliberately limited the number, to avoid turning them into an artistic activity. (He either kept them for himself, or gave them away to friends.) He later said: 'The *ready-mades* were a way of getting out of the exchangeability, the monetarization of the work of art, which was just beginning about then.'

Duchamp was a founder member of the Society of Independents, to which, in 1917, he sent a standard urinal, which he turned upside down, called *Fountain* and signed R. Mutt. When it was rejected by the society, Duchamp responded by saying that the only works of art America had given to the world were her plumbing and her bridges.

FROM DADA TO DALI

In 1915, Duchamp returned to Paris after learning of the death of his brother Raymond from war wounds. He was immediately seen by the Paris group as a forerunner of Dada. This was the artistic and literary movement that emphasized irrationality and developed as a response to the war in Europe, breaking away from the traditional cultural values. (The name Dada – French for hobby-horse – was itself apparently chosen at random.)

However, Duchamp discreetly withdrew from direct participation in the Dada group's activities and, after returning to New York in 1920, spent the rest of his life alternating between the two countries.

In New York he joined the American painter Katherine Dreier as a director of her Société Anonyme. This was her pioneering effort to educate the public with lectures and exhibitions of her growing collection (which Duchamp helped to form). He was a sensitive and knowledgeable buyer and together they built up an art collection which, upon her death in 1952, was divided, with Duchamp's help, between Yale University museum and the Museum of Modern Art in New York.

FROM PAINTING TO CHESS

Duchamp never completed *The Large Glass*. Its composition consists entirely of complicated adaptations of chance, all carried out with the same painstaking attention to detail. In its final, incomplete state it is executed in oil paint, lead wire, foil, dust and varnish on glass.

He abandoned it in 1923, and with it abandoned all artistic production, committing himself instead to chess. He later said he wanted to become the champion of the world, which he never did, but he took chess seriously and played in tournaments until 1940.

Duchamp really never left the art world. Treated with great respect by the Surrealists, he remained aloof and distant, living quietly in Paris and New York. In 1934, he published, in a limited edition, the *Green Box*, in which he gathered together – in a totally random order – all the notes and drawings he had made for *The Large Glass*. In 1942, he was responsible for setting up exhibitions for exiled Surrealists.

PROFOUND INFLUENCE

Reacting against the emotional paintings of Abstract Expressionism, the post-1945 generation were ready for the cynicism of Marcel Duchamp. The first important book on him, by Robert Lebel, appeared in 1959. In 1960 George Heard Hamilton translated the *Green Box* into English. The same year the English artist, Richard Hamilton (no relation) published a typographic version of the *Green Box* and in 1965 made a version of the *Large Glass*, approved and signed by Duchamp. He was always better received in New York than in Paris – even the Abstract Expressionists admired him. William de Kooning remarked: 'Duchamp is a one-man movement, but a movement for each person and open to everybody.' Jasper Johns and Rauschenberg both acknowledge their debt to him, as does Jim Dine. The use Warhol later made of commercial products would be unthinkable before the existence of *ready-mades*. It is impossible to believe that the whole Pop Art movement, as well as Happenings and Performance Art, could have happened without him.

Retrospectively Duchamp seems to be the artist/thinker who has had the most profound influence on the latter part of this century. Duchamp himself commented, 'The business of my being influential is very much exaggerated.

Chess enthusiast Duchamp painted Portrait of a Chess Player *in 1911.*

Whatever there is in it is probably due to my Cartesian mind. I refused to accept anything, doubted everything. So, doubting everything, I had to find something that had not existed before, something I had not thought of before . . . anyway it might be that now all of these things I did, which did not come from anything before me, have become a source for these young people to start a new step entirely on their own.' A visit to museums and galleries, anywhere in the Western world, would justify this prediction.

CHARLIE CHAPLIN 1889-1977
ICON OF COMEDY

Charles Spencer Chaplin, the son of a theatrical family, was born near the site of Shakespeare's Globe Theatre in Kennington, South London. Like Dickens before him, Chaplin experienced extreme poverty in childhood. He received the little formal education that did come his way in the school at Hanwell Poor Law Institution. Following family tradition, Chaplin was already an experienced stage performer by the age of eight and in 1914 he went to Hollywood as a member of Fred Karno's Comedy Troop. There he joined the exploding silent movie industry.

PRODUCTIVITY

In his first year in Hollywood, Chaplin made 35 films and developed his little tramp trademark. This was to persist through all his early films and turn him into a beloved figure around the world. The elements of vulnerability, slapstick, humour and sadness, combined with terrific outbursts of physical, almost balletic energy, were to produce a winning formula.

CREATIVITY

Chaplin's silent masterpieces of these early years were the films *The Kid* (1920) and *The Gold Rush* (1924). The latter includes an immortal scene in which Chaplin, starving to death in a Klondike cabin, devours a boiled shoe, and follows this up by eating the laces for dessert.

COMMITMENT AND HUMOUR

It is too easy, though, to dismiss Chaplin merely as an entertainer, a clown. In fact, his social and political conscience was as highly developed as that of Charles Dickens. This came most powerfully to the fore in Chaplin's first full sound film, *The Great Dictator* (1940). Made the year before America entered the war against Nazi Germany, this film is a satirical attack against Hitler and considered by many to be Chaplin's masterpiece. He wrote, directed and produced it as well as taking the two lead roles, those of the Jewish barber and the Great Dictator himself, Adenoid Hynkel. Here we see Chaplin's slapstick armoury employed in the service of serious purpose, alerting America to the evil aspects of Nazism.

Yet, despite its high purpose, the film also contained all the classic ingredients of Chaplinesque comedy: the little man, eternally put upon at the bottom rung of the pecking-order, with his bowler hat, feet turned out in a waddle, shoes several sizes too large, cane, artificial moustache, baggy trousers and ill-fitting jacket. Chaplin's image of the clown exudes a dilapidated quality of surreal dapperness; as a personal icon, logo or trademark, it is likely to be remembered for many centuries to come.

ENERGY

The little tramp character is overwhelmed by the complexity of modern life, yet he is always resourceful and possessed of a remarkable dexterity. When Chaplin made *The Great Dictator* he was already 51 years old, yet in various stunt sequences which he performed he displayed the physical agility of a boy.

IMAGINATION

Chaplin's previous films had either been silent and accompanied only by music – for example, *City Lights* (1931) – or part speech, part mime – as in *Modern Times* (1936). In *The Great Dictator*, audiences had the opportunity to hear Chaplin's beautifully clipped diction, as well as his manic reproduction of Hitler's oratorical style. Chaplin invented his own spoof 'German' language for his sinister and terrifying impersonation of the Führer. But two genuine German words do surface again and again in the tumult of pseudo-teutonic babble: *Strafe*, meaning punishment, and *Juden*, the Jews.

During the film, one character a thinly disguised portrait of Hitler's Minister of Propaganda, Goebbels, states: 'Today democracy, liberty and equality are words to fool the people. No nation can progress with such ideas; they stand in the way of action, therefore we frankly abolish them! In the future each man will serve the interests of the state with absolute obedience. Let him who refuses beware.'

TRUTH

As an antidote to this threatening message, the film ends with a peroration by Chaplin that is almost painfully direct and heartfelt and totally relevant to the time: '*We have developed speed, but we have shut ourselves in. Machinery that gives abundance, has left us in want. Our knowledge has made us cynical; we think too much and feel too little. Dictators free themselves, but they enslave the people. Let us fight for a world of reason, where science and progress will lead to all men's happiness. Don't give your lives to men who tell you what to do, what to think and what to feel.*' Such a sentiment links Chaplin, the supreme clown, with philosophers and writers such as Socrates, Erasmus, Milton and Spinoza, all of them fighters for freedom of speech, thought and belief, an essential quality of genius.

COURAGE

During the early 1950s, a witch-hunt was conducted in the United States against alleged Communist sympathizers. It was led by the inquisitorial Senator Joseph McCarthy. When the campaign was at its height, Chaplin cabled Picasso in Paris, hoping to enlist the aid of the great artist to join him in a public crusade against McCarthy's persecutions. The result – Picasso was permanently denied an American visa. Chaplin himself was eventually expelled from his

adopted country for his liberal views by the fanatically anti-communist head of the FBI, J. Edgar Hoover.

Chaplin sought refuge in Switzerland. This exile in a good cause established one final link between Chaplin and those great minds of the past who suffered the same fate for adhering to their principles – namely Confucius, Dante and Machiavelli. Confucius was exiled from Lu province, while Dante and Machiavelli were both exiled from their home city of Florence. Official recognition did finally come Chaplin's way; in 1975 England gave him a knighthood.

MARTHA GRAHAM 1895-1991
REINVENTING DANCE

Ballet had been developing for four centuries when Martha Graham came on the scene. In the space of one lifetime, she revolutionized dance and introduced the art of choreography to the 20th century. She brought into play every aspect of the dancer's body and mind and introduced spoken dialogue into her performances. She was devoted to dance, seeing herself as a shaman of the form. Her private life was ascetic and rigorous and she demanded equal dedication from her acolytes. For her, dance was not just for entertainment; it was also a language – almost a religion.

PARENT POWER

Brought up in Pittsburgh, Pennsylvania, Martha learned much from her father, a doctor who studied the expression of emotion through bodily movement. His investigations into anatomy led him to show his daughter how movement can reveal character. Influenced early on by yogic breathing techniques, Oriental aesthetics, Zen Buddhism and many artists, including Picasso, Graham was later to describe her own choreographic style as: 'Painting with movement . . . an explosion of the spirit . . . defiance of tradition . . . colour, line, shock and vibrancy.'

LEFT This dramatic black-and-white shot shows the entertaining silent movie star Charlie Chaplin (complete with the moustache that audiences came to expect) in a scene from The Pilgrim, *a full-length film made in 1923.*

RIGHT Martha Graham lives on as a heroine and role model. Among others, she has inspired the outrageous diva Madonna, who described meeting Graham: 'She absolutely lived up to all my expectations with her wit, intelligence and nerve-wracking imperiousness'.

EMULATING ISADORA

Isadora Duncan (1878-1927) was another major inspiration to the young Graham, who by 1926 was already committed to dance, having performed in vaudeville, revue and classical work in Manhattan. Duncan's style, based on ancient Greek art (as recorded on vase painting), was free-flowing and innovative, but undisciplined. Graham resolved to build up a body of technique which would formalize such innovations.

READING AND ANIMALS

In 1930 Martha Graham danced the lead role in Stravinsky's controversial and trail-blazing ballet, *The Rite of Spring*, and the same year she founded the Dance Repertory Theatre.

Martha read prodigiously. Like Jung, she drew extensively on history, myth and legend, as well as detailed studies of anthropology and psychology. She also studied animals in zoos, especially the pent-up violence of the big cats in their cages. As she said: *'There are times when it is almost necessary to feel an animal sensualness in dance . . . like completely primitive movements . . . dancing is animal in its source!'*

VERSATILITY

Graham's achievements after founding her own company were multifarious and extensive. Despite a lack of state funding, she still found the strength of will to develop her own technique, choreograph new dances utilizing her ideas, and train her dancers. She even had to design and make her own costumes while striving to run the company as a business. The strain of juggling these varied activities simultaneously must have been immense.

NEW TECHNIQUE

For her revolutionary choreographic language, Graham enlisted all the muscles in the body to convey emotion, even those used for coughing. Such interplay of the muscles she called 'contractions'. As her biographer Agnes de Mille has

Like the Italian educationalist Maria Montessori, dance teacher Martha Graham left a legacy of schools all over the world where her methods are still taught. Graham, seated with the bouquet, is one of many long-lived geniuses who worked with great enthusiasm well past the age when most people retire to a quieter life.

put it: 'These contractions were visible, like an intake of breath, at the back of the auditorium. She focused on the emotional aspects of her technique, angular, sharp and stunning . . . uncomfortable to behold, but they jolt the mind.'

TEACHING

Martha Graham set up schools worldwide to teach her methods. In spite of initial rejection of her work in some countries outside the United States, she persevered with a constant belief in what she was creating. When she came to London in 1954 her reception was such that she was able to set up the first contemporary dance school in Britain at The Place in London.

CREATING HER OWN LEGEND

Graham was intent on becoming a legend, so she consciously and deliberately destroyed things to do with her personal life, including letters, personal documents and even books. She then set about moulding herself according to her own designs. She always looked immaculate, dressing dramatically in either black or white.

MARTHA'S NOTEBOOK – VERBAL INTELLIGENCE

Graham believed that words and movement are inexorably linked and often express identical things. She once said: *'If you are stuck for a gesture, say the word, the sentence; the action will come.'* Words were a major source for her dance compositions. She studied dictionaries, trying to find the roots of words and, therefore, the original idea behind them.

Throughout her working life, she wrote down quotations in notebooks, which were finally published in 1973. They embrace poetry, history and literature, including geniuses cited in this book: Milton, Shakespeare, Goethe and classical authors such as Julius Caesar.

FROM ART TO INDUSTRY

In 1965, the National Endowment of the Arts was set up and Martha Graham's company at last started to receive large grants for foreign tours. She was soon in command of a dance 'industry' with funds of hundreds of thousands of dollars. There was a huge marketing drive, including sales of memorabilia, tote bags, Martha Graham T-shirts and so on. Suddenly, the financial drought was over and she had become a recognized world leader in her field. But to maintain the legend she had always to be available for interviews. Her private life evaporated since the entire enterprise relied on her brain, her output. She persevered through crippling arthritis, spurred on by her need to communicate her ideas to the world.

SPREADING THE SEED

When female dancers left Graham's company they set up schools to teach her techniques and proselytize her ideas, whereas the male dancers started their own companies and used Graham's techniques as a springboard for their own ideas. For example, Merce Cunningham (who worked closely with composer John Cage), Paul Taylor and Glen Tetley became famous choreographers in their own right.

Wherever Martha Graham travelled on her world tours, she was accorded an heroic welcome. She received over 37 national and international awards, including the 'Medal of Freedom' in 1976 from President Gerald Ford, who hailed Graham as a 'national treasure'. In 1984 she was made a Knight of the French Legion of Honour and in Tokyo in 1990, the year before she died, she received the 'Order of the Precious Butterfly with Diamond'.

AGE CANNOT WITHER

Graham was in her mid-30s when she began to establish her name in New York. She was already older than the dancers in her company, but she still surpassed them all. Her work remained illuminating, creative and brilliant until the last years of her life, in common with other geniuses who created masterpieces in their later years, such as Leonardo, Michelangelo and Picasso. At a similar age, Verdi composed *Falstaff* and *Othello*, and Goethe worked on *Faust*.

DEFYING ARTHRITIS

Graham's last performance, in May 1968, when she was aged 72 and crippled with arthritis, was called *A Time of Snow*. She choreographed it herself, and it took the theme of the medieval lovers, Abelard and Eloise, in their old age. After this triumph, she invited world-famous ballet dancers to appear as guest artists with her company. In 1975, Dame Margot Fonteyn and Rudolph Nureyev danced with her and in 1987 three Russian stars joined her company for a season: Maya Plesitskaya, Nureyev and Mikhail Baryshnikov. Her final work was *Maple Street Rag* (to music by Scott Joplin) which was created one year before she died at the age of 96.

REACHING FOR THE LIMITS

*'AT SIX I WANTED TO BE A CHEF, AT SEVEN, NAPOLEON, AND MY
AMBITIONS HAVE BEEN GROWING EVER SINCE!'*
SALVADOR DALÍ (1904-1989)

JORGE LUIS BORGES 1899-1986
PERSISTENCE

Borges was the greatest writer in the Spanish
tongue of the 20th century. Yet the Nobel Prize
Committee established a laughable annual tradition of not awarding him the prize for literature.
Borges studied in Argentina, Geneva and
Cambridge and was bilingual in both English and
Spanish – his stories read equally fluently in both
languages. With great self-deprecation, he used
to assert that his English translators had
improved on his original Spanish. In later life he
became blind – almost a blind seer like Homer
or Milton.

EXPLORING FOREVER

Borges' plots centre around the exercise of intelligence in a vast universe. Indeed, two of his
stories, *Funes, The Memorious* and *The Circular
Ruins*, are panegyrics to memory. In *Funes*, after
a riding accident the hero is crippled in body but
his imagination is jolted so that his perception
and memory become 'infallible'. Whereas others
might simply observe three wine glasses on a
table, 'Funes saw all the shoots, clusters and
grapes of the vine'.

*Borges, photographed in 1971, was often
referred to as 'the blind visionary'.*

especially his play *Doctor Faustus*. Among Borges' greatest works are *Labyrinths*, *The Book of Imaginary Beings*, *Dream Tigers* and *The Book of Sand*. He was fascinated by geometric plots and scenarios which involved the use of a double, or impinged somehow on infinity. In one story he devised a book that was infinite – one could never open it at the same page twice. Doubtless he saw in this a mirror of the infinite possibilities of creation.

MENS SANA

As a young man he spurned all advancement in Argentine society through his opposition to the regime of the dictator Perón. Refusing to compromise his principles by supporting a regime of which he disapproved, he remained a humble librarian. Another example of his independence of spirit was when in 1982 he described the Falklands War, between his native Argentina and England, as 'two bald men fighting over a comb'. Even at the end of his life, like so many of the other geniuses in this book, he was mentally extremely active and physically fit.

WALT DISNEY 1901-1966

Chicago-born Walter Elias Disney was behind the entire late 20th-century trend in cinema entertainment and education. If modern motion pictures are, to a certain extent, dominated by special effects generated either by computers, cartoon artists, or even virtual reality, it was Walt Disney who freed the wide screen image from exclusive colonization by human actors. He created the cartoon hero and paved the way for the stunning special effects of directors such as Steven Spielberg and George Lucas.

In the 1920s, when sound films were in their infancy and colour films virtually unknown, Disney had the vision to create a studio which would become not just a producer of films, but a major educational influence on the planet.

Walt Disney, at the drawing board in 1950, won an Oscar for his appealing and much-loved cartoon character Mickey Mouse in 1932.

Borges' themes explore the vastness and bewildering complexity of the universe and of eternity, but without that overwhelming fear of eternity which prevails in the work of the Austrian novelist Franz Kafka (1883-1924). Borges found this vastness and complexity, the immensity of the universe and time, inspiring – whereas Kafka found it terrifying. Indeed, one could see Borges' *Book of Imaginary Beings* almost as a symbol of his desire to explore and penetrate the uttermost reaches of the imagination and mythology.

MIND GAMES

A devotee of mind games, and of chess in particular, Borges even tried to follow chess games when he was blind. He loved to explore the roots, the meanings of words – for instance, he traced the word 'bungalow' back to a type of single-storey dwelling common in Bengal. He was a great admirer of Shakespeare and an enthusiast for Christopher Marlowe's work –

CREATIVITY

Disney is remembered in particular for his creation of Mickey Mouse, who first appeared in a black and white sound cartoon (*Steamboat Willie*) in 1928. Other popular characters, such as Donald Duck, soon hit the screen. Disney's first revolutionary full-length colour cartoon, *Snow White and the Seven Dwarfs*, appeared in 1937. There then followed *Pinocchio* (1940), *Dumbo* (1941), *Bambi* (1942), *Lady and the Tramp* (1955) and *Sleeping Beauty* (1959).

Perhaps his most amazing achievement was *Fantasia* (1940), a stunningly successful attempt to express music in both abstract and concrete cartoon images. The film interprets some of the greatest works of music – including Beethoven's *Pastoral Symphony*, Stravinsky's *Rite of Spring*, Bach's *Toccata and Fugue in D minor*, Schubert's *Ave Maria* and Tchaikovsky's *Nutcracker Suite* – in an imaginative way that was simply not possible before the advent of the colour cartoon.

IMAGINATION

Towards the end of the 1940s, Disney began directing a series of feature films in colour. One in particular was *The Living Desert* (1953), which had an extraordinary educational impact, teaching young children about animals, the environment and the world in which they lived. Disney Studios also produced a whole range of exciting adventure films, but the real icons of the Disney oeuvre are Mickey Mouse, Donald Duck and *Fantasia*.

Disney reached for the limits – he proved that film, through animation and special effects, need not be bound by human actors and could soar into a universe previously undreamed of, scaling the heights of the imagination and even abstraction. It could be argued that Disney's cartoon films represent the pinnacle of contemporary graphic art, in the same way that Leonardo da Vinci and Michelangelo did during the Renaissance. Similarly, like these two other geniuses, Disney was a perfectionist who paid great attention to the smallest details.

ATTENTION TO DETAIL

During the 1930s and 1940s, Disney personally supervised team after team of graphic artists who gave life to his cartoon characters. He insisted that his artists observe live animals close up so as to absorb their most subtle and realistic nuances of movement. In order to manipulate and manage the complex story lines – both logistical, verbal and pictorial – of his cartoon films, Disney kept the storyboard in his head. He was, above all, a brilliant visual raconteur.

COURAGE AND FREEDOM

Disney's courage, vision, determination and persistence were shown at their greatest and most forceful during the making of *Fantasia*. It was Disney's vision and goal to turn musical masterpieces by Beethoven, among others, into a car-

toon film. The film's costs exceeded initial projection so dramatically that the studio appeared on the verge of bankruptcy. But Disney insisted that the project be carried through, and in the end the picture more than justified the initial investment. Through his vision, Disney created an educational and entertainment empire that will probably endure until motion pictures become obsolete – if they ever do.

Disney's creations have sometimes been interpreted as American cultural imperialism. They represent a certain quality of life, aspirations, freedom to act and freedom of the imagination, as well as a lack of authoritarian restraint imposed from the outside. There is, indeed, a subtle hint of propaganda here, albeit a benign propaganda. However, the more serious criticism levelled against Disney as a person is that his politics were extremely right wing. He was certainly deeply hostile to Communism and sought to combat it in American society. Disney should be judged, however, by his work which has endured, which has brought pleasure and education to young and old alike across the planet, and also by his artist's eye and his intense focusing on the goal of creating an entirely new entertainment and art form – one in which anything visual and imaginative becomes possible. It is possible to see a positive connection between Disney's hatred of Communism, in any of its forms, and his work in the cinema. He saw Communism as a threat to the liberation of the individual, and his cartoon work is, in fact, the ultimate expression of freedom, since it is a medium in which anything goes. Walt Disney was the man who made cartoons famous and cartoons make the impossible achievable.

WERNER KARL HEISENBERG
1901-1978
OLYMPIAN INTELLIGENCE

Heisenberg, a brilliant theoretical physicist, played a major part in preventing the development of atomic weapons by Nazi Germany. He was born in Würzburg in the old German Empire, which had only been fully unified and recognized since the end of the Franco-Prussian War three decades earlier. His father was a Professor of Greek, and in addition to the young Heisenberg's superlative performances in mathematics and physics, he retained a lifelong love and passion for philosophy, especially that of Greek antiquity.

Heisenberg saw modern physics as an exten-

This mushroom cloud resulted from the first thermonuclear explosion in 1952.

sion of that tradition of philosophical enquiry, but armed with much more sophisticated tools than were available to the ancient Greeks. In his book, *Physics and Philosophy*, he stated that one of his aims was 'To meditate in peace on the great questions Plato raised. Questions that have, perhaps, found an answer in the physics of elementary particles'.

SYNERGY
In 1932, Heisenberg was awarded the Nobel Prize for his development of quantum mechanics. Five years later, he married a 21-year-old (Elizabeth Schumacher) who bore him seven children. From 1941 to 1945 Heisenberg was Director of the Kaiser Wilhelm Institute for Physics in Berlin and from 1945 to 1958 Director of the Max Planck Institute.

THE RIGHT FORMULA
Einstein's equation $E=MC^2$ had made the development of atomic weaponry a theoretical possibility. Heisenberg himself immediately realized that modern post-Einsteinian physics must inevitably be connected with atomic energy, whether directed to peaceful or aggressive purposes.

THE WRONG FORMULA
In Germany during the 1930s, relativity and quantum theory had come under vitriolic attack. Obvious further targets for Nazi wrath were those physicists, such as Heisenberg, who had devoted their lives to work on these theories. Heisenberg's situation was exacerbated in the eyes of German officialdom when he won the Nobel prize. Indeed, the Nazis wanted to do away with the study of what they dismissed as 'Jewish Physics'. Yet Heisenberg refused to emigrate. This is a perfect example of an ideologically rigid regime displaying its anti-genius stance by shutting down an avenue of thought.

GARBAGE IN – GARBAGE GROWS!
The advent of the Second World War, however, alerted Hitler to the fact that the enormous energy locked within the atom could be released for destructive purposes. Overnight, official Nazi policy performed a U-turn. Heisenberg was welcomed with open arms and 'invited' to develop a Nazi atomic bomb. Indeed, Heisenberg was the man most feared by the US atomic bomb experts

who were racing to complete their own pro-gramme for the construction of a thermo-nuclear device. Had Heisenberg co-operated with the Nazis, there might still have been time for their programme to catch up. Instead, over several years, Heisenberg stalled, delayed and diverted all of the Nazi atomic weapons initiatives.

Origins of the Universe

In 1952, Heisenberg helped to set up CERN, the European Council for Nuclear Research, in Geneva, which is still carrying out vital investi-gation into the creation of the universe.

Heisenberg went on to set up foundations to help and encourage young people to study sci-ence. True to his principles, in 1957 he signed the Göttingen Declaration, which amounted to a refusal by 17 German scientists to cooperate in a contemplated West German manufacture of nuclear weapons.

Mastermind Group

Heisenberg always acknowledged the training and support given him by a Mastermind Group consisting of fellow physicists Niels Bohr (1885-1962), Max Born (1882-1970) and Wolfgang Pauli (1900-58). His single most important individual contribution to quantum mechanics was the for-mulation of his famous Uncertainty Principle, or Principle of Indeterminacy, in nuclear physics. Announced in 1927, it amounted to a new direc-tion in atomic theory.

The Uncertainty Principle

To understand quantum physics, you need to know that light, X-rays and other energy waves cannot be emitted at an arbitrary rate from a hot body, such as a star. They are, in fact, emitted in packets, or quanta. This was first established in 1900 by the German physicist Max Planck (1858-1947). Light had also recently been discovered to exist in both wave and particle form.

By experimentation, Heisenberg succeeded in proving that the position and momentum of a particle cannot both be ascertained at the same time. If the particle's position is determined, then its velocity remains unknown, and vice versa.

Chance and Proportion

In a sense, Heisenberg's principle defined the ruling cast of mind of the early nuclear age – namely, massive global uncertainty and the ever-present fear of sudden and irrational destruction by atomic bombs. Science and art reflect each other at their deepest levels, so it is no accident that dominant emerging art forms at that time were the chance operations of the artist Marcel Duchamp (1887-1968) and the composer John Cage (1912-92), who both elevated indetermi-nacy in art to the level of a creative principle

Professor Stephen Hawking writes: '*The uncertainty principle had profound implications for the way in which we view the world. One cer-tainly cannot predict future events exactly if one cannot even measure the present state of the uni-verse precisely! Quantum mechanics therefore introduces an unavoidable element of random-ness into science.*'

The Quantum Leap

However, although the Uncertainty Principle proves that it is impossible to predict both the position and velocity of individual particles, quantum mechanics has been very successful in predicting general cases. It underpins nearly all of modern science and technology – including transistors, televisions and computers – and it also lies at the heart of modern biological and chemical theory.

Before leaving Heisenberg, it is worth noting that the so-called quantum leap, implying a giant leap forwards, is a misnomer. Quanta emissions are, in fact, infinitesimally minute. Perhaps the quantum leap should be redefined as the leap of the imagination associated with Heisenberg's development of quantum mechanics!

SALVADOR DALÍ 1904-1989
'Le Surréalisme C'est Moi'

Salvador Dalí's publications include *Journal of a Genius* (1965), and there is no doubt that he con-sidered himself to be one. The rest of the world, however, is divided on this. Some think that Dalí *was* a genius of art – Freud's theories made vis-ible, as it were – while others maintain he was merely a genius of self-promotion.

Eccentric Interpreter of Dreams

Dalí has described his own paintings as 'hand-painted dream photographs', and they certainly stand out through their minutely crafted detail, their filigree and virtuoso technique, their mys-terious realism and the exotic nature of their themes. On the other hand, Dalí's extravagant behaviour and eccentric lifestyle have caused him to be written off in some quarters as an avaricious exhibitionist.

His critics believe that they have plenty of

Salvador Dalí had a reputation for wildly eccentric behaviour. Here he is taking a dip in the sea, having draped his hair with seaweed and given himself a false beard as a child might. A sense of humour and the ability to relax and have fun are essential genius qualities.

ammunition. Dalí's residence in Cadaques, Spain, was an esoteric obstacle course for visitors and he was certainly prone to eccentric behaviour. For instance, he once gave a lecture in a diving suit, complete with helmet (which jammed and nearly caused his suffocation).

Whenever his imagination seemed to flag, Dalí turned to crustacea. A ubiquitous lobster, positioned tastefully on a phone, or deployed strategically on a nude model's lap could always swim to the rescue, if all else failed.

DESIGNED TO SHOCK

A final salvo in his detractors' accusations was that Dalí was given to outrageous and meaningless statements about his own work that were designed merely to shock, and that his titles were deliberately obscure – a jumble of words laced with knowingly provocative salacious innuendi, but otherwise devoid of substance.

For example, his *Young Virgin Autosodomised by her own Chastity* (1954) depicts a more or less naked girl, leaning over a balcony and surrounded by what could be either rhinoceros horns, parts of her own anatomy, or parts of the male anatomy – it is difficult to tell. Dalí himself wrote about this: 'The horn of the rhinoceros, the former uniceros, is in fact the horn of the legendary unicorn, symbol of chastity. The young virgin can lean on it and play with it morally, as was practised in the time of courtly love.'

Another example is the picture he painted from 1952-4, the full title of which is: *The Chromosome of a Highly Coloured Fish's Eye,*

Starting the Harmonious Disintegration of the Persistence of Memory. This picture harks back to one of Dalí's most famous works, *The Persistence of Memory* (1931), which features his famous soft watches. Dalí wrote of it: 'Be persuaded that Salvador Dalí's famous limp watches are nothing else than the tender, extravagant and solitary paranoic, critical, camembert of time and space.'

THE PERSISTENCE OF MEMORY

What are we to make of this? Undeniably, Dalí's images exert a shattering power – they are at once original, full of visual puns and visually arresting. Who, having once seen them could ever forget the soft watches of *The Persistence of Memory*, or Dalí's elephants on giant, spindly stilts of legs, staggering across desert landscapes?

THE REAL PROCESS OF THOUGHT

Surrealism, of which Dalí was an early advocate, intended both to show the real process of thought and also to shock, in part by juxtaposing incompatible images. Dalí took Surrealism further. He wished to reproduce faithfully the unconscious – not just dreams, but also paranoia, fears, longings, visions and entire states of mind.

In *Conquest of the Irrational* (1935), he wrote:

'My whole ambition in the pictorial domain is to materialize the images of concrete irrationality . . . In order that the world of the imagination and of concrete irrationality may be as objectively evident, of the same consistency, of the same durability, of the same persuasive, cognoscitive and communicable thickness as that of the exterior world of phenomenal reality.'

THE PEOPLE'S CHOICE

Dalí is certainly controversial. But to assess his true worth, look not at the publicity, but at his paintings; and look closely, for he is a one-off in his profundity both of artistic technique and of meaning.

On a yearly basis from 1972 to 1976, Madame Tussaud's waxwork museum in London handed out questionnaires to its customers, asking them to choose their all-time favourite artist. Picasso came first in each of the five polls, while Dalí was the only other artist – including Rembrandt and Leonardo da Vinci – who came in the top five on every occasion. He came 4th in 1972, and 3rd equal in 1973, '74, '75 and '76. So, the visiting public at Madame Tussaud's confirmed that, in their eyes, Salvador Dalí's estimation of his own genius was entirely appropriate.

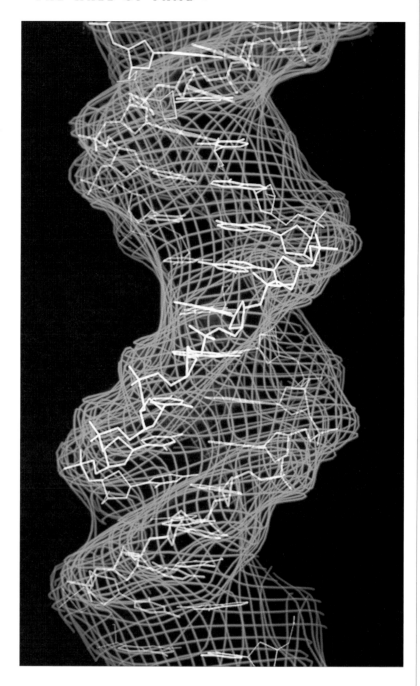

Right This is a computer graphics representation of a section of deoxyribonucleic acid (DNA) — which Crick and Watson brilliantly discovered. The two strands of the sugar-phosphate backbone (in red and yellow) are twisted into a double helix.

Left Metamorphosis of Narcissus, *painted in 1934, is one of Dalí's Surrealist works which he described as 'hand-painted dream photographs'. Dalí considered himself to be a genius and his popular reputation will doubtless continue to swing like a pendulum.*

FRANCIS CRICK (BORN 1916) AND JAMES DEWEY WATSON (BORN 1928)

SUPREME 20TH-CENTURY SCIENTISTS

Crick – a British scientist, educated at London and Cambridge Universities – was involved from 1949 in research in Molecular Biology at the Cavendish Laboratory. In 1953, with his fellow researcher, Watson, he constructed a molecular model of the complex genetic material deoxyribonucleic acid (DNA). Later researches on the nucleic acids led to far-reaching discoveries concerning the genetic code.

MASTERMIND GROUP

Crick's partner, Watson, is an American scientist who graduated from the University of Chicago, the city of his birth. He then came to England and collaborated with Crick on unravelling the structure of DNA, before becoming Professor of Biology at Harvard in 1961. His book *The Double Helix* (1968) explains the process whereby the DNA structure was discovered. It is interesting that, whereas in the past scientific discoveries could often be ascribed to one brilliant individual – such as Copernicus, Galileo or Newton –

most recent scientific achievement is more often the result of a team effort. Maurice Wilkins, a British physicist who was born in New Zealand in 1916 and educated at St John's College, Cambridge, was also involved in early research into DNA, and in 1962, Crick, Watson and Wilkins were jointly awarded the Nobel Prize for Medicine and Physiology for their work on the structure of DNA.

THEORY OF EVERYTHING (ANIMATE)

DNA has rightly been described as containing 'the building blocks of life'. As the carrier of the genetic message, it contains all the physical information that determines the making of virtually all other living organisms. It determines the colour of our eyes and hair, and whether we are short, thin, tall or fat. Everything is encoded in this fabulously complex molecule. The DNA molecule's structure is that of twin spirals – the 'double helix' – which constitute the chain that connects us, not only to our ancestors, but also to practically all animate life. DNA has also become the key to new ways of understanding and fighting disease, to advances in genetic engineering of plants and animals, and even the capture of criminals through DNA fingerprinting, which compares genetic patterns unique to each individual. Yet this blue-print of life was discovered by a team of scientists working in a back-street Cambridge laboratory with minimal funds.

PERSISTENCE

The discovery of the structure of DNA has been hailed as one of the 'pinnacles of our civilization'. Crick and his team had been working on advanced genetics for some time, but were making scant progress when they were joined in 1951 by the young Jim Watson. Crick later recalled, 'I was on the lookout for some cheap labour. We could get these young American researchers for next to nothing because they were on scholarships. I was told that there was this fellow Jim Watson who was very bright. I put him up at my house in Cambridge to start with. He had started university at 15 and he was only 23 when he turned up at Cambridge.' Watson turned out to be the catalyst who stimulated Francis Crick to start studying DNA. The two men complemented each other perfectly.

In March 1953, they finally cracked the genetic code. It was a right-handed double helix molecule – in appearance, very like two interlocking spiral staircases – with paired bases of adenine and thymine at the core and phosphates on the outside. Crick said: '*All the time, several billion years since life began, the double helix had been there.*' Now he was looking at it. He had discovered the molecule that carried hereditary information for all forms of life. Biological science was changed forever.

TEAMWORK

Watson is now a Director of the Cold Spring Harbor Laboratory, the top leading US molecular biology laboratory, and Crick is studying the visual system of the brain at the Salk Institute in San Diego, California. As well as Wilkins, other scientists who were part of the team were Max Perutz and Sir John Kendrew.

BEAUTY AND INFINITE POSSIBILITY

When the discovery was first made, one team member said: 'It is too pretty not to be true.' It is, without doubt, the supreme scientific discovery of the 20th century in the realm of biology and medicine; it revolutionized biological science and led to the billion-pound bio-technology industry.

MUHAMMAD ALI (BORN 1942)

Ali was born Cassius Marcellus Clay, but changed this on joining the Black Muslims, because he did not want to be associated with a slave name meaning dirt. He is the only man to have won the world heavyweight boxing title three times. He achieved this record, not by massive punching power, but by the exercise of intelligence, superior mobility in the ring and refined technique. Ali was in the forefront of a generation of black American sportsmen who had discovered a newly-won self-respect and confidence in their own abilities and place in society, as a result of the civil rights work of Martin Luther King (1929-68). Ali was self-confident, brash, outspoken, flamboyant and never afraid to defy authority.

DETERMINATION

Ali was born in Louisville, Kentucky. He was an amateur boxer from 1954 till 1960, when he won the Olympic gold medal in the light heavyweight division. In 1964, at his first challenge, he won the World Heavyweight Championship, the most richly endowed prize in individual sport. To do this, he had to beat the defending champion, Sonny Liston, which he did in seven rounds at Miami Beach. When threatened by fight promoters before the bout and told that he would

Ali said he would 'Float like a butterfly, sting like a bee' – and he did!

publicly have to disavow his affiliation to the Black Muslims, or risk the fight being cancelled, Ali steadfastly refused to give in, and the contest went ahead as planned.

In 1967, when Ali refused on religious grounds to be drafted into the US armed forces, he was stripped of his title and banned from boxing, two decisions he successfully overturned later in the Supreme Court. This he achieved by defending himself brilliantly without a lawyer.

BOUNCING BACK

In 1971, Ali lost the title to Joe Frazier, but after further wins against Frazier himself in 1974 and George Foreman later in the year in Zaire, Ali regained the championship. He was then beaten by Leon Spinks in a split decision in Las Vegas early in 1978, but recaptured the title on 15 September in the Superdome in New Orleans. Ali thus became the first man to win the world heavyweight title three times. This second Ali–Spinks clash attracted 63,350, which is a world record number of spectators for an indoor championship.

EMULATING GENGHIS KHAN

Ali's contribution to boxing was to import techniques of psychological warfare into the ring. Genghis Khan had demonstrated, seven centuries beforehand, that to undermine the opponent's morale before battle may facilitate a bloodless victory. Ali applied this maxim to ruthless effect in the field of sporting endeavour. The Ali shuffle, whereby he was constantly dancing out of his opponent's reach during the fight; his pre-match predictions of which round would witness a knock-out of the victim; his taunting doggerel, which he composed ad lib; his publicly orchestrated humiliation of his slower-witted opponents – all this combined to demoralize his opponents thoroughly even before the actual fight began. Many of his opponents were so psyched out that they failed to connect with a single punch. Ali refused to fight in a restricted, classical way and introduced innovative tactics and skill to the boxing ring.

DEVASTATING DOGGEREL

Before his first championship challenge against Liston, whom most experts regarded as the favourite, due to his immense size and power, Ali zapped off a whole series of poems and taunts designed to fracture the morale of his mighty opponent. For example: 'It all started 20 years past, the greatest of them all was born at last. The name of this champion I might as well say, no other than the greatest, Cassius Clay'; or: 'Sonny, you is too ugly to be the champion.'

THE GREATEST
As Ali walked into the post-match press conference room after defeating Liston, he was immediately hit with a barrage of questions. He held up his hands for silence and, as he recalls in his autobiography, *The Greatest*, the following scenario developed: '"Who is the greatest?" I asked them. Nobody answers. They look down at their pads and microphones. "Who is the greatest?" I say again. They look up with solemn faces, but the room is still silent. "For the last time," I shout, "all the eyes of the world are on us. You are a bunch of hypocrites. I told you I was gonna get Liston and I got him. I have proved all of you wrong. I shook up the world, tell me, who is the greatest, who is the greatest?" They hesitate for a minute, and finally, in a dull tone, they all answer, "You are. YES!"'

Despite his sometimes aggressive-sounding manner, when he was on tour Ali kept his hotel doors open 24 hours a day and welcomed anyone who wanted to see him. He retired from boxing in 1981 but still makes public appearances, even though he has severe Parkinson's disease (which attacks the nervous system and impairs speech and movement). He refuses to allow his disability to beat him.

In April 1994, Glyn Leach, a leading sports writer, commented: 'When Ali's name is mentioned one thinks of genius – not just in the ring, but as a human being who transcended so many barriers and helped shape modern culture.'

STEPHEN WILLIAM HAWKING (BORN 1942)
MENS SANA IN CORPORE SANO
In some ways, the physicist and cosmologist Professor Stephen Hawking is the most remarkable character in this book. Many of those in our gallery of genius have overcome immense physical adversity and disability to attain great creative heights. For instance, Alexander the Great and Julius Caesar both suffered from epileptic fits, Zizka, Milton and Borges were blind, Beethoven deaf, Nelson lost one arm and one eye in action, while Martha Graham danced on with crippling arthritis, to name but a few.

According to medical orthodoxy, however, Stephen Hawking should have been dead at least a quarter of a century ago. Although he was physically fit and an exceptional athlete as a student, since the 1960s he has suffered from a peculiarly debilitating form of the standardly terminal motor neuron disease. Today, Hawking is confined to a wheelchair and can only speak through a computer-linked voice box.

PROLIFIC ACTIVITY
Hawking's ongoing survival, his prolific activity, and his ability to travel and give lectures around the world, is attributed to his powerful vision and adamant mental stamina.

Although he and his work have long been recognized by his fellow scientists, he received public recognition in 1988, when his book *A Brief History of Time* was published. On publication, this topped the Best Seller lists for 220 weeks, an all-time record! Hawking wrote this work, which is subtitled 'From the Big Bang to Black Holes', specifically for the general reader as an introduction to theories of the cosmos. His aim was to write 'a popular book about space and time' and he undoubtedly achieved this.

BRAIN OF THE YEAR
In 1992, Hawking was made Brain of the Year by the Brain Trust Charity. Interestingly, he is connected in two ways with geniuses of preceding ages in his own subjects of physics, mathematics and astronomy. Hawking was born on the 300th anniversary of Galileo's death (1642), and he also holds Sir Isaac Newton's chair as Lucasian Professor of Mathematics at Cambridge University (he was appointed in 1979).

UNLOCKING THE UNIVERSE
Time magazine has written of Hawking: 'Even as he sits helpless in his wheelchair, his mind seems to soar ever more brilliantly across the vastness of space and time to unlock the secrets of the universe.' In 1981, Hawking gave a lecture at a conference on cosmology, organized by Jesuits in the Vatican. He relates that at the end of the conference the delegates were granted an audience with the Pope, at which His Holiness told the assembled scientists that it was all right to study the evolution of the universe after the big bang, but that they should not enquire into the big bang itself, because that was the moment of creation and therefore the work of God. In fact, the theme of Hawking's address at the confer-

ence had been the possibility that although space and time are finite, they have no boundary, which means that they have no beginning, and therefore no moment of creation.

PHYSICS REPLACING THEOLOGY

It seems that physicists are now displaying both the intellectual energy and spirit of enquiry which were once the province of the Church or of moral philosophy. Towards the close of *A Brief History of Time*, Hawking writes of the 'Origin and Fate of the Universe' and adds 'What is the nature of the universe? What is our place in it and where did it and we come from?' 'If we find the answer to that,' he concludes, 'it would be the ultimate triumph of human reason – for then we would know the mind of God.'

WILLIAM (BILL) GATES (BORN 1955)

Bill Gates' motto is 'I can do anything I put my mind to'. His faith in himself and his talent for writing computer operating systems has made him America's youngest billionaire. By enhancing computer operability, he is stretching the performance of thinking machines to their limit. In a sense, he is on the opposite side of the fence from Dr Marion Tinsley, the World Draughts (Checkers) Champion, and Garry Kasparov, the World Chess Champion. While Gates is straining the potential of computers to outperform the human brain, Tinsley and Kasparov are attempting to prove that the human brain will always be superior to the computer (on rare occasions they have both been beaten by a machine).

Hawking's brilliant mind has not been restricted by his severe disabilities.

FLEXIBILITY

One thing which sets Gates apart from some otherwise brilliant inventors of the past (like Gutenberg, whose invention of printing was not matched by his business acumen) is his brilliance and skill in operating his own financial affairs. Both intellectually and creatively 'Windows' and 'MS DOS' (Microsoft Disk Operating Systems) software are the basis of Gates' fortune. But Gates had also earlier established the Microsoft Corporation to handle his own business affairs. Gates is currently America's second richest individual, and he has already turned 2200 of his employees into dollar millionaires. His fortune is also entirely self-made, based on intelligence not inheritance.

PROLIFIC PERSISTENCE AND FOCUS

In January 1975, Gates took just five days to develop and write out an entirely new version of the computer language BASIC for the Altair Computer. He locked himself in a room of the Albuquerque Hilton for the entire period, eventually emerging with a pile of yellow legal pads covered in the new formulae and codes. A conservative estimate for a standard expert team, working conventionally on such a task, would be six months.

PETER PAN

People who have had to deal with Gates often describe him as a perpetual teenager. Even though, at the time of writing, he is 38 years old, it is that child-like joy in the brilliant speed and sheer pleasure of his own inventiveness which has driven him on. This childish playfulness has created a fortune for him of more than six billion dollars – equal in 1994 values to four billion pounds sterling.

WORK EQUALS PLAY

Gates, who includes playing with earth-moving equipment on building sites at night as one of his favourite pastimes, has been decried by his detractors as a workaholic. But, as with so many of the other great geniuses, work to him is play.

In fact, the Gatesian equation for success is 'work equals play'. Everyone enjoys playing, but the ultimate goal for most working people is to reach and enjoy the moment when they can successfully retire. Instead the key should be to achieve that critical redefinition in one's own mind that the challenge and work of one's own life equals something to be relished.

A QUIZ FOR GENIUS READERS

Now that you have read about the great geniuses in this book, test your memory (without referring back) and see if you can supply the solutions to the following questions. The answers are on page 255. Give yourself 10 points for each question that you answer correctly and then check your score. No cheating!

1 How can freedom and Beethoven's 9th symphony in D minor be linked?

2 Who crossed the River Thames and was an excellent swimmer?

3 What is the link between winter sports and a fictional detective?

4 Which writer once pulled faces in a mirror for inspiration?

5 What prompted King Archelaus of Macedonia to cut off his hair?

6 Which artists identified themselves with two American aviators?

7 What do a lightning conductor, bi-focal glasses and chess have in common?

8 Who holds the world record for the greatest number of inventions?

9 Why might Andrew Carnegie have enjoyed talking to Mary Anning?

10 Whose army never fought a battle but is still admired today?

11 Who tried to follow chess games even when blind?

12 Which Oriental thinker believed that the negative can be changed into the positive?

13 Who plays with earth-moving equipment for fun?

14 How did a bicycle wheel and bottle rack influence modern art?

15 What is the link between the size of the universe and a grain of sand?

16 What military innovation links the painter of the world's greatest artistic attraction with a blind Hussite?

17 Who used salt to start a revolution?

18 What is the black and white link between dictionaries and dance?

19 Who designed a safety lamp for miners at the same time as Humphry Davy?

20 Which sculptor used olive oil to solve a problem?

21 How did the dome of a cathedral produce musical results?

22 Which English writer employed a vocabulary of 25,000 words?

23 Which genius daydreamer was an accomplished violinist?

24 Who attracted a world record number of indoor spectators?

25 Which country gave its name to an element, thanks to a Nobel Prizewinner?

26 Whose belief in Plato and Aristotle led to death at the hands of a mob?

27 Who dared to abandon the coastline?

28 Which speed reader knew a lot about Florence?

29 Who taught deaf mutes and improved communication?

30 Which poet practised a martial art (or martial artist wrote poetry)?

31 How has Professor Stephen Hawking followed in Sir Isaac Newton's footsteps?

32 Which lecturer captivated an audience even though he was speaking in a foreign language?

33 What is the connection between cheese and an artistic timepiece?

34 Apart from writing their plays, what are Aeschylus and Shakespeare said to have had in common?

35 Who jested that a book should be banned because he was not mentioned in it?

RANKING THE GREATEST GENIUSES OF ALL TIME

*'AT THE CONCLUSION OF OUR MICROSCOPIC ANALYSIS OF THE INDIVIDUAL
QUALITIES OF THE GENIUSES, IT EMERGED THAT LEONARDO DA VINCI
SCORED TOP MARKS IN VIRTUALLY EVERY CATEGORY INCLUDING
100% IN DOMINATION IN FIELD, POLYMATHY, VERSATILITY AND ABOVE
ALL IN THE STRENGTH AND ENERGY OF HIS PERSON AND OF HIS VISION.'*

TONY BUZAN AND RAYMOND KEENE

What follows is the world's first attempt to rank the greatest geniuses of history. You are already familiar with the qualities of the great minds as set forth in the Genius Quotient questionnaire (see page 13). Under that system the qualities of persistence, commitment and subject knowledge etc. are ranked from 0 to 100. The score of 0 under any heading on the GQ questionnaire represents an exceptionally minimal aptitude in that area, whereas a score of 100 indicates world class performance.

The great geniuses of history would, by definition, all score between 90 and 100 in most categories of the GQ questionnaire. In order to distinguish between them in the ultimate ranking of the 100 greatest geniuses of all time, it was necessary to devise an even finer measuring instrument with new categories that allowed us to assess the qualities of genius-within-genius as precisely and as objectively as possible.

The categories we determined upon are as follows: Dominance in Field; Active Longevity; Polymathy and Versatility; Strength and Energy; IQ; On-going Influence; Prolificness and Achievement of Prime Goal. In each of these categories we have awarded a range of 0 to 100 points, where even a 0, because it is a ranking relating specifically to the 100 Top Geniuses, would indicate, in relation to everyone else, a very high score. We established three further bonus categories, namely Universality of Vision (bonus of 15), Outstanding Originality (bonus of 10) and a deliberate desire to create Teaching Avenues or Academies to further the genius's ideas (bonus of 10). The grand total available is a maximum of 835 possible points.

The Active Longevity category required special attention. Those geniuses who managed their personal physiques to the maximum to ensure the widest possible time span for the accomplishment of their life's visions deserved extra credit. However, so as not to overweight this category, we established this scale: a range of 16 points from youngest to eldest rewards those who 'hung in' and does not penalize those who died early; on our chart, death between the ages of 33 and 36 scores 84/100, death between the ages of 57 and 60 scores 90. Finally, a career terminating between the ages of 97 and 100 scores a maximum 100 points.

As IQ is a significant factor in genius, we included it, and provided a sliding scale with a range of only 30 points. We assumed that each of our 100 geniuses would have comfortably been able to pass Mensa's introductory tests, and therefore commenced with a minimum IQ of 140, which is basic genius level. Using a further sliding scale we awarded 70 points to an estimated IQ of 140, 88 points to an estimated IQ of 170 and 100 points to an estimated IQ of 190.

It should be remembered that all the performances assessed here are of an extraordinarily high order. Thus Hannibal's low score of 15/100 under Achievement of Prime Goal reflects the fact that he set himself the high target of annihilating the Roman Empire and narrowly but absolutely failed to achieve it. Conversely the high score of Phidias (99/100) under the heading 'Dominance in Field' represents the fact that he designed and built, almost single-mindedly, one of the greatest cities on earth, Athens, and inspired Michelangelo and Leonardo.

Fascinating conclusions have emerged from this exercise and the top ten have truly earned their place. You will notice that they are the only ones to cross the magic border of 800 points.

The statistical matrix can be explored from many different perspectives. For instance, how many of the geniuses come from which countries and which time periods? And of the dominant categories of activity, which is the *most* dominant? Writing? Art? Mathematics and Physics? Education? Or Philosophy? These conclusions are the first of their kind and with this book we now open and invite a world discussion and debate.

RANKING	THE GENIUSES Note: An explanation of the scoring system is given on page 235. Column 2 is not included in the total score.	1 DOMINANCE IN FIELD	2 LIFE SPAN IN YEARS	3 ACTIVE LONGEVITY	4 POLYMATHY/ VERSATILITY	5 STRENGTH & ENERGY	6 I.Q.	7 ON-GOING INFLUENCE	8 PROLIFICNESS	9 ACHIEVEMENT PRIME GOAL	10 UNIVERSAL VISION	11 ORIGINALITY	12 ACADEMIC	TOTAL
1	Leonardo da Vinci	100	67	92	100	100	100	98	99	98	15	10	10	822
2	William Shakespeare	100	52	88	100	98	100	100	99	98	15	10	10	818
3	Great Pyramid Builders	99	71	93	100	100	94	98	99	99	15	10	10	817
4	Johann Wolfgang von Goethe	99	84	96	100	99	100	87	100	100	15	10	10	816
5	Michelangelo	97	89	97	99	100	91	99	99	97	15	10	10	814
6	Sir Isaac Newton	100	84	96	91	97	97	100	99	95	15	10	10	810
7	Thomas Jefferson	95	83	96	99	97	97	96	98	96	15	10	10	809
8	Alexander the Great	100	33	83	99	100	94	98	100	99	15	10	10	808
9	Phidias	99	60	90	98	98	94	96	98	100	15	10	10	808
10	Albert Einstein	100	76	94	97	88	100	100	98	92	15	10	10	804
11	Thomas Alva Edison	98	85	97	99	99	97	96	99	94		10	10	799
12	Homer	98	71	93	96	95	91	95	96	98	15	10	10	797
13	Plato	87	80	95	95	97	94	98	98	98	15	10	10	797
14	Euclid	99	71	93	94	96	95	98	97	98	15		10	795
15	Elizabeth I	96	70	93	95	95	94	97	94	96	15	10	10	795
16	Archimedes	95	75	94	98	97	97	96	97	91	15	10		790
17	Aristotle	87	62	91	97	97	97	97	99	89	15	10	10	789
18	Filippo Brunelleschi	94	69	92	97	95	97	96	91	91	15	10	10	788
19	Andrew Carnegie	98	84	96	94	96	94	91	96	100		10	10	785
20	1st Ch'in Emperor	96	49	87	98	99	91	97	100	95		10	10	783
21	Sinan	92	99	100	96	98	94	86	100	96		10	10	782
22	Nicolas Copernicus	97	70	92	97	70	97	100	95	97	15	10	10	780
23	Ludwig van Beethoven	97	56	89	85	95	85	98	99	96	15	10	10	779
24	Pablo Picasso	94	92	98	90	100	91	98	100	96		10		777
25	Leon Battista Alberti	84	68	92	98	98	94	96	94	96	15		10	777
26	Ivan Pavlov	95	87	97	90	99	94	95	92	94		10	10	776
27	Michael Faraday	94	76	94	85	97	94	98	98	96		10	10	776
28	Igor Stravinsky	90	90	98	90	100	94	92	92	96		10	10	772
29	Benjamin Franklin	76	84	96	99	97	97	95	94	96		10	10	770
30	Charles Darwin	99	73	93	91	71	90	100	94	96	15	10	10	769
31	Sophocles	82	89	97	95	96	90	86	96	97	15		10	764
32	Muhammad Ali	100	71	93	85	100	75	80	99	96	15	10	10	763
33	Vyasa	81	71	93	94	94	80	87	98	94	15	10	10	756
34	Sir Arthur Conan Doyle	92	71	93	98	98	95	94	95	80		10		755

RANKING	THE GENIUSES Note: An explanation of the scoring system is given on page 235. Column 2 is not included in the total score.	1 DOMINANCE IN FIELD	2 LIFESPAN IN YEARS	3 ACTIVE LONGEVITY	4 POLYMATHY/ VERSATILITY	5 STRENGTH & ENERGY	6 I.Q.	7 ON-GOING INFLUENCE	8 PROLIFICNESS	9 ACHIEVEMENT PRIME GOAL	10 UNIVERSAL VISION	11 ORIGINALITY	12 ACADEMIC	TOTAL
35	Alexander Graham Bell	82	75	94	83	91	94	98	94	98		10	10	754
36	Salvador Dalí	80	85	96	94	96	94	94	98	90		10		752
37	St Thomas Aquinas	95	48	87	93	91	85	97	97	95		10		750
38	Jorge Luis Borges	78	87	97	99	96	95	80	82	88	15	10	10	750
39	John Milton	80	66	92	97	96	90	76	97	98		10	10	746
40	Genghis Khan	100	65	91	63	100	94	72	98	91	15	10	10	744
41	Johann Sebastian Bach	95	65	91	62	96	85	94	98	85	15	10	10	741
42	Walt Disney	98	65	91	96	78	60	99	100	98		10	10	740
43	Christopher Columbus	100	55	89	90	95	70	99	98	73	15	10		739
44	Ueshiba	92	84	96	92	100	65	75	94	90	15	10	10	739
45	Martha Graham	90	98	100	94	100	75	70	94	96		10	10	739
46	Marie Curie	69	67	92	85	96	94	86	96	100		10	10	738
47	Gottfried Wilhelm Leibniz	89	70	93	100	77	95	90	100	73		10	10	737
48	Paul Cézanne	94	68	92	71	94	76	98	94	90		10		734
49	Guglielmo Marconi	92	73	93	85	95	85	95	82	96		10		733
50	Wilbur and Orville Wright	82	64	91	78	93	85	98	95	100		10		732
51	George Stephenson	80	67	92	71	95	90	97	93	98	15			731
52	Aeschylus	76	69	92	87	96	90	80	92	92	15	10		730
53	Francis Crick and James Dewey Watson	90	75	94	80	77	90	98	90	96		10		725
54	Maria Montessori	76	82	96	95	97	80	94	90	75		10	10	723
55	Sir Christopher Wren	75	90	98	97	96	85	82	86	94		10		723
56	Werner Karl Heisenberg	92	75	94	90	85	90	96	80	85		10		722
57	Socrates	81	71	93	92	95	82	93	90	54	15	10	10	715
58	Isambard Kingdom Brunel	91	53	88	90	97	85	78	95	80		10		714
59	William Gates	88	71	93	76	82	90	88	96	90		10		713
60	Julius Caesar	72	56	89	98	100	88	98	98	45	15		10	713
61	Napoleon Bonaparte	70	52	88	94	100	94	98	98	50		10	10	712
62	Baron Joseph Lister	70	85	96	80	91	85	81	87	95	15		10	710
63	Carl Gustav Jung	80	86	97	84	95	82	85	78	82	15		10	708
64	Stephen Hawking	74	71	93	55	100	94	91	88	88	15	10		708
65	Galileo	85	78	95	85	58	94	96	95	74	15	10		707
66	Frederick Matthias Alexander	78	86	97	87	96	76	78	90	85		10	10	707

This ranking chart of the geniuses continues overleaf.

RANKING	THE GENIUSES — Note: An explanation of the scoring system is given on page 235. Column 2 is not included in the total score.	1 DOMINANCE IN FIELD	2 LIFESPAN IN YEARS	3 ACTIVE LONGEVITY	4 POLYMATHY/VERSATILITY	5 STRENGTH & ENERGY	6 I.Q.	7 ON-GOING INFLUENCE	8 PROLIFICNESS	9 ACHIEVEMENT PRIME GOAL	10 UNIVERSAL VISION	11 ORIGINALITY	12 ACADEMIC	TOTAL
67	Suleyman the Magnificent	92	72	93	91	92	82	66	96	84			10	706
68	William Pitt the Elder, the Earl of Chatham	72	70	93	82	94	94	97	91	78				701
69	Ferdinand Magellan	90	41	85	90	100	73	86	87	73	15			699
70	George Eliot	66	61	90	99	94	97	64	88	91		10		699
71	Marcel Duchamp	65	81	95	90	94	94	87	82	80		10		697
72	Marion Tinsley	96	71	93	46	98	95	59	93	99			10	689
73	Giuseppe Verdi	82	88	97	51	95	76	84	95	99		10		689
74	Charles Dickens	82	58	90	67	90	76	84	93	96		10		688
75	Confucius	79	72	93	97	76	88	87	86	46	15	10	10	687
76	Abraham Lincoln	73	56	89	62	97	88	98	84	92				683
77	Charlie Chaplin	94	89	97	69	97	70	80	95	68		10		680
78	Wolfgang Amadeus Mozart	96	35	84	78	74	82	97	98	67				676
79	Horatio Nelson	87	47	87	28	99	73	90	93	98		10	10	675
80	Euripides	70	78	95	80	71	90	87	85	80	15			673
81	Arthur Wellesley, 1st Duke of Wellington	68	83	96	51	96	73	84	94	100			10	672
82	Lao-Tzu	76	100	100	94	94	90	74	60	58	15	10		671
83	Averroës	66	72	93	97	80	91	48	89	81			10	655
84	Raphael	76	37	84	81	74	88	67	91	68	15		10	654
85	Alighieri Dante	81	56	89	81	77	91	55	91	63	15	10		653
86	Sun Tzu	69	71	93	85	96	85	71	61	82			10	652
87	Mahatma Gandhi	80	78	95	58	91	82	81	89	53			10	639
88	George Washington	72	67	92	53	92	70	95	54	100			10	638
89	As Suli	78	92	98	95	88	91	8	89	75			10	632
90	John Stuart Mill	75	66	92	98	72	97	34	78	64		10		620
91	Titian	68	96	99	33	95	73	67	91	85				611
92	René Descartes	48	54	89	75	44	91	78	78	81	15		10	609
93	Niccolo Machiavelli	83	58	90	53	65	85	91	75	45		10		597
94	Desiderius Erasmus	63	70	93	82	62	91	47	71	60				569
95	Rembrandt van Rijn	42	63	91	51	90	73	63	90	49				549
96	John Zizka	43	48	87	48	98	73	7	81	83	10	10		540
97	Hannibal	55	55	89	81	96	79	15	81	15	15	10		536
98	Johannes Gensfleisch Gutenberg	82	68	92	67	48	70	100	5	50	15			529
99	Sappho	15	71	93	50	85	85	48	60	58		10	10	514
100	Benedict de Spinoza	52	44	86	87	27	91	35	35	78				491

MENTAL WORLD RECORDS

This section includes world records achieved to date which involve the mind and memory. Anyone can strive to beat world records – and it's never too late to start. Dominic O'Brien only began brain training at the age of 30 and was World Memory Champion within five years. If you apply the principles outlined in Part One, you will be amazed at how your memory and powers of concentration can be improved. Reading through the profiles of geniuses in Part Two will give you extra inspiration and encouragement. Above all, remember that it is just as important to keep your body physically fit and to live by the genius motto *mens sana in corpore sano* (a healthy mind in a healthy body) if you want to equal or beat existing world records.

WORLD MEMORY RECORDS

*'I DEVELOPED A SYSTEM OF MNEMONICS FOR IMPROVING MY MEMORY
AND THEN DISCOVERED THAT THE GREEKS HAD BEEN DOING EXACTLY
THE SAME THING 2000 YEARS AGO!'*

DOMINIC O'BRIEN, FIRST WORLD MEMORY CHAMPION

Of all the mental skills, memory is perhaps the most important and the most tested and measured of all by psychologists. Yet memory feats historically have suffered from the notorious problems of exaggeration, poor testing, and, dare we say it, forgetting! Not until the first World Memory Championships, sanctioned by the Brain Trust in October 1991, were feats of memory in different categories tested for record-making purposes.

Photographic memory is an interesting case in point. Most memory practitioners and experts will attest to never having met anyone with true photographic memory, but will have met hundreds of people who claimed to have met someone with a photographic memory! Rather than simply ignore those feats of recall performed under less-than-rigorous circumstances, the first official ranking and rating of world memory records are recognized according to a simple three-level scale:

1 Records which have been established with the highest degree of rigour are rated AAA. Records receiving an AAA grade will have been performed under such strict conditions that there is no doubt as to their validity.

2 Those performed under less rigorous circumstances receive an AA rating.

3 Those records that are claimed without rigorous proof, or those which are reliable historically but which lack quantitative rigour, are given a single A rating.

AAA RECORDS

PLAYING CARD MEMORIZATION

SPEED MEMORIZATION OF CARDS

A single deck of 52 playing cards is thoroughly shuffled, then memorized in the shuffled order as quickly as possible. The cards are looked at once, in sequence, with no back-tracking allowed. No errors of recall are permitted.

The world record used to be held by Tariq Mamoon, who achieved a time of 44.62 seconds on 10 August 1993 in Florida, USA.

DOMINIC O'BRIEN beat this on 25 March 1994 in a record time of 43.59 seconds.

WORLD RANKINGS FOR SPEED CARD MEMORIZATION
1 Dominic O'Brien (UK)   43.59 seconds
2 Tariq Mamoon (USA)   44.62 seconds
3 Jonathan Hancock (UK) 58.79 seconds
4 James Longworth (UK)   1 minute 35 seconds
5 Creighton Carvello (UK) 2 minutes 17 seconds

MARATHON CARD MEMORY

As many packs of cards as desired are shuffled together. The memorizer must see each card only once. Once they have looked at all of the cards, they must recall them in order. DOMINIC O'BRIEN holds the world record (established 19 November 1993 in London) of 40 packs with only 1 error, and 35 packs without error.

THE ONE HOUR CARD MEMORY CHALLENGE

In 1991 JONATHAN HANCOCK of Middlesbrough, England, initiated this challenge and was able to remember four complete packs of cards with just six errors. At the 1993 Memoriad held at Simpson's-in-the-Strand, London, on 7-8 August, Hancock broke his own world record with six packs perfectly memorized within 60 minutes. Three minutes later, another competitor established the new world record: DOMINIC O'BRIEN memorized eight packs of playing cards in sixty minutes. O'Brien beat his own record at the 1994

World Memory Championships when he successfully memorized nine and a half packs – 494 cards. He in fact memorized 10 packs but misremembered one card (the scoring system knocks half a pack off the total result for every mistake).

Memorizing a pack of cards may not sound easy but it *is* possible. Try to memorize a pack and see how fast you can get with practice (you will need someone to test you). Check your timing against the grading scale below and test yourself against the world's great card memorizers. At first, try to memorize just half a pack.

26 cards in 30 minutes: Average.
52 cards in 30 minutes: A good memory.
52 cards in 15 minutes: You can out-memorize 98% of the population.
52 cards in 10 minutes: You can out-memorize 99% of the population.
52 cards in 6 minutes: Good enough to take part in national competitions.
52 cards in 5 minutes: Strong national calibre.
52 cards in 3 minutes: Good enough to compete in the next World Championship.
52 cards in 2 minutes: This puts you among the world top 10 memorizers.
52 cards in 60 seconds: This puts you among the world top four memorizers.
52 cards in under 50 seconds: Try to speed up a bit – you might break the world record!

NUMBER MEMORIZATION
MEMORIZATION OF π

It is only the *approximation* of π at ²²⁄₇ which recurs after its sixth decimal place which can, of course, be recited *ad nauseam*. The true value is a string of random numbers which are fiendishly difficult to memorize. (The average ability for memorizing random numbers is barely more than eight – many people find it difficult to memorize eight- or nine-digit telephone numbers.)

As Roger Bannister took on the 'impossible feat' of running a mile in under 4 minutes, so Professor A.C. Aitken, Professor of Mathematics of the University of Edinburgh, took on the 'impossible task' of memorizing digits of the number indicating the value of π. Until Professor Aitken came along, the best results, even with considerable effort, had been 30-40 digits. By applying his memory and basic systems, Professor Aitken was able easily to remember the first 1000 decimal places of π. He could do this not only in correct order, but in reverse order as well. Professor Aitken was one of the first memory pioneers to show that it is possible to train the memory, that memory can be improved and that when it is trained it can improve standard performance by factors of a hundred.

This was demonstrated by CREIGHTON HERBERT JAMES CARVELLO (born 1944), who established what is regarded by many as the mental equivalent of the transatlantic rowing record. He managed to quote 20,013 decimal places of π from memory without error on 27 June 1980 at Saltscar Comprehensive School in Redcar, England.

Carvello encouraged many memorizers, including Dominic O'Brien and Jonathan Hancock who both became World Memory Champions, to take up memory as a mental sport. They were inspired by his performances on national and international television shows, in which he demonstrated his ability to memorize π, as well as his ability to memorize packs of cards and telephone numbers.

A few years later, RAJAN MAHADEVAN, a young Indian, took up Carvello's challenge. He had first shown an interest in numbers as a five-year-old when he stunned guests at a family party by reciting the licence numbers from 40 of their cars. Mahadevan memorized 31,811 digits of π, breaking Carvello's record. News of Carvello's and Mahadevan's accomplishments spread around the world, and the challenge was taken up by a Japanese, HIDEAKI TOMOYORI of Yokohama (born 1932). On 9-10 March 1987 at the Tsukuba University Clubhouse in Japan, he broke Rajan's record by reciting 40,000 places of π in 17 hours 21 minutes, including breaks of 4 hours 15 minutes – a staggering achievement and a world record.

WORLD RANKINGS FOR THE MEMORIZATION OF π	
1 Hideaki Tomoyori (Japan)	40,000 places
2 Rajan Mahadevan (India)	31,811 places
3 Creighton Carvello (UK)	20,013 places
4 Philip Bond (UK)	10,000 places

THE MATRIX MEMORIZATION OF π

In the straight memorization of π, the aim is to quote as many decimal places as possible. The

THE FIRST 2000 DIGITS OF π AFTER THE DECIMAL

1	14159	26535	89793	23846	26433	83279	50288	41971	69399	37510
2	58209	74944	59230	78164	06286	20899	86280	34825	34211	70679
3	82148	08651	32823	06647	09384	46095	50582	23172	53594	08128
4	48111	74502	84102	70193	85211	05559	64462	29489	54930	38196
5	44288	10975	66593	34461	28475	64823	37867	83165	27120	19091
6	45648	56692	34603	48610	45432	66482	13393	60726	02491	41273
7	72458	70066	06315	58817	48815	20920	96282	92540	91715	36436
8	78925	90360	01133	05305	48820	46652	13841	46951	94151	16094
9	33057	27036	57595	91953	09218	61173	81932	61179	31051	18548
10	07446	23799	62749	56735	18857	52724	89122	79381	83011	94912
11	98336	73362	44065	66430	86021	39494	63952	24737	19070	21798
12	60943	70277	05392	17176	29317	67523	84674	81846	76694	05132
13	00056	81271	45263	56082	77857	71342	75778	96091	73637	17872
14	14684	40901	22495	34301	46549	58537	10507	92279	68925	89235
15	42019	95611	21290	21960	86403	44181	59813	62977	47713	09960
16	51870	72113	49999	99837	29780	49951	05973	17328	16096	31859
17	50244	59455	34690	83026	42522	30825	33446	85035	26193	11881
18	71010	00313	78387	52886	58753	32083	81420	61717	76691	47303
19	59825	34904	28755	46873	11595	62863	88235	37875	93751	95778
20	18577	80532	17122	68066	13001	92787	66111	95909	21642	01989
21	38095	25720	10654	85863	27886	59361	53381	82796	82303	01952
22	03530	18529	68995	77362	25994	13891	24972	17752	83479	13151
23	55748	57242	45415	06959	50829	53311	68617	27855	88907	50983
24	81754	63746	49393	19255	06040	09277	01671	13900	98488	24012
25	85836	16035	63707	66010	47101	81942	95559	61989	46767	83744
26	94482	55379	77472	68471	04047	53464	62080	46684	25906	94912
27	93313	67702	89891	52104	75216	20569	66024	05803	81501	93511
28	25338	24300	35587	64024	74964	73263	91419	92726	04269	92279
29	67823	54781	63600	93417	21641	21992	45863	15030	28618	29745
30	55706	74983	85054	94588	58692	69956	90927	21079	75093	02955
31	32116	53449	87202	75596	02364	80665	49911	98818	34797	75356
32	63698	07426	54252	78625	51818	41757	46728	90977	77279	38000
33	81647	06001	61452	49192	17321	72147	72350	14144	19735	68548
34	16136	11573	52552	13347	57418	49468	43852	33239	07394	14333
35	45477	62416	86251	89835	69485	56209	92192	22184	27255	02542
36	56887	67179	04946	01653	46680	49886	27232	79178	60857	84383
37	82796	79766	81454	10095	38837	86360	95068	00642	25125	20511
38	73929	84896	08412	84886	26945	60424	19652	85022	21066	11863
39	06744	27862	20391	94945	04712	37137	86960	95636	43719	17287
40	46776	46575	73962	41389	08658	32645	99581	33904	78027	59009

Matrix Memorization record requires the memorizer not only to know the actual order of the number, but also to know the digits in the correct order from anywhere in the sequence. It is a bit like learning Homer's *Iliad* and then being given a sequence of just a couple of words from it, and asked to remember the words that appear on either side.

When record-holder Philip Bond memorized 10,000 digits of π, his technique was to break this giant number into groups of five digits. The first 2000 digits listed above are just a taster for the world champions, but try to see how far you can get! The sequence should be memorized from left to right, from line 1 down to line 40. Start by trying to memorize just the first 10 or 15 numbers.

A new benchmark was established on 18 May 1994 when PHILIP BOND (born 1964) of London, England, demonstrated the ability to recall any five digits immediately before and after each of 50 groups of five digits chosen at random from the first 10,000 decimal places of π, without error. The record attempt took just 53 minutes.

Said Bond, reported in *The Times* the following day, 'I tend to associate different numbers with different colours. Threes, for example, tend to be yellow in my mind. When I concentrate on a series of numbers, the colours flash past and then the answer seems to pop out.'

Bond also associates numbers with textures and emotions. He has described the Matrix Memorization of π as 'the Everest of memory tests'.

RECALL OF A SPOKEN NUMBER

A random number is read out at the rate of one digit every two seconds. The number must be recalled without error immediately afterwards. Until the 1980s, the record had stood for 70 years since 1911 when a young mathematics professor memorized 18 digits. (A person with an average IQ and no training can remember seven!)

Demonstrating just how far the art and science of memory and mental athletics has progressed, DOMINIC O'BRIEN, in the 1994 World Memory Championships at Simpson's-in-the-Strand, London, established the new record of 142 digits.

SPEED MEMORIZATION OF RANDOM NUMBERS

The record for memorizing random digits within 15 minutes was set by DOMINIC O'BRIEN on 16 October 1991 at the first World Memory Championships held at the Athenaeum Club, London. His achievement was 266 digits perfectly memorized forwards and backwards. Since then, O'Brien has memorized 678 digits forwards and backwards in 60 minutes. At the 1994 World Memory Championships, O'Brien also won the competition in which as many random numbers as possible are memorized in 60 minutes, achieving a record 1080.

SPEED MEMORIZATION OF BINARY DIGITS

The 15-minute record for binary digits is 480 by Jonathan Hancock set at the 1994 Student Memory Championships. The 30-minute record is 1296 established by Dominic O'Brien at the 1994 World Memory Championships.

NOTABLE MENTAL FEATS

MEMORIZATION OF NAMES AND FACES

HARRY LORAYNE of New York has memorized more than 7,500,000 names and faces over a 'memorizing lifetime' of approximately 40 years. He has made over 200 personal appearances a year, memorizing between 400 and 800 people at a time, often more than 2-3 times per day, and including numerous national and international television appearances. Harry Lorayne has established such an astounding record that it may never be broken.

MUSIC MEMORIZATION

Genius composer WOLFGANG AMADEUS MOZART once went to the Vatican, where he listened to a piece of music that was only played once a year. It was always carefully guarded, so Mozart could not possibly have seen the score or heard the piece practised. Yet upon leaving the Vatican, he was able to write down the entire score, note by note, from memory!

SONG MEMORIZATION

The world record holder is BARBARA 'SQUEAK' MOORE, who performed 1852 songs from memory in Pennsylvania, USA, in 1988.

MEMORIZATION OF SPORTS FACTS

FRANK FELBERBAUM of New York, USA, set the record on 26 October 1991 at the Athenaeum Club, London, with perfect memorization of national league baseball statistics from 1876 to 1990. He memorized over 2000 items of information and data, including the year games were played, pennant winning teams, managers, total winning games for the season, and the winning percentages.

AA RECORDS

These records were not performed under such rigorous conditions as the AAA records mentioned above. However, they are generally accepted as being true feats of memory.

MEMORIZATION OF PROPHETIC SAYINGS

In the 9th century AD, IMAM AL BUKHARI memorized over 300,000 prophetic sayings amounting to approximately 21,000,000 words.

MEMORIZATION OF HOLY TEXTS
AHAND DIDAT memorized by heart the Holy Koran, and most of the 46 versions of the Old Testament in the Bible.

MEMORIZATION OF CANONICAL TEXTS
BHANDANTA VICITSARA, in Yangon, Myanmar (formerly Rangoon in Burma), recited 16,000 pages of Buddhist canonical texts in May 1974.

MEMORIZATION OF CHESS GAMES
PAUL MORPHY (1837-84), born in New Orleans, was a lawyer by profession. He became one of the great World Chess Champions and reportedly could remember every move of every game that he played throughout his championship career, including those he had played while blindfolded. His claims are backed up by the fact that nearly 400 of his games were preserved only because he was able to dictate them long after the event.

ROBERT (BOBBY) FISCHER (born 1943), one of the most formidable World Chess Champions ever, once recalled 19 games of blitz chess from memory shortly after playing them. The observing Grandmasters confirmed the accuracy of this American's memory.

GREAT MEMORIZERS THROUGH HISTORY
ANTONIO DI MARCO MAGLIABECHI (see page 52) was able to read entire books, and memorize them without missing a single word or punctuation mark. He eventually committed to memory the entire library of the Grand Duke of Tuscany.

DANIEL McCARTNEY, a 19th-century American, could tell, at the age of 54, what he had been doing on every day since early childhood. Among other things, he could remember the weather conditions and what he had eaten for breakfast, lunch and supper on any given day.

CHRISTIAN FRIEDRICH HEINECKEN was born in Lubeck, Germany, in 1721. At the age of 10 months, he was able to speak and repeat every word said to him. By the age of three he had memorized most known facts about world history and geography at the time, and had similarly learned Latin and French. He is also said to have predicted his own death, which occurred in 1725 when he was still under four-and-a-half.

THEMISTOCLES (c.523-c.458 BC), Greek soldier and statesman, was able to remember the 20,000 names of the citizens of Athens.

XERXES, King of Persia from 486 to 465 BC, was reputed to be able to recall the names of the 100,000 men in his armies.

CARDINAL MEZZOFANTI, a 19th-century linguist, was able to memorize the vocabulary of over 70 languages, including Latin, Greek, Arabic, Spanish, French, German, Swedish, Portuguese, English, Dutch, Danish, Russian, Polish, Bohemian, Serbian, Hungarian, Turkish, Irish, Welsh, Albanian, Sanskrit, Persian, Georgian, Armenian, Hebrew, Chinese, Coptic, Ethiopian and Amharic.

SENECA (c.4 BC–c.65 AD), Roman tragedian and philosopher, is said to have recalled 2000 words after a single hearing.

A RECORDS

MEMORIZATION OF TELEPHONE NUMBERS
GONG-LING HUA of China is reported by the Associated Press to have memorized more than 15,000 telephone numbers from the Chinese telephone directory.

THOMAS MORTON of England has claimed to know more than 10,000 telephone numbers.

CREIGHTON CARVELLO of England has also memorized much of the Middlesbrough telephone directory.

None of these records has been rigorously tested by the time-consuming process of quoting all of the numbers in front of witnesses or by the statistically sound method of random selection. Both Morton and Carvello have, however, given numerous demonstrations of their abilities.

MEMORIZATION OF RELIGIOUS BOOKS
THE SHASS POLLAK JEWS OF POLAND were able to remember the exact position on the page of every word in each of the 12 volumes of the Talmud. Giant religious books such as the Talmud and the even larger Vedic scriptures of ancient India were also passed down by memory.

MEMORIZATION OF TRIBE HISTORY
MAORI CHIEFS have been reported to spend as long as three days reciting the history of their tribe, passed from generation to generation.

GENERAL AND TEXT MEMORIZATION

PETRARCH (1304-74), the Italian poet who was himself a memory expert of repute, states in *Rerum Memorandarum Libri* that one of his friends had a virtually perfect memory: 'It was enough for him to have seen or heard something once, he never forgot; nor did he recollect only the subject matter but also the time and place where he had first learned it.'

SIMPLICIUS, a misnomer if ever there was one, was a friend of St Augustine (AD 354-430) who recalled 'An excellent man of remarkable memory who, when he might be asked by us for all the next-to-last verses in each book of Virgil responded in order quickly and from memory. If we then asked him to recite the verse before each of those, he did so. And we believe that he could recite Virgil backwards. If we desired a common place concerning any topic we asked him to make one and he did. If we wanted even prose passages from whatever of Cicero's orations he had committed to memory, that also he could do; he followed in order however many verses were wanted, backward and forward.'

THE BOOK OF GENIUS RANKING OF THE WORLD'S TOP MEMORY MENTATHLETES	
1 Dominic O'Brien (UK)	**8** Tariq Mamoon (USA)
2 Jonathan Hancock (UK)	**9** Frank Felberbaum (USA)
3 Hideaki Tomoyori (Japan)	**10** Melik Duyar (Turkey)
4 = Philip Bond (UK) & James Lee (UK)	**11** Creighton Carvello (UK)
6 Sue Whiting (UK)	**12** Natacia Diot (UK)
7 Rajan Mahadevan (India)	**13** Thomas Morton (Ireland)

HUMAN CALCULATION RECORDS

ROOT EXTRACTION

The fastest extraction of a 13th root from a 100-digit number is reported in *The Guinness Book of Records* as 0.15 second by JAIME GARCIA SERRANO of Bogotá, Columbia, established on 24 May 1989. We contend that it would be impossible even to speak the answer in the time attributed! We prefer Dutchman WILLEM KLEIN's record of 88.8 seconds set on 7 April 1981.

MULTIPLICATION

MRS SHAKUNTALA DEVI of India demonstrated the multiplication of two 13-digit numbers (7,686,369,774,870 × 2,465,099,745,779) picked at random by the Computer Department of Imperial College, London, on 18 June 1980 in 28 seconds. For those who want to test their multiplication skills, Mrs Devi's correct answer was 18,947,668,177,995,426,462,773,730.

SPEED READING

In most speed reading tests, the reader has to read an entire novel as fast as possible, and then give a speech including knowledgeable comments to people who have read the novel in depth.

WORLD RANKINGS FOR SPEED READING (WORDS PER MINUTE)			
1 Sean Adam (USA)	3850	**6** Luc van Hof (Netherlands)	1906
2 Kjetill Gunnarson (Norway)	3050	**7** Michael J Gelb (USA)	1805
3 Vanda North (UK)	3000	**8** Cinnamon Adam (USA)	1782
4 Cris van Aken (Netherlands)	2520	**9** James Longworth (UK)	1750
5 Mithymna Corke (Netherlands)	2100	**10** Frank van der Poll (Netherlands)	1560

THE WORLD MEMORY CHAMPIONSHIP

Raymond Keene, co-author and co-founder of this event, describes the background to the 1994 Championship and the exciting finale.

The World Memory Championship, inaugurated in 1991, was won by Dominic O'Brien. In 1993 the second World Memory Championship was held, with mnemonists, memorists and memory record holders invited to compete from all over the globe. Once again, Dominic O'Brien achieved victory. So dominant was his performance that the Brain Trust Charity, which monitors superlative mental performance worldwide, awarded him the accolade of 'Brain of the Year' (sharing the title with the American student prodigy Lana Israel).

For the 1994 World Memory Championship, held at Simpson's-in-the-Strand, London, Dominic O'Brien was again considered the overall favourite. After completion of nine of the 11 competitions in the Championship, O'Brien's lead was substantial. He had smashed a number of records which he personally had established in former years. This included an unprecedented memorization of 142 consecutive spoken digits, accurate recall of 494 playing cards in sequence and an amazing ability to memorize 1296 consecutive binary digits (0 and 1 typed in random order on a page) without error.

Then, with O'Brien's predicted victory almost within his grasp, he stumbled in the 'Round the World in 80 Days Flight Disk Challenge'. Sponsored by the Official Airlines Guide of Reed Travel Group, the major backers of the 1994 Championship, and devised by co-author Tony Buzan, the Flight Disk Challenge required memorization of 800 items of travel information in just 30 minutes. If correctly recalled this complex yet functional itinerary would enable the memorist to circumnavigate the planet in precisely 80 days.

When the results were read out, they revealed a sensation. Dominic O'Brien had misremembered a digit at the very start of his mental journey and had virtually 'crashed' on take-off from London's Heathrow Airport, thus essentially scoring zero for this competition. Meanwhile, O'Brien's great rival Jonathan Hancock, a first class honours graduate from Oxford University and silver medal winner from the first two Memory Championships, had memorized an amazing segment of the journey, sweeping him across the Atlantic, into the United States, down through

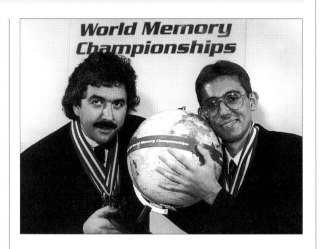

World Memory Champions first and present: Dominic O'Brien (left) and Jonathan Hancock.

Latin America and back via the Caribbean to America's West Coast. Declared the triumphant winner of the Flight Disk Challenge, Hancock had now shot into the lead, albeit a narrow one, in the main championship.

All now hung on the final test – speed memorization of a single shuffled pack of 52 playing cards. Traditionally, this was O'Brien's strong suit, a field of mental combat in which, time and again in former contests, he had obliterated his competitors. By winning the card sprint now, O'Brien could still hang on to his title.

As spectators gathered for the final showdown, Hancock seemed nervous. Starters' orders were given and Hancock sped through the cards, pausing for micro-seconds only, and with his hands visibly trembling. After just 58 seconds, Hancock signalled that he had completed his task. The rapidity was amazing. However, in his rush, had he misremembered a card?

Twenty-seven seconds later O'Brien indicated that he, too, had memorized his pack. The tension was almost unbearable as the invigilators painstakingly checked the two rivals' answers. Then came the final announcement. Under championship conditions, Hancock had set a new world record in competition for perfect speed memorization of a pack of cards. The crowded tournament hall erupted into thunderous and prolonged applause. Jonathan Hancock was the new World Memory Champion.

Dr Sue Whiting from Hertfordshire is the 1994 World Women's Memory Champion.

RESULTS OF THE 1994 WORLD MEMORY CHAMPIONSHIP

MEMORIZATION OF A 2000-DIGIT NUMBER The competitors were allowed 60 minutes to memorize the number and 45 minutes to recall it.

1 Dominic O'Brien	1080 digits
2 Jonathan Hancock	780 digits
3 Philip Bond	430 digits

MEMORIZATION OF NAMES AND FACES Competitors were shown faces with names underneath for 15 minutes. Then they were shown the faces again without names and in a new order. Competitors then had to put the memorized names to the faces within 20 minutes.

1 Jonathan Hancock	140
2 Dominic O'Brien	133
3 James Lee	81

MEMORIZATION OF RANDOM WORDS 500 words were presented in numbered columns to the competitors who memorized them for 15 minutes. They were allowed 20 minutes in which to write down the words.

1 Dominic O'Brien	102
2= Patrick Colgan	100
2= Jonathan Hancock	100

MEMORIZATION OF A NUMBER SPOKEN ALOUD 300 numbers were read out and the contestants had 30 minutes to recall the number by writing it down. The procedure was repeated three times, with each competitor's best score noted.

1 Dominic O'Brien	142
2 Jonathan Hancock	60
3 James Lee	34

MEMORIZATION OF 12 PACKS OF SHUFFLED CARDS Contestants were given 60 minutes to memorize as many packs of cards as they could. If they made a mistake in any pack, they lost half of that pack (two mistakes and they lost the whole pack).

1 Dominic O'Brien	494
2 Jonathan Hancock	384
3 Melik Duyar	199

SPEED MEMORIZATION OF A RANDOM NUMBER Competitors were given 5 minutes to memorize a string of 500 numbers and then had to write down as many as they could remember.

1 Dominic O'Brien	157
2 Jonathan Hancock	140
3 Philip Bond	90

MEMORIZATION OF PAINTINGS AND IMAGES Competitors were asked to memorize 24 images. Then they were shown 80 images including the original 24 (many of the images were similar). The competitors had to identify which of the 80 they had seen before. They also had to note whether each of the 24 images was shown as when first seen, or whether it had been flipped so that it was the opposite way round. Thus 48 maximum points were available.

1 Melik Duyar	34
2 Natacia Diot	32
3= Ian Docherty	30
3= Jonathan Hancock	30

MEMORIZATION OF A BINARY NUMBER Competitors were given 30 minutes to memorize a 2000-digit binary number (1 and 0 in a random sequence). They then recalled the number by writing it down.

1 Dominic O'Brien	1296
2 Jonathan Hancock	1140
3 Philip Bond	750

MEMORIZATION OF UNKNOWN TEXT Contestants were given 40 lines of previously unseen text to memorize within 15 minutes. They then had 15 minutes in which to recall the lines, with no spelling or punctuation mistakes. If they made an error in any line, the words in that line were not included in the final total of words memorized.

1 Natacia Diot	149
2 Jonathan Hancock	114
3 Patrick Colgan	106

FLIGHT DISK CHALLENGE Competitors had to memorize 800 items of travel information in sequence within 30 minutes and then write down as many as possible. If a competitor made a mistake, no points were scored for items correctly remembered after the error.

1 Jonathan Hancock	149
2 Kenneth Wilshire	121
3 Melik Duyar	90

SPEED MEMORIZATION OF A PACK OF CARDS A shuffled pack of 52 cards had to be remembered as fast as possible, with each card being looked at in sequence. The competitors were only allowed to look at each card once (they could not go back once the next card had been turned over).

1 Jonathan Hancock	58.79 seconds
2 Dominic O'Brien	85.36 seconds
3 Creighton Carvello	183.68 seconds

AN INVITATION TO READERS

REGISTER YOUR MENTAL WORLD RECORDS
If you know of an unrecognized mental world record or have achieved one yourself and wish to register it officially, then do the following:

1 Ensure that the record is properly verified.
2 Send a note of the record with proper authentication by at least two witnesses to:
Mental World Records, c/o Tony Buzan,
The Harleyford Manor Estate, Marlow,
Bucks, SL7 2DX.

3 Please enclose a cheque for £10.00 made payable to 'The Brain Trust' to cover the cost of registration.

Additionally, we welcome all information on geniuses, amazing mental achievements and arcana of all sorts on the great minds. We further welcome your nominations for the top 100 geniuses in any country, as well as for the overall genius of the decade, the century, the millennium, and of all time. Please note that it is only necessary to send in the registration fee if you are personally sending in a record for certification.

BIBLIOGRAPHY

We have consulted many reference works, biographies and works of literature in the course of writing this book. The following are particularly valuable and are recommended for further reading in their areas. We also encourage you to read works by the geniuses in the Hall of Fame.

A Brief History of Time by Stephen Hawking (Bantam Press, 1989)
Chambers Biographical Dictionary Editors: J.O. Thorne MA and T.C. Collocott MA (W & R Chambers Ltd, 1988)
Einstein: The Life and Times by Ronald W. Clark (A Discus Book published by Arrow Books, 1984)
Great Books Editor in Chief: Philip W. Goetz (60 volumes, Encyclopaedia Britannica, 1990)
The Great Commanders by Phil Grabsky (Boxtree Ltd, 1993)
Goethe by Richard Friedenthal (George Weidenfeld & Nicholson Ltd, 1993)
History of England by Sir Charles Oman KBE (Edward Arnold & Co, 1934)

The Lost Centuries by John Bagot Glubb (Hodder & Stoughton, 1967)
The Mahabharata by Jean-Claude Carrière, translated from the French by Peter Brook (Methuen, 1987)
Martha, The Life and Work of Martha Graham by Agnes De Mille (Vintage Books, 1992)
Nijinsky by Richard Buckle (Weidenfeld & Nicholson, 1987)
Opera by Leslie Orrey, revised by Rodney Milnes (Thames & Hudson Ltd, 1987)
The Opera Handbook by John Lazarus (Longman Group UK Ltd, 1987)
The Seafarers: The Explorers by Richard Humble (Time Life Books, 1978)
The Seafarers: Fighting Sail by A.B.C. Whipple (Time Life Books, 1978)
The Tao of Pooh by Benjamin Hoff (Mandarin Paperbacks, 1989)
The Time Life History of the World Editor: Ellen Phillips (26 volumes, Time Life Publishers, 1992)

You can read Grandmaster Raymond Keene on chess every day in *The Times* of London and each week in *The Spectator*. Among the world record 85 books he has written on chess and mind sports in general, the following are particularly recommended:

Batsford Chess Openings 2, published by B.T. Batsford, London 1993. This is the standard one volume reference work on chess openings. Since the first edition was published in 1982, the book has sold more than 100,000 copies. The co-author is the World Chess Champion, Garry Kasparov.

Chess for Absolute Beginners, also published by B.T. Batsford, London, 1993. This is the ideal introduction to the game of chess, perfect for children and adults alike, with simple, clear and easy-to-understand diagrams in colour by artist Barry Martin.

ALSO BY TONY BUZAN
BOOKS

The Mind Map Book: Radiant Thinking The comprehensive guide to Mind Mapping® by its originator. Exciting new ways to use and improve your memory, concentration and creativity in planning and structuring thought on all levels.

Use Your Head The classic BBC best seller, which has sold over a million copies. Foundation learning skills and Mind Mapping explained by their inventor. Latest information on your brain's functioning, enabling you to Learn How to Learn more effectively.

Use Your Memory An encyclopaedia of brain-related memory techniques. Provides easy-to-manage techniques for remembering names, faces, places, jokes, telephone numbers and everything you want or need to remember.

Speed/Range Reading Establish a range of reading speeds up to 10,000 wpm with good comprehension. Self-checks and practical exercises throughout.

Make the Most of Your Mind (paperback); *Harnessing the ParaBrain* (hardback) A complete course-in-book dealing with reading, memory number skills, logic, vision, listening and study. Builds to the complete Mind Map Organic Study Technique.

Master Your Memory Expands your memory systems from 10 to 10,000! Also provides basic data in 12 subject areas, including art, literature, science and languages.

Memory Vision A 'work book' to go with *Master Your Memory*, in which to record your 10,000 knowledge databases.

Spore One (poetry) Reality seen through many facets. A poetic 'work-out' for your brain.

BOOKS WITH OTHER AUTHORS

Get Ahead by Vanda North with Tony Buzan. A practical, easy and inviting introduction to Mind Mapping. How to apply it to your life to 'Get Ahead' quicker; also includes a 2-week 'Just Do It' new habit section.

Lessons From the Art of Juggling by Michael J. Gelb and Tony Buzan. Juggling is a delightful metaphor for living and learning. You will discover the secrets of transforming failure into success and mastering the art of relaxed concentration. Learn to juggle and how to learn.

Brain Power for Kids by Lana Israel with Tony Buzan. Lana, the 1994 Brain Trust Brain of the Year, explains how to make school work easier by applying the Mind Map to reports, essays, research, note-taking and exams.

AUDIO TAPES

Each 45-minute cassette is accompanied by a booklet. The seven tapes are Buzan on the Brain; Buzan on Memory; Buzan on Radiant Thinking and Creativity; Buzan on Mind Mapping; Buzan on Reading; Buzan on Success; and Buzan on Body and Mind.

In this brand new 'Buzan on' audio series, Tony is interviewed by Vanda North on a range of topics. Each audio is fast-paced Buzan wisdom, ending with ten Action Points for improvement in each specific area.

VIDEO TAPES

If At First...(one 25-minute tape with trainer booklet). Many organizations and individuals say they encourage risk-taking and making mistakes. But it is not so simple to cast aside an anxiety which has been carried with us since school. In *'If At First...'*, Buzan helps us look at the fear of failure as an event on our learning curve. Charthouse's film gives rise to group discussions that shift people's attitudes and guarantees that they become more creative and successful.

Mindpower (two 25-minute videos with a work book). Mind Mapping applications for today's business. In the BBC's new technologically superb video-led course, Tony Buzan teaches you how to use Mind Maps to clarify your thinking and make better use of your mental resources.

Developing Family Genius (four 70-minute videos). A complete, entertaining and highly participative course for the entire family or individuals, where Tony Buzan introduces you to the wonders of the human brain. Learn how to: learn; think; remember; read fast with comprehension; study effectively and easily take and pass exams.

Get Ahead (a 60-minute video with a booklet). In this fun-to-watch video, Tony introduces Lana Israel, a 16-year-old student. Lana takes students on a step-by-step demonstration of how to apply Mind Mapping to improve study, revise for exams and enhance memory.

The Enchanted Loom (a 60-minute video). Classic documentary on the brain, featuring interviews with the world's major contributors to the field. Devised by Buzan and including his pioneer work with learning-disadvantaged children.

OTHER PRODUCTS

Mind Maps® plus Software Programme The new computer thinking tool may be used on any PC compatible with VGA running DOS. The first Mind Map computer programme doubles creativity, allows flexible and instantaneous manifestation of ideas and logs levels of thought. Can translate to linear for the non-Mind Map literate.

Mind Map Pads/Kits Each printing of a Mind Map pad is covered with a limited edition Mind Map. The kit contains an A3 and A4 pad, a Buzan 4-colour pen and highlighters.

Body and Soul Poster (85 x 67 cm) A limited edition, master Mind Map style poster depicting, in a surrealist manner, all the principles of Radiant Thinking. Each numbered copy is signed by the Swedish artist, Ulf Ekberg.

SEM³ This user-friendly laminated chart of the Self-enhancing Master Memory Matrix enables the *Master Your Memory* reader to memorize up to 10,000 items with ease.

The Universal Personal Organizer (UPO) This unique approach to self/time-management is a diary system, based on the techniques created and taught by Tony Buzan and the Buzan Centres. The UPO is a living system that grows with you, and gives a comprehensive picture of your life, your desires, and your business and family functions.

The Mind Map Map This introduction to Mind Maps offers a 'How To' and 'Question and Answer' on one side and a multi-coloured Mind Map on Mind Mapping on the other.

TRAINING COURSES IN MENTAL LITERACY AND RADIANT THINKING

Full range of Radiant Thinking skills for study, work and life include courses prepared for: individuals from 5 years of age upwards; families; clubs, organizations and committees; people of all intellectual levels and abilities including the learning-disabled; corporations of any size, including directors, managers and all staff.

There are five Radiant Thinking Training Programmes.

Radiant Thinking This foundation course allows you to tap the full creative potential of your brain. Application of the Mind Map process to a range of life and business needs, i.e. problem solving; studying; communication and planning, including creative thinking and memory.

Radiant Remembering Practical application of the memory principles, rhythms and systems for remembering data, lists, faces and anything else! Saves time, money and embarrassment.

Radiant Reading Climb over that stack of information! Make informed decisions by applying information about the eyes and brain to manage all kinds of reading material with speed, efficiency, comprehension and appreciation.

Radiant Speaking Three leaders in the field give step-by-step practical applications for effective speaking with confidence and enjoyment under any circumstances.

Radiant Selling BrainSell from one brain to another. A completely new look at selling techniques, based on the functioning of the brain.

RADIANT THINKING TRAINING PROGRAMME FORMATS

Open Introductory Radiant Thinking Programmes Usually conducted over a weekend, and introducing Mind Mapping, Radiant Thinking, Reading and Memory Skills. All ages welcome.

Open Radiant Thinking Programmes One day, including a course book, focusing on either Radiant Thinking (Mind Maps), Remembering, Reading, Speaking or Selling.

Company Radiant Thinking Radiant Thinking courses are specially customized to be applicable immediately for groups of ten plus people in any one, or more, of the Radiant Thinking Programmes. The five courses can stand alone, or be combined with each other or existing company courses.

Radiant Thinking Instructor Programmes In-depth training, licensing you to teach the Radiant Thinking Programmes. Pre-course preparation prior to a full week of training. Competency based. Certification through to full diploma.

For information on training courses, products to learn how to learn and the current information pack, contact:
Buzan Centres Limited
37 Waterloo Road, Bournemouth, Dorset BH9 1BD, UK.
Telephone: + 44 (0) 1202-533593.
Fax: +44 (0) 1202-534572.
Please send a large (10 x 30 cm/8 x 12 in) stamped self-addressed envelope.
Buzan Centres USA Inc.,
415 Federal Highway, Lake Park, Florida 33403, USA.
Telephone: + 1 (407) 881-0188 or 1-(800) Y-MIND MAP
Fax: +1 (407) 845-3210

The Mind Mappers' Society You are invited to join this society, founded by Tony Buzan and organized by Buzan Centres Limited. The society's specific objective is to raise money for research into thinking and learning through The Brain Trust, charity number 1001012. Life membership to the Mind Mappers' Society is by introduction (this is yours!) and upon payment of at least £5.00/$10.00. For this you will receive a membership card, a lapel pin, knowledge that you have assisted research into thinking and learning, and fellowship into the global body of Mind Mappers. To join, send your donation to Buzan Centres Limited, along with your full name and address.

The Brain Trust/Use Your Head Club For information on how to join, see page 31.

INDEX

Note: page numbers which are printed in **bold** type indicate main references. Page numbers which are printed in *italic* refer to the illustrations.

Adam, Sean, 245
Adams, John, 158
Adler, Alfred, 197, 207
aerobic training, 34-6
Aeschylus, **73-4**, *73*, 75, 76, 104
Agostino di Duccio, 122
Aitken, Professor A.C., 241
Al Bukhari, Imam, 243
Al-Lajlaj, 94
Al-Raschid, Haroun, 93
Aladdin, 93
Albert, Prince Consort, 175
Alberti, Leon Battista, 15, 34, 60, 106, **107-8**, *108*, 123
Albertus Magnus, 99
alcohol, 39-40
Alekhine, Alexander, 61
Alexander, F.M., 37, 56
Alexander the Great, 15, 16, 66, 80, **82-4**, *82*, 86, 87, 91, 98, 120, 133, 167, 168, 170, 176, 232
Alexander Technique, 56
Alexandria, 83, **84-5**
Alexius Comnenus, Emperor, 93
Alfonsi, Peter, 95
Ali, Muhammad, 13, 16, **230-2**, *231*
Amadeity Principle, 45, 166
Ampère, André, 176
Amyntas II, King of Macedonia, 80
Anning, Mary, 181, *181*
Anokhin, Petr, 33, 42, 46
Apollinaire, Guillaume, 214
Appleton, Dr, 36
Aquinas, St Thomas, 15, 94-5, 96, **99-100**, *100*, 102
Archelaus, King of Macedonia, 76
Archimedes, 16, 51, 83, **85-6**, *86*, 138
Arensberg, Walter, 215
Aretino, Pietro, 130
Aristarchus, 66, 85
Aristotle, 15, 16, 32, 74, 77, **79-82**, *81*, 94-5, 96, 99, *100*, 101, 104, 127, 128, 176, 208
Armitage, Edward, *177*
As-Suli, **93-4**, 110
association, memory, 49
Athenaeum Club, London, 175
attitude, mental, 15-16, 41
Augustine, St, 245
auto-suggestion, 16
Averroës, 80, **94-5**, *95*, 96, 99, *100*, 127
Avicenna, 94

Babur, Emperor, 97
Bach, Johann Christian, 154
Bach, Johann Sebastian, 17, **153-4**, *153*, 224
Bacon, Sir Francis, 135, 137, 140, 141, 179
Baird, John Logie, 204
Bakst, Leon, *213*
Bannister, Roger, 241
Barrow, Isaac, 148
Baryshnikov, Mikhail, 221
Becquerel, Henri, 199
Beechey, Sir William, *168*
Beethoven, Ludwig van, 146, 154, 164, **172-3**, *173*, 196, 224, 232
Bell, Alexander Graham, **195**, *195*, 196
Bell, Alexander Melville, 195
Bellini, Giovanni, 130
Bentham, Jeremy, 178, *178*
Bergson, Henri, 209
Bernard, Emile, 194
Bernini, Gian Lorenzo, 114, 135
binary numbers, memorization of, 246, 247
Binet, Alfred, 20
Black Death, 105
Blake, William, *12*
blood, 35
Boccaccio, Giovanni, 100
body intelligence, 25-6
Boethius, 78
Bohr, Niels, 209, 226
Bol, Ferdinand, 143
Boldini, Giovanni, *185*
Boleyn, Anne, 136
Bond, Philip, 241, 242, 243, 245, 247
Booth, John Wilkes, 183
Borges, Jorge Luis, 94, 145, 146, 154, 166, 172, **222-3**, *222*, 232
Borgia, Cesare, 119
Born, Max, 226
Botvinik, Mikhail, 61
Boyle, Sir Robert, 148
brain, 32-3
 aerobic training and, 35-6
 blood supply, 35
 creativity, 51
 diet and, 39
 left and right sides of, *33*
 memory, 46-9
 mental literacy, 15, 32-3
 posture and, 56
 potential, 33
 principles, 42-4
 response to music, 166-7
 rest, 40
 and vision, 55
Brain Trust Charity, 31, 232, 246
Bramante, Donato, 123, 128, 135

Braque, Georges, 210
Braun, Karl Ferdinand, 204
Breton, André, 214
Brook, Peter, 64
Brunel, Isambard Kingdom, 60, **176-8**, *177*
Brunel, Sir Marc Isambard, 177
Brunelleschi, Filippo, 71, 73, **106**, 107, 108, 122, 123, 172
Buddha, 16, 68
Buxtehude, Diderik, 154

Caesar, Julius, 82, 83, 87, **91-2**, *92*, 120, 133, 167, 170, 221, 232
Cage, John, 221, 226
Capablanca, Jose, 61
Caravaggio, Michelangelo Merisi da, 143
Carnegie, Andrew, **188-90**, *189*
Carvello, Creighton, 240, 241, 245, 247
Catherine the Great, 93
Caxton, William, 110
Cecil, Robert (Lord Burleigh), 137
cerebral cortex, 33
CERN, 52, 226
Cézanne, Paul, 15, 154, **190-5**, *192-3*, 210
Chaplin, Charlie, 148, 209, **216-19**, *218*
characteristics of genius, 12-19
Charles I, King of England, 137, 146
Charles II, King of England, 146
Charles V, Emperor, 124, 130-1
Chaucer, Geoffrey, 66
checkers, 61-2
chess, 61, 93-4, 110-11, 156
Chigi, Agostino, 128
Ch'in Shi Huangdi, Emperor of China, 14, 83, **88-9**, *88*
Chionofuji, 16
Chocquet, 191, 194
Christina, Queen of Sweden, *141*, 142
Cicero, 86, 92, 245
Clement VII, Pope, 124
Clinton, William Jefferson, *156*, 158
Cocteau, Jean, 210
Colgan, Patrick, 247
Collins, Paul, 154
colour, and memory, 49
Columbus, Christopher, 106, 107, **110-12**, *111*, *112*, 116, 124
commitment, 14
Communism, 224
comprehension, 55
Conan Doyle, Sir Arthur, 42, **197-9**
Condell, Henry, 139
Confucius, 16, *16*, 68, **70-1**, *70*, 88, 93, 102, 117, 119, 219
Conon, 85
Constantine the Great, Emperor, 133

Constantinople, 133, 134
Cooper, Dr Kenneth, 35, 36
Copernicus, Nicolas, 15, 84, 85, 106, 116, **120-1**, *120*, *121*, 138, 148, 179, 229
Corneille, 66
Cornwallis, General, 162
Cortés, Hernando, 124
Cosway, Maria, 159
Coubertin, Baron Pierre de, 73
courage, 17
Cranach, Lucas, 130
Crassus, 91
Crawford, Professor Michael, 38-9
creativity, 17, 26-7, 50-1
Crick, Francis, 16, 181, **229-30**
Cromwell, Oliver, 146
Cubism, 194, 195, 210, 214
Cunningham, Merce, 221
Curie, Eve, 200
Curie, Marie, 60, **199-200**, *199*
Curie, Pierre, 199, *199*

Dada, 215
Dalí, Salvador, 15, 222, **226-8**, *227*, *228*
Daniele da Volterra, 124
Dante Alighieri, 80, 94, **100-2**, *101*, 117, 119, 145, 219
Darius, King of Persia, 83
Darwin, Charles, 15, 60, *179-81*, *181*, 206, 209
David, Jacques Louis, *69*, *169*
Davy, Sir Humphry, 174, 175, 176
daydreaming, 42
De Kooning, William, 215
De Witt, Jan and Cornelius, 147
Degas, Edgar, 191
Descartes, René, **141-2**, *141*, 146
desire, 13
Devi, Shakuntala, 245
Diaghilev, Sergei, 210, 213
Diaz, Bartholomeu, 124
Dickens, Charles, 16, *183-4*, *184*, 216, 217
diet, 38-9
digestive system, 36
Dine, Jim, 215
Diot, Natacia, 247
Disney, Walt, 16, 153, **223-4**, *223*
Docherty, Ian, 247
Donatello, 71, 73, 106, 107, 122, 123, 130
Dou, Gerrit, 143
Drake, Sir Francis, 137
draughts, 61-2
dreams, 40
Dreier, Katherine, 215
drugs, 39-40
Duchamp, Marcel, **214-16**, *216*, 226
Duchamp Villon, Raymond, 214, 215
Dufay, Guillaume, 107, 122, 172
Duncan, Isadora, 220
Duplessis, Joseph-Siffrede, *165*
Duyar, Melik, 245, 247

Edaljee, 198
Edison, Thomas Alva, 15, 43, 174, **195-6**, *196*
Edward VI, King of England, 136
Edward VII, King of England, 190
Einstein, Albert, 15, 16, 17, 49, 60, 93, 176, 196, 205, **207-9**, *207*, 210, 225
Eliot, George, **186-7**, *187*
Elizabeth I, Queen of England, 93, 104, 131,

133, **135-7**, *136*
energy, 17
engineering intelligence, 23-4
enthusiasm, 17
Epidaurus, *75*
Erasmus, Desiderius, **116-17**, *116*, 217
Eratosthenes, 85
Este, Alfonzo d', Duke of, 130
Euclid, 17, 82, 83, *84*, **85**, 127, 208
Euripides, 73, 74, **75-6**, 104
Evelyn, John, 142
exaggeration, and memory, 49
eyes, 52, 53-5, *54*, 57

faces, memorization of, 243, 247
faith, 14
Faldo, Nick, 16
Faraday, Michael, 13, 17, **175-6**, *177*
Farnese, Cardinal Alessandro, 131
fears, facing, 17
Felberbaum, Frank, 243
Ferdinand, King of Spain, 111
Feuerbach, Ludwig, 187
Feynman, Richard, 208
field of vision, 54-5, *54*, 56
Fischer, Bobby, 37, 61
fish, 38-9
fitness, 34-8
Fleming, Alexander, 51
Flesch, Rudolph, 50
flexibility, 17, 37
Flight Disk Challenge, 246, 247
Florence, 105, 106-7, 119
Fonteyn, Dame Margot, 221
food, 38-9
Ford, Gerald, 221
Foreman, George, 231
Francis I, King of France, 116
Franco, General, 210, 211
Franklin, Benjamin, 93, *155-8*, *155*, 159
Frazier, Joe, 231
Frederick the Great, King of Prussia, 160
French Revolution, 158
Freud, Sigmund, 164, 197, **205-7**, *206*, 209, 226
Froebel, Friedrich, 202
Fust, Johannes, 108, 109

Galileo Galilei, 60, 115, 117, 120, 121, 124, **137-8**, *138*, 142, 146, 148, 154, 229, 233
Galli, Jacopo, 122
Gama, Vasco da, 124
games, 61-2
Gandi, Mohandas K. (Mahatma), 16, **201-2**, *201*
Gardner, Professor Howard, 21
Gates, William (Bill), 15, 16-17, 109, **233**
Genghis Khan, **96-8**, *96*, *98*, 162, 168, 170, 231
Genius Quotient (GQ), 13, 18-19
Ghirlandaio, Domenico de, 122
Giorgione, 130
Giotto, 73
go (board game), 62
Goebbels, Joseph, 217
Goethe, Johann Wolfgang von, 14, *14*, 15, 45, 66, 93, **162-4**, *162*, 168, 172, 187, 206, 221
Goethendipity Principle, 45, 164, 166
Gomez, 124
Gonzaga, Frederico II, 130

Graham, Martha, 17, **219-21**, *219*, *220*, 232
grains, 38
Grant, General Ulysses S., 183
Gray, Elisha, 195
Great Pyramid, Giza, 64-6, *65*
Greene, Liz, 206
Gunnarson, Kjetill, 245
Gunnell, Sally, 16
Gutenberg, Johannes Gensfleich, **108-10**, *109*, *110*, 126, 233

Hahn, Otto, 209
Hals, Frans, 142
Hamilton, George Heard, 215
Hamilton, Richard, 215
Hancock, Jonathan, 240, 241, 243, 245, 246, 247
Hannibal, 87, **89-91**, *89*, *91*, 134, 162, 170
Harvey, William, 148
Haussmann, Baron, 191
Hawking, Stephen, 138, 150, 152, 172, 226, **232-3**, *233*
Haydn, Joseph, 172
Hazlitt, William, 145
heart, aerobic training, 34, 35
Heisenberg, Werner Karl, 209, **224-6**
Heminges, John, 139
Henry VII, King of England, 111
Henry VIII, King of England, 131, 135, 136
Herbert, Frank, 17
Herodotus, 66
Hertz, Heinrich, 203
Hill, Napoleon, 190
Hilliard, Nicholas, *136*, *139*
Hitler, Adolf, 208, 217, 225
Homer, 15, *66-8*, 80, 82, 84, 101, 102, 140, 145, 146, 154, 176, 222
honesty, 13, 17
Hooch, Pieter de, 142
Hooke, Robert, 150
Hoover, J. Edgar, 219
Hoppner, John, *161*
Horace, 70
Hoyle, Sir Fred, 153
Hughes, Ted, 48
Humanism, 106
humour, and memory, 49
Hus, Jan, 102
Hussites, 102
Huygens, Constant, 143
Huysmans, Joris Karl, 194
Hypatia, 79, *79*

Iconoclastic Movement, 142
images, memorization of, 247
imagination, 15, 49
Impressionism, 191
intelligence (IQ) tests, 20-1, *20*, 55
inter-personal intelligence, 28-9
internal role models, 17
intra-personal intelligence, 27-8
intuition, 16
Isabella, Queen of Spain, 111, *112*
Israel, Lana, 246
Ivan the Terrible, 93, 131

James, Dr Frank, 176
James, Henry, 187
Jefferson, Thomas, 15, 52, 60, 155, *156*, **158-9**

John II, King of Portugal, 111
Johns, Jasper, 215
joints, flexibility, 37
Joliot, Jean, 200
Joliot-Curie, Irene, 200
Jones, Ernest, 197
Jonson, Ben, 140
Joplin, Scott, 221
Joseph II, Emperor, 165
Jouderville, Isaac, 143
Joyce, James, 15, 66
Julesz, Bela, 55
Julius II, Pope, 123, 127, 128
Jung, Carl Gustav, 197, **205-6**, *205*, 207, 220
Justinian, Emperor, 72, 134
Juvenal, 90

Kafka, Franz, 223
Karno, Fred, 216
Karpov, Anatoly, 14, 61
Kasparov, Garry, 14, 34, 37, 61, 93-4, 233
Kendrew, Sir John, 230
Kennedy, John F., 52, 158
Kepler, Johannes, 121-2
Khufu, King of Egypt, 64-5
kinaesthetic intelligence, 25-6
King, Martin Luther, 159, 230
Klein, Willem, 245
knowledge, 15
Kobes, Dr, 36
Kublai Khan, 97

Lacourière, Roger, 211
Lamprus, 75
Lao-Tzu, 16, *16*, **68**, *68*, 87, 88, 166
Lasker, Emanuel, 61
Lastman, Pieter, 143
Leach, Glyn, 232
learning from mistakes, 15
Lebel, Robert, 215
Lee, James, 245, 247
Leibniz, Gottfried, 93, 150, **151-3**, *152*
Leo X, Pope, 115, 128
Leonardo da Vinci, 15, 34, 37, 47, 49, 52, 59, 60, *60*, 68, 71, 104, **112-16**, *113*, *114*, 122, 123, 127, 131, 135, 154, 172, 200, 221, 224, 228
Lewes, George Henry, 187
Lincoln, Abraham, 154, 159, **182-3**, *182*, 188
linguistic intelligence, 21-2
Lister, Joseph, **187-8**, 206
Liston, Sonny, 230, 231-2
literacy, mental, 15, 32-3
Livingstone, Robert, 158
Livy, 90
logical intelligence, 22-3
Lomazzo, Giovanni, 131
Longworth, James, 240, 245
Lorayne, Harry, 243
Louis II, King of Hungary, 133-4
Louis XII, King of France, 128
Louis XIV, King of France, 151
love of the task, 17
Loyola, Saint Ignatius, 117
Lucas, George, 223
Luria, Professor, 46
Luther, Martin, 117

McCarthy, Senator Joseph, 209, 217
Machiavelli, Niccolo, 70, 71, 83, 84, 102, 114, **117-20**, *118*, 219

Madonna, *219*
Magellan, Ferdinand, 116, **124-7**, *126*
Magliabechi, Antonio di Marco, 46, 52-3, 55
Mahadevan, Rajan, 241, 245
Mahler, Gustav, 172, 213
Maimonides, Moses, 95-6, *96*
Mamoon, Tariq, 240, 245
Manet, Edouard, 191
Manhattan Project, 208
Manutius, 110
Mao Tse Tung, 71, 87
Marcellus, General, 86
Marconi, Guglielmo, **203-4**, *204*
Marie Medici, Queen of France, 143
Marlborough, Duke of, 87
Marlowe, Christopher, 117, 119, 135, 137, 140, 223
Marmont, Marshal, 171
Mary, Queen of Scots, 135
Mary I, Queen of England, 136
Masaccio, 106, 107, 115, 123
Maslow, A.A., 29
Massena, Marshal, 171
Mastermind Groups, 16-17, 45
Matisse, Henri, 209-10
Matrix Memorization of π, 241-3
Matsys, Quentin, *116*
Maximilian, Emperor, 119
Maximus, Quintus Fabius, 90, 162
meat, 39
Medici, Cardinal Giulio, 128
Medici, Lorenzo de, 122
Medici family, 106, 119
Mehmed the Conqueror, Sultan, 133, 134
Melzi, Francesco, 115
memory, 15, 46-9, 51, 240-7
Mendelssohn, Felix, 154
mental attitude, 41
mental literacy, 15, 32-3
Messiaen, Olivier, 51
Michelangelo, 13, 15, 71, 101, 104, 106, 107, 115, **122-4**, *123*, *125*, 127, 128, 131, 135, 208, 221, 224
Microsoft Corporation, 233
Mill, James, 178
Mill, John Stuart, 20, 52, **178-9**, *179*
Milton, John, 17, 66, **145-6**, *147*, 148, 172, 217, 221, 222, 232
Mind Mapping, 42, 47, 51, 58-60
mind sports, 61-2
Minkowski, Professor Hermann, 208
mistakes, learning from, 15
mnemonics, 47, 51
Monet, Claude, 191
Montefeltre, Frederico, Duke of Urbino, 127
Montessori, Maria, 17, **202-3**, *203*
Montgolfier, Joseph and Jacques, 200
Moore, Barbara 'Squeak', 243
Morton, Thomas, 245
movement, memory, 49
Mozart, Leopold, 165
Mozart, Wolfgang Amadeus, 15, *44*, 45, 154, **164-7**, *165*, 172, 243
Multiple Intelligence Quotient (MIQ), 19-31
multiplication, world records, 245
muscles, 36-7
Muses, 69
music:
  brain's response to, 166-7
  memorization of, 243

Nadar, 191
names, memorization of, 243, 247
Napoleon III, Emperor, 191
Napoleon Bonaparte, 15, 64, 87, 91, 93, 97, 98, 133, 151, 162, 164, 167, **168-70**, *169*, 171, 172
Nazis, 207, 209, 211, 217, 224, 225-6
Nelson, Horatio, 16, 91, 98, 133, **167-8**, *167*, *168*, 232
Newcomen, Thomas, 174
Newton, Sir Isaac, *12*, 15, 51, 60, 142, 148, **150-1**, *151*, 152-3, 154, 208, 229, 232
Ney, Marshal, 171
Nicholas V, Pope, 108
Nichomachus, 80
nicotine, 39
Nijinsky, 213-14
Norman, Greg, 16
North, Vanda, 47, 245
number, and memory, 49
numbers, memorization of, 241-3, 247
numerical intelligence, 15, 22-3
Nureyev, Rudolph, 221
nuts, 38

O'Brien, Dominic, 15, 46, 49, 240-1, 243, 245, 246, 247
Oersted, Hans Christian, 176
Olympic Games, 72-3
O'Neill, Henry Nelson, *112*
order, and memory, 49
Ornstein, Professor Robert, 21
Ottoman Empire, 132-5
Ovett, Steve, 16
Owen, Sir Richard, 181
oxygen, aerobic training, 34-5

paintings, memorization of, 247
passion, 17
Paul III, Pope, 124
Pauli, Wolfgang, 226
Pavlov, Ivan Petrovich, 17, **197**
Pericles, 72, 75
Perón, Juan, 223
persistence, 15, 43
Perugino, 127
Perutz, Max, 230
Pestalozzi, Johann, 202
Peterlini, Domenico, *101*
Petrarch, 84, 245
Pheidias, 85
Phidias, **71-3**, 104, 106, 172
Philip, King of Macedon, 80
Philip II, King of Spain, 131, 136
photographic memory, 240
physical energy, 17
physical fitness, 34-8
Picabia, Francis, 214
Picasso, Pablo, 15, 51, 60, **209-12**, *211*, *212*, 217, 219, 221, 228
Pigafetta, Antonio, 126
Pissarro, Camille, 191, 194
Pitt, William the Elder, Earl of Chatham, 15, 155, **159-60**, *161*
Planck, Max, 208, 209, 226
planning, 14
Plato, 16, 70, 76, 77, **78-9**, *79*, 80, *81*, *100*, 102, 104, 127, 128, 225
playing cards, memorization of, 240-1, 247
Plesitskaya, Maya, 221

Plutarch, 85
poise, 37
Pompey, 91, 92
Pop Art, 215
Pope, Alexander, 66, 150
Porus, King, 83
positive attitude, 15-16, 49
posture, 56-7, *57*
printing, 108-9
Proclus, 85
prophetic sayings, memorization of, 243
Prusias, King of Bithynia, 90
Ptolemy, 83-4, 127
Ptolemy Soter I, King of Egypt, 83, 84
Pygmalion Effect, 43
Pythagoras, 127

Racine, 66
Radiant Thinking, 42, 47, 58
Raleigh, Sir Walter, 137
range reading, 54, 57
Raphael, *81*, 123, **127-9**, *129*, 131, 143
Ratdolt, Erhard, 85
Rauschenberg, Robert, 215
Rauscher, Frances, 166, 167
reading, 52-7, 245
Red Rum Brain Principle, 43, 110, 166
Reformation, 117
Rembrandt, Titus, 143, 145
Rembrandt van Rijn, 15, 66, 128, **142-5**, *144*, 228
Renaissance, 104-31
Renoir, Pierre Auguste, 191
rest, 40
Retton, Mary Lou, 16
Rimsky-Korsakov, Nikolai, 213
role models, 17, 45
Roman Catholic Church, 102, 116, 117, 121, 136, 137, 142
Röntgen, Wilhelm, 199
Roosevelt, Franklin D., 208
root extraction, world records, 245
Roxelana, 132-3
Royal Institution, 175
Royal Society, 148, 151, 156, 179, 188
Rubens, Sir Peter Paul, 115
Ruisdael, Jacob van, 142
Rushdie, Salman, 102
Rutherford, Ernest, 209

Saladin, 94
Sappho, **69-70**, *69*
Savary, A.J.M., 168
Scarburgh, Sir Charles, 148
Schiller, Friedrich, 172-3
Schubert, Franz, 224
Schumacher, Elisabeth, 225
Schumann, Robert, 154
Scipio, Publius Cornelius, *89*, 90
seeds, 38
Seki, Kowa, 152
'self-talk', 16
Selim I, Sultan, 131
sensual energy, 17
sensual intelligence, 24-5
Serrano, Jaime Garcia, 245
sexuality, 17, 41, 49
Sforza, Ludovico, Duke of Milan, 114
Shakespeare, William, 15, 17, 28, 66, 93, 104, 117, 124, 135, 137, **138-40**, *139*, *140*, 173, 184, 221, 223

Shaw, Dr Gordon, 166
Shereshevsky, 46, 47, 49
Sherman, Roger, 158
Sherman, General William Tecumseh, 183
Simonton, Dean Keith, 51
Simplicius, 245
Sinan, 132, 133, **134-5**
sitting posture, 56, *57*
Slater, Oscar, 198
sleep, 36, 40
smoking, 39
Société Anonyme, 215
Society of Independents, 215
Socrates, 16, 17, **76-8**, *77*, 79, 80, 104, 127, 148, 217
song memorization, 243
Sophocles, 69, 73, **74-5**, *74*, 76, 80, 104
spatial intelligence, 23-4
speed reading, 52-7, 245
Spenser, Edmund, 135, 137
Sperry, Professor Roger, 33
Spielberg, Steven, 223
Spinks, Leon, 231
Spinoza, Benedict de, 145, **146-8**, *147*, 151, 152, 187, 217
spiritual intelligence, 29-30
Spitz, Mark, 16
sports facts, memorization of, 243
Stael, Madame de, 168
Stein, Gertrude, 209, *211*
Stein, Leo, 209
Steinitz, Wilhelm, 61
Stephenson, George, **174-5**, *174*
Steptoe, Professor Andrew, 166
Stieler, Joseph Carl, *173*
Stoffels, Hendrickje, 145
Strassman, Fritz, 209
Strauss, David Friedrich, 187
Stravinsky, Igor, 15, **213-14**, *213*, 220, 224
strength, 36-7
subject knowledge, 15
Success Principle, 43, 166
Suetonius, 92
Suleyman the Magnificent, 16, 17, 91, **131-4**, *134*, 170
Sun Tzu, **86-7**
Surrealism, 214, 215, 228
Swift, Jonathan, 14
symbolism, and memory, 49
synaesthesia, 49
Synergistic Principle, 42-3, 166

Taborites, 102
Tamburlaine, 93, 97
Taoism, 68, 87
Taylor, Paul, 221
Tchaikovsky, Peter Il'ich, 224
Tetley, Glen, 221
text memorization, 245, 247
Theodosius I, Emperor, 72
Theodosius II, Emperor, 72
Thompson, Daley, 16
Thouless, Robert, 17, 197
Thucydides, 77
Tinsley, Dr Marion, 15, 62, 233
Titian, 15, **129-31**, *132*, 191
Tomoyori, Hideaki, 241, 245
Toscanelli, Paolo, 107, 111
Traini, Francesco, *100*
Trevithick, Richard, 174
truth, 13, 17

Ueshiba, Morihei, 32, **87-8**
Use Your Head Club, 31
Uylenburgh, Hendrik, 143

vegetables, 38
Velazquez, Diego de Silva y, 210
Venice, 129-30
verbal intelligence, 21-2
Verdi, Giuseppe, **184-6**, *185*, 221
Vermeer, Jan, 142
Veronese, Paolo, 130
Verrocchio, Andrea del, 112-14
Vespucci, Amerigo, 112, 124
Victor Emmanuel II, King of Italy, 186
Victoria, Queen of England, 170, 175
VIE Brain Principle, 45, 119-20, 166
Villon, Jacques, 214
Virgil, 102, 145, 245
vision, 13, 54-5, *54*, 56
Vitruvius, 108
vocabulary, 21
Vollard, Ambroise, 194
Volta, Alessandro, 176
Voltaire, 152, 153
Vyasa, **64**, 140

Walcott, Derek, 66
Wallace, Alfred, 179
Walsingham, Sir Francis, 137
Warhol, Andy, 215
Washington, George, 155, 158, **160-2**, *163*, 175
Watson, James Dewey, 16, 181, **229-30**
Watt, James, 60, 174
Weimar, Duke of, 164
Wellington, Duke of, 16, 91, 98, 133, 162, **170-2**, *171*, 175
Whitehead, A.N., 79
Whiting, Sue, 245, 246
Wilhelm, Kaiser, 190
Wilkins, Maurice, 230
William III, King of England, 147
Wilshire, Kenneth, 247
words, memorization of random, 247
World Memory Championships, 246-7
Wren, Sir Christopher, 135, **148-50**, *149*
Wright, Wilbur and Orville, 15, **200-1**, *200*, 210
Württemberg, Duke of, 172

Xenophon, 76

Zander, Ben, 172
Zizka, John, **102-3**, *103*, 196, 232
Zola, Emile, 191, 192

ANSWERS

VERBAL INTELLIGENCE TEST
(PAGES 21-22)

1 SEX 50 points

2 SPUMANTE (the others have been used in musical descriptions) 50 points

3 a) CORTEX
b) BRAIN
c) THINK
d) CREATIVE 100 points

4 Adulthood or maturity (NOT adultery!) 100 points

5 a) LION
b) TIGER
c) MONGREL
d) FELINE
e) CAT
= MONGREL – the only dog (all the others are related to the cat family) 150 points

6 G (the letters spell the word COGITATE) 100 points

7 POUND 50 points

8 Casals 100 points

9 ISTHMUS 150 points

10 STAKE (the word 'stake' can mean either a form of stick or a gambling bet) 150 points

NUMERICAL/LOGICAL INTELLIGENCE TEST
(PAGES 22-23)

1 23 (they each increase by three) 50 points

2 69 (they each decrease by eight) 50 points

3 200 (the figure in the left hand column is multiplied by the figure in the centre column to give the figure in the right hand column) 100 points

4 3 or 12 (each pair of diagonally opposite numbers is made up of a half and a double) 100 points

5 7 (this question decodes into A = 1, B = 2, C = 3, etc.; the word thus spells INTELLIGENT, with G (7) as the missing letter) 100 points

6 46 (one squared, two squared, three squared, four squared, etc. – but in the double digits each number is reversed) 100 points

7 7 (add the numbers at top right and top left, and divide by three: 16 + 5 = 21 ÷ 3 = 7) 100 points

8 6 (each horizontal row has two numbers that are half the other two) 100 points

9 4 (numbers in the lower squares were obtained by halving the total of the two above them) 150 points

10 45 (add 2 and 10 alternately) 150 points

ENGINEERING/SPATIAL INTELLIGENCE TEST
(PAGES 23-24)

1 1 with side c at the top 100 points

2 Eight 100 points

POETRY CHALLENGE
(PAGE 48)

The subject of *Anamnemonicker* is Shakespeare's *Hamlet*, brilliantly condensed and rendered into poetry by Ted Hughes.

QUIZ FOR GENIUS READERS
(PAGE 234)

1 Beethoven based the final movement on Schiller's *Ode to Joy*, which the German poet originally wrote as *Ode to Freedom*.

2 Julius Caesar.

3 Sherlock Holmes' creator Sir Arthur Conan Doyle also invented and popularized skiing as a sport.

4 Charles Dickens.

5 The death of Euripides.

6 Georges Braque and Pablo Picasso nicknamed each other Orville and Wilbur after the Wright brothers.

7 Both the lightning conductor and bi-focal glasses were invented by Benjamin Franklin, who was an accomplished chess player.

8 Thomas Alva Edison.

9 They shared a great interest in dinosaurs.

10 The First Ch'in Emperor's (his terracotta one).

11 Jorge Luis Borges.

12 Lao-Tzu.

13 Bill Gates.

14 They were two of Marcel Duchamp's *ready-mades*.

15 Archimedes tried to calculate the size of the universe by using his 'Sand Reckoner'.

16 An early form of tank which was invented by both Leonardo da Vinci and John Zizka.

17 Mahatma Gandhi.

18 Ballet dancer and teacher Martha Graham (who always dressed in black or white) was fascinated by words and their meanings.

19 George Stephenson.

20 Phidias.

21 Guillaume Dufay wrote a piece of music based on the mathematical ratios used by Brunelleschi when he designed the dome of Florence Cathedral.

22 William Shakespeare.

23 Albert Einstein.

24 Muhammad Ali.

25 Marie Curie named polonium after her native country, Poland.

26 Hypatia's.

27 Christopher Columbus.

28 George Eliot.

29 Alexander Graham Bell.

30 Morihei Ueshiba.

31 He holds Newton's chair as Lucasian Professor of Mathematics at Cambridge University.

32 Ivan Petrovich Pavlov.

33 Salvador Dalí described his limp watches in *The Persistence of Memory* as the 'camembert of time and space'.

34 They are both said to have acted in their plays.
35 Napoleon Bonaparte.

350-300 Congratulations! Your memory is in tune with your brain's bank of knowledge and you can consider yourself an expert on the geniuses in the Hall of Fame.

300-200 A well above average score – you are well on the way to unleashing your genius potential. Concentrate on making notes of key words as you read and you will find information easier to remember. Using Mind Maps will help you.

200-100 A good score. You are probably concentrating only on what you *think* interests you. Expand your horizons and in future practise asking yourself what you can remember after you read articles in books and newspapers.

100-50 An average score. Look again at the sections on memory and speed reading at the front of this book. You may find that it helps if you allow visual associations to come into your mind as you read. Also, try drawing Mind Maps on your favourite geniuses to clarify your thoughts.

50-0 Are you reading this book from back to front? You can do better than this! The chances are that you answered up to five questions correctly because you knew the information before you looked at this book. Be positive and try not to be distracted. Make mental notes as you read.

PICTURE ACKNOWLEDGEMENTS

The authors and publisher thank the following photographers and organizations for their kind permission to reproduce the illustrations in this book:

E.T.ARCHIVE 77, 101 (Pitti Palace, Florence), 116 (Palazzo Barberini, Rome), 141, 173 *left*; ARCHIV FÜR KUNST UND GESCHICHTE, BERLIN 139-140, 207, 211; ARCHIVE PHOTOS 91, 162-163, 182, 189, 195, 220, 222 (Eduardo Comesana); BETTMAN/UPI 223; BRIDGEMAN ART LIBRARY 12 (Tate Gallery, London); 69 (Hermitage, St Petersburg), 81 (Vatican Museums and Galleries, Rome), 112 (Wolverhampton Art Gallery, Staffs), 120 (Lauros-Giraudon/ Musée de Torun, Torun), 125 (Vatican Museums and Galleries, Rome), 129 (Giraudon), 132 (Wallace Collection), 136 (The Walker Art Gallery, Liverpool), 144 (Giraudon), 149 (Private Collection), 153 (Christies, London), 156 (City of Bristol Museum and Art Gallery), 165 *left* (Lauros-Giraudon), 168 (Guildhall Art Gallery, Corporation of London), 169 (Schloss Charlottenburg, Berlin), 177 *above* (Royal College of Physicians, London), 184 (Dickens House Museum), 192-193 (Philadelphia Museum of Art, Pennsylvania), 212 (Museum of Modern Art, New York, © DACS, London 1994), 213 (Private Collection), 216 (Louise & Walter Annenberg Collection, Philadelphia/© ADAGP, Paris and DACS, London 1994); TONY BUZAN 60; CAMERA PRESS 219; JEAN-LOUP CHARMET 138; CHRISTIE'S COLOUR LIBRARY 161; THE HULTON DEUTSCH COLLECTION 44, 70, 92, 96 *above*, 187, 200, 227 (Charles Hewitt), 231; IMAGE SELECT (Ann Ronan) 151 *left*, 188; IMPACT PHOTO 88 (Julian Calder), 65 (Yann Arthus-Bertrand/Altitude); THE MANSELL COLLECTION 75, 82, 95, 123, 126, 134, 147 *below*, 156-157, 171, 177 *below*, 178, 180, 199, 201, 204; MARY EVANS PICTURE LIBRARY 16, 67-68, 73-74, 79, 86, 96 *below*, 103, 108 *above*, 118, 121, 152, 155, 179, 196, 198, 206; THE NATURAL HISTORY MUSEUM, LONDON 181; OSTERREICHISCHE NATIONALBIBLIOTHEK, VIENNA 165 *right*; POPPERFOTO 14, 108 *below*, 147 *above*, 173 *right*, 203, 218; SCALA 84 (Palazzo Ducale, Urbino), 89 (Palazzo del Quirinale), 100 (S Caterina, Pisa), 104-105, 113 (Biblioteca Reale, Turin), 114 (Museo della Scienza e della Tecnia, Milan), 185 (Galleria d'Arte Moderna, Roma); NAOMI SCHILLINGER 246; SCIENCE PHOTO LIBRARY 109, 151 *right*, 174, 205 (National Library of Medicine), 225, 229; JULIAN SIMPOLE 62; THE TATE GALLERY, LONDON 228 (© DEMART PRO ARTE BV/DACS 1994); TOPHAM PICTURE SOURCE 233.